an introduction to data processing for business

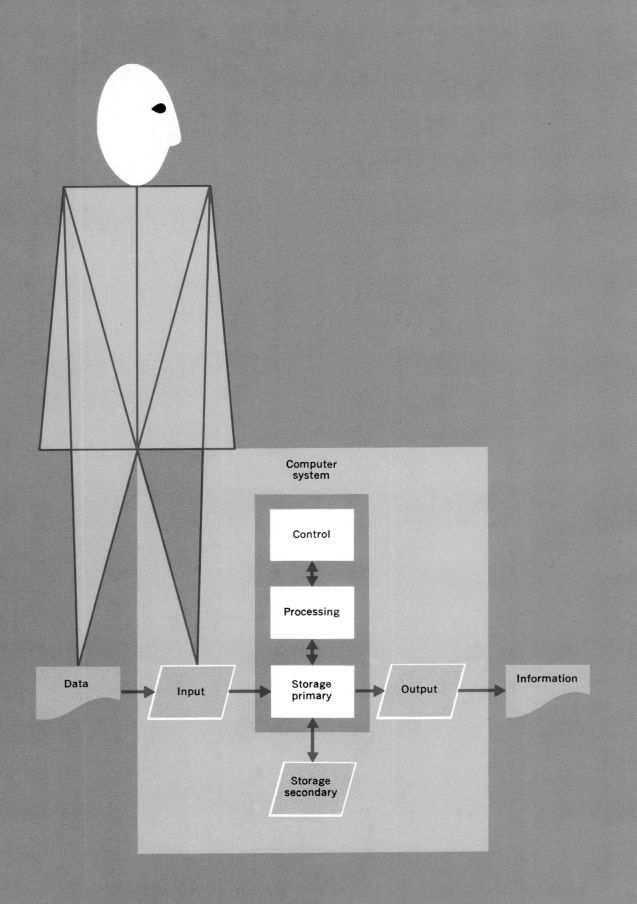

an introduction to data processing for business

robert j. thierauf

Chairperson
Department of Managment and Information Systems
D. J. O'Conor, Memorial Professor of Business Administration
Xavier University

john f. niehaus

Associate Vice President
for Finance and Computer Services
Adjunct Associate Professor of Information Systems
Xavier University

With the Assistance of
Verale Phillips
Cincinnati Technical College

John Wiley & Sons
New York   Chichester   Brisbane   Toronto

Library of Congress Cataloging in Publication Data:

Thierauf, Robert J.
An introduction to data processing for business.
Includes index.

1.   Business—Data processing.   I.   Niehaus, John F.,
joint author.   II.   Title.

HF5548.2.T443   001.6'02'4658   79-20568
ISBN 0-471-03439-8

Printed in the United States of America

10 9 8 7 6 5 4 3 2 1

**dedicated to the
D. J. O'Conor family**

about the authors

ROBERT J. THIERAUF is a professor of management and information systems at Xavier University in Cincinnati where he is the Chairperson of the Department of Management and Information Systems. He has written widely on areas related to computers, in particular, systems analysis and design, management information systems, and distributed processing systems. His highly successful *Data Processing for Business and Management* was the first basic computer book to be translated into Russian under contract agreement. His writings in other areas include those of operations research, management, and management auditing. He is the first holder of the D. J. O'Conor Endowed Chair ($600,000) at Xavier University. Prior to coming to Xavier, he received his Ph. D. degree from The Ohio State University in 1966. Also, he was staff accountant (CPA) and consultant for six years at Coopers & Lybrand, specializing in computers and accounting systems as well as computerized operations research studies. Professor Thierauf is a member of the Association for Computing Machinery, American Institute of Decision Sciences, American Institute of Certified Public Accountants, Academy of Management, and Institute of Management Science.

JOHN F. NIEHAUS is currently Associate Vice-President for Finance and Computer Science at Xavier University. Also, he is an adjunct associate professor of information systems. Prior to this time, he taught mathematics at Xavier where he received his master's degree in mathematics. Active in consulting, he specializes in small business systems and first-time users of computer systems. Professor Niehaus is an active member of the Association for Computing Machinery.

Computer data processing in a business environment can be an interesting and challenging career. In this introductory book, an insight into this field will be given by analyzing and solving business problems using a programming language. (Courtesy International Business Machines Corporation.)

This book represents a new and exciting direction in the teaching of data processing principles and practices. Specifically, the focus of its presentation, which differs from other data processing textbooks, is to have the student use the computer as early as possible. In a course where a *problem solving approach* using computers is highlighted in an interactive processing mode, our experience has shown this objective to be particularly valuable. Moreover, the participants at a recent AEDS (Association for Educational Data Systems) Workshop on college curriculums in computer science, data processing, and information systems stressed the need for student's early familiarity with the computer so that their fear of it can be overcome. Also, AED participants found that the student has more time to solve a wider range of typical business problems. We believe that the findings of our own experience and the AEDS Workshop represent an important direction for teaching the beginning data processing student of the 1980s.

Within this new framework, the book contains several student-oriented learning features. In each chapter, they include:

- *Orientation toward problem analysis and solution*—the accent is on defining and solving business problems in an interactive processing environment rather than on a technical presentation of business data processing (i.e., computer equipment, data codes utilized by computers, and the like).

- *Chapter objectives and outlines* — each chapter begins with study objectives and is accompanied by an outline of the material to follow.
- *Two full-page summaries* — halfway through each chapter as well as at the end of each chapter, a full-page summary of the prior material is given. These summaries are designed to assist the beginning student in bringing together the important material of each chapter.
- *Two full-page self-study exercises* — halfway through each chapter as well as at the end of each chapter, self-study exercises consisting of 10 true-false questions and 10 fill-ins are given. The self-study exercises not only serve as a mini-workbook but also complement the full-page summaries on the immediate preceding page.
- *Answers to self-study exercises* — all answers are given at the end of each chapter. These pedagogical tools will also assist the instructor whose time, because of large class size, may well be limited.

The principal areas covered are business information systems, essentials of computers, problem analysis and solution using computers, computer programming, programming languages, time-sharing, the feasibility of data processing, and the human element. Emphasis is placed on the BASIC language, since BASIC enables a student to program the computer in a short time. Also, many schools require that the student solve a wide range of business and scientific problems for which BASIC is well suited — especially where time-sharing terminals of a *minicomputer system* are used.

This text is appropriate for any time period in an introductory course or in one covering the fundamentals of business data processing. If it is used for a survey course, Part Five on the designing and implementing of data processing can be dropped. However, one quarter or one semester will normally allow coverage of the entire book. The text can be used for a full academic year in conjunction with selected data processing and pro-gramming manuals. In this approach, the book should be used as a general guide for the computer course. Chapters can be supplemented with various computer and language manuals. For each type of course, the text is flexible enough to accommodate most classroom situations. This text is accompanied by a full package of support materials. A Teacher's Manual and a computerized Test Bank are available for the Instructor, and a Student Study Guide has been prepared for the student.

The structure of the book follows a logical sequence for a comprehensive treatment of computer data processing for business. The major areas covered are as follows:

Part One. Introduction to Data Processing for Business. Chapter One discusses basic data processing concepts as well as the various types of computer systems developed for business organizations. The sources of data found in a typical manufacturing firm are also explored and related to computer systems.

Part Two. Problem Analysis and Operating Concepts of Data Processing for Business. Within Chapter Two, the fundamentals of flowcharts are investigated as an essential part of problem analysis using computers. In Chapter Three, the Input–Storage–Processing–Control–Output (ISPCO) cycle of computers and computer data codes are covered, with emphasis on the binary and hexadecimal systems. In addition; the execution of com-puter instructions is explored.

Part Three. Programming Languages for Business. The fast growing field of computer programming, known as computer *software*, is the subject matter of Chapter Four. The computer languages, COBOL and RPG, are surveyed and an orderly method for programming and implementing is presented. The BASIC programming language is discussed in Chapters Five and Six. Typical BASIC programs are illustrated for several functional areas in a business information system environment.

Part Four. Data Processing Equipment for Business. Batch-oriented computer equipment and related devices, or computer *hardware,* are presented in Chapter Seven. Chapter Eight is devoted to computer communications and interactive-oriented computer equipment. Minicomputers and general purpose systems, as found in various sized business organizations, are explored in Chapter 9.

Part Five. Designing and Implementing Data Processing for Business. The feasibility study is the subject matter for this part of the book, comprising Chapters Ten and Eleven. Included is a discussion of systems analysis, systems design, equipment selection, and systems implementation.

Part Six. The Impact of Data Processing on the Individual and the Organization. Chapter Twelve focuses on the key to success in business data processing — the human element. Career opportunities in the computer field are explored.

Epilogue. Future Impact of Data Processing on Society and Business. The future developments in computer data processing are discussed as they affect society and business.

We are deeply indebted to the many people who contributed their time and effort to make this book possible. We are especially grateful to Professors Richard A. Hall, Donald A. Heckerman, William M. Kramer, J. Michael Thierauf, and Thomas C. Wood. We also like to thank Professors J. Daniel Couger (University of Colorado-Colorado Springs), Barbara Fox (Rock Valley College), Ida Mason (Montgomery County Community College, PA), Verale Phillips (Cincinnati Technical College), Harice Seeds (LA City College) and Gerald Wagner (California State-Pomona) whose constructive criticism of our manuscript was invaluable.

Xavier University
January 1980

Robert J. Thierauf
John F. Niehaus

contents

part one introduction to data processing for business

Before undertaking a detailed investigation of problem
analysis and solution in a computerized business
environment per Part Two, it is helpful to have an
understanding of basic data processing terms, especially as regards information and computer systems.
This background provides a foundation for exploring
the concepts underlying the use of computers in
business information systems. It will also provide a
better understanding of the traditional sources of
business data and of typical computer applications.

chapter one
overview of data processing for business

chapter objectives

- To define the basic terms of data processing that provide the underlying structure of this book.
- To develop a general guide for relating the value of information to the cost of obtaining it.
- To set forth the important information system concepts found in business information systems.
- To examine the basic types of computerized business information systems.
- To relate the various sources of business data to typical computer applications as found in business information systems.

This book aims to give the reader an understanding of what data processing (DP) for business involves and how it can help typical organizations in planning and controlling everyday operations. Chapter One introduces the reader to the world of data processing. Basic data processing terms are then defined. Special emphasis is placed on information as output from computer systems, and in particular from business information systems. The relationship of value of information to its cost is set forth. Current system concepts are discussed along with the basic types of computerized business information systems. Lastly, the important sources of business data are explored along with typical computer applications that employ these input data.

the world of data processing

Consider the following sequence of events. It is 8:00 a.m. As the alarm clock goes off, the bedroom curtains swing apart and the thermostat raises the heat to 70° F. The percolator in the kitchen starts. The back door opens to let the dog out. The television set comes on with the news, including a selective rundown of the latest events affecting the economy. Mail, from correspondents who have dictated their messages into the computer network, is next displayed on the TV. At the press of a button, a bedside box issues a string of personal and business memos. After shower, which has turned itself on at exactly the right temperature, Mr. A dresses and saunters out to the car. The engine of the car is running.

Meanwhile, Mrs. A concentrates on the screen for a readout of comparative prices at local markets. Following visual consultations with the baker and the grocer on the TV, she depresses a button to order supplies for tonight's dinner party. Pressing keys on the kitchen terminal, she orders from the memory bank her favorite recipes, tells the machine to compute the ingredients for six servings, and directs the ovens to preheat to the correct temperature for each dish, starting at 6:30 p.m.

The Miracle Chip. Is the foregoing a George Orwell fantasy? The answer is an emphatic no. All the basic technology to accomplish the tasks described above exists. This is all possible due to the latest technological advances. We are referring to the "miracle chip" that represents a quantum leap in computer technology. The revolution it has launched promises to ease and enhance life in ways undreamed of.

Unveiled in 1971, the one-chip computer contained 2250 transistors in an area barely a sixth of an inch long and an eighth of an inch wide. Under a microscope, it resembled an aerial view of a railroad switching yard. Yet this miracle chip had a calculating capacity almost equal to the room-size ENIAC—the first fully electronic computer, completed in 1946. And it performed as well as an early-1960's IBM machine which, with all of its parts, costing $30,000. The new chip was so small and cheap for the functions it performed that it could be incorporated into cameras, vending machines, typewriters, household appliances—in almost any device that might benefit from some "thinking" power. A computer in every car is now a reality. As someone said, "To ask what the applications are is like asking what are the applications of electricity."

Computers are highly amenable to solving a myriad of business and scientific problems. The computer is capable of computing and performing logical comparisons with tremendous speed and accuracy. To get an insight into how a computer can be used in business, it is first necessary to start with some basic terms.

basic data processing terms

As with every discipline, there are a group of basic terms that the reader should be familiar with and understand. Several of the basic terms are discussed below. As new ideas and concepts are presented throughout the book, additional data processing (DP) terms will be defined. This interspersing of defined terms not only assists in clarifying a subject area, but also reduces the need for developing a long list of data processing terms in this first chapter.

Data. The term "data" (plural of datum) is defined as unstructured facts. It is the unstructured raw material of data processing. As shown in Figure 1-1, it provides the necessary inputs to a system. A telephone book, for example, can be looked upon as a collection of data.

Information. Information can be defined as selected data. The selection and organization process may be based upon the needs of the user, the particular problem to be solved, or some other criterion. Information, as illustrated in Figure 1-1, is the output of a system. Using the example of the telephone book, specific numbers in that book become information when a user refers to it.

System. A system is an ordered set of methods and procedures to achieve an objective. The primary function of a system is the conversion of data to information that will further organization objectives (Figure 1-1). If the information compiled by the system does not enhance its objectives, there is little point in making the conversion. Referring again to the telephone book illustration, the methods and procedures used by a service-oriented firm for soliciting its prospective customers via a telephone directory could be termed a system. A typical business example is an accounts receivable system that processes charges and credits against customer accounts to determine current balances.

Computer. Although systems can be manually oriented, the trend is toward the use of computers as their essential part. A computer is defined as an electronic computing machine that accepts input data, processes the data, and provides output. In certain cases, the output will be in the form of printed reports; in others it will be displayed on television-like

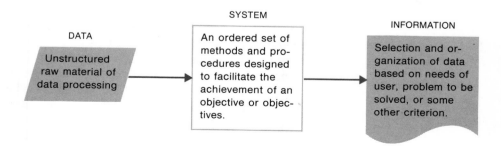

figure 1-1. An effective *system* extracts the required *data* to produce meaningful *information*.

SYSTEM

DATA

Unstructured raw material of data processing

An ordered set of methods and procedures designed to facilitate the achievement of an objective or objectives.

INFORMATION

Selection and organization of data based on needs of user, problem to be solved, or some other criterion.

figure 1-2. Relationship of *data* and *information* to the essential components of a *computer system.*

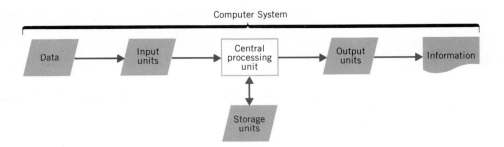

Computer System

Data → Input units → Central processing unit → Output units → Information

Storage units

devices or stored for further processing. Because a computer is capable of processing a sequence of instructions, it is capable of manipulating input data in a variety of ways. A picture of a current IBM computer is shown at the beginning of the text.

Computer System. In general, a computer can also be referred to as a computer system because it consists of one or more input devices, a central processing unit (CPU), storage devices, and one or more output devices. The relationship of data and information to these essential components of a computer system is illustrated in Figure 1-2.

There are a wide range of computer systems available, ranging from small to large. In a small-scale computer system, the CPU is modest in its processing capabilities. Relatively few input/output(I/O) and storage devices are used. In a larger-scale system, the central processing unit is considerably more powerful and may be attached to many input/output and storage devices. The components of a computer system are configured to meet the specific processing needs of a user.

Business Information System. We are now in a position to define a business information system. Fundamentally, it is a computerized system designed to meet the information needs of a business organization. More specifically, it aids in the handling, manipulating, and recording required to convert business data into timely and meaningful information. From this view, it is a tool of an organization using computers for achieving desired organization objectives. A business information system interfaces with most areas of a typical firm, namely, marketing, research and development, engineering, manufacturing, purchasing, receiving, inventory, shipping, accounting, and personnel.

information value versus cost

Having set forth the meaning and importance of information, the question of its accuracy for a reliable business information system must be answered. A logical starting point is an examination of an organization's functional areas. The need for an accuracy of 100 percent will be apparent in some areas. Activities, such as payroll, sales commissions, accounts receivable, and accounts payable, require the highest degree of accuracy. On the other hand, inaccuracies for low value inventory stock—cartons, supplies, and like items—can be tolerated since the cost of controlling these items is greater than their value. Based on these two extremes for accuracy, the general guide is to relate value of information to the cost of obtaining it. The most desirable degree of accuracy is reached when the value of

figure 1-3. Relationship of value, cost, and accuracy to information. Accuracy is increased to the point where the value of information is still greater than its cost.

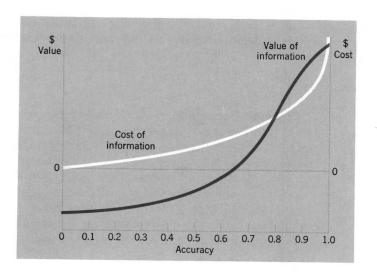

information exceeds the cost of acquiring it by the greatest margin. Logically, accuracy is increased up to the point where the value derived from the information is still greater than its corresponding cost, as illustrated in Figure 1-3.

Cost of Accuracy

The value of information to management is small or negative when its accuracy is low. Inaccurate information can lead to profit-losing decisions. As noted in Figure 1-3, the value of information rises fast as the degree of accuracy increases. This is particularly true at the higher levels. More accurate information facilitates better decisions. However, as the value of information approaches perfect information, decision making is not sensitive to slight improvements of near-perfect accuracy. In effect, costs increase rapidly for higher degrees of accuracy, and in particular, as accuracy reaches 100 percent without a corresponding increase in its value to management.

concepts underlying business information systems

Just as there are basic data processing terms, so too there are underlying concepts to business information systems. The purpose of presenting these concepts is to help the reader obtain an overview of the various approaches to business information systems. Although many system concepts have been developed over the years, the discussion will center around the following two important ones:

- the management information system concept
- the distributed processing system concept

The Management Information System Concept

A most important system approach today is one referring to a *management information system* (MIS) concept. Though it is possible to have a noncomputerized management information system, this book stresses the computer as an essential part of it. External and internal information is channeled into this single, centralized computer system. Output generated by such a system will be meaningful and effective for management's decisions.

Common Data Base. Basically, a computerized management information system means capturing originating data as close to their source as possible, feeding the data directly or almost directly into the computer system, and permitting the system to utilize common data storage files that can service several different outputs (Figure 1-4). In this type of environment, a single piece of information is entered into the data processing system once only. From then on, it is available to serve all requirements until its usefulness is exhausted. Under these ideal conditions, adequate and correct information can be presented to managers in a coordinated fashion. Likewise, such a system provides the required information on a timely basis.

To illustrate the use of a such common data base, consider the weekly time cards of production employees. Not only can these data be stored for paying employees, but they also can be used for costing company products. In turn, these data serve as a basis for updating personnel records as to total service time on the job as well as a means for producing annual earnings reports for the company, employees, and government. Thus, employee time data can serve many users.

Control Reports. Control reports include those necessary to service the basic business functions (as shown in Figure 1-4). Among these are sales forecasting, shipping and warehousing, finished goods replenishment, production control, materials management, manufacturing cost control, personnel skills and manning control, and management incentives. Other reports include short-range and long-range financial and operating budgets,

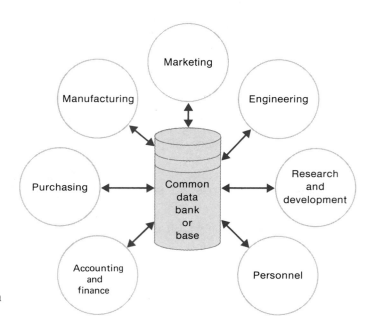

figure 1-4. An essential part of a management information system is a common data bank or data base.

monthly financial and operating statements, and various historical data for short-run to long-range planning. Sales and order entry statistics, including sales quotas, salesperson's compensation, purchasing, manufacturing, and shipping, are additional examples of output that provide input to many other systems. An essential part of any management information system is *feedback,* which shows what has happened to the financial plan in view of actual results to date or what would happen if hypothetical changes were made in the plan. Control reports, then, are concerned with monitoring actual results via feedback in order to determine whether organizational functions are proceeding in accordance with plans and standards.

Distributed Processing System Concept

One of the newer systems concepts underlying business information systems is the *distributed processing system* concept. It is actually a spin-off of the small business computer approach. In many cases, the computer equipment used is the same; however, the accent is on who is using it and how it is programmed.

Focuses on Local Processing. An essential part of distributed processing is the increased responsiveness of the DP function to the user's needs by providing data entry/inquiry capabilities, i.e., processing power at the local level. Not only does this give local managers more control over and involvement with the data and the business information system, but also a burden is taken off the central computing facility. And because more processing is done locally, the overall system now can be utilized to do what it does best, that is, repetitive processing with responsiveness improved in the process.

The distributed processing concept is an answer to difficulties experienced with earlier computer systems. The use of large centralized computers in the 1960's and 1970's created large data input bottlenecks and also created situations where the feedback of the business data necessary to run the business occurred after long delays. In effect, distributed processing arose out of the need to get data processing power where it is needed and to handle DP operations that can be done more efficiently in the field than at the home office. A good example is sales-order processing at the local level, whereby sales personnel can work directly with the order-entry clerk to ensure the proper handling of regular as well as exception items.

Relationship with Centralized Processing. The distributed processing concept still allows the use of centralized processing facilities. Those DP operations that can be best handled by the local, on-site computer stay at that level. However, summary information that is needed for higher levels of management are forwarded from the local level to the centralized computer facility for appropriate processing. A typical illustration is the summarization of weekly and monthly sales. In effect, detailed information needed for local operations remain at that level; summary information needed to control overall operations are forwarded from the local level and are handled by the central computer.

**first summary
of chapter one**

basic data processing terms:

• data—unstructured facts or raw material that is used as input to a system. Example: a telephone book

• information—selected data as output from a system. The selection process is dependent upon the user's needs. Example: a desired number from a telephone book

• system—an ordered set of methods and procedures designed to facilitate the achievement of an objective or objectives. Example: methods and procedures used by a service-oriented firm for soliciting its prospective customers via a telephone book

• computer—an electronic computing machine that accepts input data, processes the data internally within the machine, and provides output of some type. Example: picture of current IBM system in the beginning of the text

• computer system—commonly referred to as simply a computer because it consists of one or more input devices, a central processing unit (CPU), and one or more output and/or storage devices.

• business information system—a computerized system designed to meet the information needs of a business organization. Functional areas that interface with a business information system are set forth in the second half of the chapter.

information value versus cost:

Accuracy of information should be increased as long as the value of information is greater than its corresponding cost. Activities, such as payroll and sales commissions, require the highest degree of accuracy. On the other hand, inaccuracies for low-value inventory items, such as cartons and supplies, can be tolerated since the cost of controlling them is greater than their value.

concepts underlying business information systems:

• management information system—a group of computerized functional systems, such as marketing, manufacturing, and accounting, employed to fulfill the managerial information requirements necessary to control ongoing business operations. It is a system for producing and forwarding timely information that will support management in fulfilling its specific tasks. For the most part, a common data base or data bank is used where one piece of information is used by many users. Example: weekly time data of employees serve payroll, cost accounting, and personnel informational needs

• distributed processing system—an approach that places low-cost computing power at the various processing points in an organization and links these points, where necessary, with a centralized computer. It is an alternative to central processing, made possible by the declining costs of computing devices. It places computing power where it is needed for efficient and economical DP operations. Example: sales order processing at the local level where order entry personnel work directly with sales personnel to ensure proper handling of regular and exception items

first self-study exercise of chapter one

True-False:

1. ( ) Data and information mean the same thing.
2. ( ) A system is a set of methods and procedures to achieve an objective(s).
3. ( ) A business information system is concerned with internal data only.
4. ( ) The terms computer and business information system can be interchanged.
5. ( ) Information feedback should not be an integral part of business information systems.
6. ( ) Accuracy should be increased up to the point where the information value is less than its cost.
7. ( ) The cost for 100 percent accuracy is generally low in most business situations.
8. ( ) Underlying business information systems are important system concepts.
9. ( ) Another name for common data storage files is a common data base.
10. ( ) Distributed processing is not a major direction currently in information systems.

Fill-In:

11. The raw material for business data processing which must be changed in form or content to permit its effective use is called _____.
12. _____ is selected data which is meaningful to the user.
13. An ordered set of methods and procedures required to convert data into information is called a _____.
14. The handling, manipulating, and recording required to convert business data into timely and meaningful information is called a _____ _____ _____.
15. A _____ _____ consists of one or more input/output devices and a central processing unit.
16. The _____ principle is concerned with forwarding critical information to the proper personnel for modifying specific plans, organization structures, or current directives.
17. The most desirable degree of accuracy is reached where the _____ _____ exceeds the corresponding cost of acquiring the data by the greatest margin.
18. The _____ _____ _____ concept utilizes a common data base or data bank for storing business data.
19. The focus of distributed processing is on _____ _____ versus centralized processing.
20. A distributed processing environment allows _____ _____ to be forwarded from the local level to central headquarters.

Distributed data processing (DDP) is an antithesis of the general MIS concept. The focus of the latter is on large, common data bases as an essential part of a management information system. Although DDP will not replace or displace the central computer facility, it will augment centralized computing. Thus, the distributed processing concept allows the use of a centralized computer with dispersed processing at the lower levels.

basic computerized information systems for business

The terms computer and business information system are brought together as a basis for discussing various types of systems used in business today. The basic approaches to computerized business information systems are *batch processing* and *interactive processing*. Using the batch approach, transactions are accumulated and processed periodically. The items in a batch may be in sequential or random order. An example of sequential batch processing is a sorted group of inventory punched cards which will be computer processed to produce a weekly inventory report. In the interactive approach, records are stored on-line and updated as the transactions occur. On-line devices are in direct communication with the computer system and are used to reflect current activities introduced into the data processing system. A typical example is the on-line devices used by airlines to book reservations. The requirements of a computer system capable of processing on-line data are different from those for processing batch data.

File storage devices of computer systems can be two types— *sequential access,* and *direct,* or *random access.* In sequential access files, the data are stored in some predetermined order. Before a record can be read, say in the middle of the file, all preceding records must first be read. When operating with direct access file equipment, the unit is capable of locating and reading any record without having to read other records in order to obtain the desired one. An example would be the location of a specific customer account without having to read all prior accounts as found in sequential access files.

Batch Processing
The batch processing approach is characterized by the periodic processing of accumulated transactions. It is normally associated with records maintained on magnetic tape. College students, for example, submit programs to a computer center and pick them up after processing has occurred. This is an example of batch processing.

Sequential Access Files. When the files are of the sequential access type, the entire master file is updated each time it is processed on a computer system. This operation requires sorting all input data according to the same sequence as the master file (Figure 1-5). Batch processing with sequential access file storage is ideally suited for payroll and accounts payable. It usually costs less to process batches than to process each transaction, as it occurs, immediately on-line. However, for other processing runs that require timely information for immediate decisions, the on-line approach may be justified.

figure 1-5. Batch processing with sequential access file storage—magnetic tape.

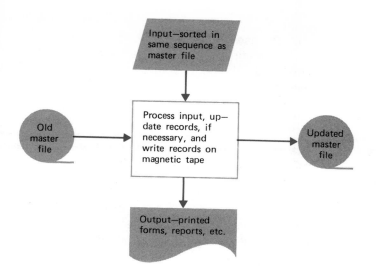

Direct Access Files. The batch approach can also use direct or random access file devices. The most common form of random access storage is the magnetic disk file which allows the direct updating of the desired record. For applications involving few transactions relative to the size of the master file, this approach is widely used. An added advantage of direct access over the sequential access approach in the batch processing mode is that there is no need to sort the input data. Thus, certain advantages of direct access make it a logical candidate for certain business applications.

Interactive Processing

The trend continues to be toward more interactive processing. Transactions and inquiries into the system are processed as they occur. An example is many students at a college sharing interactively the computing power of one computer.

Direct Access Files. In an interactive processing system, all data and inquiries are processed as they occur. Each originating point for transactions has an input/output terminal connected to the computer. All information is stored in direct access file devices that are available at all times for immediate interrogation (Figure 1-6). Applications include accounts receivable, airlines' reservation systems, bank deposit and withdrawal accounting, hotel accounting and reservations systems, law enforcement intelligence systems, patient hospital records, savings and loan deposit

figure 1-6. Interactive processing with direct access file storage—magnetic disk.

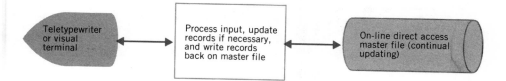

accounting, and stock market information. These applications do not exhaust those presently in operation, those currently being installed, or those contemplated. Interactive processing with direct access file storage is decidedly the continuing direction of business information system developments.

sources of data for business information systems

Data within an organization are generated as a result of daily operations and interaction with other functions. Although most activities are related to other internal functions, there is also a need to relate activities to external groups, namely, customers, vendors, banks, and governmental agencies.

As indicated in Figure 1-7, there are several basic business operations to be found in a typical manufacturing firm. Because these key operations are interrelated, large masses of data are generated on hundreds of different forms. Many of these operating forms serve as a basis for producing output reports that are necessary in making managerial decisions.

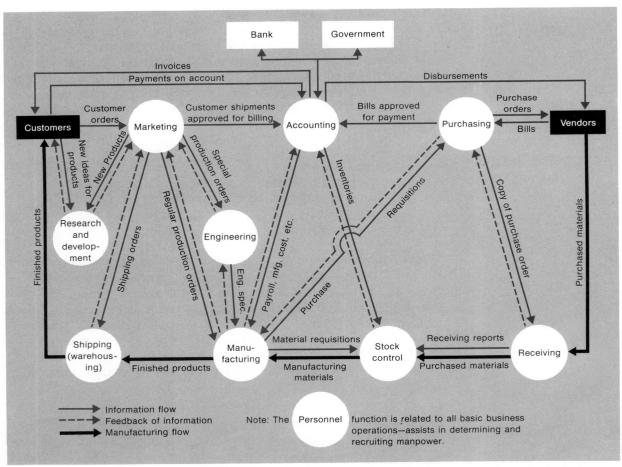

figure 1-7. The sources of data for the basic business operations of a typical manufacturing firm.

The chart in Figure 1-7 illustrates the *basic flow of goods* through a firm. It also shows other important activities—the *information flow* necessary to produce the goods. Likewise, there is the important *feedback* of critical information to the appropriate levels of management for controlling operations. To illustrate this chart, manufactured parts represent the basic flow of goods while material requisitions represent the information flow to obtain raw materials, parts etc., for manufacturing. An inventory out-of-stock condition represents feedback to purchasing for stock replenishment. Many of the operations shown in the chart are also found in service-oriented organizations.

Marketing

The primary job of the marketing department is to contact potential customers and sell merchandise through salesmen, advertising, and special promotions. If products are sold, a multicopy *sales order* is originated by a salesperson or the order section of the marketing department. Copies are distributed as follows: original copy to customer for acknowledging order; duplicate copies to the salesperson and to the manufacturing, stock control, shipping, and accounting departments. In addition, the marketing department may prepare other forms, such as *contracts, bids, back orders,* and *change orders.*

Retail sales other than regular cash transactions are recorded normally on a *sales slip* and are prepared by sales personnel. The original copy is given to the customer and other copies are distributed to the shipping, stock control, and accounting departments. Other sales documents can be prepared by various types of selling institutions. No matter what kind of organization is involved, the marketing department generally starts the product information flow, and is therefore an initial source of data.

Research and Development

Often the marketing department receives inquiries regarding a new product. It will initiate a *research and development (R & D) order* for its development if marketing prospects look promising. Similarly, the marketing research section may have its own ideas on what new products should be developed. This, too, will result in an R & D order. At other times, the firm will want to use the talents of another firm for pooling research talents. This is necessary in order to obtain a larger contract which neither is capable of undertaking individually.

Engineering

Before manufacturing operations can commence, it is necessary to design the products as agreed upon by the marketing department in conjunction with the research and development department. This means designing the product from scratch, after which the engineering specifications are forwarded to the manufacturing department. The *engineering blueprints* form the basis for producing the parts, subassemblies, frames, and the like. The requirements for the product to be manufactured are summarized on *bills of materials.* This forms the basis for exploding bills of materials, that is, determining the number of detailed items for the production order.

With engineering specifications and appropriate bills of materials prepared, these data can be forwarded to the production control department.

Manufacturing

The manufacture of finished products involves many steps. Not only must plant, equipment, and tools be provided but also appropriate personnel must be hired and trained to use the manufacturing facilities. Raw materials and goods-in-process must be available as needed. Production must be planned, scheduled, routed, and controlled for output that meets certain standards.

The firm's products can be produced in anticipation of demand, manufactured upon receipt of customer's orders, or some combination of the two. If goods are being produced to order, a sales order copy may, in many cases, be the *production order*. The usual arrangement is to have the production planning or control department initiate action on factory orders. The production order is also distributed to the stock control, shipping, and accounting departments. The original copy is kept in the production department files.

Manufacturing materials can be obtained from within or outside the firm (See Figure 1-7). If a *purchase requisition* is prepared, it is forwarded to the purchasing department for vendor purchase. On the other hand, if materials are available from the stock control department, a *materials requisition* is prepared. Other records and forms are *periodic production reports, tool orders, material usage reports, material scrappage reports, inspection reports, labor analysis reports, cost analysis reports,* and *production progress reports.*

Purchasing

Purchasing is concerned with procuring raw materials, equipment, supplies, utilities, as well as other products and services required to meet the firm's operating needs. Purchasing is generally centralized in one department. The procurement process generally begins with the completion of the purchase requisition in duplicate. One copy is forwarded to the purchasing department and one is retained by the originator.

Based on the purchase requisition form, the purchasing department locates the supplier(s). If the desired information is not available, the buyer may send a *request for quotation* to prospective vendors. Once the outside supplier has been determined, a *purchase order* is typed and mailed to the vendor. It contains the items to be shipped, prices, specifications, terms, and shipping conditions. Generally, the original is forwarded to the vendor and duplicate copies are distributed to the purchasing, receiving, stock control, accounting, and preparing departments.

Receiving

As soon as goods are received from suppliers, they are checked and verified against the copy of the original purchase order by the receiving department. Once the receiving clerk is satisfied that the goods correspond to those on the purchase order, a *receiving report* is prepared noting any discrepancies between the order and material received. Sometimes, an *inspection record* may be prepared by the receiving department along with the receiving report. Copies of both are sent to purchasing, stock control, manufacturing, and accounting. A carbon copy is retained by the receiving department.

Goods are delivered by the receiving department to the stock control department or any other department that has ordered them. Generally, the department that takes possession of the materials acknowledges receipt by signing a copy of the receiving report.

Inventory Control

The function of inventory control is to store and protect all materials and supplies not required for current usage. The transfer-in of materials from an outside vendor is documented as mentioned earlier. The transfer-out of goods to the manufacturing department is authorized by the materials requisition, also noted previously. Materials are issued in response to current manufacturing needs.

A most important source of data is the *inventory records* or *stock records* maintained by the department. Since it is responsible for materials flowing in and out of stock, it has all the necessary data for determining inventories. Stock records may be in the form of visual records, punched cards, or computer storage. If stored on-line, input/output devices are generally used to keep inventory data up-to-date.

Inventory control has the added function of replacing stock when it reaches a minimum level, often referred to as a reorder point. The stores clerk prepares a purchase requisition and forwards it to the purchasing department. Inventory control is thus an important source of data.

Shipping

The finished products must be packed, labeled, and transported to the customer. The *shipping order,* which authorizes shipment, is delivered with or in advance of the goods. If delivery is made directly to the customer, the receipt of goods will be acknowledged by a signed copy of the shipping order which is then filed in the shipping office.

Shipments made via public carriers must be accompanied by a bill of lading; actually a contract between the consignor and the carrier. One copy each goes to the customer and the public carrier, a third copy is filed in the shipping department as proof of shipment.

Accounting

After shipping, the accounting department must prepare *customers' invoices.* These not only serve as a record of charges, but also are the basis on which the seller can legally claim payment for goods or services. Generally, the first two copies are sent to the customer. Remaining copies are distributed to the marketing department, salesperson, and are held in the accounting department's billing file.

Depending upon the terms of the invoice, payments from customers are deposited in the firm's bank account. These payments are recorded in the *cash receipts journal* as documented evidence of their receipt. Periodically, *statement of accounts* are mailed to inform customers of the status of their accounts. The usual time for mailing statements is at the end of each month. Whenever there is a large number of accounts, billing is spread throughout the month.

The accounting department is also concerned with disbursing funds, mainly for payroll and for goods and services. *Time cards* are the originating source for paying salaries and wages. Time cards may also be used for making labor distribution charges to various departments. *Payroll checks* and *earnings statements* are the end result of payroll procedures.

The second type of disbursement involves checking the vendor's invoice against the purchase order and receiving reports initially. Upon approval of payment by the purchasing department, *voucher checks* are prepared. A voucher check is a check with an attached voucher that contains sufficient space for date, purchase order number, vendor number, description, amount, discount, and net payment. The first copy is mailed to the payee on designated days of the month according to stated terms of the vendor's invoice. Duplicate copies are used for data processing. When processing is complete, voucher checks are filed.

The foregoing accounting functions are not complete until all legitimate governmental forms have been prepared and the proper voucher checks drawn for the respective amounts due. Federal, state, and local governments require the preparation of specific tax forms. These include *federal income tax returns, reports on social security taxes withheld, federal and state unemployment compensation returns, state income tax returns, personal property tax returns,* and *city income tax returns.* Other governmental information returns that form the basis for statistical data on the United States are also required. Government requirements can place a substantial extra load on a firm.

Personnel
Although the personnel function is not shown graphically in Figure 1-7, it is interconnected with all the basic business operations shown. Its basic task is to determine personnel needed. A combined personnel and payroll file on-line can assist in recruiting personnel internally for new positions before going to outside sources. Various personnel forms can be employed, such as *personnel history and promotion records* and *personnel requisition forms.*

computer applications for business information systems

In order to visualize the uses of the foregoing sources of data, it would be helpful to relate them to computer applications for business information systems. Fundamentally, a computer application represents one or more operations of a system to which a computer solution can be applied. Although applications may vary, there is generally some type of input data that is manipulated by the computer to produce some form of output. Computer applications presented below include sales analysis, inventory control, and accounts receivable.

Sales Analysis

The net result of processing marketing data is to produce meaningful output for sales management and accounting purposes. Output can be used to answer such questions as: what are total monthly sales in terms of products, what are monthly sales by salespeople and, what are monthly sales commissions by salespeople? Computer output can also answer questions such as: who are the highest producing salespeople, what products are showing a decline in sales and, should a product be dropped?

MONTHLY SALES REPORT BY PRODUCTS
Month Ending 2-28-xx

| | | Sales | Year-to-Date Sales | | |
Product Name	Inventory Number	This Month	This Year	Last Year	Inc./ (Dec.)
Electric Skillets—s.	10010	48,750	81,825	78,655	3,170
Electric Skillets—m.	10020	42,830	82,105	81,265	840
Electric Skillets—l.	10030	43,735	88,490	89,470	(980)
Toasters—Two Slices	10100	23,330	44,950	45,280	(330)
Toasters—Three Slices	10110	21,415	41,468	38,955	2,513
Toasters—Four Slices	10120	46,410	90,510	86,645	3,865

MONTHLY SALES REPORT BY SALESPEOPLE
Month Ending 2-28-xx

Salesperson Name	Salesperson No.	Total Sales
Atwood	10	125,380
Crawford	25	143,540
Dalton	33	68,050
Graham	45	49,750
Greely	48	85,160
Hanover	52	82,260
McVay	62	98,775
Moran	70	93,275

figure 1-8. Typical monthly sales analysis reports—monthly sales report by products and monthly sales report by salespeople.

Two typical sales analysis reports shown in Figure 1-8 illustrate sales computer applications, namely, total monthly sales by products and monthly sales by salespeople. The first computer report gives the sales by product for the current month and compares year-to-date sales with the previous year-to-date sales. By examining the large decreases, the sales manager can determine where sales losses have occurred, and how to overcome anticipated losses in the future. The second computer report lists total sales by salespersons.

Sales analysis enables marketing management to decide where its sales efforts need to be improved. Without adequate information, marketing management cannot make effective decisions for the future.

Inventory Control

Inventory control has two goals: (1) to keep the investment in inventory as low as possible, and (2) to provide an adequate level of customer service. Emphasis here will be on monthly inventory reports that relate to the second goal — service to the customer.

Emphasis in Figure 1-9 is on the service level percent for a given month and on the year-to-date service level. Those inventory items that are experiencing a less than 100% service level for the current month should be analyzed. It may well be that the amount of safety stock, i.e., inventory to protect against stock outages, is too small based upon increased demand for a specific product. Hence, adjustments may be necessary to increase the overall inventory level for this item in order to reduce the number of back orders throughout the coming month.

Computerized inventory control applications tend to be complex. However, they can be an important means of increasing profits. Use of computer systems has been justified by their capability to control inventory more effectively. Thus, computerized inventory control systems can have a positive effect on the typical company.

MONTHLY INVENTORY SERVICE-LEVEL REPORT
Month Ending 2-28-xx

| Product Name | Inventory Number | This Month | | | Year-to-Date Service Level |
		Value Ordered	Back Ordered	Service Level	
Electric Skillets — s.	10010	48,750	—	100.0%	94.5%
Electric Skillets — m.	10020	42,830	1,075	97.5%	86.0%
Electric Skillets — l.	10030	43,735	—	100.0%	100.0%
Toasters — Two Slices	10100	23,330	—	100.0%	97.5%
Toasters — Three Slices	10110	21,415	1,475	93.1%	88.8%
Toasters — Four Slices	10120	46,410	—	100.0%	97.5%

figure 1-9. Typical monthly inventory service-level report.

Accounts Receivable

Numerous sources of accounting data were presented previously in the chapter. Emphasis here will be on accounts receivable. Because accounts receivable refers to amounts owed, its computer application centers on keeping records of amounts owed by customers as well as providing information that will help an organization control these amounts.

To control the amounts owed, accounting management needs information as illustrated in Figure 1-10. The aged accounts receivable report shows the amounts owed by each customer and the length of time these amounts have been owed. Within the report are separate columns for current and delinquent amounts. Column values agree with the "total balance" column in each case.

The second computer report shows customers whose debts are over 60 days. Also contained in this report is information regarding the number of times the customer has been past due.

AGED ACCOUNTS RECEIVABLE REPORT

Month Ending 2-28-xx

Customer Name	Customer Number	Total Balance	Current	Over 30 Days	Over 60 Days	Over 90 Days
A. & B. Stores	2055	2,827.25	2,827.25			
Ayres Stores, Inc.	2150	5,109.66	2,742.00	296.91		2,070.75
All Stores	2257	5,261.70			5,261.70	
Arnold's Stores	2350	1,129.00	1,129.00			
Big Stores	2435	1,550.90	1,550.90			
Campus Stores	2654	1,781.70	1,781.70			
Consolidated Stores	2750	1,915.15	812.65		1,102.50	
Downtown Stores	2810	1,399.00	1,399.00			
General Stores	3258	2,049.50	2,049.50			

DELINQUENT ACCOUNTS RECEIVABLE REPORT

Month Ending 2-28-xx

Customer Name	Customer Number	Last 12 Months Times Over 30 Days	Last 12 Months Times Over 60 Days	Amount Over 60 Days
Ayres Stores, Inc.	2150	7	3	2,070.75
All Stores	2257	2	1	5,261.70
Consolidated Stores	2750	5	2	1,102.50

figure 1-10. Typical monthly accounts receivable control reports—aged accounts receivable report and delinquent accounts receivable report.

The foregoing accounts receivable computer application not only produces accurate information, but also provides accounting management with up-to-date information that can be of significant help in reducing the amount of delinquent balances.

summary

Initially, the chapter focused on defining basic data processing terms, with emphasis on information and business information systems. The relationship of information value to its cost was also discussed. The most desirable degree of information accuracy is reached when its value exceeds the cost of acquiring it by the greatest margin.

Next in the chapter, accent was placed on exploring the underlying concepts of business information systems. This was followed by a discussion of the basic types of computerized business information systems found in organizations today. Such a presentation served as a background for exploring the sources of data and typical computer applications as found in business organizations. Hence, this overview to computerized business information systems gives the reader an introduction to various subject areas that will be explored in more detail in subsequent chapters.

**second summary
of chapter 1**

basic computerized information systems:

• batch processing—transactions are accumulated and processed periodically; the items in the batch may be in sequential or random order. Sequential or direct access files are used. Example: college students submitting computer programs to the computer center and picking them up after processing has occurred

• interactive processing—transactions and inquiries into the system are processed as they occur. Direct access files are used. *Example:* college students sharing interactively the computing power of one computer

sources of data for business information systems:

Business data are generated as a result of daily operations and interaction with other functions. The basic business functions that are the sources of data for a typical manufacturing firm are:

• marketing—its primary task is to contact potential customers and sell merchandise through salespersons, advertising, and special promotions. Sample form: sales order

• research and development—its major role is to develop new products and processes to sustain the organization's planned growth rate. Sample form: research and development order

• engineering—its principal function is to design new products and processes that have been agreed upon by the marketing and research and development departments. Sample form: engineering blueprint

• manufacturing—its chief role is to produce finished goods in anticipation of demand, upon receipt of customer's orders, or both. Sample form: production order

• purchasing—its assigned task is to procure raw materials, equipment, supplies, etc. required to meet the organization's operating needs. Sample form: purchase order

• receiving—its major function is to check and verify the receipt of goods and materials from outside vendors. Sample form: receiving report

• inventory control—its assigned task is to store and protect goods and materials as well as issue items to the appropriate departments. Sample form: inventory record

• shipping—its principal task is to ship finished goods to customers or company-owned warehouses. Sample form: shipping order

• accounting—its primary job is to record, classify, and report company activities that are of a financial nature. Sample form: customer invoice

• personnel—its principal role is to place the right person in the right job at the various levels in an organization. Sample form: personnel history and employment form.

second self-study exercise

True-False:

1. (   ) Sequential and direct access files are one and the same.
2. (   ) Files for a batch-processing mode may be sequential or direct access.
3. (   ) Interactive processing is not available for student purposes at a college.
4. (   ) Accounting is a very important source of financial business data.
5. (   ) Planning, organizing, directing, and controlling are the sources of business data.
6. (   ) Research and development and engineering perform the same functions.
7. (   ) Bills of materials are used to determine the number of items for a production order.
8. (   ) A purchase requisition and materials requisition can be used interchangeably.
9. (   ) Voucher checks are only used for payroll purposes.
10. (   ) The personnel function is the least important of all the basic business functions.

Fill-In:

11. Two basic types of computer information systems for business are _____ _____ and _____ _____.
12. Batch processing lends itself to _____ access and _____ access files.
13. Interactive processing utilizes _____ or _____ access files.
14. An interactive processing mode is widely used in airline _____ _____.
15. Business data are generated as a result of daily operations and _____ with other functions.
16. The initial source of data that starts the product information flow is the _____ department.
17. A _____ _____ is forwarded to the purchasing department for placing orders with outside vendors.
18. A _____ _____ is used to document the actual amount of goods received from a vendor.
19. A _____ _____ is a check with an attached form that contains date, amount, discount, net payment, and other relevant items.
20. _____ _____ and earnings statements are the basis for paying organization employees.

questions

1. Define the following terms:
   a. a business information system   d. information
   b. data   e. feedback
   c. data base

2. Why is the concept of a business information system so important to a manager? Explain.

3. What general system rule can be used to determine the most desirable level of information accuracy?

4. Differentiate between the management information system concept and the distributed processing system concept.

5. Distinguish between the basic types of computer access file systems.

6. Differentiate between a batch processing mode and an interactive processing mode.

7. What are the basic sources of data to be found in any organization regardless of the system employed?

8. What is the relationship of sources of business data to computer applications?

answers to first self-study exercise

1. F 2. T 3. F 4. F 5. F 6. F 7. F 8. T 9. T 10. F 11. data 12. information 13. system 14. business information system 15. computer system 16. feedback 17. value received 18. management information system 19. local processing 20. summary information

answers to second self-study exercise

1. F 2. T 3. F 4. T 5. F 6. F 7. T 8. F 9. F 10 F 11. batch processing and interactive processing 12. sequential and direct 13. direct and random 14. reservation systems 15. interaction 16. marketing 17. purchase requisition 18. receiving report 19. voucher check 20. payroll checks

part two

problem analysis and operating concepts of data processing for business

For a computerized business program to produce the desired results, it is necessary first to analyze it, that is, define the problem and prepare the appropriate flowcharts. This is done in Chapter 2. To assist in a better understanding of writing and testing an operational program (the subject matter of Part Three), the internal operating concepts of computers are presented in Chapter Three.

chapter two
problem definition and preparation of flowcharts

In the opening section of the previous chapter, reference was made to a typical scenario of the future. Here, we will deal with computer processing capabilities as used today. For example, let us consider Joe Cosgrove, a blue collar worker, in a manufacturing plant. When the factory buzzer signals the end of the shift at 4:30 p.m., Joe heads for the parking lot. Before doing so, he punches his time card. By punching his time card, Joe has sent a message to the company's computer, that he left work at 4:30 p.m. today.

This information plus all others about clocking in and out for the entire week is used in preparing his following week's pay. The computer has totaled his hours worked and calculated his total pay. Additionally, it has calculated the appropriate mandatory deductions, such as federal and state income taxes, as well as voluntary ones, such as union dues and hospitalization, for determining net pay. This weekly pay information is used for determining year-to-date payroll figures, providing valuable information for costing the company's products, updating total service times for the personnel department, and similar items. However, before processing can occur, there is need for analyzing payroll processing (problem analysis) and determining the detailed steps in preparing the weekly payroll checks (preparation of flowcharts).

In this chapter, problem analysis is explored as a logical starting point for programming and implementing an operational computer program. A typical business example is given to illustrate this initial phase of computer programming. Next, flowcharts are discussed and illustrated. In addition, an alternative method to flowcharting is presented, namely, decision tables.

solving business problems using computers

Before business problems can be solved by a computer approach, they must be recognized as such. Problems may be brought to the attention of management, in particular, DP management, by organization personnel, outside consultants, or company customers. By and large, recognition of business problems that are solvable by computer technology is the result of systematic observation by lower, middle, and top management. For example, the need of timely management information by marketing managers, the need to determine more efficient ways of preparing monthly financial statements, and the need for prompt feedback to customers on the status of their orders, to name a few, are problem types that must be detected before a solution can be started.

Once the problem has been detected and determined to be solvable by a computerized solution, there is need to study the problem in detail. This is known as *problem analysis*—a process whereby the problem is defined and all of the information needed for the problem's solution is identified. Since the problem is oriented toward utilizing a computer program—a set of instructions to perform a specific processing task—it includes two basic steps. They are:

- defining the problem
- preparing the program flowchart(s)

which are discussed below.

defining the problem

Developing a precise definition of the problem is the initial undertaking before an operational computer program can be implemented. This entails determining what its relationship is to the overall system; what information is required from the system, particularly in the form of reports; where the input is obtained, including a list of all required and available inputs; what data files are involved; whether results are needed upon inquiry or otherwise; what exceptions must be considered in processing; and similar considerations. These important items are stressed in Figure 2-1. Even if

figure 2-1. Step 1 of problem analysis for developing an operational computer program consists of defining the problem. Systems personnel are discussing the problem to be solved.

Problem Analysis of a Computer Program

Step 1: *Defining the Problem.* The problem to be solved is carefully studied and defined. As shown below, system personnel are discussing the problem to be solved. Determination must be made regarding what input data are to be processed, what files are to be used, what output is to be desired, and how the data are to be manipulated to produce the desired output.

IBM 1403 PRINT CHART

IBM

PROGRAM TITLE: SALES REP

PROGRAMMER OR DOCUMENTALIST: JACK NIEHAUS

CHART TITLE: REPORT 1

PAGE 1   DATE 10/23/8

MONTHLY SALES REPORT BY PRODUCTS

MONTH ENDING MM-DD-YY

| PRODUCT NAME | INVENTORY NUMBER | SALES THIS MONTH | --YEAR-TO-DATE SALES-- | | INC./ |
			THIS YEAR	LAST YEAR	(DEC.)
XXXXXXXXXXXXXXXXXXXXXXX	XXXXX	XXX,XXX	XXX,XXX	XXX,XXX	XXX,XXX
XXXXXXXXXXXXXXXXXXXXXXX	XXXXX	XX,XXX	XX,XXX	XX,XXX	XX,XXX

figure 2-2. Print chart for a monthly sales report by products.

a specific area is being converted as is, answers to these questions must be obtained since any business information system has far-reaching effects on other parts of the system. The necessity to define the problem precisely cannot be overemphasized. Without this process, the problem may not be solved in a manner commensurate with the overall system objectives.

Computer Monthly Sales Report Application

To illustrate this first step in business problem analysis, a monthly sales report by products (refer to Figure 1-8 in the prior chapter) is to be programmed. In order to know exactly what the computer program is supposed to do before it can be written, certain information is needed. For this batch-processing program, the following areas must be defined:

1. The input source for product name, inventory number, sales this month, year-to-date sales this year, and year-to-date sales last year.
2. The checking of input data to ensure that all inventory numbers are in the proper sequence.
3. The number of lines to be printed for each inventory item, assuming that there may be more than one input source for each item.
4. The spacing on the monthly sales report.
5. The method of calculation for determining the increase and decrease in year-to-date sales.

These and other questions must be defined completely for a thorough understanding of what the computer program will be doing.

As a way of defining this monthly sales reports by products report, normally a print chart is supplied, like the one pictured in Figure 2-2. If one is not supplied, the programmer should have little difficulty in developing one. In addition, it is necessary to know the punched card format of input data. Illustrated in Figure 2-3 is the record layout form for recording sales data by the computer system. An understanding of what the foregoing input data are, what the foregoing output of the computer program must be, and what calculations and totals must be made in deriving the output from the input provides a means of defining the problem precisely.

| **preparing the program flowchart(s)** | To express the defined problem for computer solution, one or more program flowcharts are prepared. As noted later in the chapter, program flowcharts are a means for showing graphically the flow of computer program steps. They include all the possible alternatives of the defined problem. However, in some cases, one or more decision tables are developed. As stated later in the chapter, decision tables are a means for showing logical choices of computer program steps. This is particularly true where there is a myriad of decisions that must be undertaken by the program. Still in other situations, a combination of program flowcharts and decision tables is the answer. By having computer program steps stated concisely and briefly in decision tables, accurate flowcharts can be constructed that includes all of the possible alternatives.

Whether program flowcharts, decision tables, or a combination of the two are utilized, these programming aids depict the overall flow of program steps. One or more levels of detailed flowcharts or decision tables should |

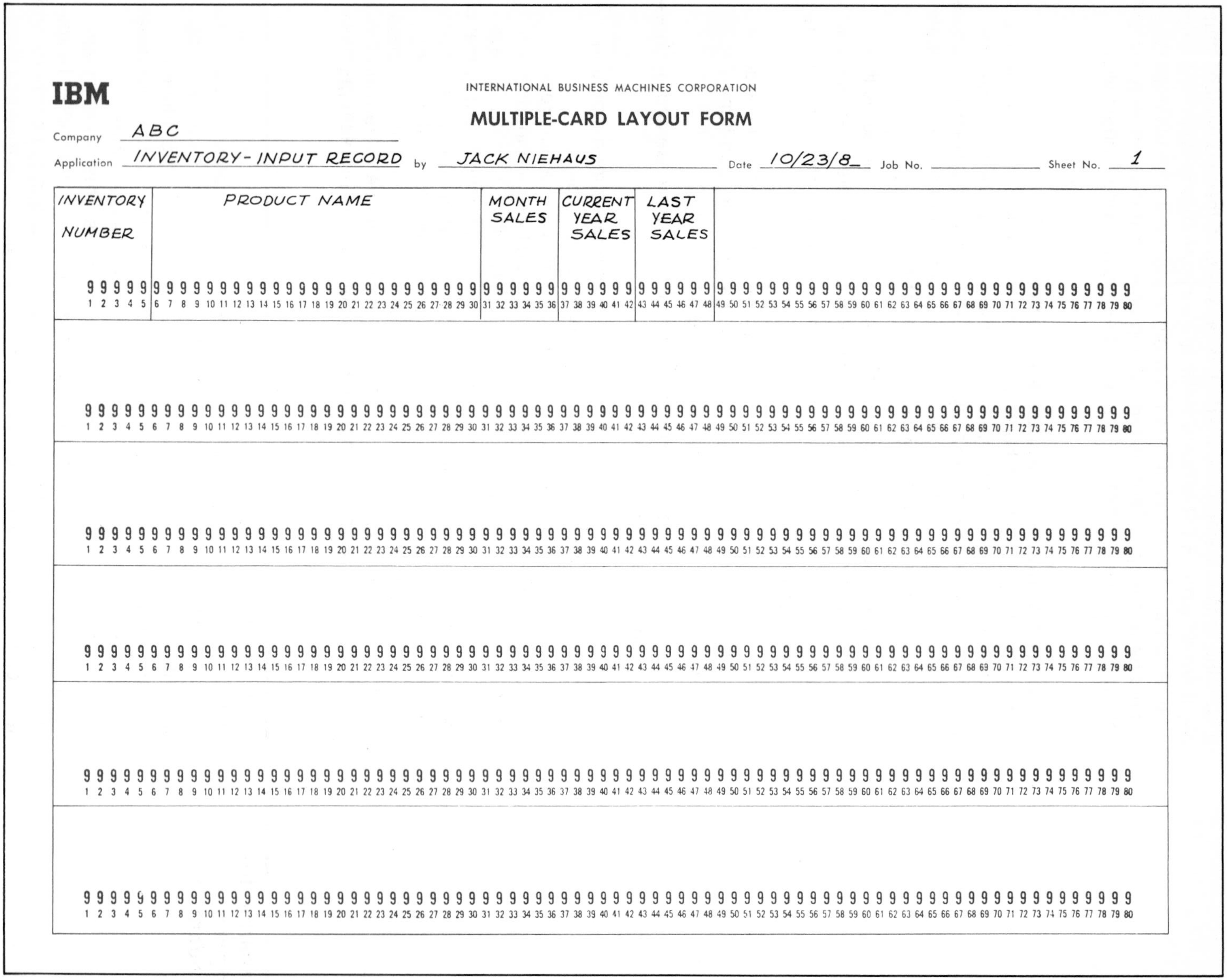

figure 2-3. Record layout for monthly sales cards by products.

figure 2-4. Step 2 of problem analysis for developing an operational computer program consists of preparing the program flowcharts. A programmer is checking punched cards (representing the steps in the flowchart) against a computer prepared flowchart.

be supported by an overview approach to the defined problem. Not only do these programming aids allow the programmer to visualize the overall flow of work, but also they provide the necessary detail for coding the computer problem under study. A summary of this second step is set forth in Figure 2-4.

Problem Analysis of a Computer Program

Step 2: *Preparing the Program Flowcharts.* Once the problem has been defined, one or more program flowcharts are prepared manually. However, program flowcharts can be produced by the computer using punched card input. As illustrated below, a programmer is checking a computer prepared flowchart. In some cases, one or more decision tables are developed. Using either method or a combination of the two, the individual reduces the problem to a series of discrete programming steps. Program flowcharts illustrate graphically the flow of program steps while decision tables depict logical choices of program steps.

Computer Monthly Sales Report Application (continued)
To illustrate the preceding monthly sales report computer program (being programmed in a batch-processing mode), a program flowchart is found in Figure 2-5. Although program flowcharts will be discussed in more detail later in the chapter, it can be seen that a sequence of instructions is used. Similarly, logic is involved to derive the desired output, i.e., the monthly

figure 2-5. Program flow-chart for printing monthly sales report by products.

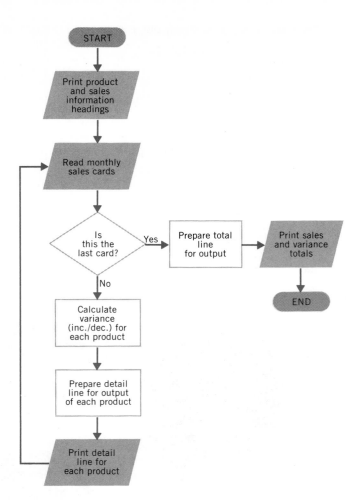

sales report by products from the monthly sales card input. In essence, the program flowchart determines what must be done to solve the problem, that is, to produce the monthly sales report.

As depicted in Figure 2-5, the first step in the program flowchart is to print product and sales information headings (refer to Figure 1-8). Next, the first monthly sales card is read. Since this is the first card and not the last card, the variance for this product is calculated and all information to be contained on the report is printed. The program logic goes to reading the second card and performing the necessary operations, then the third card, and so forth. After the last card is read by the computer, sales and variance totals are printed. This printing of totals ends the computer program. Thus, the preparation of a program flowchart for this simple problem illustrates the second step of business problem analysis—deciding what must be done to solve the problem defined in step one.

Programming and Testing

Problem analysis, which consists of defining the problem and preparing program flowcharts and/or decision tables, is the first of a series of steps that are necessary for programming and testing an operational computer

figure 2-6. Programming of an operational computer program in a batch and an interactive processing mode. A programmer is coding from a program flowchart.

Programming of a Computer Program

Steps for a Batch-Processing Mode: The series of discrete programming steps set forth in flowcharts and/or decision tables are coded as a group of computer instructions in a programming language. As shown below, a programmer is coding from a program flowchart. Standard coding sheets and language manuals assist in the programming effort. After the program has been written, the programmer desk checks the program for errors after which each line on the coding sheets is converted to a punched card. These program cards are used as input for compiling, that is, they are converted to machine language—a language that the computer understands. All errors noted by the compiling process are corrected and the computer program is recompiled.

Steps for an Interactive Processing Mode. Since most programs used in this mode are straightforward, the program is entered through the keyboard of a typewriter or a visual display terminal. Corrections are made as directed by the computer. Hence, an interactive processing mode has fewer steps than a batch-processing mode.

program. The additional steps are conditioned upon the type of processing mode—batch or interactive. If programming is performed in a batch-processing mode, i.e., if data are batched and processed in this manner, there are several steps involved, namely, writing the computer program, desk checking the program, preparing punched cards of the program, compiling or converting the program cards to machine language instructions, correcting errors as noted by the computer during the compiling process, and recompiling the program. On the other hand, if an interactive processing mode is used for programming, the program is entered through the keyboard of a typewriter or a visual display terminal. Corrections are made by the operator as indicated by the computer. The steps for programming in a batch and an interactive processing mode are set forth in Figure 2-6.

Testing of a Computer Program

Steps for a Batch-Processing Mode. The recompiled computer program is tested against sample transactions. As illustrated below, a group of programmers are watching for printed output using sample test data. Errors are corrected during this testing process. If a large number of errors is noted, the program is again recompiled. Sample data are processed again to insure that all program errors are corrected.

Steps for an Interactive Processing Mode. Testing in an interactive processing mode is similar to a batch-processing mode, except that testing is performed on a typewriter or visual display terminal. Generally, the testing time is faster in an interactive mode.

figure 2-7. Testing of an operational computer program in a batch and an interactive processing mode. A group of programmers are watching for printed output using sample test data.

When testing the program in a batch-processing mode, sample transaction data are used to remove errors from the program. All known errors are corrected. Generally, the program is recompiled, especially when a large number of errors are noted. After recompiling the program, sample data are again processed to insure that all corrections have been made properly. In a similar manner, testing is performed in an interactive processing mode, except that a typewriter or a visual display unit is employed. This user/machine interaction is faster than for a batch-processing mode. The essentials of testing are given in Figure 2-7.

The foregoing steps for programming and testing for an operational computer program in both processing modes are explored in more detail in Chapter 4 along with the steps for implementation. Additionally, documentation is covered which include flowcharts, decision tables, computer programs, program language printouts, write-up on computer programs, and similar items. Only the second step, i.e., the preparation of flowcharts, and decision tables is explored in more detail in the remainder of this chapter.

flowcharts

A *flowchart* is defined as a graphical representation of the definition, analysis, or solution of a problem using symbols to represent operations, data flow, equipment, and the like. In essence, a flowchart is a diagrammatic representation of a series of events.

Because a flowchart is a pictorial representation of data flow, the flow of data and paper work from the input stages through the many intermediate stages, including complex computer programs, to the final outputs must be explicitly detailed for effective implementation. Otherwise, it is difficult to follow the logical flow of data processing activities.

The procedures an individual follows in performing a job can be flowcharted. In a similar manner, the routines an individual follows when getting up in the morning, getting to work, and the like can be flowcharted. For example, when the alarm rings in the morning, the individual turns it off and gets out of bed. After showering, brushing teeth, combing hair, etc., the person is ready for breakfast. In effect, a series of end-to-end activities take place where a certain number of decisions must be made. If it is raining, a decision must be made whether to wear a raincoat, take an umbrella, or both. Similarly, the individual could decide if groceries are needed before returning home, resulting in the need for extra money.

Values of Flowcharts

It has been said that "a picture is worth a thousand words." The same can be said for a flowchart since it is a picture of some part of a data processing system.

Aids Understanding. A flowchart shows explicitly what is happening, in what order, and has the ability to detect gaps in procedures or overlaps in system activities. It is much easier to comprehend what is occurring with diagrams than with a written description. In a diagram of a data processing procedure, errors or omissions stand out.

Effective Communicator. The flowchart is an effective communicator to other personnel. The interworkings of a new method, procedure, or system can be communicated to others. Likewise, a chart is a succinct presentation of data flow to management and operating personnel for controlling the organization's activities.

Permanent Record. A third value of flowcharting is that it is a permanent record which does not depend on oral communication. Since the chart is written, it is available for review purposes in terms of accuracy and completeness. It also provides a basis for analyzing and comparing present and proposed systems so that efficiency, cost, timeliness, or other relevant factors may be improved.

flowchart symbols

Over the years, there has been a concerted attempt to standardize flowcharting symbols. Standardization allows anyone to interpret accurately the work of another. This is particularly important today because of the high

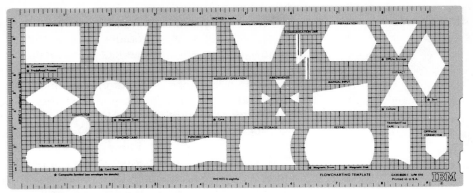

figure 2-8. Template for drawing flowchart symbols.

job mobility of systems personnel. The person preparing the flowchart today may not be the one interpreting it tomorrow. If standard flowcharting symbols are used, confusion is kept to a minimum. Thus, standardized flowchart symbols have been developed by the United States of America Standards Institute (USASI) and the International Standards Organization. These approved flowcharting symbols are discussed below.

Standard Flowchart Symbols

Standard flowchart symbols that indicate the type of operations to be performed by computer and punched card equipment consist of general and specialized symbols. A template, such as that pictured in Figure 2-8, aids in drawing those symbols. Generally, these symbols can be classified in three main categories:

- basic
- input/output and file
- processing

This classification, along with typical payroll examples, is illustrated in Figures 2-9 through 2-11 respectively.

To illustrate the foregoing categories, the following are presented. A typical example for employing *basic* symbols is the payment of sales commissions where sales cards are computer processed to produce the monthly sales commissions report:

Input/Output Symbol   Process Symbol   Input/Output Symbol

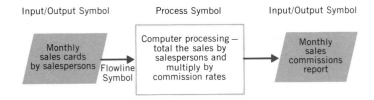

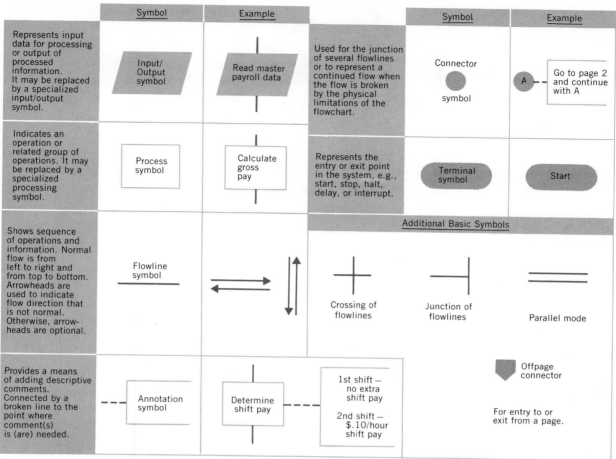

figure 2-9. *Basic* flowchart symbols and illustrated payroll examples along with additional basic symbols.

An example of utilizing *input/output* and *file* symbols is the weekly editing of payroll for factory employees. The input is punched time cards which are computer processed against a master payroll file to produce a weekly payroll error listing:

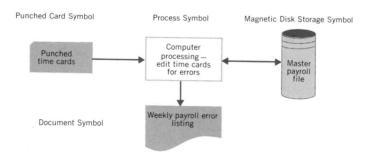

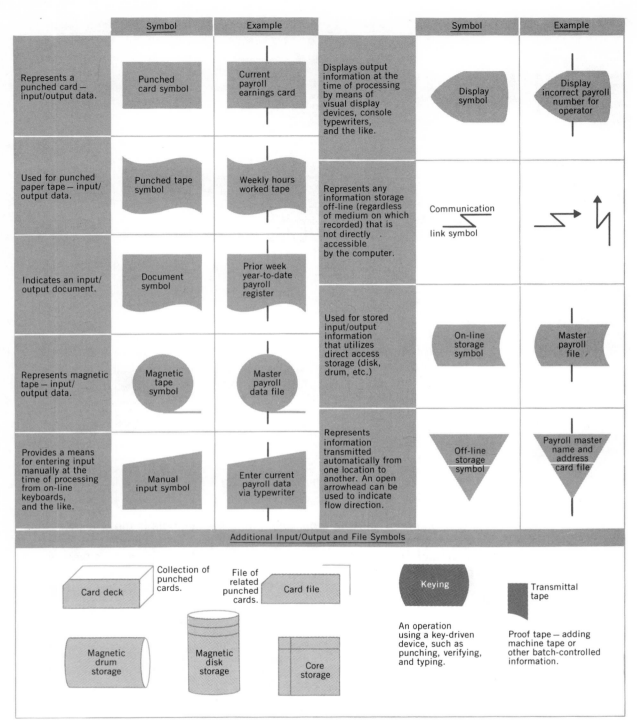

	Symbol	Example		Symbol	Example
Represents a punched card — input/output data.	Punched card symbol	Current payroll earnings card	Displays output information at the time of processing by means of visual display devices, console typewriters, and the like.	Display symbol	Display incorrect payroll number for operator
Used for punched paper tape — input/output data.	Punched tape symbol	Weekly hours worked tape	Represents any information storage off-line (regardless of medium on which recorded) that is not directly accessible by the computer.	Communication link symbol	
Indicates an input/output document.	Document symbol	Prior week year-to-date payroll register	Used for stored input/output information that utilizes direct access storage (disk, drum, etc.)	On-line storage symbol	Master payroll file
Represents magnetic tape — input/output data.	Magnetic tape symbol	Master payroll data file	Represents information transmitted automatically from one location to another. An open arrowhead can be used to indicate flow direction.	Off-line storage symbol	Payroll master name and address card file
Provides a means for entering input manually at the time of processing from on-line keyboards, and the like.	Manual input symbol	Enter current payroll data via typewriter			

Additional Input/Output and File Symbols

Card deck — Collection of punched cards.

File of related punched cards. — Card file

Keying — An operation using a key-driven device, such as punching, verifying, and typing.

Transmittal tape — Proof tape — adding machine tape or other batch-controlled information.

Magnetic drum storage

Magnetic disk storage

Core storage

figure 2-10. *Input/output* and *file* flowchart symbols and illustrated payroll examples along with additional input/output and file symbols.

An illustration of *processing* symbols is the weekly comparison of hours worked by factory employees to determine the amount of overtime:

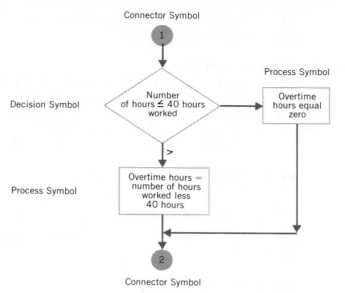

Flow of Symbols. No matter what combination of above flowchart symbols are used, flowcharts are constructed to follow our natural tendency to read from left to right and from top to bottom. At times, it is desirable to deviate from this pattern in order to achieve symmetry and to emphasize important points. *Solid flowlines* are drawn to indicate the direction of the flow while *dotted flowlines* depict a transfer of information as well as annotated information. In either case, flowlines can be drawn horizontally, vertically, or diagonally, as needed, for a meaningful flowchart.

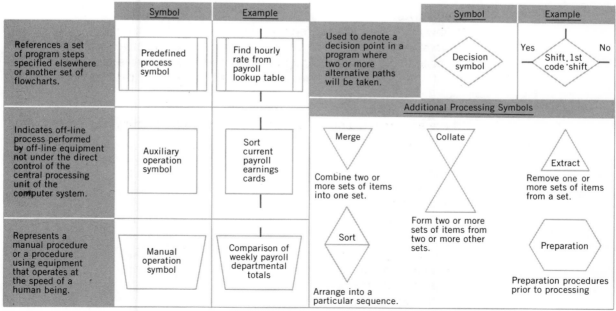

figure 2-11. *Processing* flowchart symbols and illustrated payroll examples along with additional processing symbols.

**first summary
of chapter 2**

solving business problems with computers:
Before business problems can be solved using a computer, there must be a recognition that they exist. Problems can be uncovered by a systematic observation of the organization.

defining the problem:
The first step centers on understanding the problem to be solved, that is, what the computer program will be doing in terms of what the inputs are, what the outputs of the program are, and what calculations and other programming procedures must be followed in deriving the desired outputs. Example: computer monthly sales report application

preparing the program flowchart(s):
The second step focuses on reducing the defined problem per the first step to a sequence of logical program instructions to produce the desired output. Hence, program flowcharts and/or decision tables decide what must be done to solve the defined problem. Example: computer monthly sales report application (continued)

programming and testing:
For a batch-processing mode, a series of program steps are coded as a group of computer instructions. In turn, program cards are prepared and the program is compiled for conversion to machine language instructions. Once all known program errors have been corrected, the program is tested with sample test data. The programming and testing steps in an interactive processing mode are somewhat similar to a batch-processing mode, except that the program is entered through the keyboard of a typewriter or visual display terminal. Similarly, all test data are entered via the keyboard for verifying the accuracy of the program.

flowcharts:
A flowchart is a pictorial representation of data flow. It aids not only in understanding what is happening, but also is an effective communicator to those using it as well as a permanent record. Example: a series of end-to-end activities that involves decision making in performing a job

flowchart symbols:
There are three major categories of standard flowchart symbols. They are:
- basic symbols
  - input/output
  - process
  - flowline
  - annotation
  - connector
  - terminal
- input/output and file symbols
  - punched card
  - punched tape
  - document

- magnetic tape
- manual input
- display
- communication link
- on-line storage
- off-line storage
- processing symbols
  - predefined process
  - auxiliary operation
  - manual operation
  - decision

**first self-study
exercise
of chapter 2**

True-False:

1. (   ) The final step in developing an operational computer program is flowcharting.
2. (   ) Problem analysis is the same for both batch and interactive processing modes.
3. (   ) Generally, testing is not needed for a typical computer program.
4. (   ) A decision table is a pictorial representation of data flow.
5. (   ) By and large, there are no official flowcharting symbols.
6. (   ) An example of a flowline symbol is an arrow.
7. (   ) Crossing of flowlines is not allowed in program flowcharting.
8. (   ) The magnetic tape storage symbol is the same as for the magnetic drum.
9. (   ) The on-line and off-line storage symbols are the same.
10. (   ) The inverted triangle symbol means to combine data into one set.

Fill-In:

11. The first step in developing an operational computer program is _____ the _____.
12. The second step in developing an operational computer program is preparing _____ _____.
13. An alternative to using program flowcharts is developing _____ _____.
14. _____ always precedes testing of a computer program whether it be in a batch or an interactive processing mode.
15. A _____ is a pictorial representation of data flow within an organization.
16. A flowchart has certain important values. It aids understanding, is an effective _____, and serves as a permanent _____.
17. The basic _____ symbol is represented by a rectangle.
18. The basic _____ symbol is represented by a small circle.
19. A management report can be represented by a _____ symbol.
20. A diamond indicates a _____ symbol.

flowchart types

There are several types of flowcharts found in a data processing installation. Among the most frequently used are system flowcharts and program flowcharts. A *system flowchart* depicts the flow of data through the major parts of a system with a minimum of detail. Generally, it shows where input enters the system, how it is processed and controlled, and how it leaves the systems in terms of storage and output. A program *flowchart* depicts the flow of processing steps in a computer program and is generally more detailed than a system flowchart. Since a computer must be directed according to a detailed set of instructions called a program (stored internally in the computer), these flowcharts are a necessity for programming computer applications.

The amount of detail will depend upon the purpose for which the flowchart will be used. However, for a successful installation of any data processing equipment, all methods and procedures must be flowcharted in detail. This lowest level of detail is also the basis for issuing instructions to company personnel.

System Flowchart

System flowcharts, sometimes referred to as *procedural flowcharts,* show the sequence of major activities that normally comprise a complete operation. They are generally prepared to assist all organizational personnel, in particular the systems analyst, in understanding some specific data processing operation as well as obtaining an overview of the operation itself. Before a system flowchart can be drawn, the area under study must be clearly defined. Questions relating to the type and number of inputs (source documents), exceptions, transactions, files, and reports, must be answered. Similar questions refer to the relationship of the area under study to other functional parts of the data processing system, the timeliness of data, and the source of various data. Answers to these typical questions provide the necessary information for the initial system flowchart.

A very simple system flowchart, illustrated in Figure 2-12, involves the procedures necessary to maintain an individual's bank account at a minimum level of $200. The purpose of maintaining this amount is to save monthly banking charges as well as charges on each check written. The initial procedure is totaling the new checks written and subtracting them from the current bank balance for a new bank balance. A comparison is made to $200 (cutoff point for saving bank charges). If the new bank balance is greater than or equal to $200, checks are mailed and processing is completed. However, if the comparison results in a less-than condition, a deposit must be made to bring the new balance up to a level of $200 (or more). Checks are then mailed and processing ends.

Raw Material Inventory Illustration. A typical system flowchart is found in Figure 2-13. Inspection of this flowchart indicates that current transactions are updated as they occur. These include raw materials receipts from vendors, in-plant transfers to finished goods inventory, physical inventory count changes, and miscellaneous adjustments—based on spoilage, scrappage, obsolescence, shrinkage, and similar items. Also, automatic purchasing of raw materials is performed on-line. Cards are punched

figure 2-12. System flow-chart for maintaining an individual's bank balance at a level of $200 or more.

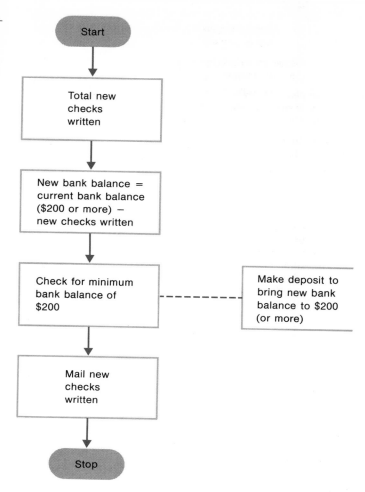

to signal excess inventory and certain inventory errors that are the result of previously mentioned on-line activities. In essence, this approach to raw material inventory allows inquiry into the system at any time.

Program Flowchart

Program flowcharts, sometimes referred to as *block diagrams,* describe the specific steps and their sequence for a particular computer program. When a program is extremely simple, a flowchart may not be necessary. However, for most programs, it is necessary to have a sequence of operations and decisions that detail the computer program steps. Otherwise, the programmer would have a difficult task in coding the program properly. In a similar manner, the program flowchart provides an excellent means of documenting the program. The program flowchart, then, has three important uses.

- aids program development
- serves as a guide for coding
- is a basis for documentation

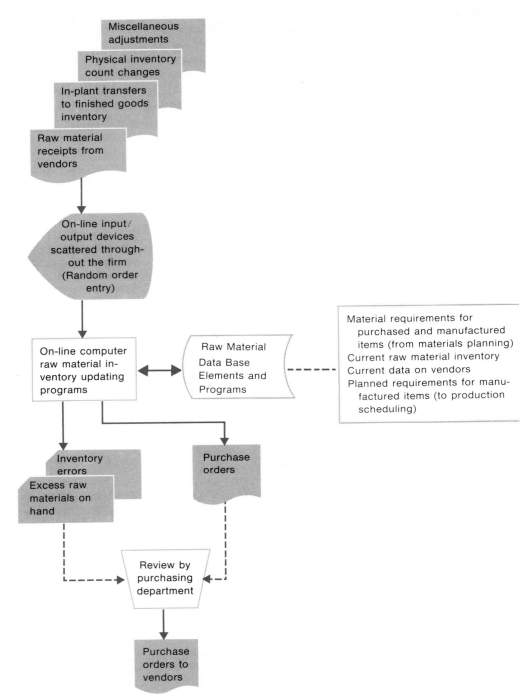

figure 2-13. System flowchart for a computer raw material inventory updating run.

Figure 2-14 illustrates a simple example of a program flowchart. This example would normally be a part of a larger program flowchart. The example illustrates the program steps needed to add weekly pay (regular) and weekly pay (overtime) together in order to store the results for total

figure 2-14. Program flowchart for adding R (weekly pay—regular) and O (weekly pay—overtime) together and storing the results in T (total weekly pay).

weekly pay. Computer instructions to add the two values and store the results are illustrated in Chapter Three.

Compute Voluntary Deduction Illustration. A computer program flowchart for computing voluntary deductions is depicted in Figure 2-15. The program consists of a series of operations and decisions regarding the proper weekly voluntary payroll deductions. In the first processing symbol, union dues of $5.00 are deducted for each employee. This value is added for all employees. For the first set of decision symbols, if the insurance code is 1, then $2.50 will be deducted. Similarly, if the insurance code is 2, $3.00 will be deducted. Otherwise, the insurance deduction will be $2.00. In all cases, each insurance deduction is added for a grand total. In the last set of decisions, a comparison is made to determine whether the code is 1, 2, or 3. The amount deducted for these codes is $5.00, $7.50, and $10.00 respectively. As before, each amount is added for a grand total. Thus, within this program flowchart, comparisons are made to determine the deductions for insurance premiums and savings bonds while union dues of $5.00 are deducted for all employees.

Computer Prepared Program Flowchart. An extremely helpful flow-charting technique is utilization of the computer itself with a special flowchart writing program. Using asterisks and other special symbols, the printer plots the outlines of the symbols and converts them as if they were flowcharted manually. The advantage of such a method is that revisions can be made easily once the initial table is written and cards have been correctly punched. The updating process consists of repunching cards that represent program flowchart changes. This approach can keep the laborious task of updating complex program flowcharts to a minimum. An example of this approach was illustrated previously in Figure 2-4.

decision tables

A *decision table* is similar to a flowchart in its use and construction. It can be used independently of or to complement a flowchart. A decision table shows conditions and actions in a simplified and orderly manner. By presenting logical alternative courses of action under various operating conditions, a decision table enables one to think through a problem and present its solution in compact notation. It allows a computer problem to be divided into logical segments that provide a multilevel structure in the problem's analysis. At the highest level, decision tables can be used for an overall system by referencing to lower-level tables.

Tax rate and insurance rate tables are forms of decision tables. Likewise, the price list of various product lines, expressed in terms of quantity discounts, package sizes, and product specifications, is another example.

Values of Decision Tables

Many values can be derived from decision tables. Like flowcharts, decision tables require a complete statement of the problem. Several studies have shown that approximately 50% of total costs related to computer system development have been attributed to poor problem definition as well as to ineffective documentation.

figure 2-15. Compute
Voluntary Deductions
program flowchart.

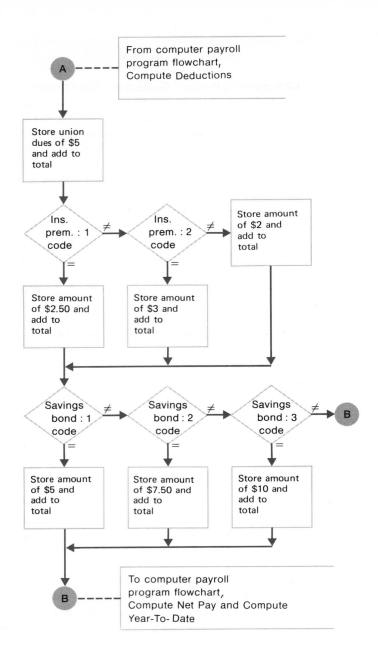

Compact Notation. Many pages of a computer program flowchart can be condensed in a single logic table. Studies indicate that persons with no previous computer experience have programmed applications in less time with decision tables than experienced programmers who fail to make use of decision tables. Likewise, those who must review a program need not go through page after page of flowcharts to follow the logic of the program. Also, decision tables are generally easier for the nonsystems person to understand.

Easy to Modify Program. Another important value of the decision table's compact notation is that it is easy to modify and update a program. Adding new conditions or changing a given decision rule action will not require substantial reformulation. In addition, introduction of new decision tables will not require substantial revision of system flowcharts.

Ability to Produce a Machine Language Program. Today, a most significant value of decision tables is their ability to produce a machine language computer program. In such cases, a translator converts the decision rules into a programming language without human intervention and has the ability to convert this language into the appropriate machine language.

Compatibility with Flowcharts. Although decision tables have many advantages over program flowcharts, they are not complete substitutes in a business data processing environment. Business processing is still primarily a sequential process of using input data to process controlled tasks, revise storage files, and prepare output. Flowcharts are still needed to show this sequential process and are useful when there are few conditions and simple conditions only or when presenting the combined system of decision logic, programs, and computers. Instead of showing each branch representing an individual decision, flowcharts can include a single block representing a complete decision table. From this viewpoint, decision tables and the various types of flowcharts complement and supplement each other in a business information system.

---

decision table components

A decision table is divided into four basic elements. Provision is made for other information that may be helpful in interpreting final results. This is shown below.

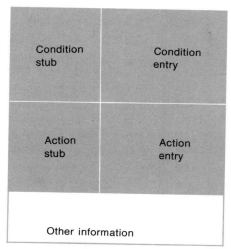

If: (condition statement)	Condition stub / Condition entry
Then: (action statement)	Action stub / Action entry
	Other information

All conditions are listed in the upper part of the decision table and represent the contents of decision and branching symbols on a program flowchart. Since this represents the condition of the computer at a particular time (an "if" condition), it may be necessary to perform a specific operation on data at this time. Actions taken correspond to the processing symbols on a flowchart (a "then" action) and are listed in the second half

DECISION TABLE	TABLE NAME: INVENTORY LEVEL CHECKING		PAGE 1 OF 1
	CHART NO: INVENTORY—5	PREPARED BY: ROBERT J. THIERAUF	DATE: NOV. 5, 198–

CONDITION	RULE NUMBER											
	1	2	3	4	5	6	7	8	9	10	11	12
Inventory available ≥ ordered amount	Y	N	N	N	N	N	N	N	N			
Inventory available < ordered amount	—	Y	Y	Y	Y	Y	N	N	N			
Partial shipment of goods	—	Y	Y	N	N	—	—	—	—			
Back order of goods	—	Y	N	Y	N	—	Y	N	—			
Additional goods due in next day	—	N	N	N	N	Y	N	N	Y			
ACTION												
Item shipped	X	—	—	—	—	—	—	—	—			
Partial shipment	—	X	X	—	—	—	—	—	—			
Back order unshipped balance	—	X	—	X	—	—	X	—	—			
Out of stock notice sent	—	—	X	—	X	—	—	X	—			
Order held for entire day	—	—	—	—	—	X	—	—	X			
Other Information:												

figure 2-16. Decision table for checking inventory level.

of the decision table. It should be noted that a condition cannot appear in the action area nor can an action appear in the condition area.

Symbols and Rules. Various symbols can be used in a decision table for the condition entry, namely, yes (Y), no (N), greater than (>), equal to (=), less than (<), and blank (—). The action entry to be performed is an X or a blank (—). A blank in either case means that the condition or action is not applicable. Each column in the decision table makes up a rule that corresponds to one of the many possible paths of a program flowchart. Basically, a decision table relates given conditions to the appropriate actions, with a column of entries that forms a rule. Alternative conditions which result in other actions that constitute other rules in a decision table are written side by side.

Checking Inventory Level Illustration

An example of a decision table is found in Figure 2-16. The example checks the inventory level for incoming orders. The decision table was first developed by determining the possible conditions. After exhausting the condition list, the action entries are listed. For the first rule, if the inventory is greater than or equal to the order amount (Yes condition), the item ordered would be shipped as noted by the "X" in the appropriate space. Since the remaining actions are not relevant for this condition, the "—" appears in the first column. The next eight rules are interpreted in a similar manner. In total, the decision table shows nine separate decision rules.

An inspection of Figure 2-16 indicates there is little difference between rules 6 and 9 since both result in the same action, that is, both hold an order for one day. In such cases, the two rules can be combined into one. The combined rule is:

Decision Rule 6	Decision Rule 9	Combined Rule
N	N	N
Y	N	—
—	—	—
—	—	—
Y	Y	Y

summary

Initially, this chapter concentrated on problem analysis as a beginning approach to problem solving in a computerized environment. Its principal methods of defining and analyzing a problem consist of preparing flowcharts and/or decision tables. Although there are many values to be realized from flowcharts, greater values may be obtained from decision tables for complex computer programs. However, for simple and straightforward computer programs, the use of program flowcharts might be the better method. This is particularly true of the type of problems presented in an introductory computer text. Thus, the utilization of flowcharts, decision tables, or a combination of the two depends upon the problem to be solved by the business information system.

**second summary
of chapter 2**

flowchart types:

• system flowchart or procedural flowchart—depicts the flow of data through the major parts of a system with a minimum of detail. For the most part, it shows where input enters the system, how it is processed and controlled, and how it leaves the system in terms of storage and output. Example: procedures necessary to maintain an individual's bank account at a minimum level of $200.00

• program flowchart or block diagram—portrays the various arithmetic and logical operations as well as their sequence. It has three important uses:

- • aids program development
- • serves as a guide for coding
- • is a basis for documentation

Example: procedures for adding together weekly pay—regular and over-time—for total pay

decision tables:

A decision table, which can be used in the place of a flowchart, combines "conditions" (if) to be considered in the description of a problem along with the "actions" (then) to be undertaken. It allows a computer problem to be divided into its logical segments in compact notation.

decision table components:

A decision table is divided into four basic elements with provision for other information that may be helpful in interpreting the results. These components are:

- • if (condition statement): Condition   Condition
  stub   entry
- • then (action statement):   Action   Action
  stub   entry
- • other information

Symbols used for the "condition entry" are:

- • Y (Yes)
- • N (No)
- • > (greater than)
- • = (equal to)
- • < (less than)
- • — (blank)

Symbols used for the "action entry" are:
- • X (applicable)
- • — (blank)

Simplified forms of decision tables are tax rate tables, insurance rate tables, and price lists.

**second self-study
exercise
of chapter 2**

True-False:

1. ( ) Another name for a program flowchart is a decision table.
2. ( ) A system flowchart shows what operations are performed by a computer program.
3. ( ) System flowcharts are rarely used today in a new system project.
4. ( ) A block diagram aids in developing an operational computer program.
5. ( ) Generally, flowcharts are not used for documentation purposes.
6. ( ) A decision table is similar to a flowchart in its use.
7. ( ) Only two symbols are allowed for the "condition entry" in decision tables.
8. ( ) For the most part, decision tables are easy to modify.
9. ( ) Decision tables are capable of being converted directly to machine language.
10. ( ) Decision tables are not compatible with flowcharts.

Fill-In:

11. Popular types of flowcharts used currently are _____ _____ and _____ _____.
12. Another name for a program flowchart is a _____ _____.
13. Program flowcharts aid program development, serves as a guide for _____, and is a basis for _____.
14. As illustrated in Figure 2-15, the _____ symbol is used to determine which path to follow during processing.
15. A _____ _____ shows conditions and corresponding actions that are logically related.
16. The most significant feature of decision tables is their _____ _____.
17. The top half of a decision table represents "_____" _____ while the second half refers to "_____" _____.
18. The _____ _____ to be performed must be represented by an X.
19. In addition to the symbols represented by greater than, equal to, less than, and blank, other symbols allowed for the "condition entry" are _____ and _____.
20. Decision tables and various types of _____ complement and supplement each other in a business information system.

questions

1. How important is problem analysis in developing a business information system?

2. Can the first step (defining the problem) in programming and implementing an operational computer program be ignored? Explain.

3. What are the advantages of using flowcharts in a computer installation? Explain.

4. Distinguish between a system flowchart and a program flowchart.

5. Can the computer be used in program flowcharting?

6. (a) What is the primary purpose of a decision table?
   (b) How does a decision table differ from a program flowchart?
   (c) Which should be preferred when programming and why?

flowchart and decision table exercises

1. Develop an appropriate program flowchart and the corresponding decision table for the following:
   (a) Compute gross pay (total hours = regular hours + overtime hours at time and a half).
   (b) Compute saving bonds deduction (amount equal to 5% of gross pay or $3.00 a week, whichever is less).
   (c) Compute credit union deduction (amount equal to 10% of gross pay or $15.00 a week, whichever is less).

2. Develop an appropriate program flowchart and the corresponding decision table for each of the following:
   (a) Compute gross pay (regular hours are based on a 35-hour week and overtime hours at $1\frac{1}{2}$ times the regular hourly rate).
   (b) Compute FICA amount (use current figures).
   (c) Compute mandatory taxes (state income tax rate of gross pay—2%, city income tax—1%, and federal income tax—consult current rate table).
   (d) Compute voluntary deductions (refer to Figure 2-15).
   (e) Compute current net pay and year-to-date amounts (refer to a, b, c, and d above).

answers to first self-study exercise

1. F 2. T 3. F 4. F 5. F 6. T 7. F 8. F 9. F 10. T 11. defining and problem 12. program flowcharts 13. decision tables 14. programming 15. flowchart 16. communicator and record 17. process 18. connector 19. document 20. decision

answers to second self-study exercise

1. F 2. F 3. F 4. T 5. F 6. T 7. F 8. T 9. T 10. F 11. system flowchart and program flowchart 12. block diagram 13. coding and documentation 14. decision 15. decision table 16. compact notation 17. "if" conditions and "then" actions 18. action entry 19. Y(Yes) and N(No) 20. flowcharts

chapter three

internal operating concepts of computers

chapter objectives

- To show the relationship of the ISPCO cycle to the various hardware components in a computer system.
- To examine computer data codes that are found in computer systems today.
- To illustrate the use of the "stored program" concept in computers.
- To show examples of the single-address and multiple-address instruction formats of computers.
- To demonstrate how machine language instructions accomplish the desired processing within a computer program.

Joe Cosgrove has received his paycheck on Friday for the prior week's work. He stops at his local bank. While waiting in line to use an automated teller, he notices the strangely shaped block numbers at the bottom of his paycheck and deposit slip. The numbers, which are printed with a special magnetic ink, allow the bank's computer to read the document. When it is Joe's turn, he inserts his plastic bank card into the slot of the 24-hour automated teller and types in his personal code number. In response, the metal cover rises and exposes a set of push buttons.

From this point on, Joe is interacting on line with the bank's computer. He pushes the button marked "Checking Account Deposit" and drops his paycheck and deposit slip through the slot. Next, he depresses the appropriate buttons indicating his desire to withdraw $100 in cash to meet daily expenses. In turn, the machine dispenses the money. The method of instructing computers internally will be explored before their programming methods are set forth.

Within this chapter, after relating the input-storage-processing-control-output (ISPCO) cycle to the various units in a computer system, numbering systems and coding methods are developed for processing data under computer control. This is followed by an explanation of the stored program concept for a fixed-word length, a variable-word length, and a byte-addressable combination computer. Sample machine language instructions are used to demonstrate how a computer actually operates.

input-storage-processing-control-output (ISPCO) cycle

The basic data processing functions, i.e., methods and procedures for relating input to output in a system, also comprise the input-storage-processing-control-output (ISPCO) cycle of computers. As shown below, this ISPCO cycle approach to computers is a meaningful way of identifying their major components.

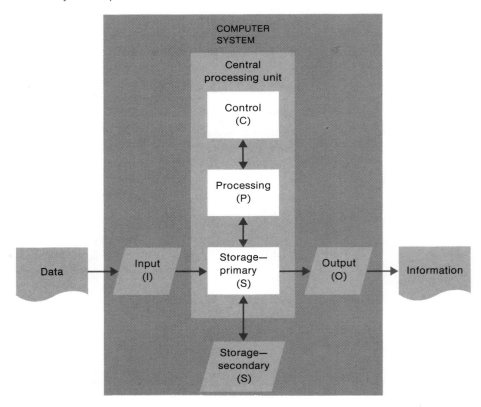

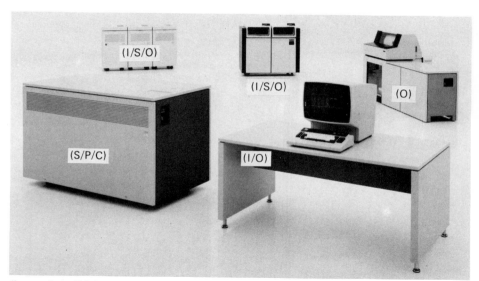

figure 3-1. ISPCO cycle applied to the IBM 4331 system — a small-scale computer system. (Courtesy International Business Machines Corporation)

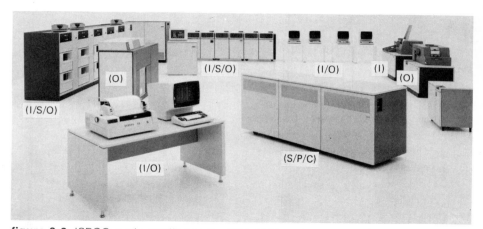

figure 3-2. ISPCO cycle applied to the IBM 4341 system — a medium-scale computer system. (Courtesy International Business Machines Corporation)

This approach is shown in Figure 3-1 for a small-scale computer system. A medium-scale system is shown in Figure 3-2. Both systems use hardware that centers around input, storage, processing, control, and output. Note that several of the computer devices serve several data processing functions, that is, magnetic tape and magnetic disk units serve as input, storage, and output devices.

The input-storage-processing-control-output functions are applied to the individual hardware components in Figure 3-3. Each component performs an essential function and is as follows:

- *Input* devices convert instructions and data from user-readable code to machine-readable code.
- Primary *storage* (memory) stores instructions and data, and transfers them for use by the arithmetic/logical unit.

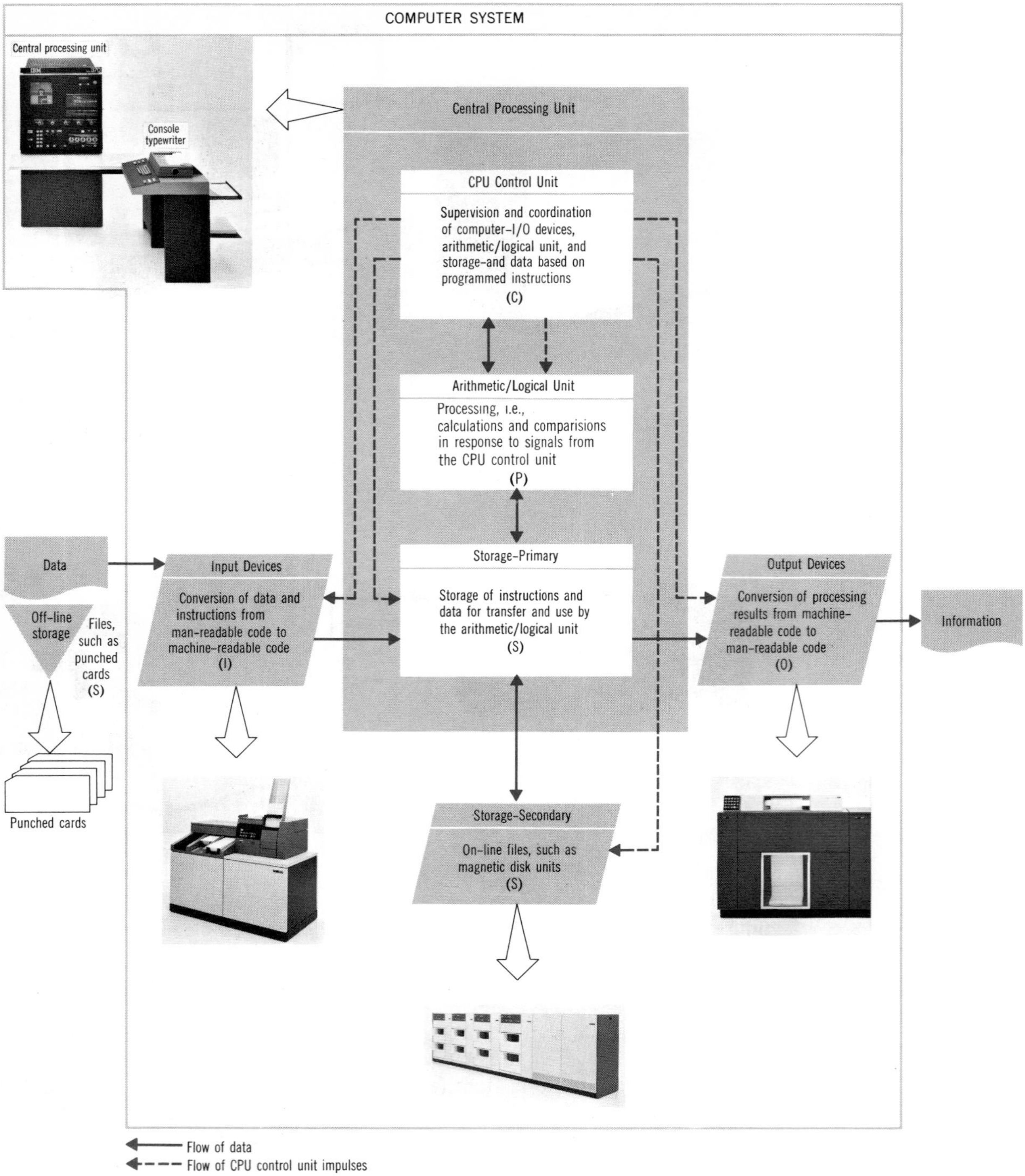

figure 3-3. Input-storage-processing-control-output units of a magnetic disk-oriented computer system.

- Secondary *storage* (files) stores large amounts of data for on-line processing.
- Arithmetic/logical unit performs the necessary *processing*, i.e., calculations and comparisons, in response to signals from the CPU control unit.

- CPU *control* unit supervises and coordinates the computer system and data in accordance with the programmed instructions.
- *Output* devices convert processing results from machine-readable code to user-readable code.

The solid lines in Figure 3-3 represent the flow of data. The dotted lines indicate the flow of control impulses by the CPU control unit.

Emphasis in this chapter will be on the arithmetic/logical unit (P) and the CPU control unit (C). However, a more detailed explanation of the input (I), storage (S), and output (O) units shown in these first illustrations will be given later in the text. In Chapter 7, computer equipment that is batch oriented will be surveyed. Similarly in Chapter 8, interactive computer equipment with emphasis on time sharing will be examined.

coding systems

Data input and output for computer processing consists of the decimal number system, 26 alphabetic characters, and special characters. Computations and manipulations made internally by the computer are represented by a special computer notation. Depending upon the machine's design, the computer coding system can be one of several types.

An overview of the conversion process from alphanumeric characters to computer code and back to alphanumeric is shown as follows:

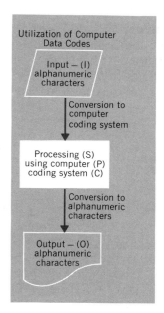

While input (I) and output (O) per the above can be referenced directly to Figure 3-3, processing per the above is related to the central processing unit (in Figure 3-3), that is, primary storage (S), arithmetic/logical unit (P), and CPU control unit (C), plus secondary storage (S). The ISPCO cycle, then, is applicable to the conversion process from one system to another.

Computer coding systems are based upon an *absolute value* and a *positional* value. The radix or the base of the system determines how many absolute values are a part of that system. The positional values are found for the specific system by raising the base to the power of the position. These basic concepts of a number system will be illustrated below.

Decimal System

The decimal system is presented although it is not used in a computer system. It has 10 absolute values—0 through 9, indicating a system with a *base* or *radix* of 10. Once these 10 values have been used, it would be impossible to go any further without inventing more values. The process of counting higher than 9 is obtained by moving one position to the left, writing down the number 1, and beginning all over again with the digits 0 through 9. Each time all possible combinations of values have been used, notation takes place again by moving one position to the left. For example, when the number 156 is written, the digits 1, 5, and 6 are written in sequence. This is actually shorthand notation for one times ten to the second power, $1 \times (10)^2$, plus five times ten to the first power, $5 \times (10)^1$, and plus six times ten to the zero power, $6 \times (10)^0$. Expressing the foregoing statement mathematically, the results are:

$$1(10)^2 + 5(10)^1 + 6(10)^0 = 156$$
$$(1 \times 10 \times 10) + (5 \times 10) + (6 \times 1) = 156 \qquad \text{(Any number raised to the}$$
$$100 + 50 + 6 = 156 \qquad \text{zero power equals 1)}$$

In essence, as each place to the left is taken (positional notation), the digits are multiplied by increasing powers of 10 in order to find the actual value. If the number had included three values to the right of the decimal point, the first digit to the right (of the decimal point) would be multiplied by 10^{-1}, the second digit by 10^{-2}, and the third digit by 10^{-3}.

Decimal Positional Values. As stated previously, the base or radix of the decimal system is 10. Several of the positional values found in the base 10 system are found in Figure 3-4. Positive values are positioned to the left of the decimal point and negative amounts to the right of the decimal. It should be obvious that this table of positional values was used in determining the above value, 156.

Position number	4	3	2	1	0	.	−1	−2	−3	−4
Base 10 position value	10^4	10^3	10^2	10^1	10^0	.	10^{-1}	10^{-2}	10^{-3}	10^{-4}
Amount represented by position value	10,000	1,000	100	10	1	. decimal point	1/10	1/100	1/1,000	1/10,000

figure 3-4. Selected positional values in the decimal system.

Binary System

An integral part of computer coding systems is the binary system. It has 2 as its base with only two digits, 0 and 1 employed. Thus the base of the binary system is 2. The value 156 expressed in binary notation, is 10011100, shown as follows:

$$1(2)^7 + 0(2)^6 + 0(2)^5 + 1(2)^4 + 1(2)^3 + 1(2)^2 + 0(2)^1 + 0(2)^0 = 156$$
$$128 + 0 + 0 + 16 + 8 + 4 + 0 + 0 = 156$$

Hence, the binary number 10011100 has a decimal equivalent of 156.

DECIMAL	BINARY				
	16	8	4	2	1
0		0	0	0	0
1		0	0	0	1
2		0	0	1	0
3		0	0	1	1
4		0	1	0	0
5		0	1	0	1
6		0	1	1	0
7		0	1	1	1
8		1	0	0	0
9		1	0	0	1
10		1	0	1	0
11		1	0	1	1
12		1	1	0	0
13		1	1	0	1
14		1	1	1	0
15		1	1	1	1
16	1	0	0	0	0
17	1	0	0	0	1
18	1	0	0	1	0
19	1	0	0	1	1
20	1	0	1	0	0
21	1	0	1	0	1
22	1	0	1	1	0
23	1	0	1	1	1
24	1	1	0	0	0
25	1	1	0	0	1
26	1	1	0	1	0
27	1	1	0	1	1
28	1	1	1	0	0
29	1	1	1	0	1
30	1	1	1	1	0
31	1	1	1	1	1

figure 3-5. Comparison of decimal and binary numbers, 0 through 31.

Binary Positional Values. The concepts of absolute value and positional value are applicable to the binary system as they are to the decimal system. A comparison of decimal and binary numbers for 0 through 31 is given in Figure 3-5. These values plus more of the positional values in the binary system are depicted in Figure 3-6. The values of the binary bit—smallest unit of information in the binary number system— are often called the "0 bit" and the "1 bit." In a similar manner, these two binary values can mean a "no bit," described by the 0 state, and the "bit," described by the 1 condition.

Arithmetic computations are performed with binary numbers following the same basic rules as for the decimal system. The only real difference is that the binary system requires more frequent carries since there is need for a carry to the next column every time the total exceeds one. This is in contrast to the decimal system where a carry to the next column is required whenever the total is greater than nine.

Binary Addition. Binary addition is carried out in much the same manner as decimal addition. The difference is that this arithmetic calculation consists of four rules:

$$0 + 0 = 0$$
$$0 + 1 = 1$$
$$1 + 0 = 1$$
$$1 + 1 = 0 \quad \text{with a carry of 1}$$

Examples of addition in the decimal and binary systems are:

Decimal	Binary	Decimal	Binary
4	100	18	10010
+3	+ 11	+11	+ 1011
7	111	29	11101

The values for the binary system have been taken from Figure 3-5.

Binary Subtraction. Binary subtraction is similar to binary addition except that the procedures are reversed. Instead of using a method by which one digit can be carried, it becomes necessary to subtract a larger digit from a smaller one. In binary subtraction, this can occur only when 1 is subtracted from 0. It is therefore required to borrow a 1 from the next position to the left and the remainder is 1. The rules for binary subtraction are:

$$0 - 0 = 0$$
$$0 - 1 = 1 \quad \text{with a borrow of 1}$$
$$1 - 0 = 1$$
$$1 - 1 = 0$$

Position number	8	7	6	5	4	3	2	1	0	.	−1	−2	−3	−4	−5	−6	−7	−8
Base 2 position value	2^8	2^7	2^6	2^5	2^4	2^3	2^2	2^1	2^0	.	2^{-1}	2^{-2}	2^{-3}	2^{-4}	2^{-5}	2^{-6}	2^{-7}	2^{-8}
Amount represented by position value	256	128	64	32	16	8	4	2	1	. binary point	1/2	1/4	1/8	1/16	1/32	1/64	1/128	1/256

figure 3-6. Selected positional values in the binary system.

Comparative examples for the decimal and binary systems are:

Decimal	Binary	Decimal	Binary
10	1010	25	11001
− 6	− 110	−12	− 1100
4	100	13	1101

Decimal to Binary Conversion. The decimal to binary conversion can be accomplished by taking the decimal number, dividing it by two each time, and writing the remainders each time until there is nothing left to divide. The binary answer is given by reading the remainders, starting with the bottom figure. Examples of these procedures are given below.

Decimal	Binary	Decimal	Binary
31/2 = 15 with a remainder of 1		72/2 = 36 with a remainder of 0	
15/2 = 7 with a remainder of 1		36/2 = 18 with a remainder of 0	
7/2 = 3 with a remainder of 1		18/2 = 9 with a remainder of 0	
3/2 = 1 with a remainder of 1		9/2 = 4 with a remainder of 1	
1/2 = 0 with a remainder of 1		4/2 = 2 with a remainder of 0	
		2/2 = 1 with a remainder of 0	
		1/2 = 0 with a remainder of 1	

The binary equivalents for 31 and 72 are 11111 and 1001000 respectively. All binary values are read from bottom to top.

Binary Coded Decimal System

When the binary system is used, it represents two basic conditions: either 1 or 0, on or off, something or the absence of something. As indicated above, numerical value can be represented by a group of 1's and 0's. By using only four positions of place values—8, 4, 2, and 1—the decimal digits 0 through 9 can be represented. Going one step further, if this group of four-bit values is assigned units, tens, hundreds, thousands, and the like, any decimal number can be expressed. This extension of the binary system whereby a four-bit set can be used for each decimal digit is called the binary coded decimal (BCD) system. A comparison of the binary and BCD system for two values (53 and 163) is illustrated in Figure 3-7.

The binary coded decimal simplifies the task of programming business problems on the computer. This method provides fast conversion from and

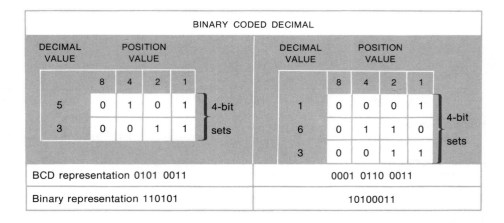

figure 3-7. Comparison of binary coded decimal (BCD) and binary representation for decimal figures 53 and 163.

Character	EBCDIC* Zone	Numeric
0	1111	0000
1	1111	0001
2	1111	0010
3	1111	0011
4	1111	0100
5	1111	0101
6	1111	0110
7	1111	0111
8	1111	1000
9	1111	1001
A	1100	0001
B	1100	0010
C	1100	0011
D	1100	0100
E	1100	0101
F	1100	0110
G	1100	0111
H	1100	1000
I	1100	1001
J	1101	0001
K	1101	0010
L	1101	0011
M	1101	0100
N	1101	0101
O	1101	0110
P	1101	0111
Q	1101	1000
R	1101	1001
S	1110	0010
T	1110	0011
U	1110	0100
V	1110	0101
W	1110	0110
X	1110	0111
Y	1110	1000
Z	1110	1001

figure 3-8. Comparison of numerics and alphabetics to the Extended Binary Coded Decimal Interchange Code (EBCDIC).

* Extended Binary Coded Decimal Interchange Code.

to decimal form for input/output conversion. However, this usually occurs at the expense of internal operating speeds. It should be remembered that business applications typically involve very little manipulation for each record processed. This is in contrast to the straight binary computer where internal computational speeds are faster than with the binary coded decimal. Generally, the regular binary system is used in scientific computers where the accent is on fast internal processing speeds and not on reading large volumes of input data or producing vast amounts of output.

The rules for binary coded decimal arithmetic, sometimes called decimal arithmetic or packed decimal, are not too different from binary arithmetic. The rules allow a decimal type carry when the results from adding two digits exceed 9.

Extended Binary Coded Decimal Interchange Code System

The Extended Binary Coded Decimal Interchange Code (EBCDIC) system employs eight binary positions to present a single character of information (Figure 3-8) and is the basis for many current computers. The use of eight bits has many advantages. Eight binary positions provide for up to 256 (2^8) different bit combinations; they can be used for both upper-case and lower-case letters, numerals, and many special characters for programming. An 8-bit field can store two decimal values, which results in a greater utilization of primary and secondary storage than the BCD format.

EBCDIC Character Codes. Although not pointed out previously, most character codes are a composite of zone and numeric segments. The EBCDIC (pronounced ee bee dick or ib se dick) system is no exception and divides each storage location, known as a *byte*, into equal parts. Each byte consists of 8 bits—4 zone and 4 numeric, as shown in Figure 3-8, plus a parity bit. A parity bit is a binary check digit appended to a group of bits to check the accuracy of the information. The sum of all the bits are always odd or always even, depending upon the requirements of the equipment.

Since the zone positions are constructed and utilized differently from other codes, Figure 3-9 illustrates how the zone portion of the EBCDIC byte is used. The IBM System/370 series of computers employ the 8-bit byte which is, actually, the EBCDIC character code.

The EBCDIC system allows for packing digits under programmed instruction, resulting in a more efficient utilization of storage. The packed format uses the numeric portion of a byte to represent one digit and the zone portion to represent a second digit. Packing also speeds up arithmetic calculations and improves rates of data transmission.

Hexadecimal System

One of the difficulties encountered in communicating with a computer is the necessity of interpreting long strings of 0s and 1s. Because this process is prone to error and very tedious, it can be simplified by using the hexadecimal system (base 16) which has become a standard communication notation.

By way of review, a numbering system requires as many different values as there are in the base of the system. Since the hexadecimal system has a base of 16, 16 different symbols are required. A comparison of this code with the decimal and binary system is given in Figure 3-10. The hexa-

figure 3-9. Various uses of zone portion of EBCDIC byte.

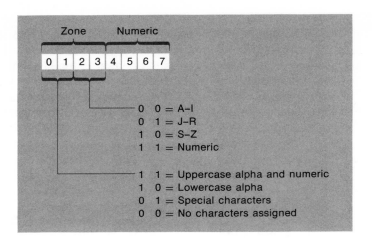

decimal system includes the familiar 0 through 9 and letters A through F whose place values, 0 through 15, are assigned in ascending order (0 through 9 and then A through F symbols).

Hexadecimal Positional Values. The process of counting higher than 15 is obtained by carrying 1 to the next position to the left in order to

DECIMAL		BINARY					HEXADECIMAL	
10	1	16	8	4	2	1	16	1
	0		0	0	0	0		0
	1		0	0	0	1		1
	2		0	0	1	0		2
	3		0	0	1	1		3
	4		0	1	0	0		4
	5		0	1	0	1		5
	6		0	1	1	0		6
	7		0	1	1	1		7
	8		1	0	0	0		8
	9		1	0	0	1		9
1	0		1	0	1	0		A
1	1		1	0	1	1		B
1	2		1	1	0	0		C
1	3		1	1	0	1		D
1	4		1	1	1	0		E
1	5		1	1	1	1		F
1	6	1	0	0	0	0	1	0
1	7	1	0	0	0	1	1	1
1	8	1	0	0	1	0	1	2
1	9	1	0	0	1	1	1	3
2	0	1	0	1	0	0	1	4
2	1	1	0	1	0	1	1	5
2	2	1	0	1	1	0	1	6
2	3	1	0	1	1	1	1	7
2	4	1	1	0	0	0	1	8
2	5	1	1	0	0	1	1	9
2	6	1	1	0	1	0	1	A
2	7	1	1	0	1	1	1	B
2	8	1	1	1	0	0	1	C
2	9	1	1	1	0	1	1	D
3	0	1	1	1	1	0	1	E
3	1	1	1	1	1	1	1	F

figure 3-10. Decimal, binary, and hexadecimal equivalents.

Position number		5	4	3	2	1	0	.	−1	−2	−3	−4	−5
Base 16 position value		16^5	16^4	16^3	16^2	16^1	16^0	.	16^{-1}	16^{-2}	16^{-3}	16^{-4}	16^{-5}
Amount represented by position value	1,048,576	65,536	4,096	256	16	1		.	1/16	1/256	1/4,096	1/65,536	1/1,048,576

Hexadecimal
point

figure 3-11. Selected positional values in hexadecimal system.

represent the decimal number 16. The next number to the left is then 16 times larger or 256. This progression continues in a positive or negative direction, as illustrated in Figure 3-11.

Binary to Hexadecimal Conversion. Binary to hexadecimal conversion and vice versa is a straightforward process since there is a direct four to one relationship between the base 2 and base 16 systems. Every four binary digits become a single hexadecimal digit. In like manner, each hexadecimal digit becomes four binary digits. For example, convert the binary code 0011 1011 1000 to hexadecimal code:

```
0011   1011   1000
  3      B      8
```

The conversion of the hexadecimal 3B8 to the binary code is the same value as given above (0011 1011 1000). If there is any doubt about the conversion, refer to Figure 3-10.

Decimal to Hexadecimal Integer Conversion. Decimal to hexadecimal integer conversion is accomplished by dividing the decimal number repeatedly by 16 until a zero quotient is obtained. Next, the decimal remainders 10 through 15 are converted into the appropriate hexadecimal symbols A through F. The first remainder is the least significant hexadecimal digit while the last remainder is the most significant digit. For example, the decimal values 210 and 1726, converted to hexadecimal notation, are:

Decimal	*Hexadecimal*	*Decimal*	*Hexadecimal*
210/16 = 13 with a remainder of 2	2	1726/16 = 107 with a remainder of 14	E
13/16 = 0 with a remainder of 13	D	107/16 = 6 with a remainder of 11	B
		6/16 = 0 with a remainder of 6	6
210 = D2		1726 = 6BE	

Hexadecimal to Decimal Integer Conversion. Hexadecimal to decimal integer conversion consists of expansion of the hexadecimal number in powers of 16, using decimal arithmetic for the calculations. Under this direct method, multiply the decimal equivalent of each hexadecimal digit by the place value of the digit, expressed in decimals, and add their products to obtain the equivalent decimal. To prove the validity of the hexadecimal values D2 and 6BE for decimals 210 and 1726 respectively, their values are:

$$D2 = (D \times 16^1) + (2 \times 16^0)$$
$$= (13 \times 16) + (2 \times 1)$$
$$= 208 + 2$$
$$= 210$$

$$6BE = (6 \times 16^2) + (11 \times 16^1) + (14 \times 16^0)$$
$$= (6 \times 256) + (11 \times 16) + (14 \times 1)$$
$$= 1536 + 176 + 14$$
$$= 1726$$

first summary of chapter 3

input-storage-processing-control-output (ISPCO) cycle:

The ISPCO cycle is a meaningful way of applying the basic DP functions to the individual components of a computer system. These computer components are:

• input devices read data into the computer system.

• storage is available as *high-speed primary storage* for storing program instructions and data and as *slower secondary storage* for storing file data.

• processing of program instructions and data is accomplished through the arithmetic/logical unit.

• control over processing is provided by the computer's *CPU control unit*.

• output devices convert processing results from the computer system to printed or some form of stored output.

relationship of ISPCO cycle to computer coding systems:

An overview of the input-storage-processing-control-output components that use some type of computer coding system is shown as follows for a typical computer system:

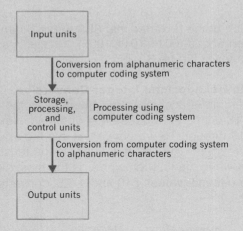

Input units

Conversion from alphanumeric characters to computer coding system

Storage, processing, and control units

Processing using computer coding system

Conversion from computer coding system to alphanumeric characters

Output units

coding systems:

• decimal system—has 10 absolute values—0 through 9, indicating a system with a base or radix of 10.

• binary system—has a base of 2—0 and 1. The values of the binary bit are often called the "0 bit" and the "1 bit."

• binary coded decimal system—uses four positions of place values—8, 4, 2, and 1—for representing 10 absolute values—0 through 9.

• extended binary coded decimal interchange coding system—uses the 0 and 1 for storing data as bytes. Each byte consists of 4 zone and 4 numeric bits plus a parity bit for storing numeric and alphabetic data.

• hexadecimal coding system—has 16 characters—numeric 0 through 9 and letters A through F, indicating a system with a base or radix of 16.

**first self-study
exercise
of chapter 3**

True-False:

1. (   ) Primary storage stores large amounts of file data for on-line processing.
2. (   ) Arithmetic/logical unit supervises and controls the entire computer system.
3. (   ) Computer coding systems are optional features of computer systems.
4. (   ) The decimal system with a base ten uses 10 different alphabetics.
5. (   ) The 0 state of a binary value can be described as a "no bit."
6. (   ) Binary subtraction is similar to binary addition, except the procedures are reversed.
7. (   ) The binary coded decimal system uses only four place values—8, 4, 2, and 0.
8. (   ) In EBCDIC character codes, a bit consists of 8 bytes plus a parity byte.
9. (   ) The EBCDIC system does allow for packing data under programmed instruction.
10. (   ) The process of counting higher than 15 in the hexadecimal system is obtained by carrying one to the next position to the left.

Fill-In:

11. The _____ _____ _____ oversees the computer system and data being processed in accordance with the programmed instructions.
12. _____ _____ stores instructions and data, and transfers them for processing by the arithmetic/logical unit.
13. Each coding system has a _____ or _____ which indicates the number of digits used.
14. The number 10 is different from the value 01 although the same digits are used. The difference in value is determined by the _____ of the digits.
15. The complexity of electronic circuitry for utilizing the decimal system has resulted in a simpler two-digit system for computers. This system, having a base of two or 0 and 1, is called the _____ system.
16. Since the positions of the digits 0 and 1 determine their value in the binary system, this system is like the decimal system in that it is a _____ numbering system.
17. _____ _____ is similar to binary addition, except the procedures are reversed.
18. The _____ _____ _____ system uses four positions of place values, that is, 8, 4, 2, and 1 to represent numbers 0 through 9.
19. In order to overcome the long strings of 0- and 1-bits to represent large numbers, the _____ system coding system (base 16) was developed for operator notation.
20. The _____ _____ _____ _____ employs binary positions to represent a single character of information.

the stored program

This section and subsequent discussions center on the computer's internal operations. The "stored program" concept refers to storing within the memory of the computer a series of coded instructions that is used to accomplish the desired processing. The program is read into the computer, stored in memory, processed as directed, and its output is produced according to some planned format. The function of the machine's memory is not only to accumulate data to be processed and associate it with other related data, but also to instruct the computer as to what it must do in a very precise manner. Its set of instructions represent basic operations. When the computer begins operation, the first instruction is taken to the control unit and interpreted. The operation specified by the instruction is carried out. The second instruction is moved to the control unit where it is interpreted and executed. In a similar manner, all other instructions follow the same procedure. When the final instruction has been completed for the initial transaction, the process is repeated again for each transaction following. The method of instructing a computer will be described in the following sections. Before doing so, the word structure available with current computers is discussed.

Fixed-Word Length

In fixed-word length computers, all storage locations in memory are capable of holding only so many digits, say 10 digits and a plus or a minus sign. All stored data use the full 10-digit positions whether they are needed or not. If the number 4 is stored, for instance, it would appear as 0000000004 in a specified memory location. Just as data are stored in 10-digit lengths, so are the computer's instructions. At times, the fixed-word length requirement for data and instructions makes it difficult to distinguish between the two in memory.

Bit (Storage Unit). When referring to a fixed-word length computer, every storage location is identified by an address that specifies a certain number of storage representations. For example, a fixed-word length machine might be 24, 30, 36, 48, 54, etc. bits where a bit (binary digit) is a single character in a binary number. Once the computer designer determines the word size, all addresses represent storage areas containing that number of bits. If a computer is developed as a 36-bit word machine, each reference to a single memory location will access the same number of bits.

Byte (Storage Unit). For the IBM System/370, these systems process data in multiples of an 8-bit byte (Figure 3-12). Each 8-bit unit of data is called a byte, the basic building block for both systems. A ninth bit is the *parity* or *check bit* that indicates whether the total number of binary "1" digits is odd or even. It is transmitted with each byte and carries an odd parity in the byte. Byte locations in main storage are consecutively numbered, starting with 0. Each number is the address of the corresponding byte. A group of bytes in storage is addressed by the left-most byte of the group.

Words (Storage Units). Bytes may be handled separately or grouped in fields. The halfword, word, and doubleword are fields of consecutive bytes. A halfword has two bytes (or 16-binary bits), a word has four bytes

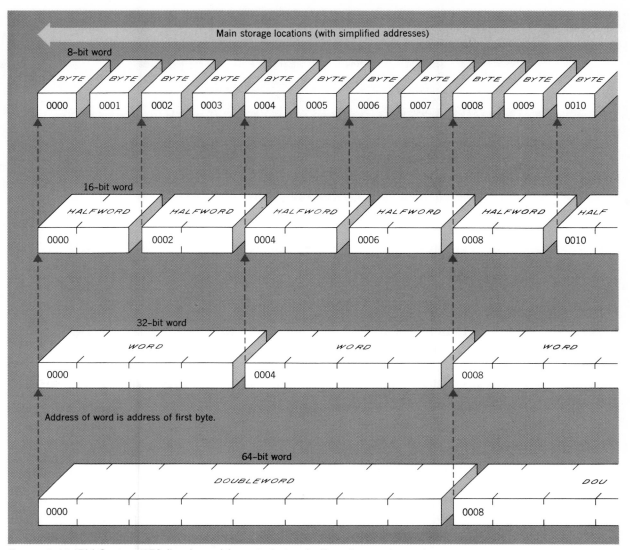

figure 3-12 IBM System/370 fixed-word formats-bytes, halfwords, words, and doublewords in main storage. (Courtesy International Business Machines Corporation.)

(or 32-binary bits), and the doubleword has eight bytes (or 64-binary bits), as illustrated in Figure 3-12. These fields make up the basic fixed-length data formats.

Variable-Word Length

Instead of recording information in memory in words of a specific length, several computer systems are able to handle each field (a single character or many characters) as an individual unit of information. In some computers, a field is addressed by its right-most position (low order) in memory while, in others, the left-most position (high order) is designated. Regardless of the approach used in addressing the field of information, the end of the field can be indicated in several ways. One is that the length of the field can be specified in the instruction. Another method is to have the end

figure 3-13. IBM System/370 variable-length format —(a) standard and (b) binary coded decimal or packed decimal.

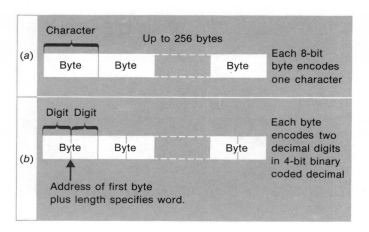

of the field indicated by a special character, by a special bit position in the character, by sensing the sign of the field, or by some comparable scheme.

Standard and Packed Decimal Formats. The IBM System/370 encodes one character with each 8-bit byte for the variable-word format, as is the case for the fixed-word format. The variable-length fields may start on any byte location and may contain up to 256 bytes, as shown in Figure 3-13a. The binary coded decimal or packed decimal code can also be used for variable-word formats where each byte encodes two decimal digits in a 4-bit binary coded decimal. The address of the first byte plus length specifies the size of the word. The coding scheme is depicted in Figure 3-13b.

The Byte-Addressable Combination

Both fixed-length and variable-word length computers have their advantages and corresponding limitations. Fixed-word length is easier to program than variable-word length since the size of the field is always constant, thereby reducing the need for special methods to control word sizes. On the other hand, variable-word length can store more information in memory. Instead of allocating a certain size word length for one or a few digits of information, data can be packed into a smaller area of memory. The variable-word length computer, then, is capable of utilizing memory in a more efficient manner, which can be critical for larger programs. In view of these facts, several manufacturers have designed computer systems that have both fixed and variable address formats. This is accomplished by incorporating the byte-addressable combination in the computer's hardware. The IBM System/370 is an example of both fixed- and variable-word address formats in a byte-addressable computer.

execution of computer instructions

For processing to occur within a computer system, a program must reside in the central processing unit. To be more specific, a program must reside in the memory or primary storage under the direction of the CPU control unit. The instructions of an operational program are in machine language. The format of the instructions will vary depending on how the manufacturer designed the machine. Data and instructions, stored in the computer's memory, are indistinguishable. If data are called from a memory location in place of an instruction—caused by an error in programming—the CPU control unit would translate the data as an operating command. In such a case, the computer could enter into a loop, indicate an error condition, or show some other abnormal operating condition.

Requirements for Each Computer Instruction

The program, being a set of instructions for the computer to follow, processes data on this basis. Each instruction, generally, includes the following three items.

1. The operation code specifies the operation to be performed or what the computer is to do.

2. One or more *operands,* sometimes called *data addresses,* indicate the address or addresses of the data to be worked on or where data are to be taken. They designate the address or addresses of the data needed for the operation code.

3. The last part of the instruction is the location of the next instruction, sometimes referred to as the *instruction address.*

Based upon the foregoing general format, an instruction is basically an operation code plus operands and an instruction address. The operation codes for one computer will be completely different from all others. In like manner, the method of using operands and their number vary from computer to computer.

Single-Address Instruction Format

A common instruction format is the one- or single-address that is generally associated with a fixed-word length computer. The instruction word is fixed at one and, sometimes, at one-half word. To simplify the discussion on a single-address instruction format, all storage locations for this computer (5000 word computer) are capable of holding 10 characters of information plus a sign (plus or minus). All data use the full 10-digit positions whether they are needed or not. This is in contrast with instructions that must contain 10 digits of information for a valid instruction. Each instruction is made up of three items: the operation code (positions 9–10), operand or data address (5–8), and instruction address (1–4) as described above.

Single-Address, Fixed-Word Length Illustration. To illustrate the operation of a single-address, fixed-word length computer, the problem of adding weekly regular pay—R—and weekly overtime pay—O—to obtain the total weekly pay—T— which then must be stored in a specified location, is set forth. Programming this problem in machine language requires four instructions as follows:

Operation Code

20   RESET accumulator to zero and LOAD contents of operand (data address) location into accumulator.

25   ADD contents of operand (data address) location to data in accumulator.

40   STORE contents of accumulator in storage location specified by operand (data address).

10   JUMP To another instruction of the program.

The above instructions are for a hypothetical fixed-word length computer.

In this sample problem, four storage locations, 2000 to 2003 (chosen arbitrarily) will contain the instructions. The value R will have been stored previously in location 0500 and the value O in location 0501. Both the values for R and O require ten-digit words as well as the value to be stored in location 1500 for T although their actual values will require less space in memory. The reason is that a fixed-word length computer is being utilized.

The four instructions that are required to solve for R + O = T are given below.

| Storage Location of Instruction | Instruction | | | Explanation |
	Oper- ation Code	Operand (Data Address)	Instruc- tion Address	
2000	20	0500	2001	RESET accumulator to zero, LOAD R into accumulator, and GO To next instruction at 2001
2001	25	0501	2002	ADD O to R and GO To next instruc- tion at 2002.
2002	40	1500	2003	STORE contents of accumulator (T) in address 1500 and GO To next instruction at 2003.
2003	10	3000	—	JUMP to next instruction at 3000.

Note that in the above program, the number to be added is not the number in the four-digit operand address segment of the instruction, but the ten-digit number in memory represented by those four digits. Thus, data in this computer come in ten-digit groups whereas the location of data is specified by only four digits.

Multiple-Address Instruction Format

Another instruction format is the multiple-address system found in many computers currently. The two-address instruction format contains two operands that normally reference two storage locations. For example, the instruction "add 1750 2060" would be interpreted (by some computers) to mean, "add the contents of storage location 2060 to location 1750 and store the results in 1750." In a three-address system, the first two addresses would reference the location of the data to be acted upon and the third address would specify where the result of the operation is to be stored. Generally, variable-word length and byte-addressable combination are used for the multiple-address instruction format.

Two-Address, Variable-Word Length Illustration. Referring to the preceding example under the single-address format, the same set of instructions will be used for a two-address, variable-word length format (with a word mark bit), except that the 25 instruction needs to be modified. Assuming the values for R and O are stored in locations 0500 and 0501 respectively and the results, T, are to be placed in location 0501 instead of 1500, instructions start in location 2000 as follows.

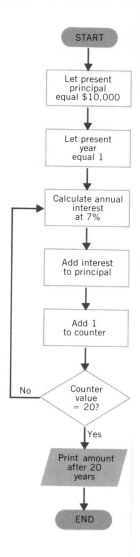

Storage Location of Instruction	Instruction				Explanation
	Operation Code	1st Operand	2nd Operand	Instruction Address	
2000	→ 25	0501	0500	2001	ADD R (location 0500) to O (location 0501), STORE automatically the result (T) at location 0501 (destroying previous contents), and GO To next instruction at 2001.
2001	└→ 10	3000	—	—	JUMP To next instruction at 3000.

Word mark bit—
beginning of instruction.

If one of the values must be saved (O in the example), it would be necessary to have an additional instruction. This added instruction would store the value (O) in an appropriate location (for later use in the program).

Single-Address Instruction Versus Multiple-Address Instruction. From the foregoing machine language instruction examples, the two-address instruction format does have an advantage over the single-address format. The number of instructions that must be executed to process a program is considerably reduced. In the example, the single-address instruction format required three lines of machine language to add R and O, storing the resulting value T, while the storage-to-storage approach required only one line of machine coding. However, the two-address instruction format destroys the initial value of the first operand by storing the answer in its place. Also, the multiple-address format is slower than the single-address method.

Computer Instructions Illustration

Although the foregoing material on how computer instructions are executed has been simplified, it is a good representation of the actual operations of a computer. Based upon this simplistic presentation, two important concepts which have been discussed previously should have been observed by the reader. First, referring to the input-storage-processing-control-output cycle of computers, data are read in by input devices for storing temporarily in an input area. Similarly, before information can be read out, it must be arranged properly in an output storage area for that device before output can occur. Second, a program flowchart adequately represents the instructions of a computer program. As noted in the prior chapter, the I/O symbol represents input and output operations. While the process and decision symbols represent arithmetic data-movement and logic instructions respectively, the flowlines of a program flowchart depict the consecutive execution of computer instructions as well as the various branching instructions within a program.

To illustrate a program flowchart that represents computer instructions, reference is made to Figure 3-14—a program for calculating a future amount. Basically, interest is calculated each year at a 7% rate and added

figure 3-14. Program flowchart for calculating a future amount (20 years hence) based upon a beginning principal of $10,000 and an annual rate of 7%.

to the principal; then one is added to a counter for the current year. This sequence of instructions is repeated until the counter value, representing years, is equal to 20. At that time, the principal after 20 years is printed and the computer program terminates.

Although this sample problem is simple and straightforward, it would take some time to solve if done manually. However, when this program is executed by a computer via internally stored instructions, the calculations take a matter of seconds or less. Thus, this type of program illustrates how the computer is capable of extending human capabilities.

second summary of chapter 3

The stored program concept refers to the storage of coded instructions within the memory of the computer for accomplishing the desired processing. Storage in memory can be one of the following:
• fixed-word length—all storage locations in memory are capable of holding so many digits, say 10 digits and a plus or a minus sign. Fixed-word formats include bytes (8-bit word), halfwords (16-bit word), words (32-bit word), and doublewords (64-bit word).

• variable-word length—all storage locations in memory are capable of varying in length to meet the needs of the particular application program.

• byte-addressable combination—all storage locations in memory are capable of utilizing both fixed- and variable-word length formats.

execution of computer instructions:
A computer program is a set of instructions to perform a specific processing task. Each instruction includes these three items:

| *operation code* specifies what operation is to be performed | *operands or data addresses* indicate the address or addresses to be worked on or where data are to be taken | *instruction address* specifies the location of the next instruction |

Each computer utilizes a particular instruction format for processing a set of instructions, i.e., a program. The two basic types of instruction formats are:
• single address—each instruction consists of the operation code, an operand or data address, and the instruction address.

Example:

	operation code	*operand*	*instruction address*
STORE contents (T) at location 1500 and GO TO next instruction at 2003	40	1500	2003

Note: memory location of this instruction is 2002

• multiple address—each instruction consists of the operation code, two or more operands, and the instruction address.

	operation code	1st operand	2nd operand	instruction address
Example:				
ADD R (location 0500) to O (location 0501) and store results (T) at 0501 and GO TO next instruction at 2001	25	0501	0500	2001

Note: memory location of this instruction is 2000

---

second self-study exercise of chapter 3

True-False:

1. (   ) The stored program concept refers primarily to the storage of data files.
2. (   ) The largest unit of storage for many computers is the halfword.
3. (   ) Each 8-bit unit of data is called a byte.
4. (   ) The newer computers utilize storage that is a fixed-word length size.
5. (   ) More data can be stored in packed decimal format than the standard format.
6. (   ) A variable-word length computer utilizes its memory more efficiently than a fixed-word length computer.
7. (   ) Operands tell the computer what processing is required.
8. (   ) Data addresses and instruction addresses are processed in the same manner by the computer.
9. (   ) The single-address instruction format is found in most computers today.
10. (   ) Multiple-address instruction format is too slow for computer processing.

Fill-In:

11. A _____-_____ _____ computer indicates that a storage location will always be a specific length regardless of the size of input data or other considerations.
12. The smallest unit of storage is the _____.
13. For many computers, a _____ is an 8-bit unit of data while a _____ is defined as so many bits or bytes.
14. A _____-_____ _____ computer handles each field of information as a separate unit in order to conserve memory space.
15. A computer that has the capability of fixed-word and variable-word length formats is called a _____-_____ computer.
16. The _____ _____ specifies the operation to be performed while the _____ indicates the address or addresses to be worked on or where data are to be taken.
17. The last part of the instruction is the location of the next instruction which is called the _____ _____.
18. The _____-_____ _____ format is generally used on a fixed-word length computer.
19. In a _____-_____ _____ format, two operands normally reference two storage locations.

20. In a _____-_____ _____ format, the first two addresses would normally reference the location of the data to be acted upon.

summary

After applying the ISPCO cycle to the various hardware components, computer coding systems were presented in order to illustrate how the arithmetic/logical operations are handled by a computer system. Coverage was comprehensive enough to obtain an overview of how the computer operates internally. It should be pointed out that it is not necessary to comprehend the coding scheme used by the machine when programming. This will be apparent in the next three chapters.

The stored program concept was followed by a presentation of machine language instructions and how they are executed. The concept of addressing as related to single-address and multiple-address instruction formats was discussed in terms of the word structure for the computer employed. While past-generation and current-generation computers have been either fixed-word length or variable-word length, the present trend is the byte-addressable combination that incorporates the advantages of both.

questions

1. What is the relationship of the ISPCO cycle to the central processing unit?
2. What is the basic advantage and the basic limitation of the binary system?
3. Contrast the similarities and differences among the following computer systems:
   (a) binary coded decimal (BCD)
   (b) extended binary coded decimal interchange code (EBCDIC)
4. Why is the hexadecimal system used as an operator notation form?
5. Of the computer coding systems illustrated in this chapter, which one results in the most efficient utilization of the computer's memory?
6. State the rules for binary addition and subtraction.
7. Distinguish among the following: a word, a byte, and a bit.
8. (a) What is a computer instruction? Explain.
   (b) Are computer instructions the same for all computers?
9. Differentiate between single-address and multiple-address instruction formats.

answers to first self-study exercise

1. F 2. F 3. F 4. F 5. T 6. T 7. F 8. F 9. T 10. T 11. CPU control unit 12. primary storage 13. base and radix 14. position 15. binary 16. positional 17. binary subtraction 18. binary coded decimal 19. hexadecimal 20. extended BCD interchange code.

answers to second self-study exercise

1. F 2. F 3. T 4. F 5. T 6. T 7. F 8. F 9. F 10. F 11. fixed-word length 12. bit 13. byte and word 14. variable-word length 15. byte-addressable 16. operation code and operand 17. instruction address 18. single-address instruction 19. two-address instruction 20. three-address instruction

part three

programming languages for business

Programming and implementing computer languages—the subject matter of Chapter 4—are presented in a batch and an interactive processing mode. For batch-processing the computer program must first be written and converted to a machine language. For interactive processing, the program can be written and tested at an input/output terminal. Interactive processing is stressed with BASIC, a time-sharing language presented in Chapters 5 and 6.

chapter four
programming and implementing computer languages

Joe Cosgrove and his wife, Claudia, stop at their local department store. After selecting three items, they wait in line for a few minutes. Claudia then presents the store's credit card. The clerk inserts the card into a small machine. Within a few seconds, a green light goes on, indicating that the credit sale has been approved.

The machine has sent Claudia's credit card number to the store's computer. The computer checks whether Claudia has paid her bills on time. The computer also checks a list of stolen credit cards. If the account had been past due or if the card had been stolen, a red light would have been flashed. In this case, another set of programmed instructions would have been followed. Overall, a series of computer programmed steps have been followed to approve or reject the sale.

This chapter describes programming in a batch processing mode or on interactive processing mode. Alternative programming approaches are discussed. Current programming languages, COBOL and RPG are presented. Chapters 5 and 6 will concentrate on BASIC in some detail.

program classifications

The overall process from logical analysis through detailed program coding testing is called computer programming. Although it has many steps, it can be divided into two basic types: *applications programming* and *systems programming*. Both types are essential for an efficient and economical computer system, and they complement one another. Applications programs is the main thrust of this book.

Applications Programs

Applications programming is undertaken by those programmers whose purpose is to accomplish specific data processing tasks. Applications programs may involve accounting, finance, engineering, manufacturing, marketing, personnel, purchasing, and research and development. Typical examples are payroll, raw materials inventory, and accounts receivable programs.

Many general application programs have been written by the computer manufacturers in the form of program libraries. Other general programs have been developed by software houses. Applications programs are oriented toward solving computer processing requirements for specific business problems.

Individuals are generally knowledgeable about problems they are analyzing. The programmers may have been hired and trained by a company. Or, the services of a software house or the assistance of the computer manufacturer may be used to accomplish the applications programming. The task of the programmers is to produce an efficient and effective program.

Systems Programs

Systems programming involves those programs which control the computer. Many computer routines are developed by the equipment manufacturers. Such system programs are often referred to as control or supervisor program packages. They include control programs which operate the input and output equipment; utility programs which control output formats; diagnostic programs which examine electrical and mechanical malfunctions; and programs for conversion to a machine language.

Systems programming is an invaluable aid to programming. When an applications programmer comes to a point in a program that requires reading or writing specific data, a control program can be used. The time to develop applications programs is thus speeded up considerably.

With the aid of such languages as BASIC and COBOL, the applications programmer, who possess only minimal knowledge of hardware functions, can put together an extremely efficient program. The systems programmer, however, must know how the machine functions; its memory capacity, retrieval and processing speeds; its input and output capabilities; and its electronic limitations. An academic background in a scientific discipline is consequently valuable here.

types of programming languages

An important part of systems programming today is the development of translator or processor programs. Instead of having applications programmers code in a machine language for a specific computer, they can instruct a computer in a language closer to English and normal mathematical notation. The program can then be translated into the machine language of the specific computer. There are several types of language being used for these translator programs, the more important ones being:

procedure-oriented language
problem-oriented language

Procedure-Oriented Languages

Procedure-oriented languages allow the programmer to describe the set of procedures by which the problem is to be solved. Examples are BASIC, COBOL, FORTRAN, and PL/1.

Problem-Oriented Languages

Problem-oriented languages describe the problem itself, that is, the programming language approximates the language of the problem to be solved by the computer. Examples are RPG and simulation languages.

Translation Process

Within each group of major programming languages set forth above, there are many different languages, each requiring a separate program *compiler*, sometimes referred to as a *translator*, to produce the desired machine language. Each programming language includes a set of allowable words, symbols, and characters as well as a set of rules for using this vocabulary to define the problem. The translation process is basically the same for all languages.

As shown in Figure 4-1, programming language instructions are entered

figure 4-1. Translating a programming language program (input) into a machine language program (output).

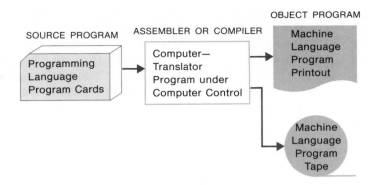

SOURCE PROGRAM   ASSEMBLER OR COMPILER   OBJECT PROGRAM

Programming Language Program Cards → Computer—Translator Program under Computer Control → Machine Language Program Printout

Machine Language Program Tape

as input into the computer. The translator or processor program causes the computer to convert these instructions into machine language output. The machine language program, written on magnetic tape, is read into memory just as if it had been written directly by the programmer.

The programming language program as read in is known as the *source program*. The computer program that performs the translation is referred to as the *compiler* (for procedure-oriented and problem-oriented languages). The machine language program that results is called the *object program*.

computer programming and implementation

Because there are two basic types of computer processing modes, there are also two computer programming and implementation approaches:

- batch processing
- interactive processing

batch processing approach

The task of preparing a computer program for daily operations is not simple and straightforward for a batch-processing computer. The steps are long and drawn out. The steps provide an accurate program when processing is complete.

Define the Problem and Prepare the Program Flowcharts

Problem analysis entails two separate steps. These include defining the problem and preparing the program flowchart(s) and/or decision table(s). As noted in Figure 4-2, these are the first two steps in preparing an operational computer program in a batch-processing environment. Also, they are the first steps for developing a program in an interactive processing mode.

Write the Computer Program

Coding is the process of writing the actual computer instructions. The programmer studies previously prepared flowcharts in order to become familiar with the program to be written. The individual should think not only

Problem Analysis (Treated in Chapter 2)	1. Define the problem. 2. Prepare the program flowcharts.
Programming and Implementation	3. Write the computer program. 4. Desk check the program. 5. Prepare program cards. 6. Compile source program. 7. Correct errors and recompile program. 8. Test (debug) program with sample transactions. 9. Correct errors and recompile program. 10. Test program using systems testing. 11. Test program using parallel operations. 12. Conversion to daily operations. 13. Documentation.

figure 4-2. Problem analysis, programming, and implementation process for an operational computer program—batch processing mode.

in terms of the problem to be solved, but also of the end result—the computer's language. Consideration should be given to how the program will be compiled by the translator program.

Before the programmer undertakes the detailed coding, the program should be segmented into a series of logically independent *modules* or *subprograms*. If these program modules can be compiled separately, there are many benefits that will accrue. Work can be divided among several programmers. Programs can be tested prior to all modules being written, thereby, reducing the testing time at a later date. Changes can be made independently of other unaffected modules.

When writing a program, program packages and special programs developed by equipment manufacturers, software houses, consulting firms, users groups, and service bureaus are available. Consulting services may be provided by many of these same sources.

Desk Check the Program

Once the program has been written, it is highly unlikely that it will be free of error. Most computer programs are checked by another programmer or supervisor for errors. Despite the efforts of the most expert programmer, errors are generally found at this stage also and appropriate corrections made. Two major types of errors are found in the typical program, logical and clerical errors.

Logical errors are difficult to uncover since a thorough understanding of the program flowcharts and program is necessary. Basically, they refer to those conditions in the program that do not adequately represent the data processing operations required within the program. For example, the amount of an employee's deductions in a payroll program cannot produce a negative net pay even though the deductions may be legitimate. Additional logical tests are necessary to insure this negative condition never occurs.

Clerical errors include the assignment of the same symbol for two different sets of data, the omission of an instruction, or the misuse of an operation symbol.

Prepare Program Cards

Preparing program cards is the next step in computer programming and implementation in a batch-processing mode. Key verification is recommended. Simple misreading at the keypunching stage can cause errors, especially if there are characters that look alike. There always seems to be confusion regarding O and zero, i and 1, and z and 2. It is recommended that the programming language program be printed after keypunching and key verifying. In this manner, the programmer can visually check for errors caused by illegible handwriting misinterpreted at the keypunching stage. One noticeable error that comes to light when a printed listing is available centers around the incorrect keypunching of data fields, where the wrong card columns are being punched.

Compile Source Program

Compilation of the source program occurs under computer control. Compilation is the translation of a procedure-oriented or problem-oriented language into machine language. Programs written in BASIC, COBOL, FORTRAN, PL/1, and RPG are compiled to produce an object program. The object program, in turn, is a machine language program which performs the instructions originally represented by the coding.

During the compilation process, the processor that produces the object program checks for clerical errors or omissions. An invalid operation symbol, symbols not properly defined, labels omitted in the program, various types of keypunching errors, and other errors can be brought to the attention of the programmer at this stage. It is not advisable to punch an object program deck or write an object program on magnetic tape or disk. The normal procedure is to print the source program only.

Correct Errors and Recompile Program

Having made the necessary corrections to the program deck, recompilation of the source program is undertaken. During this second computer pass, the printed source program should be devoid of any clerical errors that are capable of detection by the translator program. Since the source program is as correct as possible at this point, a machine language program is produced for testing the sample data. It should be noted that for very simple programs, this step is generally not needed.

Test (Debug) Program with Sample Transactions

To make each test session as productive as possible, the programmer should have all materials necessary for efficient debugging. These include an operating run manual, a machine language program of the problem to be tested, and the test data itself. Computer paper, blank cards, magnetic tape reels, and magnetic disk packs, required by the program, should also be readily available. An operating run manual should contain the original flowcharts, a list of operating instructions, input and output requirements, a complete list of all stop instructions and the reasons for reaching that portion of the program, and a list of the expected results from the test data employed. Thus, the exact testing sequence to be followed for each run, the purpose of each test, the data requirements, and the expected results should be determined before going on the computer.

Program Test Deck. The ultimate test of the object program is to determine how accurate its results are when processed on the computer. This can be determined by applying hypothetical data which are representative of the real world. The data should be varied enough so that when the program has been successfully tested, all parts of the program will have been checked against every combination and sequence of data conceivable under actual operating conditions. Large quantities of test data do not necessarily insure good test data.

Basically, these input data are designed to test the various branches and parts of the program. The correct output for these hypothetical input transactions should be predetermined. In this manner, a comparison can be made between the expected and actual results. In many cases, it is quite helpful to test for intermediate results in order to detect various types of errors. The most important errors uncovered are those where certain program paths have been omitted.

Test Modules. An important consideration when debugging a complex program is to break the program into component parts or modules and test each section separately. Even if a program does not use the modular approach, the major segments of a large complex program can be tested by entering intermediate results and starting at the beginning of the area(s) to be tested. The purpose of this approach is to localize the clerical and/or logical errors in the program.

Correct Errors and Recompile Program

Program errors found during the testing or debugging phase are corrected. After the program is as error free as possible, it is advisable to reassemble or recompile the program. Generally, an extensive amount of patching is made to a complex program for the various errors found. Sometimes, the changes and documentation become very difficult to read and understand. In such cases, not only should a new object program be produced, but also the same test deck should be rerun for the program. Only in this manner can the programmer be assured of a program that is the same after numerous corrections have been made.

Test Program Using Systems Testing

Before parallel operations are undertaken, it is recommended that systems testing be employed. Systems testing involves using actual past data so that the computer program can be tested. Regular transactions and exceptions are tested against the computer program for reliability. Depending upon the type of system, this phase could be short or somewhat lengthy.

Test Program Using Parallel Operations

Despite the many months of hard work by a group of experienced programmers, there is still the question of how well the program handles all regular and exception items. To gain confidence in the program and related data processing procedures, it is customary to run parallel operations. Cross-checking between the old and new data processing systems will establish confidence in the new system. Discrepancies will be brought to light without the loss of valuable data and operating efficiency.

Initially, parallel operations are restricted to a small volume of data. For example, in a cycle billing accounting system, only one or two cycles out of twenty will be converted in order to test the accuracy of the new program and procedures. These dual operations may extend over a period of several months if major difficulties arise. The problems expected in all cycles are expected to show up when converting one or two cycles.

Personnel Considerations. The problems encountered in dual processing involve more than the program and related procedures. Personnel difficulties can be significant since someone must process the information in the old way while someone must handle it in the new manner. It is necessary to coordinate these operations for best results. A work force that may be reduced because of more computer mechanization may have to be increased for the period of dual operations. This duplication of effort may occur within or outside the DP system.

The process of parallel operations can be very trying on people. A substantial resentment of newer data processing methods can be engendered by the changes taking place. Often, disgruntled employees seize this opportunity to discredit the new programs and procedures and all other changes associated with them. In such situations, it takes all the cooperation and efforts of programmers and department heads to overcome the problem. It is best to convert one area at a time so that disruption and confusion can be kept to a minimum.

Conversion to Daily Operations

Conversion to daily operations can be more hectic than parallel processing. The reason is that large volumes of activities are involved versus a limited amount for dual operations. In addition, there is a problem that unusual exception items show up in large volume processing which is not always true of small volume operations during parallel processing. Likewise, the work habits of people have been changed. Only after a period of time can minor changes be undertaken to satisfy employees who are unhappy with the new system.

Experience has shown that the long hours required for converting to daily operations can affect the performance of the average employee. Long hours tend to make employees irritable and unreceptive. For the most part, organizations are extremely happy to have conversion activites behind them.

Documentation

Documentation is the final step in programming and implementation. This phase is not a step in the sense of the preceding ones since it is an integral part of those mentioned previously. It consists of gathering all documents associated with the program and placing them in a program manual. A typical program manual might include the following items: problem description, program flowcharts, decision tables, input and output record and file formats, printed copy of the program (in coding language), copy of object program, test data deck used during the debugging phase, and program change control log. Also, a copy of the operating instructions or computer run book used by the computer operator should be an essential part of the documentation process.

Continual Updating Process. The documentation phase does not end when the program has become operational. It must be maintained on an up-to-date basis as changes occur within the system. At all times, documentation should represent the program in its current state rather than its previous status. As many organizations have found, it is much easier to modify a well-documented computer program while it is almost impossible to modify a poorly documented or undocumented one. In many cases, organizations have found it easier to reprogram the entire job rather than attempt to modify a program that lacks adequate documentation.

Relationship Among the Steps

The overall process of programming and implementation has involved the foregoing steps. Although the process is rather lengthy, this systematized procedure leads to better results.

A close examination of these steps reveals that they are a part of an *error correcting process.* When a problem arises, the process loops back to a prior step which, in turn, means correcting all subsequent steps up to the point where the problem occurred. With these interrelationships, it is necessary to return to an earlier step so that previous work can be redone. For example, logical errors discovered during the testing or conversion process can force a return to the problem definition step. This means considerable reworking of all intervening steps. Errors of this type are not only time consuming to correct, but also point out the need for a thorough and complete job from start to finish. Data processing personnel must sacrifice speed in the interest of obtaining accuracy and getting the detailed information needed for a problem's solution. They must be capable and thorough in their efforts.

| **interactive processing approach** | Computer programming and implementation in an interactive processing environment differs from that of a batch-processing mode. Since interactive processing is designed for on-line processing, this orientation results in a conversational mode with the computer. Access to input/output terminals decreases the time needed to set up a computer program. Organizational personnel who must solve computer problems quickly can employ an interactive processing language such as BASIC. An interactive processing approach is well suited for those company personnel who must write their own programs that may be used infrequently. It is also well suited for experienced programmers who must develop programs that will be used for day-to-day operations. |

Programming and Implementation Steps

Since the interactive processing approach is basically used for writing somewhat straightforward programs at on-site and remote terminals, its programming and implementation steps differ somewhat from those set forth above for a batch-processing approach (Figure 4-2). Its initial two steps are alike, that is, defining the problem, and preparing the program flowcharts. However, it should be noted that these two steps will not be as difficult as in the batch-processing mode since the problem is generally straightforward. Hence, for very simple problems, an individual may well sit down at an I/O terminal and begin with the next step.

To initiate the programming and implementation phase, the individual will enter (write) the computer program at the terminal. For complex programs, the program will have been written and reviewed for completeness as well as logical and clerical errors. As the program instructions are entered, the computer will ask certain questions about the program if clerical errors are noticed. Hence, as the program is entered, corrections to the program as indicated by the computer are made by the individual.

Once the program has been entered and all corrections have been made by the operator, test data can be processed against the computer program. In the testing process, computer program errors may develop. This means that the program must be corrected for such errors. Once the individual is satisfied that all test data are processed correctly according to the program, the next step is to resort to systems testing. This means that past real world data are processed against the program to increase its validity. If the program meets the test of previous real-live data correctly, the remaining steps are the same as with batch processing. Otherwise, appropriate corrections must be made to the program. It is recommended that a second pass of all real world data be undertaken if errors are discovered at this step.

As with the batch-processing approach, parallel operations are employed to test the computer program. Conversion to daily operations is then undertaken. As always, there is need for proper documentation of the program and its related procedures.

The preceding steps for programming and implementing an operational computer program in an interactive processing mode are summarized in

Problem Analysis (Treated in Chapter 2)	1. Define the problem. 2. Prepare the program flowcharts.
Programming and Implementation	3. Enter (write) the computer program at the terminal. 4. Make corrections as directed by the computer. 5. Test (debug) program with sample transactions. 6. Correct errors. 7. Test program using systems testing. 8. Test program using parallel operations. 9. Conversion to daily operations. 10. Documentation.

figure 4-3. Problem analysis, programming, and implementation process for an operational computer program—interactive processing mode.

Figure 4-3. Although the foregoing procedures were based upon the implementation of a computer program that is used for daily DP operations, many other programs operating in an interactive processing mode are not used daily, but rather infrequently. Thus, the latter steps of systems testing, parallel operations, and conversion to daily operations may not be required.

alternative programming approaches

To make the job of programming and testing easier, several approaches have been developed over the past few years. Among these are:

- modular programming
- top-down programming
- structured programming

Emphasis in this book will be placed on modular programming because it is a logical method for simplifying the programming process. Also, it is an essential part of the other two programming approaches.

Modular Programming

Modular programming refers to the technique of programming in which the logical parts of a problem are divided into a series of individual routines or modules so that each routine may be programmed independently. This approach to programming enables complex problems to be divided into sections. Access to individual routines is controlled by a single routine, commonly known as the mainline program in a batch-processing mode. The mainline routine makes all decisions governing the flow of data to the processing routines (see Figure 4-4).

In a modular programming approach, a program consists of several program modules where each module is generally limited from two to six pages of coding. A program module passes control to a calling program; control is returned to the calling program when processing is completed by the module. Decisions may be made in a module which will cause a change in the flow of the system, but the module will not actually execute the branching. It will communicate the decision to the calling program which executes the branching. The creation of a modular design is relatively easy since a computer problem consists of a number of functional data processing modules.

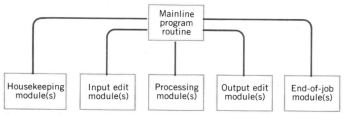

figure 4-4. An overview of modular programming in a batch-processing mode — mainline program routine makes all decisions governing the flow of data to and from the many modules.

program classifications:

• applications programming—undertaken by those programmers whose primary purpose is to accomplish specific data processing tasks. Business application programmers develop computer programs for an organization's functional areas.
Examples: payroll, raw materials inventory, and accounts receivable programs.

• systems programming—undertaken by those programmers whose primary task is to write programs that control computer operations. Typical control programs operate input and output devices, determine output formats, and convert applications programs to a specific machine language.
Examples: control programs that operate input/output devices and convert programs to a specific machine language.

types of programming languages:

• procedure-oriented languages—allow the programmer to describe the set of procedures by which the problem is to be solved.
Examples: BASIC, COBOL, and FORTRAN.

• problem-oriented languages—permit the programmer to describe the problem in a programming language that approximates the language of the problem itself.
Examples: RPG and simulation languages.

translation process:

• source program—programming language program which serves as input to the translator program.

• compiler—computer program which translates the source program into the object program. It is also known as a *translator*.

• object program—machine language program which is the result of the translation process.

computer programming and implementation:

Since there are two basic types of computer processing modes, there are the same number of computer programming and implementing approaches. These approaches differ in their steps for developing an operational computer program. Their steps are as follows:

Batch Processing
• define the problem.
• prepare the program flowcharts.
• write the computer program.
• desk check the program.
• prepare program cards.
• compile source program.
• correct errors and recompile program.
• test (debug) program with sample transactions.
• correct errors and recompile program.

Interactive Processing
• define the problem.
• prepare the program flowcharts.
• enter (write) the computer program at the terminal.
• make corrections as directed by the computer.
• test (debug) program with sample transactions.
• correct errors.
• test program using systems testing.
• test program using parallel

Batch Processing
- test program using systems testing.
- test program using parallel operations.
- conversion to daily operations.
- documentation.

Interactive Processing operations.
- conversion to daily operations.
- documentation.

first self-study exercise of chapter 4

True-False:

1. ( ) The greatest demand in terms of number of positions is for applications programmers.
2. ( ) The only type of programming languages are those that are procedure-oriented and problem-oriented.
3. ( ) RPG is an example of a procedure-oriented language.
4. ( ) An object program is input for a compiler or a translator program.
5. ( ) Programming is always faster with a batch-processing approach rather than with an interactive one.
6. ( ) Problem analysis includes defining the problem and preparing program flowcharts.
7. ( ) An example of a logical error is the misuse of an operation code.
8. ( ) Accent of a program test deck should be on the quality of data.
9. ( ) Parallel operations follow systems testing.
10. ( ) An integral part of all programming and implementing steps is documentation.

Fill-In:

11. _____ _____ is directed toward the solution of computer processing requirements for an organization while _____ _____ is oriented toward those computer routines that are common to many different programs.
12. Languages which allow the programmer to describe the set of procedures by which the problem is to be solved are _____-_____ _____.
13. Languages which are oriented toward the specification of a particular class of problems are _____-_____ _____.
14. The _____ _____ converts the source program into an object program. It is referred to as a _____ for higher-level languages.
15. The object program that results from a translator program is a _____ _____ _____.
16. The first step in _____ and _____ a computer program is defining the problem clearly.
17. Before the computer program is written, one or more _____ should be prepared.
18. Desk checking the computer program for _____ and _____ errors is highly recommended.
19. In a batch-processing mode, the object machine language program can be debugged for accuracy by utilizing a _____ _____.
20. One of the last steps in programming and implementing is running _____ _____ for a period of time in order to check the new system against the old one.

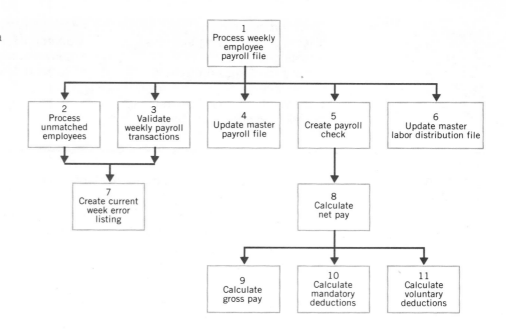

figure 4-5. Major programming modules for a typical weekly payroll program.

To illustrate the modular programming concept, a typical weekly payroll program is broken down into eleven modules (see Figure 4-5). These individual modules are separate tasks that vary in size and complexity. For example, the highest-level module represents the solution to a weekly payroll program. The next and succeeding levels solve one of the tasks to be performed in order to process the program. Within this sample programming project, four programmers handle several modules within the same program, except the lead programmer, as depicted in Figure 4-6. Each programmer is responsible for coding and testing specific modules

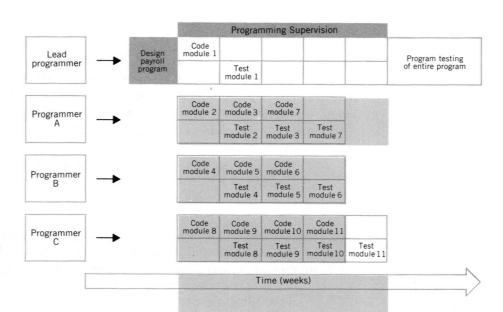

figure 4-6. Organization of modular programming for a typical weekly payroll program — based upon Figure 4-5.

while the lead programmer supervises and is responsible for final program testing.

The foregoing has described only one approach to modular programming —that where every transference of control is made in a mainline program. However, for an interactive environment, a more important type exists. For the sake of speed and efficiency, each module controls the program flow by ordering an ICP (interactive control program) to call in another module. An ICP is not a mainline program as its function is that of a "housekeeper" and does not control the logical system flow. We have, then, a type of modular programming where the flow continues on a smooth path through a chain of modules rather than going in and out of the mainline control program.

Top-Down Programming

Top-down programming essentially means proceeding by refinement from the highest level down to the lowest level. At each level, the function to be performed is defined and then expressed in terms of functional units at a lower level, continuing the process until the level is reached at which the programmer can write the computer program. This approach can be applied at any stage of the programming process—design, coding, or testing. However, one of its strengths is the way that top-down programming allows the stages to be combined. For example, once a certain module has been defined, it can be programmed and tested.

The parts that comprise a module will eventually be the functions to be performed. For these, routines, called stubs, can be substituted. Although a stub has the same name as the object it substitutes for, it does not perform the actual function it represents. A stub provides similar input-output behavior to the module which references it. This allows one to test the module by itself and then test it plugged into the rest of the system which has been so far developed. One advantage of this phased approach is that there is a partial system which is operative, thereby giving the programmer a good picture of what the final system will be. Also, this partial system serves as a test method for the next module to be completed.

A very important advantage of the top-down approach is that requirements of a system usually change before the project is finished. Since changes are inevitable, they do not have to ruin the project and its related programming. Thus, the top-down programming approach allows planning for and working with changes as they occur.

Structured Programming

Structured programming is a discipline or a method of organizing and coding a computer program that makes it easily understood and capable of being modified. Its fundamental approach is "simplifying the control paths" within a program so as to minimize program errors. In a similar manner, structured programming maximizes the ease with which errors are corrected and modifications are made. Within the framework of structured programming, the concept of modular programming is applicable, since a structured program consists of a series of program modules. The program structuring governs the transfer of their contents (modules) between different parts of the program.

Much of programming complexity arises from the fact that the program contains many jumps (GO TO's) to other parts of the program, that is, jumps are made both forward and backward in the code. These jumps make it hard to follow the program's logic. Similarly, it is difficult to insure at any given point of the program what conditions are present. Furthermore, as a program undergoes changes during its development period, the complexity of the program can grow at an alarming rate. In some cases, new coding is added because the programmer cannot find a program code that performs the desired operation, is not sure how the coding works, or is afraid to disturb the existing code.

In a structured programming environment, any program function can be performed using one of three control structures: (1) sequence, (2) selection, and (3) repetition. Any kind of processing, any combination of decisions, or any sort of logic can be accommodated with one of these control structures or a combination of these structures. Each structure is characterized by a simple and single point of transfer of control into the structure, and a single point of transfer out of the structure. These structures can be combined to form a program that is very simple in the sense that control flows from top to bottom or from beginning to end. Thus, structured programming reduces a program's complexity and increases its clarity during the programming and testing phases and later during the program maintenance phase.

higher-level programming languages

Higher-level programming languages permit a computer program to be written in a minimum of time. These various languages consist of abbreviated words or symbols that can be easily associated with the English language. This similarity, together with familiar mathematical notation, makes it quite easy to read and comprehend what is happening. Such programming languages facilitate the communications process for DP personnel.

Factors in Language Developments. According to some data processing enthusiasts, an effective programming language should be easy to learn, use, and implement. It should be machine independent, quick to compile, lead to efficient object programs, and be general purpose or applicable to a wide variety of problems. As the language is simplified so that it is easier to learn, it becomes less valuable to the experienced programmer. It is almost impossible to please the beginner in solving simple problems and the expert in solving very complex problems. The more machine independent and general purpose the language is, the harder it is to implement by writing an efficient compiler. Also more time and space are consumed by the compilation process. To obtain more efficient object programs, features which give preference to one or another computer and make assumptions about the class of problems to be handled must be incorporated into the language. In essence, a programming language that is suitable for solving problems in the most efficient manner is not feasible at this time. For this reason, there is a variety of programming languages to serve different problem needs.

Higher-Level Languages. An overview of higher-level languages will be given for COBOL and RPG. In the next two chapters, BASIC will be presented as currently used in a minicomputer environment. These languages, excluding RPG, are procedure-oriented since they refer to a set of procedures by which the problem is to be solved. The procedural notation used to write a program in COBOL resembles English, while BASIC is a compromise between English and pure computer languages. The problem-oriented language of RPG is well suited for small-computer users.

Restrictions that are present in English and mathematics also exist in the notation of these higher-level languages. Only a specified group of numbers, letters, and special characters can be used in writing a computer program. Likewise, special rules must be followed for punctuation and blanks. Despite these important constraints, a program written in a procedure-oriented language is more flexible in form than a machine-oriented language of a specific computer.

COBOL Language

COBOL, an acronym for COmmon Business-Oriented Language, was the first major attempt to produce a truly business-oriented programming language. It was developed by the Conference on Data System Languages (CODASYL) Committee that consisted of several large users, computer manufacturers, the Federal government, and other interested groups. Their report contained the first version, called COBOL-60, where 60 represented the year of issuance. Since that time, several newer versions have been developed by the Programming Language Committee (PLC), whose job is to review and recommend changes. The version below is based upon COBOL 74.

Language Components. The COBOL character set consists of the numerals 0 through 9, the letters of the alphabet, and 12 special characters. The language consists of names for identification purposes, constants and literals, operators that indicate some action or relationship, key words to establish the meaning of a statement, expressions containing the foregoing, statements using a verb and an item to be acted on, and sentences composed of one or more statements properly punctuated.

Program Divisions. A COBOL program is divided into four divisions:

1. Identification—identifies the program itself.
2. Environment—describes the equipment being used.
3. Data—specifies the form and format of the data files.
4. Procedure—depicts the processing steps to be undertaken.

Basically, the Procedure Division, being the actual processing instructions, is interpreted by the equipment described in the Environment Division as well as the files and records described by the Data Division. The Identification Division is required for documentation and is not affected by the other three divisions.

Identification Division. The Identification Division is used to identify the program and to furnish other pertinent information. It can run from one to seven paragraphs, where each paragraph represents a sentence or a group of sentences and can be identified as follows:

```
IDENTIFICATION DIVISION.
PROGRAM-ID. —Program-Name.
AUTHOR. —Author-Name.
INSTALLATION. —Any sentence or group of sentences.
DATA-WRITTEN. —Any sentence or group of sentences.
DATA-COMPILED. —Any sentence or group of sentences.
SECURITY. —Any sentence or group of sentences.
REMARKS. —Any sentence or group of sentences.
```

Only the PROGRAM-ID paragraph is required and must appear as the first paragraph of the program. The other Identification paragraphs are optional. This first division is depicted in Figure 4-8 (lines 1–3) for the sample "HOUR-PAY" program.

Environment Division. The Environment Division has two main sections —the Configuration Section and the Input-Output Section, shown in Figure 4-8 (lines 4–11). The names of these sections are fixed and must start by the beginning of their respective sections. Likewise, the names of the paragraphs following each section are fixed and their names must be given at the beginning of any paragraph used. The structure of the Environment Division is given below. Note the use of periods.

```
ENVIRONMENT DIVISION.
  CONFIGURATION SECTION.
    SOURCE-COMPUTER. Computer-Name.
    OBJECT-COMPUTER. Computer-Name.
    SPECIAL NAMES. DEVICE-NAME.... Switch-Name.
  INPUT-OUTPUT SECTION.
    FILE-CONTROL. SELECT ...
    I/O-CONTROL. APPLY ...
```

Configuration Section. The Configuration Section identifies the computer on which the program is to be compiled (source computer) and the computer on which it is to be processed (object computer). Generally, they are the same. An optional paragraph, as indicated above, can be used to assign special names to equipment items, such as card reader, printer, and sense switches.

Input/Output Section. The Input/Output Section may consist of two paragraphs. The File-Control paragraph relates files with the devices on which they are to be read or written as well as the processing mode. While the first paragraph is required, the second paragraph or I/O Control is optional. The I/O Control paragraph defines special control techniques to be applied to the object program.

Data Division. The Data Division is used to define the characteristics and format of the data to be processed. Every data name referred to in the procedure division must be defined in this division, except figurative constants. While items and records are described by record description entries, files are referenced by file description entries. The Data Division may consist of four sections. All of them, however, need not be used in a specific program. They are:

```
DATA DIVISION.
  FILE SECTION.
  WORKING-STORAGE SECTION.
  REPORT SECTION.
```

File Section. Description of the files to be utilized follow the File Section heading and will be preceded by FD (File Description). The File Description will generally include a name for the file, a description of the input to the file, a description of the size of each individual record in the file, and the name of the tape (disk or drum) if the input or output is desired on magnetic tape (disk or drum). If the file record is a punched card or paper tape, the following statements should be written with the File Description—LABEL RECORDS ARE OMITTED. Referring to Figure 4-8, lines 13–37 illustrate the File Section.

Picture Clauses. Each item of information, a record, and a file within the record must be given a distinct name so that it may be specifically identified. In addition, it is necessary to describe their format by picture clauses. A picture clause indicates the size of an item, its class, the presence or absence of an operational sign, and/or an assumed decimal point. The word PICTURE with identifying numbers and symbols follow each file description entry. The following characters are used for input items, working storage items, and constants:

Picture Character	Used to Represent
9	A numerical digit
V	The position of an assumed decimal point (for internal calculations only)
S	The presence of an operational sign
A	An alphabetic character or a space
X	Any character in the computer's character set
Z	The zero suppression of the indicated characters
$	A dollar sign character

Examples of how different pictures might look when utilizing the above picture character symbols are found in Figure 4-7.

An entry name FILLER is used to indicate the unused portions of the record. This is required since the entire word must be taken into account. For example, when reading an 80-column card, the blank columns are referenced as filler pictures.

Working-Storage Section. The Working-Storage Section is used to describe the areas of storage where intermediate results and other items are to be stored temporarily. It describes the records and individual data items which are not part of input or output files. However, these data values are developed and used when required by the program internally. The working storage locations required for Figure 4-8 are shown on lines 38 through 43.

PICTURE	ACTUAL DATA	DATA WILL BE PRINTED AS	PICTURE CHARACTER CLASS
99999	45921	45921	Numeric
99V99	8250	8250	Numeric
S999V99	−65921	−65921	Numeric
AAAAA	NAMES	NAMES	Alphabetic
XXXXX	456AB	456AB	Alphanumeric
ZZZ99	00045	45	Numeric edited
$999V99	39521	$39521	Numeric edited

figure 4-7. Examples of picture characters.

```
LINE NO.  SEQ. NO.            SOURCE STATEMENT

     1       1      IDENTIFICATION DIVISION.
     2       2      PROGRAM-ID. HOUR-PAY.
     3       3      REMARKS. PROGRAM TO COMPUTE WEEKLY GROSS PAY.
     4       4      ENVIRONMENT DIVISION.
     5       5      CONFIGURATION SECTION.
     6       6      SOURCE-COMPUTER. IBM-370.
     7       7      OBJECT-COMPUTER. IBM-370.
     8       8      INPUT-OUTPUT SECTION.
     9       9      FILE-CONTROL.
    10      10          SELECT CARD-INPUT ASSIGN TO SYS007-UR-2540-S.
    11      11          SELECT PRINT-OUTPUT ASSIGN TO SYS009-UR-1403-S.
    12      12      DATA DIVISION.
    13      13      FILE SECTION.
    14      14      FD  CARD-INPUT,
    15      15          RECORDING MODE IS F,
    16      16          RECORD CONTAINS 80 CHARACTERS,
    17      17          LABEL RECORDS ARE OMITTED,
    18      18          DATA RECORD IS WEEKLY-PAYROLL-CARD-INPUT.
    19      19      01  WEEKLY-PAYROLL-CARD-INPUT.
    20      20          02 EMPLOYEE-PAYROLL-NUMBER PICTURE IS 99999.
    21      21          02 FILLER PICTURE IS X(2).
    22      22          02 HOURS-WORKED PICTURE IS 99.
    23      23          02 HOURLY-PAY PICTURE IS 9V99.
    24      24          02 FILLER PICTURE IS X(68).
    25      25      FD  PRINT-OUTPUT,
    26      26          RECORDING MODE IS F,
    27      27          RECORD CONTAINS 133 CHARACTERS,
    28      28          LABEL RECORDS ARE OMITTED,
    29      29          DATA RECORD IS PRINT-LINE.
    30      30      01  PRINT-LINE.
    31      31          02 FILLER PICTURE IS X.
    32      32          02 EMPLOYEE-PRINT PICTURE IS 9(5).
    33      33          02 FILLER PICTURE IS X(5).
    34      34          02 HOURS-PRINT PICTURE IS 99.
    35      35          02 FILLER PICTURE IS X(5).
    36      36          02 GROSS-PRINT PICTURE IS $$$9.99.
    37      37          02 FILLER PICTURE IS X(108).
    38      38      WORKING-STORAGE SECTION.
    39      39          77 GROSS-PAY PICTURE IS 999V99.
    40      40          77 STRAIGHT-TIME PICTURE IS 999V99.
    41      41          77 OVERTIME PICTURE IS 999V99.
    42      42          77 OVERTIME-HOURS PICTURE IS 99V99.
    43      43          77 OVERTIME-PREMIUM PICTURE IS 999V99.
    44      44      PROCEDURE DIVISION.
    45      45      START-PROG.
    46      46          OPEN INPUT CARD-INPUT, OUTPUT PRINT-OUTPUT.
    47      47      READ-A-CARD.
    48      48          READ CARD-INPUT, AT END GO TO LAST-CARD.
    49      49          MULTIPLY HOURLY-PAY BY HOURS-WORKED
    50      50          GIVING STRAIGHT-TIME ROUNDED.
    51      51          DIVIDE 2 INTO HOURLY-PAY GIVING  OVERTIME-PREMIUM.
    52      52          SUBTRACT 40 FROM HOURS-WORKED GIVING OVERTIME-HOURS.
    53      53          MULTIPLY OVERTIME-HOURS BY OVERTIME-PREMIUM
    54      54          GIVING OVERTIME ROUNDED.
    55      55          ADD STRAIGHT-TIME, OVERTIME GIVING GROSS-PAY.
    56      56          MOVE EMPLOYEE-PAYROLL-NUMBER TO EMPLOYEE-PRINT.
    57      57          MOVE HOURS-WORKED TO HOURS-PRINT.
    58      58          MOVE GROSS-PAY TO GROSS-PRINT.
    59      59          WRITE PRINT-LINE AFTER ADVANCING 1.
    60      60          MOVE SPACES TO PRINT-LINE.
    61      61          GO TO READ-A-CARD.
    62      62      LAST-CARD.
    63      63          CLOSE CARD-INPUT, PRINT-OUTPUT.
    64      64          STOP RUN.
```

figure 4-8. COBOL program to compute weekly gross pay for each employee.

Report Section. The Report Section describes the content and format of reports to be generated by the COBOL report generator.

Procedure Division. Basically, the Identification Division, the Environment Division, and the Data Division describe the program, the equipment, and the data to be utilized in a particular program respectively. It is in the Procedure Division where the actual programming of the problem takes place. In this division, the coder specifies what is to be accomplished with the data described in the preceding division. The program is expressed in terms of statements, sentences, paragraphs, and sections.

Program and Processor Verbs. Action verbs form the basis of the Procedure Division where each COBOL sentence must end with a period. They fall into two major categories—program verbs and processor verbs—which are listed as follows:

	Program Verbs	Processor Verbs
Input/Output	CLOSE	ENTER
	DISPLAY	EXIT
	OPEN	NOTE
	READ	
	WRITE	
Arithmetic	ADD	
	SUBTRACT	
	MULTIPLY	
	DIVIDE	
	COMPUTE	
Data Manipulation	EXAMINE	
	MOVE	
Sequence Control	ALTER	
	GO TO	
	PERFORM	
	STOP	

While program verbs revolve around the steps that will be performed by the object program, processor verbs direct the processor in its work. Examples of program verbs are illustrated in Figure 4-8, lines 46 through 64.

Program Structure. The smallest unit of expression is the statement when utilizing these action verbs. Sentences, paragraphs, and sections are the larger units of expression. A statement consists of a COBOL verb or the word IF or ON, followed by an appropriate operands (data-names, file-names, or literals) and other COBOL words that are necessary to complete a statement. On the other hand, a sentence is a single statement or a series of statements that is ended by a period and followed by a space. A paragraph consists of one or more sentences and a section is composed of one or more successive paragraphs. The latter must begin with a section-heading.

Types of Statements. There are four types of statements. The *compliler-directing* statements instruct the compiler to take certain actions when being compiled. *Imperative* statements indicate unconditional actions that are to be taken by the object program. *Conditional* statements contain a condition which is to be tested. They determine which alternate path is to be taken in the program. Lastly, *note* statements are allowed for comments about the program. They are not translated into the object program.

COBOL Illustration. The foregoing divisions of the COBOL language are illustrated for computing gross pay in Figure 4-8 (as noted previously).

Identification Division. The Identification Division contains the name of the program (lines 1–3), namely, HOUR-PAY. A brief description of the program is found under REMARKS—PROGRAM TO COMPUTE WEEKLY GROSS PAY.

Environment Division. The Configuration Section of the Environmental Division, lines 5 through 7, indicates that an IBM 370 computer will be used to compile the program as well as process the object program. The Input-Output Section is used to name each file, identify its contents, and assign it to one or more input-output devices. Lines 10 and 11 identify the card-input device as a card reader, known as SYS007 (manufacturer number for this device is 2540) and the print-output device as a line printer, known as SYS009 (manufacturer number for this device is 1403).

Data Division. In the Data Division, the File Section, lines 13 through 37, has two File Description (FD) entries. The first, statements 14 through 18, describe the card input as a 80 column card where magnetic tape labels are not needed. The first entry is identified as a WEEKLY-PAYROLL-CARD-INPUT and is divided into several fields per lines 20 through 24. Card columns 1 through 5 contain the employee-payroll-number while columns 8 through 9 and 10 through 12 contain the hours-worked and hourly-pay respectively. The term "picture" identifies the coded description of the particular field. For example, the picture clause 9V99 on line 23 describes the hourly-pay as a three-position numeric field containing an assumed decimal point. In the second FD entry, the statements on lines 25 through 37 describe the print-output file named PRINT-LINE. The printed output with appropriate spacing contains the employee-payroll-number, hours-worked, and gross-pay for each person on the weekly payroll.

The Working Storage Section, lines 38 through 43, reserves storage locations for five fields—gross-pay, straight-time (amount), and overtime (amount, hours, and premium). It describes them as numeric fields containing appropriate decimal places.

Procedure Division. The Procedure Division, starting on line 44 and ending on line 64, has no section headings but has three paragraph headings. The first paragraph, starting on line 45, reads START-PROG. Here, the input and output files are opened and the Print-Line is cleared of any data that may be present when the program is read in. In the second paragraph, READ-A-CARD, the following programming takes place. The statement on line 48 requires the program to read input cards and, when the final card has been read, to go to (branch) the LAST-CARD paragraph (line 62) which is the third and final one in the Procedure Division.

The statements on lines 49 through 55 make the actual calculations for gross pay. This consists of determining the straight-time amount (statement on lines 49 and 50). Next, the hourly-pay rate is divided by two in order to give an overtime-premium rate (statement on line 51). The value 40 hours is subtracted from the hours-worked this week which results in overtime-hours (statement on line 52). Then, overtime-hours are multiplied by an overtime-premium rate for an overtime amount (statement on lines 53 and 54). Lastly, the straight-time amount and overtime amount are added for gross-pay (statement on line 55).

The next three statements (lines 56 through 58) cause data to be moved to the output print-line. It should be pointed out that these three names—

Employee-Payroll-Number, Hours-Worked, and Gross-Pay are related directly to the names in the File Section of the Data Division. The statement on line 59 causes the data which were moved in the preceding three lines to be printed after spacing the paper. The last two lines (60 and 61) in this second paragraph cause the print-line to be cleared and the program to branch to the paragraph headed READ-A-CARD.

The instructions in the LAST-CARD paragraph are activated by a branch operation which occurs after the last card has been read. The statement on line 63 informs the system that processing of the files has been completed. The final statement on line 64 in this payroll program stops the processing run.

Evaluation of COBOL. Currently, COBOL is widely used for programming business applications. Its logical structure of files, records, and elements approximates business practice. One of its important characteristics is that internal processing functions are stated in English. It has the added advantage of documentation in the source program itself. The quality of documentation is considered superior to other languages since programs are much easier to read. Use of data names, maximum of 30 characters, allow more detailed description of the data. Lastly, COBOL is readily adaptable to batch-type and interactive applications.

One of the major drawbacks of COBOL is its relatively elementary structure which can require extensive programming to accomplish relatively simple tasks. In the example, statements appearing on lines 49 through 55 for the READ-A-CARD paragraph could have been expressed as one line in other higher level languages. Thus, the COBOL language can tend to be wordy and drawn out when compared to other programming languages.

RPG Language

The RPG (Report Program Generator) language is one in which the programmer writes the specifications for the problem and the compiler generates an output program from the specifications. Being a problem-oriented language, it is well suited for programs that are run on a small computer. Each version of RPG varies by manufacturer. The RPG program written for one computer is generally not compatible with another computer.

Procedural Steps. The detailed steps in developing a RPG program are given in Figure 4-9. Evaluation of the problem at hand includes the determination of the input files and the output reports (1). The programmer must make the required entries on the various specification sheets, namely, control card and file description, input, calculation, and output-format (2). The source deck is key punched from the various specifications sheets (3). In the next step, the program specifications contained in the card deck are converted into machine language instructions. Storage areas are automatically assigned, constants and other reference factors are included, and linkage to routines for input-output operations and other functions are produced (4). The machine language instructions created in the prior step are executed under control of RPG. The user's input data files are used to generate the desired reports or output files (5).

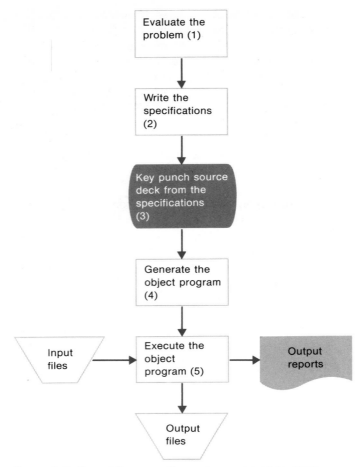

figure 4-9. Report Program Generator preparation steps.

RPG Illustration. The RPG illustration is a program designed to print a monthly accounts receivable register (A/RREG). The specification sheets to accomplish this printout from punched cards are found in Figures 4-10 through 4-13. Each input punched card contains summary data for sales made to customers throughout the month. Specifically, information in each 80 column card for this program is as follows:

Field Name	Description	Card Columns
CARDC	Card code	1–2
INVNO	Invoice number	3–7
DATE	Billing date	8–13
NAME	Customer name	14–33
ADDRES	Customer address	34–53
CTYSTA	Customer city, state, and zip code	54–73
INVAMT	Invoice amount	74–80

Control Card and File Description Specifications. The control *card specifications* sheet (Figure 4-10) contains an H (heading) in position 6. On the second half of this form or the *file description specifications*

IBM

International Business Machines Corporation

RPG CONTROL CARD AND FILE DESCRIPTION SPECIFICATIONS

GX21 9092 1 U/M050
Printed in U.S.A.

Date FEB,/198-
Program FIGURE 4-10
Programmer THIERAUF

Page $\phi1$

Program Identification A/RREG

Punching Instruction — Graphic ϕ O — Punch NUMALPHA

Control Card Specifications

Line	Form Type	Core Size to Compile	Object Output	Listing Options	Core Size to Execute	Debug				
0 1	H ϕ									

Refer to the specific System Reference Library manual for actual entries.

File Description Specifications

Line	Form Type	Filename	File Type	File Designation	End of File	Sequence	File Format	Block Length	Record Length	Mode of Processing	Length of Key Field or of Record Address Field	Record Address Type	Type of File Organization or Additional Area	Overflow Indicator	Key Field Starting Location	Extension Code E/L	Device	Symbolic Device	Labels (S, N, or E)	Name of Label Exit	Core Index	Extent Exit for DAM	File Addition/Unordered	Number of Tracks for Cylinder Overflow	Number of Extents	Tape Rewind	File Condition U1-U8
0 2	F	CARDIN	I	P	E		F	8ϕ	8ϕ								READ4ϕ	SYS$\phi\phi7$									
0 3	F	PRINTOUTO	O				F	132	132					OF			PRINTER	SYS$\phi\phi9$									
0 4	F																										
0 5	F																										
0 6	F																										
0 7	F																										

figure 4-10. RPG Control Card and File Description Specifications for printing monthly accounts receivable register (A/RREG).

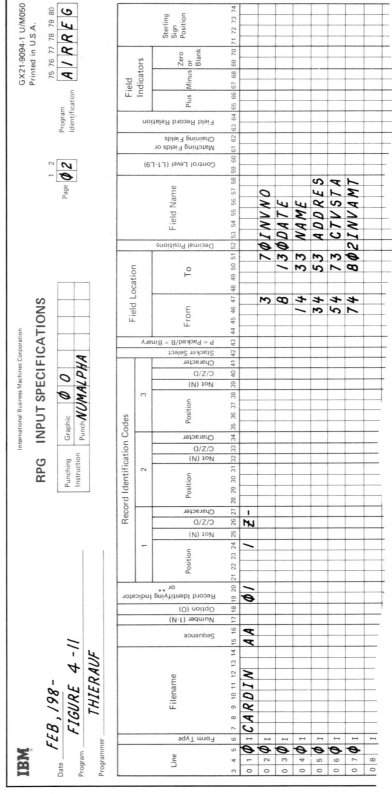

figure **4-11.** RPG Input Specifications for printing monthly accounts receivable register (A/RREG).

sheet, two files—input and output are described. The input file (CARDIN) is the primary (P, position 16) file which must provide for an end of file condition. The E in position 17 takes care of this condition. Input data are fixed (F, position 19) in length. Also, the block length is 80 (positions 22–23) as is the record length (positions 26–27). On the same first line, positions 40 to 52 show that the input device is a model 2540 card reader, assigned the symbolic name SYS007.

On the next line of the file description form, the output file (PRINTOUT) is defined as follows: format is fixed (position 19); block length is 132 (positions 21–23); and the records are 132 characters in length (positions 25–27). The entry OF (positions 33–34) allows for an overflow condition in the output file. Contained in positions 40–52 is the output unit or a printer, assigned the symbolic name SYS009.

Input Specifications. The *input specifications* sheet (Figure 4-11) describes the input requirements, such as the record layouts, fields used, and the like. In the illustration, if column 1 of the input card file contains the zone of a minus, the Record Identifying Indicator 01 is set on, indicated by the entries in positions 19–20, 24, and 26–27. The locations of the field names (set forth above) are entered in positions 44 through 51 while the names themselves are contained in positions 53 through 58.

Calculation Specifications. The *calculation specifications* sheet (Figure 4-12) describes the processing steps involved in the program: add, subtract, multiply, and divide. The sample problem specifies that the invoice amount (INVAMT, positions 18–23) be added (ADD, positions 28–30) to the total field (TOTAL, positions 33–37), storing the results in TOTAL. In positions 51 and 52, the field length and decimal positions are defined.

Output-Format Specifications. The *output-format specifications* sheet (Figure 4-13) identifies the printing positions, carriage control, and like items which will determine the final format of the report. The name of the file (PRINTOUT) to be printed is entered under Filename on the first line of the sheet. In position 15, the output types (H, D, and T) are entered which designate the heading, detail, and total lines respectively. The OR, entered in positions 14 and 15 of the second line, allows for printing the heading line (ACCOUNTS RECEIVABLE REGISTER) on the first page (1P, positions 24–25) or an overflow condition (OF, positions 24–25).

When the Output Indicator 01 is on per line 6 (positions 24–25), the detail fields entered in the Field Name (positions 32–37) will be printed on the high-speed printer per the columns indicated (positions 40–43). The Z in position 38 means that zero suppression occurs on invoice number, date, and invoice amount. Referring to the last part of the program, zero suppression also occurs when printing the total amount of accounts receivable sales cards for the month. The final total is printed when the last record (LR, positions 24–25) indicator is on.

When the invoice amount and the total amount of all billed customers are printed, constants are used (positions 45–59) to improve readability. They include the dollar sign, the comma, and the decimal point. Lastly, an asterisk is used as a constant to set off the total monthly accounts receivable amount.

IBM International Business Machines Corporation GX21-9093-1 Printed in U.S.A.

RPG CALCULATION SPECIFICATIONS

Date FEB, 198-

Program FIGURE 4-12

Programmer THIERAUF

Punching Instruction: Graphic Ø O; Punch NUMALPHA

Page (1 2) Ø3

Program Identification (75–80) A/RREG

Line (3–5)	Form Type (6)	Control Level (L0-L9, LR, SR) (7–8)	Indicators: Not (9)	(10–11)	And: Not (12)	(13–14)	And: Not (15)	(16–17)	Factor 1 (18–27)	Operation (28–32)	Factor 2 (33–42)	Result Field (43–48)	Field Length (49–51)	Decimal Positions (52)	Half Adjust (H) (53)	Resulting Indicators: Arithmetic Plus / Compare High 1>2 / Lookup Table (Factor 2) is High (54–55)	Minus / Low 1<2 / Low (56–57)	Zero / Equal 1=2 / Equal (58–59)	Comments (60–74)
01Ø	C								INVAMT	ADD	TOTAL	TOTAL	9	2					
02	C																		
03	C																		

figure 4-12. RPG Calculation Specifications for printing monthly accounts receivable register (A/RREG).

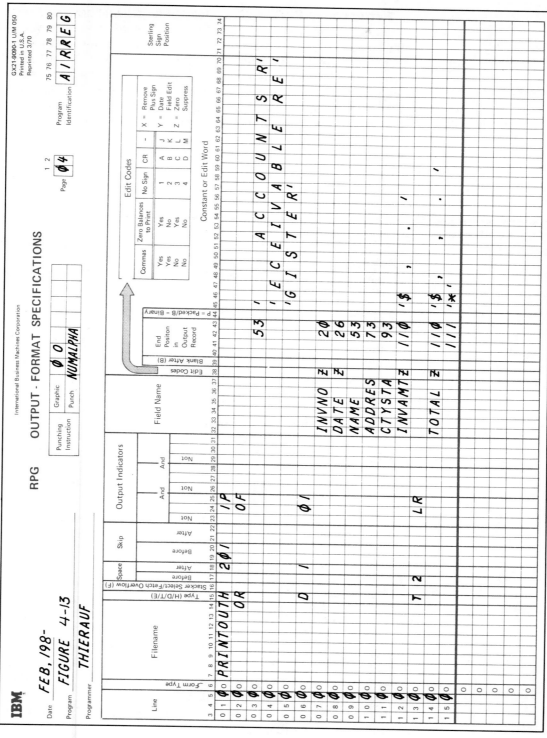

figure 4-13. RPG Output-Format Specifications for printing monthly accounts receivable register (A/RREG).

Evaluation of RPG. RPG is intended for straightforward applications. Those programs that require complex programming are not well suited to this language. The programmer would be much better off with one of the procedure-oriented languages. In terms of efficiency, RPG does not produce coding output as efficient as one written in a machine-oriented language. However, most of the problems that utilize RPG are limited by the speed of the input and output units, thereby making this consideration relatively unimportant. Thus, programming language is suited for simple problems that involve relatively uncomplicated programming.

second summary of chapter 4

alternative programming approaches:
• modular programming—a technique of writing computer programs in which the logical parts of a problem are divided into a series of individual modules so that each module can be programmed and tested independently.

• top-down programming—a technique for developing operational computer programs starting at the highest level down to the lowest level that allows planning for and working with changes as they occur.

• structured programming—a technique for organizing and coding a computer program such that control paths are simplified in order to minimize programming complexity and resulting program errors.

higher-level programming languages:
Typical higher-level programming languages which consist of abbreviated words that are easily associated with the English language and familiar mathematical symbols are:
• COBOL language—requires the programmer to develop four divisions, the hierarchy being:

- Identification—identifies the program itself.
- Environment—describes the equipment being used.
- Data—specifies the form and format of the data files.
- Procedure—depicts the processing steps to be undertaken.

Of these, the Procedure Division does the actual processing of the computer instructions. It should be noted that the Identification Division is required for documentation and is in no way affected by the other three divisions when producing an *object program.*
• RPG language—requires the programmer to write the specifications for the problem which are:

- Control and file description specifications sheet—describes the heading and the input and output files.
- Input specifications sheet—sets forth the input requirements, such as record layouts and columns used.
- Calculation specifications sheet—describes the mathematical operations to be performed.
- Output-format specifications sheet—identifies the printing positions, carriage control, etc. of printed reports.

**second self-study
exercise
of chapter 4**

True-False:

1. ( ) Modular programming enables complex programs to be divided into sections.
2. ( ) A program module normally consists of one page of computer coding.
3. ( ) Computer control of modular programs is the same for both batch processing and interactive processing.
4. ( ) Top-down programming and structured programming are one and the same.
5. ( ) Structured programming is not widely used by applications programmers.
6. ( ) COBOL, for the most part, resembles mathematical procedures.
7. ( ) The Environment Division of a COBOL program describes the equipment being used.
8. ( ) In COBOL programs, the word PICTURE is followed by identifying numbers and symbols.
9. ( ) In a COBOL program, documentation is found in the source program.
10. ( ) The RPG language is oriented toward large-sized, general-purpose computers.

Fill-In:

11. _____ _____ allows a program to be divided into a series of individual modules for the purpose of programming and testing.
12. _____ modules perform the real tasks of a computer program using the modular programming approach.
13. In a modular programming environment, each programmer is responsible for coding and testing specific modules while the _____ _____ is responsible for final program testing.
14. A very important advantage of _____-_____ _____ is that it allows planning for and working with changes as they occur.
15. The principal feature of _____ _____ is its ability to simplify control paths within a program in order to minimize programming complexity and errors.
16. A higher-level programming language which is truly business oriented is the _____ language.
17. Before a COBOL program can be compiled, all four _____ _____ must be completed with the appropriate coding and data.
18. While the _____ _____ of COBOL defines the data to be referenced and processed, the _____ _____ specifies what processing steps are to be undertaken.
19. In COBOL, the _____ _____ references data as to their size, class, operational sign, and decimal point.
20. The _____ language is one in which the programmer writes the specifications for the problem and the compiler generates an output program from the specifications.

summary

The use of programming languages to produce machine language instructions is taken for granted these days. Procedure-oriented languages allow the problem to be expressed in a form somewhat different from the machine language. This makes it possible to program with only a general knowledge of the computer itself and a minimum of training when compared to machine language programming.

The steps for programming and implementation for an operational computer program are long and drawn out in a batch-processing mode. However, the use of on-site or remote on-line input/output devices in an interactive processing mode can reduce the time and steps involved in programming. Hence, conversational programming is providing the needed thrust to break the programming bottlenecks in many organizations today.

While nonprogrammers have been reluctant to employ computers in the past due to the complex languages, the same is not true today with the many simplified programming languages available. The ease of use and simplicity of languages, such as BASIC, allow company personnel the opportunity to solve short problems quickly and effectively via an I/O terminal. Thus, time-sharing capabilities fill the programmer's gap. It frees the experienced programmer for solving large-scale computer problems while allowing non-programmers the ability to solve relatively simple problems in an interactive mode. Not only is there an awareness of the computer's capabilities with this enlightened approach to data processing, but it also brings a greater degree of computerization to the average organization.

questions

1. Define the following terms:
   (a) source program   (c) object program
   (b) translator   (d) compiler

2. What are the essential differences among the following: machine language programming, procedure-oriented programming, and problem-oriented programming?

3. Distinguish between applications programming and systems programming.

4. What are the steps involved in getting a program "on the air" in a batch-processing mode versus an interactive processing mode?

5. What are the four divisions of COBOL and what purpose does each serve?

6. What is the purpose of specifications sheets in the RPG language?

7. Name the four basic types of instructions found in most programming languages.

8. Why are logical instructions so important to the operations of a computer?

9. What might be the future direction of higher-level programming languages?

answers to first self-study exercise	1. T 2. F 3. F 4. F 5. F 6. T 7. F 8. T 9. T 10. T 11. applications programming and systems programming 12. procedure-oriented languages 13. problem-oriented languages 14. translator program and compiler 15. machine language program 16. programming and implementing 17. flowcharts 18. logical and clerical 19. test deck 20. parallel operations
answers to second self-study exercise	1. T 2. F 3. F 4. F 5. F 6. F 7. T 8. T 9. T 10. F 11. modular programming 12. processing 13. lead programmer 14. top-down programming 15. structured programming 16. COBOL 17. program divisions 18. Data Division and Procedure Division 19. picture clause 20. RPG

chapter five

essential elements of the BASIC language with business applications

In the last chapter, Joe and Claudia Cosgrove had purchased items at a local department store. After shopping, they are on their way to the late night races. Having exceeded the speed limit, Joe was stopped for speeding by a state patrol officer, Sergeant Richard Brand. To verify Joe's driver's license and automobile registration, the police officer radios these numbers back to the district police station. In turn, the district clerk uses a CRT 'erminal to interrogate central headquarters computer files where a fast check indicates that the car has not been listed as stolen and that Joe's record indicates no recent traffic violations. This information is radioed back from the district station to the officer. Since the officer has no reason for detaining Joe and his wife, he issues a citation for speeding.

Because the speeding ticket must be paid within one week, Joe must present the ticket along with the required $25. At the district police station, the citation has been entered on the central headquarters computer files that evening for payment. When Joe pays the fine, the computer file will be deleted and the traffic conviction will be transferred to the traffic violation file.

For both of the foregoing situations, there has been an interaction between the user and the computer. In the first case, the police officer via the CRT terminal operator at the district station has interacted with the central computer system. In the second case, the clerk who receives payment from Joe will have interacted directly on line with the central computer. Interactive processing is the type mode found in BASIC and its essential elements.

An Introduction to BASIC

BASIC, an acronym for Beginner's All-purpose Symbolic Instruction Code, was developed in 1963 by a small group of undergraduate students at Dartmouth College under the direction of Professor John Kemeny. It was developed at a time when interest in time sharing focused on large research-oriented experimental systems. Time sharing is defined as an interactive processing system designed to serve the problem solving needs of many users. Since that time, many improvements in the BASIC language have occurred; the newer versions are better suited for a wider class of business problems. Hence, the language has increased in power while retaining its simplicity.

Since there are many versions and levels of the BASIC language available from manufacturers of time-sharing systems, this chapter will present those items of BASIC that are fundamental to most versions of the language, in particular, those that use minicomputers and microcomputers. Specifically, the structure of BASIC, elementary statements, input to program statements, conditional and unconditional branching, and loop structures will be presented along with selected business applications for these areas. From this view, the reader will have sufficient knowledge of the BASIC language to program simplified business problems at a time-sharing terminal. Also, this material is necessary to understand the additional features of BASIC presented in the next chapter.

BASIC program to machine language program

In a batch-processing mode, the BASIC language must first be translated into the computer's own machine language. This is accomplished by a BASIC compiler or a translator program which accepts the program written in BASIC, i.e., source program as input, and produces as output a machine language program, i.e., object program. This translation process in a batch-processing mode is as follows:

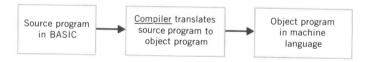

In the process of compiling, the computer checks for programming errors, thereby providing information (computer diagnostics) about the validity of program instructions. Since the process of compiling is very fast, it is customary to think of the BASIC program as the computer program, disregarding the short process of translation from the source program to the object program.

In a somewhat similar manner, a BASIC program written for an inter-active processing mode, i.e., a time-sharing mode, must be translated into the machine language of the specific computer being employed. For example, if a minicomputer is employed, an *interpreter* converts the source program as it is entered by the user into a pseudo machine language. As the computer interprets the program being entered via either a CRT unit or teletypewriter terminal, the program is converted to a pseudo machine language from the BASIC language. For a *time-sharing mode,* the conversion process is as follows:

If errors are detected by the computer during the entry of the time-sharing program, they will be noted for the user while entering the program. Once the entire program has been entered and the appropriate errors have been corrected at the terminal, the user is ready to enter the appropriate data for processing of the desired output.

access method to time-sharing system

Before exploring the important components of BASIC, it is helpful to set forth the procedures for accessing and using the time-sharing system. Once the terminal power unit has been turned on and the telephone number of the time-sharing system has been properly dialed, the user places the receiver in an acoustic coupler. If the line is available, the sign-on banner (headings) is issued by the system. Otherwise, if the line is busy, the user must hang up and try again in a few minutes. Once a successful connection has been made with the computer, the receiver is placed in the acoustic coupler. An alternative approach to dialing the computer is de-pressing the ON button for a terminal that is hard wired to the computer, i.e., there is a permanent connection between the terminal and the computer.

No matter what approach is used to get on the system, the user types HELLO and presses the RETURN (or NEW LINE) key. (In all cases where the system requests or gives an answer, the carriage RETURN key must be depressed.) The computer responds in a conversational mode by typing information and requests information from the user. Normally, this information consists of account number and password. After entering the requested data, the system will ask about the program to be entered, that is, is it a new or old program? The individual enters NEW to create a new program or OLD to retrieve a program that was previously saved by the system on some auxiliary storage device.

Once this *sign-on* procedure has been completed, the system responds by typing READY, indicating that the user should continue. For a new program being entered, the individual enters the program via the terminal keyboard. If an error is made when entering the program, that is, the wrong key was depressed, the RUB OUT (or DELETE) key can be depressed to replace the incorrect character. If several errors are made on one line, the entire line can be retyped, thereby replacing the incorrect line.

After the program has been entered, one of two things can happen. If the program has been correctly entered (no errors have been detected by the computer), the terminal will print READY and the user will then type RUN, indicating the need to process certain data against the program. On the other hand, if the computer system detects errors, the user will correct the errors as indicated, after which the terminal will type READY.

Once certain data have been processed against the program and the desired output has been processed, the system responds by printing READY. At this point, the user is ready to disconnect the terminal from the computer system, commonly known as a *sign-off* procedure. This entails typing the word BYE. The system responds by typing the word CONFIRM. To be disconnected from the system, a letter, like Y, is typed to the system, indicating a sign off from the system. Lastly, the computer system answers with information about the time required to process the program, files saved, and the like. If the system fails to respond to the BYE command, the program is probably still working. Depending upon the computer being used, specific procedures can be used to disconnect the user from the system. If no one is waiting to use the terminal, the user should turn the terminal off and hang up the telephone if one was used.

BASIC language structure

BASIC has a simple English vocabulary and few grammatical rules while resembling ordinary mathematical notation. Although the language is fundamentally simple, it is a powerful language, providing arithmetic capabilities, logic comparisons, subscripting, common mathematical functions, file organization, editing, etc. Likewise, provision can be made to use a particular part of the program repeatedly by calling for it whenever needed. Below, the fundamental elements of the language structure are explained.

Line Numbers (Statement Format)

There are several rules to follow in terms of statement format. Each statement in the program begins with a line number, i.e., an integer value between 1 and 9999. (Some computer systems allow larger line numbers.) Letters and special symbols are not permitted as part of a line number. Not only do these numbers identify the statements within the program, but also specify the order in which the executable statements are to be followed by the computer. Although the choice of the line numbers is arbitrary, consecutive line numbering is not recommended since it does not permit the insertion of additional statements which may have been overlooked during the original writing of the program. When adding a statement to an existing program, it is not necessary to place the statement in the proper sequential location since the computer does this prior to executing the program. Also, spaces have no significance since spaces are used arbitrarily to make a program more readable.

The next item after the line number is the actual BASIC statement. These statements consist of constants, strings, variables, and expressions which are explained below. In addition, they can be labels, headings, or messages as well as special BASIC words that have an inherent English meaning.

Constants

A numeric constant is any real number which may be positive or negative and may contain normally from six to sixteen digits. It may be expressed as a whole number or be in decimal form. If the number exceeds sixteen digits, the computer rounds off the value. However, further flexibility can be gained by using the letter E (exponentiation) which stands for "times ten to the power." Thus, values that exceed sixteen digits can be written with the E notation.

When a series of constants are entered as input they must be separated by commas. Commas are not permitted within the constant itself. The comma following the last constant is optional. Examples of numeric constants are:

    1000   −41500   38.5E4   −1.423E4

Strings

A string is a sequence of characters, including letters, numbers, and certain special characters, such as +, −, *, /, =, $, ., etc. Blank spaces are allowed in a string while single quotation marks are not. Depending upon the version of BASIC, the number of characters for a string will vary. In some versions, a string cannot exceed 15 characters while others allow up to several thousand characters. Its basic purpose is to represent information, such as names and addresses. Likewise, it is useful for printing textual messages. Examples of the latter are:

    THE ANSWER IS   TYPE A VALUE FOR R   ANNUAL
        INTEREST RATE

Variables

A variable is defined as a quantity that may take on different values at the various stages within a program. A computer memory location stores the present value of the named variable. The name or identification of a *numeric variable* (unsubscripted*) may consist of a single letter or a single letter followed by a single digit. Examples are:

R   S   T   X   Y   A1   B2   C3   F2

On the other hand, a *string variable* (unsubscripted*) is used to store alphanumeric data. Alphanumeric strings are combinations of alphabetics, numerics, and special characters which are generally enclosed in single quotes. A string variable name may consist of one letter, or one letter and a single digit (like the numeric variable), but also must be followed by a dollar sign ($). Examples are:

R\$ S\$ T\$ X\$ Y\$ A1\$ B2\$ C3\$ F2\$

However, it should be noted that certain versions of BASIC do not allow inclusion of one digit between the letter and a dollar sign. Thus, the last four examples would be invalid.

Expressions (Arithmetic Operations)

One of the primary functions of the BASIC language is to perform arithmetic operations within an expression. An expression is the assignment of values from one side of an equal to sign represented by a constant, string, or variable. Examples are $S = 100$ and $I = .08/4$.

The five arithmetic operations that are used to write an expression are listed as follows:

Symbol	Arithmetic Operation
+	Addition
−	Subtraction
*	Multiplication
/	Division
↑	Raise to the power

When using the above arithmetic operators, care must be used in writing parentheses to make certain that terms are formed as intended for making the appropriate calculation. Also, an expression using the above arithmetic operators must be written on a single line.

Priority Rules. The rules that are followed in BASIC in terms of the order of priorities for arithmetic operations are:

1. The formula inside the parentheses is computed before the parenthesized quantity is used in further computation.

2. In the absence of parentheses in a formula involving addition, multiplication, and raising to a power, the computer first raises the number to the power, then performs the multiplication, and the addition last. Division has the same priority as multiplication, and subtraction the same as addition.

3. In the absence of parentheses in a formula involving only multiplication and division, the operations are performed from left to right as is the case for addition and subtraction.

4. If a term is negative, it is considered as being subtracted from zero.

* Subscripted variables will be explained in the next chapter.

elementary statements

Elementary statements that employ the basic elements set forth above are those used most frequently when writing a BASIC program. They include the LET, PRINT, REM, END, and STOP statements, which will be explored below.

LET Statement. One of the most important statements in BASIC is the LET statement. Specifically, the LET statement is used to assign values to variables. The general form for this statement is:

line no. LET variable = expression

Although the foregoing includes an equal to sign, it does not represent per se an algebraic equation, but rather is interpreted as the assignment of the expression on the right-hand side to the variable on the left-hand side. To state it another way, replace the value of the variable on the left-hand side of the "equal to" sign with that found for the value on the right-hand side. Thus, the LET statement is often referred to as an *assignment* instruction. Examples are as follows:

```
100 LET S=100
200 LET I=.08/4
```

Although the LET statement has become optional in many versions of BASIC, a useful variation of this elementary statement is the *multiple* LET statement which allows the programmer to assign a single expression (or formula) to a number of variables in one statement. If four variables are to be set equal to zero, it is allowable to write the expression as follows:

```
100 LET A,B,C,D, = 0
```

Here again, the LET statement indicates an assignment process and not an algebraic equation.

PRINT Statement. Printing output in BASIC is accomplished by the PRINT statement. Like with the LET statement, there are different uses of the PRINT statement. First, it permits the value of a constant, variable, or an expression to be printed. Its first general form is:

line no. PRINT (constants, variables, or expressions, separated by commas)

Several examples are:

```
100 PRINT X, Y, Z
200 PRINT R$, T$
300 PRINT 4*X+Y
```

Second, the PRINT statement serves to type a message or label enclosed in single quotation marks.* Its general form is:

line no. PRINT (a message or label, enclosed by single quotation marks)

Spaces for this second use of the PRINT statement are important, that is, spaces are included within the single quotation marks as if they are valid

---

* In some versions of BASIC, string data are enclosed in double quotation marks. Other versions allow either single or double quotation marks.

characters. The reason is that spacing helps to provide readable titles, headings, etc. Two examples are:

```
100 PRINT'PERIOD PRINCIPAL   PERIOD INTEREST'
200 PRINT'TOTAL MONTHLY SALES IS'
```

Third, this statement combines variables, expressions, labels, or messages, resulting in the following general form:

line no. PRINT (variables, expressions, labels, or messages, separated by commas)

Examples of this combined PRINT statement are:

```
100 PRINT 'SUM=', S, 'AVERAGE=', S/N
```

where S and N are variables defined previously in the program.

```
200 PRINT 'TOTAL=', S, 'GRAND TOTAL=', T
```

where S and T are variables defined previously in the program.

A fourth use of the PRINT statement is to skip a line or allow a blank line. Its general form is:

line no. PRINT

which permits formatting of the desired output. To illustrate, it is normal to leave a blank line between the columnar heading and the data below it. An example of this fourth general form is:

```
100 PRINT
```

The preceding has described how the PRINT statement operates, but not how the data are printed across the page or CRT screen. Although the terminal determines the number of available printing positions per line, many terminals (hardcopy or visual) have 72 printable positions. In the BASIC language, these positions are divided into five fields. When printing constants, variables, expressions, messages, or labels separated by commas, the first item is printed in position 1 of field 1, the second item appears in position 15 (1st position of field 2), and so forth—position 29 (field 3), position 43 (field 4), and position 57 (field 5). Where spacing is 14 positions wide for a minicomputer, i.e., PDP-1/45 time-sharing system, there are 70 printable positions. If there are more than five values in the PRINT statement, the sixth item starts a new line at position 1, the seventh item in field 2, and so forth.

While the foregoing rules are applicable to *commas,* these rules must be revised when *semicolons* are utilized. The semicolon packs the data more closely, thereby allowing more than five output quantities to be printed on one line. Additionally, the semicolon serves another function as is the case with a comma. The insertion of a comma or semicolon at the end of a PRINT statement suppresses the carriage return/line feed operation. In such cases, the next output from the system will be typed on the same line. For example, if the program output were as follows:

```
100 PRINT 'A'
110 PRINT 'B'
120 PRINT 'C'
```

the printed output would be on three separate lines:

A
B
C

If a comma were inserted at the end of each line above, the output would be:

A   B   C

However, if a semicolon were used to end each line, the output would appear very closely packed, such as:

AB C

Notice that no spaces are found in the output. If spaces are wanted, they should be inserted within the single quotes, as shown below:

```
100 PRINT 'A    ';
110 PRINT 'B    ';
120 PRINT 'C    ';
```

When using PRINT statements, several other rules are applicable. Decimal points for integer values and insignificant zeros to the right of the decimal point are not printed. In a similar manner, when a decimal number is greater than six digits in length, the computer system will print the exponential form. To illustrate, consider the following:

1234567890   0.0000123456

which become

.123457E+10 or 1.23457E+9   .123456E−4 or 1.23456E−5

In these forms, the decimal point either appears first followed by six most significant digits or the first significant digit is followed by a decimal point and five digits. Also, the last digit is rounded.

REM Statement. A common way to introduce remarks in a BASIC program is to employ the REM (REMARK) statement. REM statements provide a convenient way for the programmer to document a program, i.e., identify a program and its important variables. They consist of a statement number followed by the word REM and a textual message. Their general form is:

line no. REM (textual message)

As an illustration, the first line of a program contains a remark statement:

```
100 REM THIS PROGRAM DETERMINES COMPOUND INTEREST
200 REM THIS MODULE CALCULATES AMOUNT OF INTEREST
```

Although REM statements are not executable instructions for the computer system, they are listed with all the other statements in the correct sequential order for a listing of the program.

END and STOP Statements. The END Statement must be physically the last line of the program. Its general form is:

line no. END

This statement serves two purposes: it indicates the end of a program and it serves to terminate final computer processing of the program.

On the other hand, the STOP statement not only can stop processing of a program, but also there can be any number of them in a program. The general form of this statement is:

line no. STOP

Its basic purpose is to stop processing when deemed necessary by the programmer. Also, it can be used in conjunction with subroutines (refer to Chapter 6).

savings account application — elementary statements

To demonstrate the use of the LET, PRINT, REM, and END statements, a program flowchart (Figure 5-1) is utilized that results in a BASIC program (Figure 5-2). Initially, the current quarterly deposit or S ($100), the current savings rate or I (five percent per annum divided by 4), and the current savings account balance or B ($5,000) are entered on lines 10 through 30. While these first three LET statements define specific values for S, I, and B respectively, the next three LET statements solve for the current savings account balance before calculating savings interest amount (X value), current savings interest amount (X1 value), and the current savings account balance after adding savings interest income (X2 value). Per line 70, 'THE INTEREST INCOME FOR THE QUARTER IS' printed along with the calculated amount. Similarly, 'THE NEW SAVINGS ACCOUNT BALANCE FOR THE QUARTER IS' is printed per line 80 with the determined value. Lastly, the END statement on line 90 is required as the last line of the program. Hence, within this simple business application, elementary BASIC statements have been illustrated.

In addition to the BASIC program per Figure 5-2, sample output data are shown. Based upon the first quarter calculation, interest income on the savings account is $63.75, while the new ending quarter savings balance is $5,163.75 ($5,000 principal + $100 deposit + $63.75 interest income).

input to program statements

Although the LET statement was the first method shown to define data for simple BASIC programs, a preferred approach is using the INPUT statement and the READ-DATA statement which are the second and third methods for defining or entering input data. Both are discussed below.

INPUT Statement

The INPUT statement is preferable to the LET statement for one important reason. While the LET statement allows the programmer to assign specific values *prior to* running a program, the INPUT statement goes one step further by permitting the user to enter data *during* the running of the program. Thus, when subsequent runs of the same program occur, various values can be assigned to the same input variables.

The general form of the INPUT statement is as follows:

line no. INPUT (variable or a group of variables, separated by commas)

Whenever the computer system comes to an INPUT statement during processing, a question mark (?) is typed by the teletypewriter unit or CRT unit and the computer stops processing until input data are entered as required by the program. Hence, the system will not continue processing until the appropriate data have been entered and the user has depressed the RETURN key.

To avoid having problems with the INPUT statement, it is advisable to have a PRINT statement immediately preceding the INPUT instruction. An example of a PRINT statement with an INPUT statement is shown as follows:

```
40 PRINT'ENTER TYPE OF COMPOUNDING,1=ANNUAL,
   2=SEMI-ANNUAL,3=QUARTERLY'
60 INPUT T
```

Thus, the user must enter the constant 1, 2, or 3 for processing to continue. The PRINT statement contains a message that identifies what information is required for subsequent processing.

To demonstrate the use of the question mark for the preceding example, the output from these statements is:

```
ENTER TYPE OF COMPOUNDING,1=ANNUAL,
2=SEMI-ANNUAL,3=QUARTERLY
? 3
```

where the programmer has entered the value 3 for a quarterly compounding basis. If a semicolon had been used at the end of line 40, the question mark would have been printed on the same line as the message with the number 3 entered after the question mark.

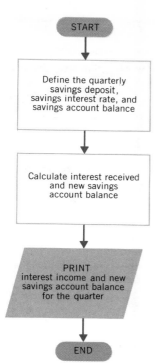

figure 5-1. Program flowchart for computing quarterly savings interest amount and new savings account balance for the quarter.

```
CHAP52   08:07            23-Oct-78
05 REM THIS PROGRAM COMPUTES QUARTERLY INTEREST AND NEW BALANCE
10 LET S=100
20 LET I=.05/4
30 LET B=5000
40 LET X=S+B
50 LET X1=X*I
60 LET X2=X+X1
70 PRINT'THE INTEREST INCOME FOR THE QUARTER IS';X1
80 PRINT'THE NEW SAVINGS ACCOUNT BALANCE FOR THE QUARTER IS';X2
90 END

Ready




RUN
CHAP52   08:08            23-Oct-78
THE INTEREST INCOME FOR THE QUARTER IS 63.75
THE NEW SAVINGS ACCOUNT BALANCE FOR THE QUARTER IS 5163.75

Ready
```

figure 5-2. BASIC program (based upon Figure 5-1) for computing the new savings account balance at end of the quarter as well as sample output.

**first summary
of chapter 5**

BASIC language structure:

• line number—each statement in BASIC begins with a line number.

• constant—any real number which may be positive or negative and may contain from six to sixteen digits.
Examples of numeric constants: 1000 and −41500

• string—a sequence of characters that is used for representing information or printing a textual message.
Examples: THE ANSWER IS and TYPE A VALUE FOR R

• variable—a quantity that may take on different values during processing of the program. There may be *numeric* or *string* variables.
Examples of numeric variables: R S A1 B2
Examples of string variables: R$ S$ A1$ B2$

• expression—assignment of values from one side of an equal to sign represented by a constant, string, or variable.
Examples: S=100
          I=.08/4

• arithmetic operations—five arithmetic operations are allowed in BASIC, namely, addition (+), subtraction (−), multiplication (*), division (/), and raise to the power (↑).

elementary statements:

• LET statement—used to assign values to variables.
Examples: 100 LET S=100
          200 LET I =.08/4

• PRINT statement—The first general form permits the value of a constant, variable, or an expression to be printed.
Example: 100 PRINT X,Y,Z

—The second general form serves to type a message or label enclosed in single quotation marks.
Example: 200 PRINT 'PERIOD PRINCIPAL   PERIOD INTEREST'

—The third general form permits a variable, expression, label, or message to be combined.
Example: 100 PRINT 'Sum=', S, 'AVERAGE=', S/N

—The fourth general form is used to skip a line or to allow a blank line.
Example: 100 PRINT

• REM statement—provides a convenient way to document a program.
Example: 10 REM THIS PROGRAM DETERMINES COMPOUND INTEREST

• END statement—represents physically the last line of the program.
Example: 90 END

• STOP statement—used to stop the processing of a program.
Example: 300 STOP

**first self-study
exercise
of chapter 5**

True-False:

1. (   ) An object program is just another form of the source program.
2. (   ) The compiler and the interpreter perform basically the same function.
3. (   ) Each statement in a BASIC program ends with a line number.
4. (   ) A constant may be expressed as a whole number or in decimal form.
5. (   ) The arithmetic operator (*) represents raising to a power in BASIC.
6. (   ) Another name for the LET statement is the assignment instruction.
7. (   ) The PRINT statement has only one general form in BASIC.
8. (   ) Semicolons pack the data more closely in a PRINT statement.
9. (   ) The END and STOP statements perform the very same function in BASIC.
10. (   ) The exponential form can be found as output in a PRINT statement.

Fill-In:

11. For a minicomputer system, an _____ converts the input program into the required pseudo machine language for internal computer processing.
12. Every line in a BASIC program must contain a _____ _____ along with an appropriate statement or instruction.
13. A numeric _____ is any real number which can be either positive or negative.
14. THE COMPOUND INTEREST RATE IS is an example of a _____.
15. The _____ _____ is used to store alphanumeric data and must be followed by a _____ _____ for it to be valid.
16. The BASIC ↑ (arrowhead pointing upward) means to _____ _____ _____ _____—a form of arithmetic operation.
17. An _____ in a LET statement means to assign its contents to the variable on the other side of the equal to sign.
18. A _____ LET statement allows the user to assign a single expression to a number of variables in one statement.
19. A method of skipping a line in the BASIC language is to utilize the _____ _____.
20. On the one hand, the _____ _____ is employed to terminate computer processing at a certain point in a program; on the other hand, the _____ _____ indicates the terminal point of the program.

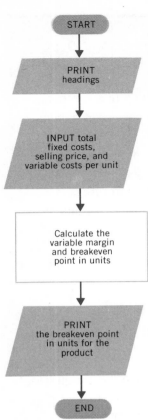

START

↓

PRINT
headings

↓

INPUT total
fixed costs,
selling price, and
variable costs per unit

↓

Calculate the
variable margin
and breakeven
point in units

↓

PRINT
the breakeven point
in units for the
product

↓

END

figure 5-3. Program flowchart for calculating the breakeven point in units for a single product organization.

READ-DATA Statements

In addition to the LET and INPUT statements for entering input data, a third method for entering information is using the READ-DATA statements. Actually, the READ and DATA statements are used jointly where the specific value or values from a DATA statement are obtained for the READ statement. Their general form is:

line no. READ (variable or variables, separated by commas)
line no. DATA (constants, separated by commas)

When the program is being executed, the computer assigns constants to the variables in the READ statement by referencing the related DATA statement. The first constant in the instruction DATA is assigned to the first variable in the READ statement. In a similar manner, the second constant is assigned to the second variable, etc. For example, the following READ-DATA statements are:

```
100 READ X,Y,Z
110 DATA 4, 8, 12
120 PRINT X,Y,Z
130 END
```

The constants 4, 8, 12, contained in the DATA statement, are assigned to the variable X, Y, and Z respectively in the READ instruction.

Although the READ statement is an executable statement, the DATA statement is not. It is useful for referencing data needed by the READ instruction. Also, it should be noted that the DATA statement can be placed anywhere in the program prior to the END statement.

In summary, the READ statement must be accompanied by at least one DATA statement. Both statements must reference the same type of data. The combined READ-DATA statements are best suited for inputing large quantities of data. Also, the READ statement is executable while the DATA statement is not.

---

breakeven application— input to program statements

A breakeven problem that illustrates the use of elementary statements as well as the INPUT statement is flowcharted in Figure 5-3. Likewise, the BASIC program to calculate the breakeven point for a single product organization is set forth in Figure 5-4. Rather than explain the easy-to-follow flowchart, it would be helpful to examine the BASIC program and its output per Figure 5-5 that incorporates representative data.

As shown in Figure 5-4 per lines 10 and 20, THIS PROGRAM WILL CALCULATE THE BREAKEVEN POINT IN UNITS FOR A SINGLE PRODUCT ORGANIZATION. The PRINT statements on lines 30, 40, and 50 relate to the amount of total fixed costs for the firm. The INPUT statement (INPUT F) on line 60 is combined with the preceding PRINT statements to clarify what value is being requested, namely, the total amount of fixed costs, defined by the variable F. These combined PRINT and INPUT statements are found also on lines 70 through 90 and lines 100 through 130 for selling price (S) and variable costs per unit (V) respectively.

In the first LET statement (M=S−V) on line 140, the variable margin (M) or contribution to fixed costs and profit is computed. On line 150, the REM statement provides a comment about the M value for use in the next LET statement (line 160). The LET B=F/M statement means that the answer

figure 5-4. BASIC program for calculating the breakeven point in units for a single product organization.

```
CHAP54   08:25              23-Oct-78
10 REM THIS PROGRAM WILL CALCULATE THE BREAKEVEN POINT
20 REM IN UNITS FOR A SINGLE PRODUCT ORGANIZATION.
25 PRINT
30 PRINT'CALCULATE THE TOTAL FIXED COSTS THAT MUST BE'
40 PRINT'COVERED BY THIS PRODUCT. ENTER THIS AMOUNT'
50 PRINT'AFTER THE QUESTION MARK'
60 INPUT F
70 PRINT'ENTER THE SELLING PRICE PER UNIT AFTER THE QUESTION MARK'
90 INPUT S
100 PRINT'WHAT ARE THE TOTAL VARIABLE COSTS ASSIGNABLE TO EACH'
110 PRINT'UNIT SOLD? IE. COSTS THAT WOULD NOT BE INCURRED IF A'
120 PRINT'UNIT WERE NOT PRODUCED AND SOLD.'
130 INPUT V
140 LET M=S-V
150 REM  M IS THE VARIABLE MARGIN
160 LET B=F/M
165 PRINT
170 PRINT'THE BREAKEVEN POINT FOR THIS PRODUCT IS';B;'UNITS'
180 END
```

obtained from the division (on the right-hand side of the expression) is to be assigned as the answer for the specified variable (B). Thus, the PRINT statement on line 170 before the END statement specifies the breakeven point for the product in 'UNITS'.

After the program has been entered per Figure 5-4, the operator types RUN (and depresses the RETURN key) and the system responds by typing certain identifying information, as shown in Figure 5-5. Values are entered for each question. The values—fixed costs (F) of $20,000, selling price (S) of $40, and variable costs per unit (V) of $13—are entered manually through the keyboard. The breakeven point is found to be 740 (740.741) units, calculated as follows:

$$B = \frac{F(\text{Total Fixed Costs})}{S(\text{Selling Price}) - V(\text{Variable Costs per Unit})}$$

$$= \frac{\$20,000}{\$40 - \$13}$$

$$= \frac{\$20,000}{\$27}$$

$$= 740.741 \text{ units}$$

figure 5-5. Representative data used in the BASIC program for calculating the breakeven point in units for a single product organization.

```
Ready

RUN
CHAP54   08:26              23-Oct-78

CALCULATE THE TOTAL FIXED COSTS THAT MUST BE
COVERED BY THIS PRODUCT. ENTER THIS AMOUNT
AFTER THE QUESTION MARK
? 20000
ENTER THE SELLING PRICE PER UNIT AFTER THE QUESTION MARK
? 40
WHAT ARE THE TOTAL VARIABLE COSTS ASSIGNABLE TO EACH
UNIT SOLD? IE. COSTS THAT WOULD NOT BE INCURRED IF A
UNIT WERE NOT PRODUCED AND SOLD.
? 13

THE BREAKEVEN POINT FOR THIS PRODUCT IS 740.741 UNITS

Ready
```

**conditional and
unconditional
branching**

When programming in BASIC, it is often necessary to branch or transfer processing from one section (module) of the program to another or to perform a process several times. For such situations, there are three instructions for branching which are the GO TO statement, the IF-THEN statement, and the ON-GO TO statement. The first is an unconditional transfer while the last two are conditional transfer statements.

GO TO Statement

As indicated previously, the computer executes program statements by starting with the lowest numerical statement and going up to the highest numerical statement, namely, the END statement. However, it may be necessary to bypass certain instructions or branch to others. In such cases, the GO TO statement provides an unconditional branch or transfer to the desired section of a program. Its general form is:

line no. GO TO (line no.)

where transfer of control within the program is to the line number shown to the right of the GO TO statement. The line number specified must be located somewhere in the program.

The function of the GO TO statement is not only to bypass certain instructions for a one-way branch, but also is to construct loops that are terminated under the control of the programmer/operator. An important function of looping is to reduce the number of statements required to program and execute a particular application.

An example of the GO TO statement is:

```
100 GO TO 200
```

Program control is unconditionally transferred from line 100 to line 200 for additional processing within the program. Thus, the GO TO statement in this example and others can be looked upon as an unconditional transfer of control, i.e., an unconditional branch instruction.

IF-THEN Statement

While the GO TO statement provides for an unconditional transfer within a program, the IF-THEN statement permits a conditional transfer. To state it another way, the GO TO statement, is a *one-way* branch instruction while the IF-THEN statement is a *two-way* branch instruction. The latter is dependent upon a condition—the result of comparing constants and variables or the result of making certain calculations. The general form of the IF-THEN statement is:

line no. IF (expression) relational operator (expression) THEN (line no.)

where the expression may be constants, variables, or formulas. The relational operator may be one of the following:

    $=$ is equal to
    $>$ is greater than
    $<$ is less than
   $<>$ is not equal to
  $>=$ is greater than or equal to
  $<=$ is less than or equal to

The IF-THEN statement involves a conditional transfer of control. If the relation or logic test is true, control is transferred to the line number following THEN. If the test is not met or false, control is transferred to the next executable instruction in the program. In contrast to the GO TO statement, control is automatically transferred to the line number to the right of the GO TO instruction. Also, as with the GO TO statement, loops can be developed for the IF-THEN statement.

Examples of IF-THEN statements are:

```
50 IF A > 1000 THEN 100
150 IF A = B THEN 200
300 IF A <= Y THEN 400
```

ON-GO TO Statement

A second instruction that permits a conditional transfer within a program is the ON-GO TO statement. The primary purpose of this statement is to provide a multi-branched (i.e., two-way, three-way, etc.) conditional transfer as opposed to a *two-way* conditional transfer only for the IF-THEN statement. Hence, program control is transferred to one of a series of statements. The general form of the ON-GO TO statement is:

line no. ON (expression) GO TO (first line no., second line no., . . . last line no.)

where control is passed to the first line number to the right of the GO TO instruction if the value of the expression is 1. Similarly, computer control is transferred to the second line number if the value is 2; and so forth to the last line number. The only limitation to the use of the ON-GO TO statement is the number of line numbers that can fit on one line.

If the value of the expression is outside the range of the line numbers, the program will terminate with an error message. Outside the range means that the value of the expression is greater than or less than the number of line numbers set forth to the right of the GO TO instruction. If the expression yields a noninteger value, the computer truncates the results.

An example of this type statement is:

70 ON T GO TO 100,200,300

This multi-branched conditional transfer instructs the program to go to one of the three line numbers, depending upon the T value—the type of compounding, 1=annual, 2=semi-annual, and 3=quarterly. If the value is 1, control is passed to line 100. In a similar manner, if the value is 2, control is transferred to line number 200 while a value of 3 transfers control to line 300.

---

depreciation application— conditional branching

To illustrate conditional branching, a business application for computing depreciation by two different methods is used. The program flowchart is shown in Figure 5-6; the BASIC program is set forth in Figure 5-7. In addition, sample calculations for the straight-line method and the double-declining balance method are found in Figure 5-8.

The REM statements on lines 1000 and 1010 of Figure 5-7 pertain to the computation of depreciation by two different methods. Lines 1020

figure 5-6. Program flowchart for computing and printing depreciation by two different methods — straight-line and double-declining balance.

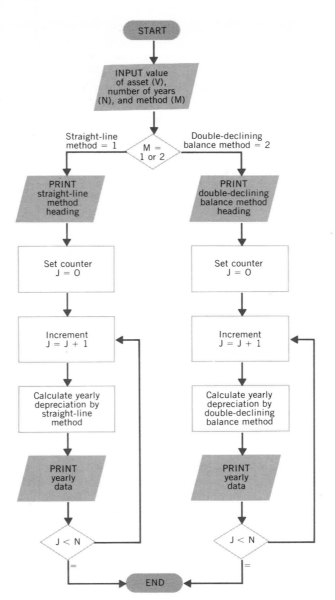

through 1050 relate to entering variable data as the program is processed. However, on line 1070, a conditional ON-GO TO instruction is found; it directs processing to the method chosen.

Starting with line 1080, the title for the straight-line method is printed. At line 1100, title headings are printed while a counter is set equal to zero (J=0) per line 1110. Appropriate calculations are made on lines 1120, 1130, and 1140. After the yearly output is printed at line 1150, a test is made at line 1160 to check whether the program has processed the number of years of useful life for the asset. If it has not, control is sent to line 1130; if it has, the processing is terminated per line 1170, that is, control is transferred to line 1270, an END statement.

For the other method, the programming process is repeated. To be more specific, the LET statements provide the means for determining yearly

figure 5-7. BASIC program for computing depreciation by two different methods — straight-line and double-declining balance.

```
CHAP51  08:30            23-Oct-78
1000 REM THIS PROGRAM COMPUTES DEPRECIATION BY TWO
1010 REM METHODS.  IT ASSUMES A ZERO SCRAP VALUE FOR THE ASSET.
1020 INPUT'ENTER THE VALUE OF THE ASSET';V
1030 INPUT'ENTER THE USEFUL LIFE OF THE ASSET';N
1040 PRINT'ENTER THE METHOD TO BE USED. 1=STRAIGHT LINE,2=DOUBLE DECLINING'
1050 INPUT 'BALANCE';M
1060 PRINT
1070 ON M GO TO 1080,1180
1080 PRINT'STRAIGHT LINE METHOD
1090 PRINT
1100 PRINT'YEAR        DEPRECIATION    CURRENT VALUE'
1110 LET J=0
1120 LET D=V/N
1130 LET J=J+1
1140 LET V=V-D
1150 PRINT J,D,V
1160 IF J<N THEN 1130
1170 GO TO 1270
1180 PRINT'DOUBLE DECLINING BALANCE METHOD'
1190 PRINT
1200 PRINT 'YEAR        DEPRECIATION    CURRENT VALUE'
1210 LET J=0
1220 LET J=J+1
1230 LET D=(2/N)*V
1240 LET V=V-D
1250 PRINT J,D,V
1260 IF J<N THEN 1220
1270 END

Ready
```

figure 5-8. Representative data used in the BASIC program for computing depreciation by two different methods —(1) straight-line and (2) double-declining balance.

```
RUN
CHAP51  08:30            23-Oct-78
ENTER THE VALUE OF THE ASSET? 10000
ENTER THE USEFUL LIFE OF THE ASSET? 5
ENTER THE METHOD TO BE USED. 1=STRAIGHT LINE,2=DOUBLE DECLINING
BALANCE? 1

STRAIGHT LINE METHOD

YEAR    DEPRECIATION    CURRENT VALUE
 1          2000            8000
 2          2000            6000
 3          2000            4000
 4          2000            2000
 5          2000            0

Ready

RUN
CHAP51  08:31            23-Oct-78
ENTER THE VALUE OF THE ASSET? 10000
ENTER THE USEFUL LIFE OF THE ASSET? 5
ENTER THE METHOD TO BE USED. 1=STRAIGHT LINE,2=DOUBLE DECLINING
BALANCE? 2

DOUBLE DECLINING BALANCE METHOD

YEAR    DEPRECIATION    CURRENT VALUE
 1          4000            6000
 2          2400            3600
 3          1440            2160
 4          864             1296
 5          518.4           777.6

Ready
```

depreciation values, the PRINT statement what is to be printed during the processing run, and the IF-THEN statement determines the correct number of lines to print for the desired number of years. As with all BASIC programs, the END statement is used to end computer processing.

Once the program has been correctly entered into the computer system, the user is ready to enter data for processing to occur. As shown in Figure 5-8, the value of the asset to be depreciated is $10,000 for both methods. Likewise, the number of years is five. The appropriate schedules for the straight-line method and the double-declining balance method are determined. Thus, a comparison can be made between the methods which might be helpful in determining the best approach for minimizing a firm's federal income taxes in the future.

loop structures

Loop structures were introduced in the previous section on branching. In addition, there are other methods for developing program loops. These include the FOR-NEXT statement and the Nested FOR-NEXT loops. The FOR-NEXT statement is used for program looping, in particular, for incrementing a counter. For loops that are contained within one another, the nested FOR-NEXT loops approach is best employed to simplify the programming process. Each of these approaches is explained below along with branching out of loops.

FOR-NEXT Statement

To simplify the process of performing the same operations over and over for a given set of instructions, the FOR-NEXT statement is used. While the FOR statement is placed at the beginning of the program loop, the NEXT statement is located at the end of the loop. The statements between FOR and NEXT determine the range of the loop. The general form of this looping process is:

line no. FOR variable = (expression-1 TO expression-2 STEP expression-3)
line no. NEXT variable

Only constants, numeric variables, or expressions are allowed in the statements. Since the variable in the FOR instruction is the incrementing part, generally referred to as the *index* of the loop, that same variable must appear in the NEXT statement. *Expression-1* per the above general form is the initial value of the index; it may be a constant, variable, or formula. *Expression-2* is the highest value that the index is allowed to reach; it also may be a constant, variable, or formula. The word TO is required between the two expressions. Because STEP is optional, an increment step of plus one is assumed. However, if some other increment is desired, STEP and *expression-3* are required for a correct looping process.

As indicated, the FOR and NEXT statements must be inserted as a pair for program looping. To illustrate, a FOR-NEXT statement is as follows:

```
210  FOR K=1 TO M
220  LET I9=I*P
230  LET P=P+I9
240  PRINT K,P,I9
250  NEXT K
260  END
```

At line 210, the K value of the counter was equal to one. After the instructions have been completed per lines 220 to 240, i.e., calculating and printing the compounding period (K), the principal (P), and period interest (I9), the NEXT statement at line 250 loops the program back to line 210 for incrementing the counter (K). This looping process is repeated until the counter (index) reaches a value equal to or greater than, at which control is passed to the statement immediately following the NEXT statement. Since line 260 is accessed, the program is terminated per this END statement. In this example, the FOR-NEXT statement has provided the capability of printing the desired number of periods for compounding interest.

In the following example, the use of the step option is illustrated:

```
100 REM SUM ALL ODD NUMBERS FROM 1 TO 20
105 LET S=0
110 FOR J=1 TO 20 STEP 2
115 LET S=S+J
120 NEXT J
125 PRINT S
130 END
```

For the first time through this loop, the value of J would be 1 and the value of S would be 1. The second time through the loop, J would be 3 and S would be 4. This process would continue until J equals 19. An equivalent method of accomplishing the same task would be to replace statement 110 with FOR J=19 TO 1 STEP −2.

Nested FOR-NEXT Loops

Due to a problem's structure, it may be necessary at times to enclose one or more program loops within another program loop. Such an arrangement is called *nesting*. When one pair of FOR-NEXT statements reside within the range of another pair of FOR-NEXT statements, there exists a pair of nested FOR-NEXT loops. Depending upon the BASIC version employed, various types of nesting is permitted.

Examples of valid nested FOR-NEXT loops are:

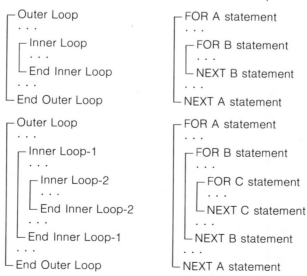

As evident in the above examples, nested loops cannot overlap the field of another loop or cross the field of another.

To illustrate the use of nesting, a company totals separately the sales for its three different product lines. Within this framework, each product line is totaled separately with subtotals. Likewise, a grand total is accumulated for all product lines. Hence, looping is used to total the desired information. It should be noted that as many as fourteen nested loops are allowed in some systems.

Branching Out of Loops

At times, the programmer may wish to terminate a loop prior to its completion if a given condition occurs. Consider the following modification to the FOR-NEXT loop given previously.

```
210  FOR K=1 TO M
220  LET I9=I*P
230  LET P=P+I9
240  PRINT K,P,I9
245  IF P>10000 THEN 255
250  NEXT K
255  PRINT 'PRINCIPAL HAS EXCEEDED $10,000'
260  END
```

In this case, if the principal exceeds $10,000, the loop is terminated by the conditional branch per line 245. This is true regardless of whether the index K has reached the value M.

---

second summary of chapter 5

input to program statements:
• INPUT statement—allows the user to enter data during the running of the program.
Example: 40 PRINT 'ENTER TYPE OF COMPOUNDING, 1=ANNUAL,
   1=SEMI-ANNUAL, 3=QUARTERLY'
   60 INPUT T

• READ-DATA statement—provides another way of entering data to the program. The READ and DATA statements are used jointly where the specific value or values from a DATA statement are obtained for the READ statement.
Example: 100 READ X,Y,Z
   110 4,8,12

conditional and unconditional branching:
• GO TO statement—provides an unconditional branch or one-way transfer to the desired section of a program.
Example: 100 GO TO 200

• IF-THEN statement—provides a conditional transfer in a program, that is, it is a two-way branch instruction while the GO TO statement above is a one-way branch instruction.
Example: 50 IF A>1000 THEN 100

• ON-GO TO statement—provides a multi-branched conditional transfer as opposed to only a two-way conditional transfer for the prior IF-THEN statement.
Example: 70 ON T GO TO 100, 200, 300

loop structures:

• FOR-NEXT statement—used for program looping, in particular, for incrementing a counter.

Example: 210 FOR K=1 TO M
250 NEXT K

• Nested FOR-NEXT loops—used to enclose one or more program loops within another program loop. Examples of valid nested FOR-NEXT were illustrated in the chapter.

• Branching out of loops—used to terminate a loop prior to its completion if a given condition occurs.

---

second self-study exercise of chapter 5

True-False:

1. (   ) The INPUT statement is a method for producing output data.
2. (   ) The INPUT statement allows the user to assign values prior to running a program.
3. (   ) The READ statement can be placed anywhere in the program.
4. (   ) The DATA statement is a non-executable statement.
5. (   ) The GO TO statement is a multi-branched instruction.
6. (   ) A conditional transfer is permitted by an IF-THEN statement.
7. (   ) The relational operation (< =) means "is greater than or equal to."
8. (   ) The ON-GO TO statement provides for a two-way conditional transfer only.
9. (   ) The FOR-NEXT statement is widely used for program looping.
10. (   ) Nested FOR-NEXT loops are not allowed in BASIC.

Fill-In:

11. The _____ _____ allows the user to assign specific values prior to running a program.
12. The _____ _____ permits the user to enter data during the processing of the program.
13. The combined _____-_____ _____ allows the programmer to input values that will be obtained from a specific source.
14. The _____-_____ _____ provides a two-way branch while the _____ _____ _____ allows a one-way branch.
15. The symbol >= represents a _____ _____ or _____ _____ condition found in an _____-_____ _____.
16. The ON-GO TO statement provides a _____-_____ conditional transfer within a BASIC program.
17. In a FOR-NEXT statement, the _____ _____ is located at the end of the loop.
18. In a _____ _____, an increment of plus one is assumed.
19. A method for incrementing a _____ is to use the FOR-NEXT statement.
20. _____ _____-_____ _____ allow the programmer the flexibility of determining sub-totals for various groups of data within the program.

summary

The important elements of the BASIC language in a time-sharing mode have been covered in this chapter. They include language structure, elementary statements, input to program statements, conditional and unconditional branching, and loop structures. Although the BASIC language does vary from one computer system to another, the fundamentals as presented can be used with few modifications. Differences required by a specific computer system can be learned in a very short time.

A most important advantage of BASIC is that it greatly facilitates programming for the average business user. It can be learned in a short time, thereby allowing more personnel the opportunity to use computers at all levels of operation. In the next chapter, additional refinements to BASIC will be found. These additional features of BASIC allow a wider range of business applications.

questions

1. a. Distinguish between constants and variables.
   b. Distinguish between constants and strings.
2. Why are the LET, PRINT, and END statements called elementary statements?
3. What is the major difference between the INPUT statement and the READ-DATA statement?
4. a. In what way is the GO TO statement similar to the IF-THEN statement?
   b. In what way is the GO TO statement dissimilar to the IF-THEN statement?
5. a. Why are the IF-THEN statement and the ON-GO TO statement used for conditional branching?
   b. Can these two statements ever be used for unconditional branching?
6. Distinguish between the IF-THEN statement and the FOR-NEXT statement.
7. What is the rationale for not allowing nested loops to overlap or cross the field of another loop?
8. What are the primary benefits of programming in BASIC over other higher-level languages?

programming exercises

1. Referring to the problem in the chapter for calculating the breakeven point in units for a single product organization, add the lines of coding that are necessary to allow the program to continue for calculating another breakeven point.
2. Referring to the problem in the chapter for computing depreciation by two different methods, write a program to accomplish the same results for the sum-of-the-years digits.
3. Prepare a program flowchart and a corresponding BASIC program to calculate the total gross payroll for all of a company's production workers. Input data are employee's payroll number (five digits), the hours worked this week (four digits, includes a decimal point), and

current hourly rate of pay (four digits, includes a decimal point). All hours worked in excess of 40.0 hours are to be paid at the rate of one and one-half of the regular rate. The program is to print each employee payroll number, regular pay, overtime pay, and gross pay. Also, the program is to print the grand totals for regular pay, overtime pay, and gross pay. Although the formatting of output data is left to the programmer, every attempt should be made to make the total gross payroll report as readable as possible. Once you are satisfied that the program is operational after correcting logical and clerical errors, process sample data, say for four employees. Compare the results with predetermined results.

4. Prepare a program flowchart and a corresponding BASIC program to calculate the annual amount of interest on loans and to print the account loan number and principal plus the amount of annual interest. Also, the total interest on all loans is to be totaled. The fields of the input data are: five digits for account loan number, six digits for principal (includes a decimal point), and four digits for annual rate of interest (includes a decimal point). Output formatting is left to the programmer. However, the final report should be spaced so as to make it readable.

   After debugging the program for all possible errors, run sample data for five loans. Compare the computer results with manual figures to insure program accuracy.

5. Prepare a program flowchart and develop a corresponding BASIC program to calculate monthly finished good production requirements. The format of the final production schedule of finished goods is left up to the programmer. Input for the program is the finished goods inventory number, the current number of finished goods on hand and on order as well as the forecasted number of finished goods needed for the next period. The production requirements for next period equals the forecasted number of finished goods less the units on hand and on order. If the calculated production requirements are plus, a production order for finished goods must be placed by printing the finished goods inventory number and the finished goods production requirements. Otherwise, if the production requirements calculates to be minus or zero, no production order is to be placed.

   To determine the accuracy of the program written, process sample data, say twenty computations against the program. It is advisable to compare predetermined results with computer output.

6. Prepare a program flowchart and a corresponding BASIC program to calculate the pay of salespeople based on their weekly net sales and pay code. Net sales are computed as gross sales less returned merchandise. Level one pay code receives a base amount of $200.00 plus 3% of net sales while level two receives a base of $175.00 plus 2% of net sales. Input data to the program are salesperson name, weekly gross sales, value of returned merchandise, and pay code. The program is to print the name of the company, the salesperson's name, pay code, gross sales, returns, net sales, and pay. Final totals for net sales and pay for the total group are to be printed.

   After debugging the program, run sample data for six salespeople and compare the results with predetermined figures.

**answers to
first self-study
exercise**

1. T 2. T 3. F 4. T 5. F 6. T 7. F 8. T 9. F 10. T 11. interpreter 12. line number 13. constant 14. string 15. string variable and dollar sign 16. raise to a power 17. expression 18. multiple 19. PRINT statement 20. STOP statement and END statement.

**answers to
second self-study
exercise**

1. F 2. F 3. F 4. T 5. F 6. T 7. F 8. F 9. T 10. F 11. LET statement 12. INPUT statement 13. READ-DATA statement 14. IF-THEN statement and GO TO statement 15. greater than, equal to, and IF-THEN statement 16. multi-branched 17. NEXT statement 18. FOR statement 19. counter 20. Nested FOR-NEXT loops

chapter six additional elements of the BASIC language with business applications

As we noted in the preceding chapter, Joe and Claudia Cosgrove were given a citation for speeding on their way to the night horse races. Arriving there minutes ahead of the first race, Joe places a $2 bet on *Ready to Go*—number 7. Also, Claudia places a $2 bet on the daily double, deciding on the number 25 (the amount of the speeding fine). For this first race as well as succeeding ones, their attention is focused on a large electronic board where the rapidly changing odds on each horse are flashed. The track's computer recalculates these odds every 60 seconds. Its calculations are based on the actual amount of money bet on each horse. Despite a thorough analysis of the racing form to select *Ready to Go*, Joe's horse comes in last; the winner is horse number 2.

Based on the total amount bet, the computer has determined the amounts to be paid for the win, place, and show positions. Needless to say, Joe is not interested in the results, but his wife is since she could have won $10.60 on a $2 bet. In the next race, Joe bets $2 to win on *Show Me*— number 8. He is really excited because the odds are considerably higher than those shown in the racing form. Claudia is not so optimistic about number 5, since it has unusually high odds. As one might guess, Joe's horse finishes last while Claudia's horse wins. Claudia is overwhelmed with the high payoff to be posted shortly by the computer. Visions of ways to spend the money race through her mind. Unfortunately, her horse has been disqualified for running interference. Although picking the correct numbers to win initially in both races, Claudia has failed to include a fudge factor for the way in which the numbers were obtained. Because of the complexity of the horse racing computer programs, additional elements of a language are needed for programming such sophistication.

In the prior chapter, the most frequently used statements in the BASIC language were set forth in a time-sharing mode. Using these as building blocks, additional elements of BASIC are presented in this chapter. They include the use of output formatting, subscripted variables, matrix statements, internal (library) and user-generated functions, subroutines, and sorting. An understanding of these elements gives the user expanded capabilities with the BASIC language. As in the previous chapter, business applications will be presented in the chapter. A thorough understanding of these will assist the reader in solving sample business problems at the end of the chapter. Likewise, comprehension of the illustrative applications will enable an individual to solve a wider range of problems found in a business and industrial environment.

output formatting

Although the PRINT statement was presented under the elementary statements in the prior chapter, there are two other forms of output that will be discussed below. They are PRINT USING and PRINT TAB. The first instruction provides the capability to designate a particular columnar format for computer output. The second instruction gives the user the ability to begin printing computer output at a specific position.

PRINT USING Statement
Since the user generally wants to specify a particular format, the PRINT USING statement is capable of performing such a function.* In the previous

* STRING, IMAGE, and PRINT USING statements are not standard on all versions of BASIC.

examples of the PRINT statement, the information printed by the computer has not been under the programmer's control, but rather was controlled by the particular version of BASIC used. For example, exponentiation was used by the computer for values longer than six digits while decimal points were not always aligned vertically. To provide for a specified format, the PRINT USING statement utilizes the following general form:

line no. PRINT USING (STRING), (output list, separated by commas)

where the STRING next to PRINT USING relates to a corresponding statement whose general form is:

line no. STRING = 'LINE IMAGE'

The string or line image indicates to the computer system what actual print format is desired.

The STRING statement is used to specify six different types of fields: namely, (1) integer, (2) decimal, (3) dollar sign, (4) exponential, (5) alphanumeric, and (6) literal. These fields are defined by format control characters inserted in the STRING line. These format control characters include:

- Period (.) — indicates where the decimal point is to be printed.
- Exclamation point (!) — establishes a one character alphanumeric field.
- Alphabetic (E) — indicates a continuation character that must be preceded by an apostrophe, such as 'EEE. Useful for widening field to the right when data overflows the field.
- Alphabetic (L) — indicates a continuation character that must be preceded by an apostrophe, such as 'LLL. Useful for printing data to the left, but does not provide for widening a field when an overflow condition occurs.
- Alphabetic (R) — indicates a continuation character that must be preceded by an apostrophe, such as 'RRR. Useful for printing data to the right, but does not provide for widening a field when an overflow condition occurs.
- Alphabetic (C) — indicates a continuation character that must be preceded by an apostrophe, such as 'CCC. Useful for centering data within a field when the field is exceeded.
- Pound sign (#) — establishes a numeric format.
- Four upward arrows (↑↑↑↑) — used for establishing a scientific notation field.
- Dollar sign ($) — causes the sign to be printed immediately to the left of numeric data.

In some versions of BASIC, formatting is accomplished by using the IMAGE statement. To allow for a specified format, the PRINT USING statement uses the following general form:

line no. PRINT USING line no. (output list, separated by commas)

where the line number next to PRINT USING relates to a corresponding IMAGE statement whose general form is:

line no.: line image or line format

The *colon* is required after the line number to indicate that an IMAGE statement is to follow. The line image or line format indicates to the computer system what actual format is desired. As with the STRING statement, the IMAGE statement can be used to specify six different types of fields.

To utilize the foregoing image control symbols, several requirements are necessary. First, all PRINT USING commands must reference either an image line or a previously defined string variable. Second, an image line or string variable can be referenced by multiple PRINT USING statements. Third, numeric fields require one pound sign for each digit to be printed plus another for the algebraic sign. (Integer fields use pound signs without decimal points; decimal fields use pound signs and one decimal point; dollar sign fields use dollar signs and/or dollar signs followed by integer or decimal fields; and exponential fields use decimal fields followed by four upward arrows.) Fourth, depending upon the version of BASIC used, alphanumeric fields are defined in several forms. Fifth, a literal field is transmitted to the terminal exactly as it appears in the image line. Sixth, when the PRINT USING lines have more variables than the number of fields in the image, the image line is reused, resulting in a second line of output. Seventh, as indicated previously, an image line is identified by a colon placed immediately after the line number.

Examples of STRING and PRINT USING statements are:

(1) integer
10 LET A$ = '### ###'
20 PRINT USING A$,A,B
(2) decimal
10 LET B$ = '##.## ####.##'
20 PRINT USING B$,X,Y
(3) dollar sign
10 LET C$ = '$#.## $###.##'
20 PRINT USING C$,Y,Z

Examples of IMAGE and PRINT USING statements are:

(4) exponential
10: #.###   #.###
20 PRINT USING 10, E, F
(5) alphanumeric
10:'   'L   'R
20 PRINT USING 10, S, T
(6) literal
10: U V
20 PRINT USING 10

Although these are simple examples, they do show the potential of the PRINT USING statement in designating a particular format for output. Typical business examples will be illustrated later in the chapter.

PRINT TAB Statement

The TAB function in a PRINT statement allows the terminal to begin printing at a specific position. The X value of the PRINT TAB statement, called the *argument* of the function, specifies the exact printing position. The X value can be any constant, variable, or expression. All variables either used alone or in an expression must have been previously assigned in the program. The general form of the statement is:

line no. PRINT (label or expression; TAB(X); label or expression; TAB(X+10); label or expression)

or

line no. PRINT (label or expression: TAB(X); label or expression; TAB(Y); label or expression)

In actuality, the TAB function is similar to that of a typewriter, that is, it causes the output device (teletypewriter or CRT unit) to skip to a desired position as indicated by the values of X and X+10 or X and Y (where Y is greater than X). It should be noted that semicolons are used since they serve as a delimiter. If commas were used, the computer system would print not more than five fields per line, thereby not adhering to the TAB function.

An example of the PRINT TAB statement is as follows:

```
100  READ A,B,C
110  PRINT A;TAB(10);B;TAB(30);C
120  DATA 5,10,15
```

Hence, typical examples include the spacing of output for printing managerial and internal operating reports.

---

subscripted variables

In the preceding chapter, the focus was on unscripted variables. However, it is possible within the BASIC language to provide for the manipulation of subscripted numeric and string variables. Additional computing capabilities are available with subscripted variables when processing lists, tables, arrays, matrices, i.e., any group of homogeneous information. Within this framework of subscripted variables, single and double subscripts and the DIM (dimension) statement are treated.

Single and Double Subscripts

Generally, single or double subscripted variables only are permitted. They are formed by listing valid variable names, followed by subscripts. Also, the subscripts must be enclosed within parentheses; they may be constants, variables, or expressions. The purpose of subscripts is to identify specific data in any group of related information, i.e., a list, table, array, or matrix.

When the *single* subscript is used, the variables reference a one-dimensional list or table, i.e., a number of rows but only one column, shown as follows:

	A
1	3
2	7
3	13
4	42
5	96
6	15

To reference the above list, typical single numeric subscripted variables are:

$$A(1) = 3 \qquad A(2) = 7 \qquad A(3) = 13$$

which are read as "A sub-1," "A sub-2," and "A sub-3." These foregoing subscripted variables should not be confused with A1, A2, and A3 which are examples of unsubscripted variables. Other examples of single subscripted variables are:

$$A(N) \qquad A(2^*N) \qquad A(12^*N)$$

which identify specific locations in a list or table. It should be noted that the foregoing values are truncated if they were not integer values previously.

While the single subscripted variable has one subscript enclosed in parentheses, the double subscripted variable has two subscripts shown in parentheses. The first subscript references the row while the second one refers to the column. Hence, the subscripted variables reference an array or matrix containing rows and columns, such as:

A	1	2	3	4	5	6
1						
2						
3						
4						
5						
6						

To reference the above matrix, typical double subscripted numeric variables are:

$$A(1,6) \qquad A(2,5) \qquad A(5,6)$$

where the value in the parenthesis represents the row position, the column position. These subscripted variables are read as "A sub-1, comma, 6," "A sub-2, comma, 5," and "A sub-5, comma, 6."

Referring to the prior examples for single subscripted variables, typical double subscripted variables are:

$$A(N,1) \qquad A(2^*N,4) \qquad A(12^*N,6)$$

which identify specific locations in a matrix. These variables are valid only if the expressions result in integer values.

Although one-dimensional string variables are valid for most versions of BASIC, the same cannot be said for two-dimensional string variables. Some versions do not permit the latter type of subscripted variables.

DIM (Dimension) Statement

To utilize single and double subscripted variables, it is necessary to specify the maximum number of elements to be referenced.* The DIM (dimension) statement accomplishes this task. The general form of the DIM statement for a one-dimensional list or table is:

line no. DIM variable (constant), variable (constant), . . .

where the constant identifies the maximum number of elements.

In a similar manner, the general form of the DIM statement for a two-dimensional array or matrix is:

line no. DIM variable (constant, constant), variable (constant, constant), . . .

where the first constant refers to the maximum row value of the array or matrix while the second constant references the maximum column value.

To illustrate the DIM statement for a series of one-dimensional tables, consider the following statement:

```
100 DIM A(10), B(11), C(12), D(13)
```

which identifies numeric variables A through D in memory with a maximum number of locations, starting at location 1. These tables in memory would appear as:

	A		B		C		D
1	0	1	0	1	0	1	0
2	0	2	0	2	0	2	0
3	0	3	0	3	0	3	0
4	0	4	0	4	0	4	0
5	0	5	0	5	0	5	0
6	0	6	0	6	0	6	0
7	0	7	0	7	0	7	0
8	0	8	0	8	0	8	0
9	0	9	0	9	0	9	0
10	0	10	0	10	0	10	0
		11	0	11	0	11	0
				12	0	12	0
						13	0

* In some versions of BASIC, the zero row and the zero column can be used.

figure 6-1. Program flow-chart for aging accounts receivable.

Initially, the tables would contain zeros until specific values are assigned by the program during processing.

An example of a DIM statement using string variables for a series of one-dimensional tables is:

```
100 DIM A$(11), B$(12), C$(9), D$(10)
```

with a maximum of 11 locations for A$ (A$(1), A$(2), . . . A$(11)); 12 locations for B$ (B$(1), B$(2), . . . B$(12)); 9 locations for C$, and 10 locations for D$. In memory initially, the tables would contain blanks until specific strings are assigned:

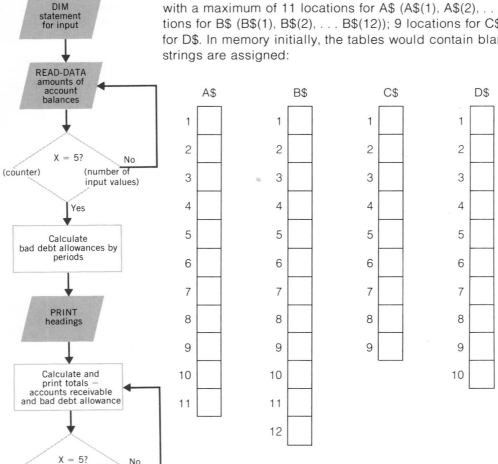

For subscripted variables that reference a table 1 through 10, the DIM statement is optional. If there is a subscripted variable without an accompanying DIM statement, the variable is assumed to have a dimension of 10 (1 through 10 elements).

As indicated above, the DIM statement is also used to determine the size of a two-dimensional array or matrix. As an example of a DIM statement, consider the following:

```
100 DIM A(2,2), B(2,3), C(3,3), D(3,4)
```

where their matrix structure for variables A, B, C, and D respectively would appear as follows in memory:

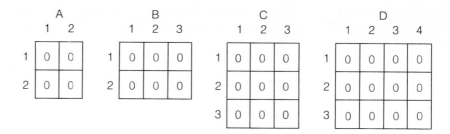

An examination of the above matrices indicates that the numeric variable A has a maximum number of 4 locations (A(1,1), A(1,2), A(2,1), and A(2,2)). Similarly, B, C, and D have a maximum of 6, 9, and 12 locations respectively. Each location in memory is initially zero and remains at such until assigned a specific value by the computer program during processing.

In order to reference an array or matrix, two subscripts must be given where the first subscript is the row indicator and the second subscript is the column indicator. To illustrate, consider the following section of a program:

```
100 DIM A(2,2), B(2,3), C(3,3), D(3,4)
110 A(1,2)=1
120 B(1,2)=2
130 C(1,3)=3
140 D(1,3)=4
150 PRINT A(1,2) + B(1,2) + C(1,3) + D(1,3)
```

where the subscripts of 1 and 2 for lines 110 and 120 refer to the first row and second column while the subscripts of 1 and 3 for lines 130 and 140 relate to the first row and third column.

Just as with one-dimensional lists and tables, the absence of a DIM statement for arrays and matrices assumes a certain size. Specifically, if the DIM statement was not present for the above example, the arrays for A, B, C, and D would have been assumed to have a dimension of 10 by 10 (10 rows and 10 columns).

accounts receivable aging application — subscripted variables

A typical business illustration using subscripted variables is the aging of accounts receivable. The program flowchart is set forth in Figure 6-1 while the corresponding BASIC program is found in Figure 6-2. Initially, the program utilizes a DIM statement on line 20 for the account balances by age (A(5)) and estimated percentages of collection (B(5)). The remaining lines of coding represent a series of DATA, LET, and PRINT statements along with two FOR-NEXT statements. Briefly, data concerning the length of the aging periods and their respective rates of computation to be printed during processing (per Figure 6-3) are represented by the READ-DATA statements on lines 60 through 90. The LET statements on lines 110 through 150 provide for calculating the amount of bad debt allowances by periods. While the first loop is found on lines 30 and 50 for reading five input values, the second loop on lines 180 and 220 provides for calculating the total accounts receivable balances and total bad debt allowance requirements for

```
CHAP62   08:34              23-Oct-78
10 REM THIS PROGRAM AGES ACCOUNTS RECEIVABLE FOR FIVE ACCOUNTS.
20 DIM A(5),B(5),C(5),A$(11)
30 FOR X=1 TO 5
40 READ A$(X),B(X)
50 NEXT X
60 DATA '1-30 DAYS OLD',0.01
70 DATA '31-60 DAYS OLD',0.02
80 DATA '61-90 DAYS OLD',0.08
85 DATA '91 DAYS -6 MONTHS OLD',0.2
90 DATA 'OVER SIX MONTHS OLD',0.5
100 INPUT A(1),A(2),A(3),A(4),A(5)
110 LET C(1)=A(1)*B(1)
120 LET C(2)=A(2)*B(2)
130 LET C(3)=A(3)*B(3)
140 LET C(4)=A(4)*B(4)
150 LET C(5)=A(5)*B(5)
160 PRINT'AGE OF ACCOUNTS            BALANCES      EST %     BAD DEBT ALLOWANCE'
170 LET B$='\              \#####.##       #.##        #####.##'
180 FOR X=1 TO 5
190 LET D=D+A(X)
200 LET G=G+C(X)
210 PRINT USING B$,A$(X),A(X),B(X),C(X)
220 NEXT X
230 PRINT
240 PRINT
270 LET C$='TOTAL ACCOUNTS RECEIVABLE    #######.##'
280 LET D$='TOTAL BAD DEBT ALLOWANCE     #######.##'
290 PRINT USING C$,D
300 PRINT USING D$,G
310 END

Ready
```

figure 6-2. BASIC program (based upon Figure 6-1) for aging accounts receivable.

the same five values. The last part of the program prints the individual and total values in the program.

Utilizing the program per Figure 6-2, typical input data are entered for processing—shown in Figure 6-3. The program prints the five aging periods along with the account balances, estimated percentages for aging, and bad debt allowances. Also, the output shows the totals for accounts receivable and bad debt allowances. Although not shown, the program in Figure 6-2 could have been coded to determine the overall percent of bad debt allowances. If the coding had been included, the results in Figure 6-3 would have included this calculation.

```
RUN
CHAP62   08:35              23-Oct-78
? 100,200,300,400,500
AGE OF ACCOUNTS             BALANCES      EST %     BAD DEBT ALLOWANCE
1-30 DAYS OLD                100.00       0.01             1.00
31-60 DAYS OLD               200.00       0.02             4.00
61-90 DAYS OLD               300.00       0.08            24.00
91 DAYS -6 MONTHS OLD        400.00       0.20            80.00
OVER SIX MONTHS OLD          500.00       0.50           250.00


TOTAL ACCOUNTS RECEIVABLE       1500.00
TOTAL BAD DEBT ALLOWANCE         359.00

Ready
```

figure 6-3. Representative data used in the BASIC program for aging accounts receivable.

matrix statements

In this part of the chapter, various types of matrix statements will be discussed, in particular, the MAT READ statement, the MAT INPUT statement, and the MAT PRINT statement.

MAT READ Statement

A frequently used matrix instruction is the MAT READ statement whose purpose is to read and store data in a matrix of specified dimensions. Its general form is:

line no. MAT READ (one or more matrix variable names, separated by commas)

where each matrix has been specified by a DIM statement or has been implied to be 10 by 10. If a fewer number of data items is supplied by a DATA statement, an "out of data" error condition occurs during the read. When the proper number of data items is specified in the DATA statement (as they should be), the data are assigned to the matrix row-by-row, that is, items are assigned to all columns in the first row first, then the second row, and so forth. This process continues until the matrix is completely filled.

A second method to read and store data in matrix form allows the matrix's size to be defined or redefined during the operation. Its general form is:

line no. MAT READ matrix variable (no. of rows, no. of columns), . . .

where the number of rows and columns can be valid numeric constants, variables, or expressions. The re-dimension of the matrix cannot be greater than the locations that were reserved previously in the DIM statement.

To illustrate, the following program contains two MAT READ statements where the first one reads data in one matrix format while the second one restructures the matrix format:

```
100 DIM A(1,2), B(2,2), X(4,1), Y(1,2)
110 DATA 1, 2, 3, 4, 5, 6
120 MAT READ A, B
130 PRINT A(1,2), B(2,2)
140 DATA 1, 2, 3, 4, 5, 6
150 REM SET X AS A 4 BY 1
160 REM SET Y AS A 1 BY 2
170 MAT READ X(4,1), Y(1,2)
180 PRINT X(2,1), Y(1,2)
190 END
```

Based upon the foregoing program, the computer would store the data as follows:

$$
\begin{array}{cccc}
A & B & X & Y \\
[1 \quad 2] & \begin{bmatrix} 3 & 4 \\ 5 & 6 \end{bmatrix} & \begin{bmatrix} 1 \\ 2 \\ 3 \\ 4 \end{bmatrix} & [5 \quad 6]
\end{array}
$$

Also, the data to be printed per line 180 are: 2 and 6.

first summary of chapter 6

output formatting:
• PRINT USING statement—provides the capability to designate a particular columnar format for computer output.

• STRING or IMAGE statement—used to specify six different types of fields, namely,

STRING:

(1) integer: example—10 LET A$ = '### ###'
                                20 PRINT USING A$,A,B

(2) decimal: example—10 LET B$ = '##.## ####.##'
                                20 PRINT USING B$,X,Y

(3) dollar sign: example—10 LET C$ = '$#.## $###.##'
                                20 PRINT USING C$,Y,Z

IMAGE:

(4) exponential: example—10: #.###   #.###
                                20 PRINT USING 10,E,F

(5) alphanumeric: example—10:'   'L   'R
                                20 PRINT USING 10,S,T

(6) literal: example—10:U V
                                20 PRINT USING 10

• PRINT TAB statement—allows the programmer to start printing at a specific position.
Example: 110 PRINT A; TAB(10); B; TAB(30); C

subscripted variables:
• Single and double subscripts—formed by listing valid variable names, followed by subscripts.

A single subscripted variable references a one-dimensional list or table.
Examples: A(1), A(N)

A double subscripted variable references a two-dimensional array or matrix.
Examples: A(1,6), A(N,1)

• DIM (Dimension) statement—defines the elements of a list, table, array, or matrix in terms of its maximum elements. If the dimension statement is not used, the variable is assumed to have a dimension of 10 (1 through 10).

Example for a one-dimensional list or table:
100 DIM A(10), B(11), C(12), D(13)

Example for a two-dimensional array or matrix:
100 DIM A(2,2), B(2,3), C(3,3), D(3,4)

**first self-study
exercise
of chapter 6**

True-False:

1. (   ) The PRINT TAB instruction provides for printing a columnar format.
2. (   ) The IMAGE statement is always used with the PRINT TAB instruction.
3. (   ) A colon (:) represents an IMAGE statement identifier.
4. (   ) A pound sign (#) establishes a numeric format in a STRING or an IMAGE statement.
5. (   ) The X value of the PRINT TAB statement specifies the exact printing position.
6. (   ) A single subscript references a two-dimensional matrix or table.
7. (   ) A double subscripted variable has one subscript shown in parentheses.
8. (   ) A DIM statement can be used for a one-dimensional list or table.
9. (   ) String variables are not allowed in one-dimensional tables.
10. (   ) The absence of a DIM statement for an array assumes a certain size.

Fill-In:

11. The _____ _____ _____ main purpose is to specify a particular format for output.
12. The STRING or _____ _____ indicates to the computer what actual print format is wanted.
13. All PRINT USING commands must reference either an image line or a previously defined _____ _____.
14. The _____ _____ in a PRINT statement allows the terminal to begin printing at a specific location.
15. The form of Y(2,2) is an example of a _____ _____ _____ while the form of Y(2) illustrates a _____ _____ _____.
16. The statement—100 DIM Y(22), Z(24)—is an example of the _____ _____ being used for a series of _____-_____ _____.
17. The adding of the dollar sign behind a subscripted variable in a DIM statement indicates that the program will be processing a _____ _____ from a list or table.
18. If there is a subscripted variable without an accompanying DIM statement, the variable is assumed to have a dimension of _____.
19. In order to reference an _____ or _____, two subscripts must be given where the first subscript is the row indicator while the second subscript is the column indicator.
20. The absence of a _____ _____ for arrays and matrices assumes a certain size, that is, 10 by 10.

MAT INPUT Statement

The basic purpose of the MAT INPUT statement is to allow the programmer to enter data via the keyboard during the running of the program. It operates in the same manner as the INPUT statement by causing a question mark to be typed. After the question mark, the user must supply the correct size matrix values. For example, the following program will total eight matrix values and find an average of these values.

```
100 DIM A(8,1)
110 MAT INPUT A
120 FOR X = 1 TO 8
130 T = T + A(X,1)
140 NEXT X
150 PRINT
160 PRINT 'TOTAL'; T, 'AVERAGE VALUE'; T/8
170 END
```

Using the foregoing program, sample data would be entered after the question mark as follows:

? 22, 45, 61, 36, 19, 44, 71, 38

The program would print the following:

```
TOTAL 336    AVERAGE VALUE 42
```

On several time-sharing systems, a special function NUM can be utilized. To illustrate (revision of above program), read the number of values in the table A:

```
100 DIM A(100)
110 MAT INPUT A
120 FOR X = 1 TO NUM
130 T = T + A(X)
140 NEXT X
150 PRINT
160 PRINT 'TOTAL' ; T, 'AVERAGE VALUE' ; T/NUM
170 END
```

Hence, the NUM function contains the number of data values read for a one-dimensional array.

MAT PRINT Statement

To simplify the process of printing data stored in a two-dimensional array or matrix, the MAT PRINT statement is used. Thus, matrix data can be printed without referencing each element of the matrix individually. Its general form is:

line no. MAT PRINT (one or more matrix variables, separated by commas or semicolons)

When commas separate the matrix variables, the data are printed according to the five-field format (set forth in the prior chapter). Otherwise, if semicolons are used, the output is spaced compactly on each line.

The MAT PRINT statement causes the matrix elements to be typed row by row across each line, with each new matrix row causing a new line to be printed. When there is more than one matrix to be printed, the new matrix is separated from the prior matrix by two blank lines. To illustrate, the following example is used:

```
100 DIM A(2,2), B(2,6)
110 MAT READ A, B
120 DATA 1, 2, 3, 4, 5, 6, 7, 8, 9, 10, 11,
    12, 13, 14, 15, 16
130 MAT PRINT A,
140 MAT PRINT B,
150 END
```

The preceding data would be stored in memory with the following format:

$$
\begin{matrix} A \\ \begin{bmatrix} 1 & 2 \\ 3 & 4 \end{bmatrix} \end{matrix}
\qquad
\begin{matrix} B \\ \begin{bmatrix} 5 & 6 & 7 & 8 & 9 & 10 \\ 11 & 12 & 13 & 14 & 15 & 16 \end{bmatrix} \end{matrix}
$$

In terms of output, matrix A would be printed as it appears in memory with a blank line separating their row values. Two blank lines would separate matrix A from matrix B. However, when matrix B is printed, the sixth value will appear on the next line. The blank line after the 10 is printed indicates that a new matrix row begins.

Using the above program, the output would be:

```
1          2
3          4

5          6          7          8          9
10

11         12         13         14         15
16
```

However, if semicolons were used, the output would be a packed format, such as:

```
1          2
3          4

5          6      7      8      9      10
11         12      13      14      15      16
```

---

internal (library) functions

Mathematical operations, such as finding the square root of a number and the sign of a number, are normally furnished by the BASIC language interpreter. Depending upon the version of BASIC used, common internal or library functions, as set forth in Figure 6-4, can be specified in statements. By inserting one of the three character names within a statement, a specific function can be performed. In effect, a particular function can be accessed by stating its name, followed by whatever information must be supplied to the function—enclosed in parentheses. Once the library function has been accessed, the desired processing will occur automatically from a library function stored in the computer's memory. Needless to say, internal functions relieve the programmer of detailed programming for complex mathematical calculations.

Although the foregoing may appear to be oriented toward the discipline

Function	Description	Example
SQR(X)	Find the square root of X.	10 LET A = SQR(B)
SGN(X)	Find the sign of X. A +1 is returned if X is positive; a 0 is returned if X is zero; and a −1 is returned if X is negative.	10 LET A = SGN(B)
INT(X)	Find the greatest integer value not greater than X.	10 LET A = INT(B)
RND(X)	Generate a random value between 0.0 and 1.0.	10 LET A = RND(B)
ABS(X)	Find the absolute value of X.	10 LET A = ABS(B)
LOG(X)	Find the natural logarithm of X.	10 LET A = LOG(B)
EXP(X)	Raise e to the x-power (e^x).	10 LET A = EXP(B)

figure 6-4. Table of common internal (library) functions in the BASIC language that are helpful in solving business problems.

of mathematics, this is not entirely true since quantitative business models utilize many of the foregoing functions for solving a wide variety of business problems. For example, the simulation of an inventory or waiting line problem utilizes the RND function. Finding the square root is a common practice found in mathematically oriented business problems. In the example below, a typical business application for square roots is found. Thus, many uses can be found for these library functions in a typical business environment.

inventory application— internal function

An example of the SQR function is to be found in determining a series of economic order quantities (EOQ) for purchasing inventory from suppliers on an optimum basis. The program flowchart for computing a series of EOQ values is found in Figure 6-5. The BASIC program to accomplish the calculation and printing of desired economic order quantities is illustrated in Figure 6-6.

On lines 10 and 20, specific remarks about the EOQ program are set forth. For calculating and printing a series of economic order quantities, the program starts on line 50. On lines 50, 60, and 70, parameter values for demand and ordering costs are entered along with a specific value for carrying costs. The PRINT statement on line 80 determines the output headings while the LET statement on line 110 makes the calculation for EOQ, thereby making use of the SQR function. Although a PRINT statement on line 130 specifies how the data are to be arranged when printed, the two FOR-NEXT statements on lines 90, 100, 140, and 150 determine the number of values to be calculated and printed. As usual, the final instruction is an END statement.

In order to visualize the processing of the preceding program, representative data for computing and printing a series of EOQ values are set forth in Figure 6-7. Similarly, this figure illustrates a series of EOQ computations for the parameters set forth. Within this example, the square root function is an integral part of the program.

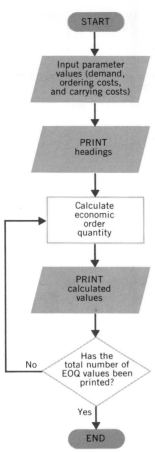

figure 6-5. Program flow-chart for computing a series of EOQ values.

```
CHAP66   08:38           23-Oct-78
10 REM THIS PROGRAM WILL DETERMINE THE ECONOMIC ORDER QUANTITY
20 REM GIVEN A SET OF DEMANDS, ORDERING COSTS, AND A VALUE FOR CARRYING COST.
50 INPUT'STARTING DEMAND, ENDING DEMAND, AND DEMAND INCREMENT';D1,D2,D3
60 INPUT'START ORDER COST, END ORDER COST, AND ORDER COST INCREMENT';O1,O2,O3
70 INPUT'CARRYING COSTS';C
80 PRINT'   DEMAND      ORD COST        CAR COST         EOQ'
90 FOR S=D1 TO D2 STEP D3
100 FOR R=O1 TO O2 STEP O3
110 LET Q=SQR(2*R*S/C)
120 LET A$='######.##          ###        #.###    ######.##'
130 PRINT USING A$,S,R,C,Q
140 NEXT R
150 NEXT S
160 END

Ready
```

figure 6-6. BASIC program (based on Figure 6-5) for determining a series of economic order quantities (EOQ) for purchasing inventory from suppliers on an optimum basis.

```
RUN
CHAP66   08:39           23-Oct-78
STARTING DEMAND, ENDING DEMAND, AND DEMAND INCREMENT? 100,200,25
START ORDER COST, END ORDER COST, AND ORDER COST INCREMENT? 5,10,2
CARRYING COSTS? 3
     DEMAND      ORD COST        CAR COST         EOQ
     100.00         5             3.000          18.26
     100.00         7             3.000          21.60
     100.00         9             3.000          24.49
     125.00         5             3.000          20.41
     125.00         7             3.000          24.15
     125.00         9             3.000          27.39
     150.00         5             3.000          22.36
     150.00         7             3.000          26.46
     150.00         9             3.000          30.00
     175.00         5             3.000          24.15
     175.00         7             3.000          28.58
     175.00         9             3.000          32.40
     200.00         5             3.000          25.82
     200.00         7             3.000          30.55
     200.00         9             3.000          34.64

Ready
```

figure 6-7. Representative data used in the BASIC program for computing a series of EOQ values.

user-generated functions

In addition to the foregoing internal (library) functions furnished by the BASIC language, the user has the option of creating internal functions, commonly called *user-generated functions*. The most common ones are the DEF (define) statement and the Multiple-Argument function. Each of these are discussed below.

Define Statement

The DEF (define) statement is a single-line function used to avoid repeated programming of the same calculations, like that demonstrated above for library functions. The general form of the DEF statement is:

line no. DEF FN variable (zero, one, or more arguments) = expression

where the name of the function is given by these characters—FN plus a variable. The variable must be one letter of the alphabet; thus, there can be as many as 26 × 11 separate functions in a single program. The argument(s) within the parentheses are *dummy* arguments since no values are assigned to them in the DEF statement. As with the library functions, values of the arguments are determined during the "call" of the function. To state it another way, in order to evaluate the function, it is necessary to reference that function name somewhere in the program.

To illustrate the DEF statement, the following example is used:

```
100 DEF FNC(A,B) = (30*A+40*B)/70
110 LET S = 5
120 LET T = 6
130 LET R = FNC(S,T)
```

Although the function has been defined on line 100, execution of line 130 will cause the function to be evaluated.

Multiple-Argument Function

User-generated functions need not be restricted to one line, but can be extended over a number of lines. Hence, a multiple-argument function, i.e., *subgroup* can be created by the programmer. The first statement of the DEF subprogram has the general form:

line no. DEF FN variable (zero, one, or more arguments)

where the variable may be one of the letters of the alphabet. This first statement is identical to a DEF function for a single-line function, except that no equal sign or expression follow the dummy argument list.

Immediately following the define statement are the program statements that define the multiple-argument function. In this part, a function name must be assigned a value, such as:

line no. FN variable = expression

The last statement in this subprogram must be:

line no. FNEND

To illustrate the multiple-argument function, the following BASIC program contains a subprogram to determine the smallest of a pair of numbers:

```
100 DEF FNC(A,B)
110 LET FNC=A
120 IF A<=B THEN 140
130 LET FNC=B
140 FNEND
150 INPUT Q,R
160 LET S=FNC(Q,R)
170 PRINT 'SMALLEST IS'; S
180 END
```

If the above program were run and the values, 4 and 6, entered after the question mark, the resulting output, 'SMALLEST IS', becomes 4.

---

subroutines

For those parts of a BASIC program that require a particular segment of statements more than once, it is more efficient to use a program subroutine than to recode the same statements repeatedly. For this purpose, the

GOSUB and RETURN statements are used. In addition, this section will explore the RESTORE statement and the CHANGE statement.

GOSUB and RETURN Statements

The GOSUB and RETURN statements are used in BASIC as a means of entering and exiting from a particular segment of statements. In particular, they are used for subroutines. A *subroutine* is defined as a group of program statements that are executed one or more times (accent on the latter) when referenced by the main body of the program. The general form of a subroutine is:

> line no. GOSUB line no.-1

where the line no.-1 is the first statement of the subroutine.

The GOSUB instruction is quite similar to the GO TO statement (unconditional transfer per Chapter 5) since it directs the computer system to start processing at a specific line number (start of the subroutine). On the other hand, the GOSUB statement is different since it provides for a transfer back to the line immediately following in the main program. A branch back to the main program occurs when the system encounters a RETURN statement in the subroutine. The form of the RETURN statement is:

> line no. RETURN.

Thus, the GOSUB statement initiates a transfer from the main program to a subroutine while the RETURN statement transfers control back to the main program to the line immediately following the GOSUB statement.

An overview of the relationship between the main program and the subroutine is found in Figure 6-8. As shown in the illustration, GOSUB statements appear on lines 240 and 350 which transfers control to line 600. Once the processing of the subroutine has been completed, the RETURN statement on line 710 transfers control to the line immediately following the GOSUB statement in the main program. In this example, control is transferred to line immediately following 240 or 350, depending upon the transfer in the main program.

```
line no. 5 REM MAIN PROGRAM
       .          .
       .          .
       .          .
line no. 240 GOSUB 600
       .          .
       .          .
       .          .
line no. 350 GOSUB 600
       .          .
       .          .
       .          .
line no. 595 REM SUBROUTINE
line no. 600
       .          .
       .          .
       .          .
line no. 710 RETURN
line no. 999 END
```

---

figure 6-8. An overview of the relationship between the main program and the subroutines when using the GOSUB and RETURN statements.

RESTORE Statement

Since it is desirable at times to read or use the same data values more than once, the RESTORE statement allows the program to reread the same data values any number of times within the same program. Data may be stored in lists, tables, or arrays. The general form of this statement is:

line no. RESTORE

In a typical program, one or more blocks of data are processed by a READ statement. By using the RESTORE statement, the computer system goes back and rereads the same data. Business situations where the program reads the same data and makes various calculations different ways is a typical use of the RESTORE statement. For example, use the same data for determining the arithmetic mean, median, and mode of current monthly sales. The restore instruction, then, would appear with the appropriate line number, such as:

```
100 RESTORE
```

CHANGE Statement

On certain time-sharing systems, the CHANGE statement is offered. Its purpose is to convert string variables or characters to numeric values. Also, conversion from numeric values to string characters is allowed. The first form of the CHANGE statement is:

line no. CHANGE (string variable) TO (numeric variable)

For example, the following statements change two string variables to an array of internal numeric values:

```
100 CHANGE A$ TO A
110 CHANGE B$(1) TO B
```

The second form of the CHANGE statement is:

line no. CHANGE (numeric variable) TO (string variable)

For example, the following lines of coding change two numeric variables to string variables:

```
100 CHANGE A TO A$
110 CHANGE B TO B$(1)
```

sorting

Sorting is widely used in business. It is employed to sort input data before, during, or after processing. For example, monthly sales reports could include a breakdown of the lowest to the highest commissions paid to salespersons; monthly sales could be sorted by invoice number or by amounts; monthly inventory reports could be sorted by inventory number or by amount; and so forth. Hence, there is a great need for sorting in typical business applications.

Subscripted variables are used in sorting, that is, data items in a table are rearranged in a certain sequence—ascending or descending order.

Normally, data are first read into a table. Next, it is rearranged into the desired sequence. The following table T is to be sorted:

T

1	22
2	35
3	71
4	90
5	65
6	62
7	59
8	50
9	42
10	37

As a starting point in Figure 6-9 (program flowchart) to sort the above data, it is first necessary to define the size of the table and then read input data into the table. After this process, a nested loop structure is used to find the smallest element in the list and interchange it with the first element. This process continues by finding the next smallest value and replacing the second table element with it and so forth. Thus, the sorted table T is:

T

1	22
2	35
3	37
4	42
5	50
6	59
7	62
8	65
9	71
10	90

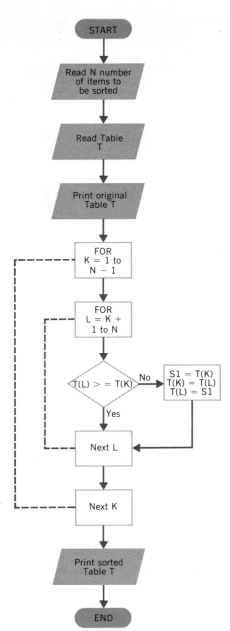

figure 6-9. Program flowchart for sorting table in ascending order.

The program for sorting numerical data in an ascending order is found in Figure 6-10. The original values before the sort and the sorted table in ascending order is also found in Figure 6-10.

```
CHAP61 _08:41          23-Oct-78
10 REM PROGRAM TO SORT A TABLE OF NUMBERS INTO ASCENDING ORDER
20 REM THE MAXIMUM SIZE OF THE TABLE IS FIFTY ELEMENTS.
30 DIM T(50)
40 REM THE FIRST ELEMENT IN THE DATA LIST DEFINES THE SIZE
50 REM OF THE TABLE
60 READ N
70 FOR J=1 TO N
80 READ T(J)
90 NEXT J
100 PRINT'ORIGINAL TABLE VALUES BEFORE SORT'
110 FOR J=1 TO N
120 PRINT T(J);
130 NEXT J
135 PRINT
140 REM THE FOLLOWING NESTED LOOPS INTERCHANGE ELEMENTS UNTIL
150 REM THE LOWEST ELEMENT IS PLACED IN THE REQUIRED LOCATION.
160 FOR K=1 TO N-1
170 FOR L=K+1 TO N
180 IF T(L)>=T(K) THEN 230
190 REM IF CONDITIONS ARE PROPER, THE SWAP IS MADE.
200 LET S1=T(K)
210 LET T(K)=T(L)
220 LET T(L)=S1
230 NEXT L
240 NEXT K
250 PRINT'SORTED TABLE IN ASCENDING ORDER'
260 FOR J=1 TO N
270 PRINT T(J);
280 NEXT J
290 DATA 10,22,35,71,90,65,62,59,50,42,37
300 END

Ready

RUN
CHAP61  08:41          23-Oct-78
ORIGINAL TABLE VALUES BEFORE SORT
 22   35   71   90   65   62   59   50   42   37
SORTED TABLE IN ASCENDING ORDER
 22   35   37   42   50   59   62   65   71   90
Ready
```

figure 6-10. BASIC program for sorting numeric data per the program flowchart of Figure 6-9.

---

summary

This chapter has built upon the essential elements of the BASIC language presented in the prior one. The additional features of BASIC which were presented included output formatting, subscripted variables, matrix statements, internal and user-generated functions, subroutines, and sorting. Even though there are variations from one BASIC version to another, the material as presented can be modified easily.

As with the prior chapter, several business applications were illustrated to demonstrate the versatility of BASIC. This easy to program language can be used for a wide variety of computer business programs. More specifically, BASIC programs can be written for the following areas: corporate planning, marketing, research & development, engineering, manufacturing, inventory, purchasing, physical distribution, finance, accounting, and personnel. Thus, a wide range of business functions are logical candidates for using a relatively easy to learn programming language.

**second summary
of chapter 6**

matrix statements:
• MAT READ statement—The first general form provides a means for reading and storing data in a matrix of specified dimensions.
Example: 120 MAT READ A,B

The second general form allows the matrix's size to be defined or redefined:
Example: 170 MAT READ X(4,1), Y(1,2)

• MAT INPUT statement—allows the user to enter data in a matrix form (via the keyboard) during the processing of a program.
Example: 110 MAT INPUT A

• MAT PRINT statement—provides a method for printing matrix data without referencing each element of a matrix individually.
Example: 130 MAT PRINT A,
140 MAT PRINT B,

internal (library) functions:
Functions supplied by the system—provides a means for accessing desired functions, such as square roots and random numbers, from a library stored in memory.
Example: 110 LET Q=SQR(2*R*S/C)

user-generated functions:
• DEF (Define) statement—gives the user the opportunity to develop one's own internal single-line functions.
Example: 100 DEF FNC(A,B)=(30*A+40*B)/70

• Multiple-argument function—gives the user the capability to develop a subprogram for internal multiple-line functions.
Example: 100 DEF FNC(A,B)
110 LET FNC=A
130 LET FNC=B
140 FNEND

subroutines:
• GOSUB and RETURN statements—gives the user the capability to enter a subroutine that is used often and return to the main program when processing is completed within the subroutine.
Example: 240 GOSUB 600
710 RETURN

other statements
• RESTORE statement—allows the program to reread the same data values any number of times within the same program.
Example: 100 RESTORE

• CHANGE statement—used to change string variables to numeric variables and vice versa.
Example: 100 CHANGE A$ TO A
100 CHANGE A TO A$

sorting:
Provides a means for arranging numeric and alphabetic data items in a certain sequence, either ascending or descending order.

second self-study exercise of chapter 6

True-False:

1. ( ) The MAT PRINT statement is used to read data in a matrix form.
2. ( ) The MAT INPUT statement allows data to be entered during the running of the program.
3. ( ) The MAT PRINT statement causes matrix elements to be typed row by row.
4. ( ) Another name for internal functions is library functions.
5. ( ) The define statement is used to avoid repeated programming.
6. ( ) The arguments within a DEF statement are called dummy arguments.
7. ( ) A multiple-argument function is called a subroutine.
8. ( ) A branch back to the main program is required in a subroutine.
9. ( ) The RESTORE and CHANGE statements can be substituted for each other.
10. ( ) Data files can be sorted only in ascending sequence.

Fill-In:

11. The _____ _____ _____ is used to read and store data in a matrix of specified dimensions.
12. The _____ _____ _____ causes the matrix elements to be typed row by row across each line.
13. After the question mark, the user supplies correct size matrix values for the _____ _____ _____.
14. If _____ are used in the MAT PRINT statement, output will be packed compactly.
15. The _____ _____, namely, SQR(X) means to find the square root of X.
16. _____-_____ _____ need not be restricted to one line, but can be extended to several lines.
17. Another name for a multi-argument function is a _____.
18. To improve efficiency in programming, _____ are used for a particular module of statements that appear more than once.
19. The _____ _____ must always be found in the main program while the _____ _____ must be contained in the subroutine.
20. The _____ _____ allows the program to read the same data elements a number of times in the same program.

questions

1. How does the PRINT statement differ from the PRINT USING and PRINT TAB statements?
2. Can the PRINT USING statement be used like a PRINT TAB statement? Why or why not?
3. Differentiate between single and double subscripted variables.
4. If a dimension statement is not used, what assumption can be made about the size of a list or an array?

5. What is (are) the difference(s) between the MAT READ statement and the MAT INPUT statement?

6. a. Of the many internal or library functions set forth in the chapter, which ones are oriented toward business?
   b. Give at least three examples where they can be used in a business environment.

7. What is the purpose of user-generated functions when standard library functions are supplied by the system?

8. Explain the relationship of a subprogram to a multiple-argument function.

9. a. What is the function of a subroutine?
   b. How are the GOSUB and RETURN statements used in the main program and subroutine?

10. Distinguish between the RESTORE and the CHANGE statements.

---

programming exercises

1. Referring to the problem in the chapter for aging accounts receivable, change the program to allow for the aging of up to twenty accounts. Rerun the program on this basis.

2. Referring to the problem in the chapter for determining the economic order quantity for inventory, run the program such that ordering costs and carrying costs are constant while demand is variable.

3. Prepare a program flowchart and a corresponding BASIC program to determine the optimum number of orders per year for a company to place for its outside purchases. The formula is as follows:

$$N = \sqrt{\frac{AI}{2S}}$$

where N = optimum number of orders per year to minimize total inventory costs
   A = total dollar amount of annual usage
   I = inventory carrying costs, expressed as a percentage of the value of average inventory.
   S = ordering costs

Include in your program the capacity to calculate different values for N. Test the accuracy of your program by running five examples for calculating N and comparing with predetermined results.

4. Prepare a program flowchart and a corresponding BASIC program to compute F.I.C.A. (Social Security) withholding for a company of ten employees. Use a subroutine to perform the withholding calculations. Test the accuracy of your program by running sample data for the ten employees.

5. Prepare a program flowchart and a corresponding BASIC program to sort 25 two-digit values. The sorted data are to be arranged in descending order. Also, the program is to print the data in the prescribed order; the output format is left to the programmer.
After you are satisfied that the program is operational upon correcting logical and clerical errors, run the sample data of 25 values. Check your output for correctness.

**answers to
first self-study
exercise**

1. F 2. F 3. T 4. T 5. T 6. F 7. F 8. T 9. F 10. T 11. PRINT USING statement 12. IMAGE statement 13. string variable 14. TAB function 15. double subscripted variable and single subscripted variable 16. DIM statement and one-dimensional tables 17. string variable 18. ten 19. array and matrix 20. DIM statement

**answers to
second self-study
exercise**

1. F 2. T 3. T 4. T 5. T 6. T 7. F 8. T 9. F 10. F 11. MAT READ statement 12. MAT PRINT statement 13. MAT INPUT statement 14. semicolons 15. library function 16. user-generated functions 17. subprogram 18. subroutines 19. GOSUB statement and RETURN statement 20. RESTORE statement

part four

data processing equipment for business

The number of computer peripheral devices has grown to meet user needs. A central processing unit plus a configuration of computer devices comprise a computerized business information system. Typical batch-oriented computer equipment is presented in Chapter 7 while typical interactive, that is, time sharing, equipment is illustrated in Chapter 8. Additionally, minicomputers and general-purpose business computer systems, operating in both processing modes, are explored in chapter 9.

chapter seven
batch-oriented computer equipment

chapter objectives

- To demonstrate the various ways of preparing input for a batch-oriented computer system.
- To explore the present direction of "distributed data entry."
- To relate the "ISPCO cycle" to the components of a batch-oriented computer system.
- To illustrate the various types of input/output devices found in computer systems.
- To explore the various types of primary storage (memory) and secondary storage devices.

Throughout the month, Joe Cosgrove and his wife Claudia receive a stack of bills for payment. Monthly bills for electricity, gas, the mortgage, and department store purchases as well as periodic payments on home insurance, car insurance, magazine subscriptions, and similar items are received via mail. Each of these bills have been addressed and prepared by a computer in a batch-processing mode. At the end of the month, Joe writes a check for each bill. Actually, each check represents a message to his bank's computer to cover a specific bill. Next, he puts the check and the bill into the preaddressed return envelope.

Claudia notes that Joe has spent over two hours performing this monthly chore. She suggests that their time could be better spent on a hobby together. Hence, she calls and signs up for the new bill-paying service being offered by their progressive bank. In this manner, the bank will transfer the funds at the proper time from their checking account to pay the appropriate bills. Here again, the computer is in charge of making the transfer of funds in a batch-processing mode. This banking service is a part of the bank's Electronic Funds Transfer System, sometimes called Electronic Money.

Within this chapter, the punched card and the various types of data-entry equipment are first covered. The major components of a computer system—input/output devices, central processing unit, plus primary and secondary storage devices—are explored. This equipment represents the ISPCO (input-storage-processing-control-output) cycle of computers, as set forth previously in Chapter 3. Also, the various types of computer equipment oriented toward a batch-processing mode are illustrated. In the next chapter, equipment oriented toward an interactive processing mode will be presented.

The process of determining which pieces of computer equipment are required within a specific business information system is based on the user's needs. Similarly, consideration must be given to the equipment available from the computer manufacturer. The task for the proper selection of computer equipment is an important part of a computer feasibility study, the subject matter for Part Four—Designing and Implementing Data Processing for Business.

the punched card

Input for many batch-oriented computer systems is punched cards, containing either 80 or 96 columns of information. The 80 column card (using the Hollerith code) is a thin piece of cardboard that measures $7\frac{3}{8}$ by $3\frac{1}{4}$ inches and is .007 inches thick. (These dimensions correspond to our paper currency in the period of development of the punched card and so were chosen arbitrarily.) The more recent 96 column card, on the other hand, is approximately one-third the size of the 80 column card. The corners may be either sharp or rounded, depending upon the application. Generally, one corner is cut to align cards right end up (refer to Figure 7-1).

80 Column Card

The 80 column card, shown in Figure 7-1, is divided into 80 columns (numbered 1 through 80), going from left to right. Each column, in turn, is divided into 12 rows or punching positions. The punching positions, from

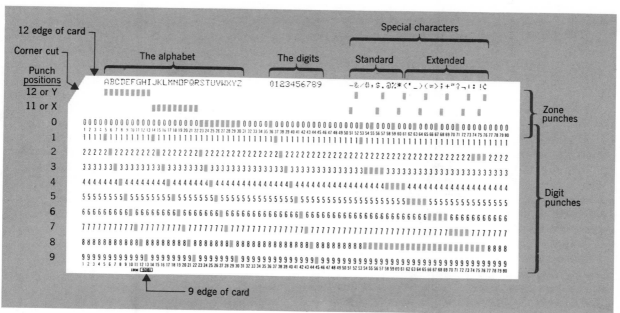

figure 7-1. 80 column punched card.

the top of the card to the bottom, are 12 or Y, 11 or X, and 0 through 9. While the top three punching positions of the card—12, 11, and 0—are the zone punches, the 0 through 9 are the digit punches. It should be noted that the zero punch position may be either a zone punch or the digit 0. The top edge of the card is called the "12 edge" and the bottom of the card is the "9 edge" while the printed position of the card is called the face. (The edge of the card is important since some computers process cards 9 edge first while others process cards 12 edge first.)

If a number or digit is to be coded, say 5, the position 5 is punched. All other numbers are punched in a like manner. For the alphabetic characters A through Z, more than one punch is required in each column. The alphabetic combinations have a logical structure, as can be seen in Figure 7-1. The first nine letters (A through I) are coded with the 12 punch and a digit. For example, the C is a combination 12 or Y punch and a digit punch 3. Likewise, the letters J through R use the 11 or X punch combined with an appropriate digit. The letters S through Z utilize the 0 punch and consecutive digits, starting with digit 2. Special characters are shown at the right-hand side of the card in Figure 7-1. They are recorded by one, two, or three punches in a column.

96 Column Card

The 96 column card can hold 16 more characters than an 80 column card (a 20% increase) and up to 128 characters can be printed on the face of the card (a 60% increase over an 80 column card). These differences for a card about one-third the size of the 80 column card are shown in Figure 7-2. Regarding the card's structure, the punching area is divided into three parts: upper half—columns 1 through 32, middle half—columns 33 through 64, and lower half—columns 65 through 96.

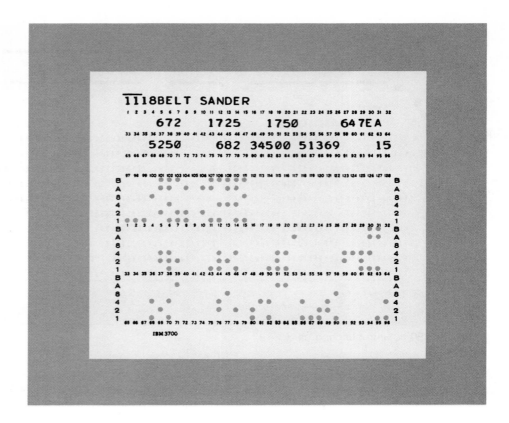

figure 7-2. 96 column punched card.

6-Bit BCD System. The method used for coding the 96 column card is the 6-bit binary coded decimal (BCD) system or B-A-8-4-2-1. The B-A combination represents the zone punches while the numerics are used for the digit punches and the alphabetics. As you will recall from Chapter 3, the BCD system is one of the most common variations of the binary system, employing only the four binary positions of 1, 2, 4, and 8. Any numeric from 0 through 9 can be represented by a combination of these four values. For example, the value 3 is a combination of binary 2 and 1 positions while the value 7 is represented by binary 4, 2, and 1 positions. In a similar manner, any alphabetic characters can be represented by a combination of zone and numeric punches. The zone or binary punches for the alphabetic characters A through I are a 1 1 combination (12 zone punch for 80 column card), J through R are a 1 0 arrangement (11 zone punch), and S through Z are a 01 combination (0 zone punch). Also, the binary numeric positions that appear for 0 to 9 are applicable again to the three sets of alphabetics (the same is true of the 80 column card). For example, a C is represented by two binary 1's for the zone positions (96 column card) versus a 12 zone punch position (80 column card) and by binary values 0 0 1 1 (value of 3) for the numeric positions (96 column card) versus a 3-digit punch position (80 column card).

data-entry equipment

Today, there are several methods for capturing data from originating documents and sources. Data-entry devices include: keypunching with a card-punch machine, keypunching to magnetic tape or disk, keyboard data-entry recording, and similar methods. Of these methods, the keypunch method has been the most widely used. However, data punching directly onto magnetic disk and tape is rapidly being used to replace key-punch machines because it saves time and expense.

Card Punch. The most common method (in the past) of converting source data into punched cards is the use of the card punch or key punch machine. Basically, the operator of this machine reads a source document and transcribes the data into punched holes by depressing the appropriate keys on the keyboard. In order for the operator to perform an efficient job during keypunching, the key punch feeds, positions, and eject cards automatically. The card punch stores two different card formats and operates in the 10 to 15 stroke per second range. Shown in Figure 7-3a is the IBM 29 Card Punch. The operation of the 29 punch is discussed in Appendix A. The use of the program unit and program codes are also covered.

Key Verifier. The most widely used verifying method for the card punch is the card verifier machine, such as the IBM 59 Card Verifier (Figure 7-3b). The verifier looks similar to the card punch, but does not punch holes. As the second operator or verifier duplicates the original card punching process by reading from the same source document and depressing the same keys (as the first key punch operator did), the card verifier compares each depressed key with the punched hole already in the card. This is accomplished by the sensing mechanism which has 12 pins rather than 12 punching dies. If the entire card is correct, then a notch is put in the extreme right-hand portion of the card between the 0 and 1 horizontal punching positions. However, if a verifier key is depressed and a difference is found between it and the card (indicates an error), the keyboard locks immediately and a red light comes on. The operator has two more chances to obtain agreement between the verifying and original keypunching. If there is none after three tries, the top of the card is automatically notched in the column of the error. This method identifies the column error so that the card punch operator can prepare a new card to replace the one punched in error. It should be noted that an error can occur at the key punch or at the key verifier.

When cards are removed from the card stacker, all correct cards that have been notched on the right-hand side can be easily identified. If not notched, the error cards will stand out. These can be removed, corrected by repunching new cards, and returned to the group after repunching and verifying.

Data Recorder. An addition to 80 column card punching is the IBM 129 Card Data Recorder, equally capable of verifying cards. Resembling the IBM 29 Card Punch, it has a memory that serves as a buffer before the cards are punched. This approach means that the operator can key data continuously while another card is being punched and stacked. Since corrections can be made before a card is punched, the entire card does not have to be repunched because of a single mistake. In addition, the 129's memory will store up to six different card formats, enabling the operator to change from one format to another without interrupting the work flow. Options include an "accumulate" feature that will total selected card fields plus a count of key strokes and cards. Having the familiar 29 keyboard, an operator does not need extensive training to use it.

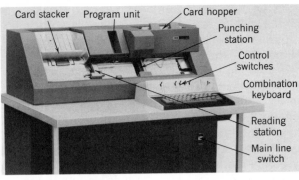

Card stacker Program unit Card hopper
Punching station
Control switches
Combination keyboard
Reading station
Main line switch

(a) IBM 29 Card Punch. (Courtesy International Business Machines Corporation.)

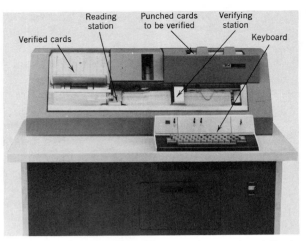

Reading station Punched cards to be verified Verifying station
Verified cards Keyboard

(b) IBM 59 Card Verifier. (Courtesy International Business Machines Corporation.)

(c) IBM 5496 Data Recorder. (Courtesy International Business Machines Corporation.)

(d) Honeywell Keytape (stand-alone unit). (Courtesy Honeywell Information Systems.)

figure 7-3. Various types of data-entry equipment.

(e) IBM 3741 single-station data-entry unit. (Courtesy International Business Machines Corporation.)

The IBM 5496 Data Recorder (Figure 7-3c) is the basic punching device for the 96 column card. Its distinguishing characteristics are: buffered storage, four control program levels, and the ability to punch directly from data written on the face of the card. Buffered storage stores the complete contents of a card image before any punching or printing takes place. This feature permits the operator to correct any known errors before the card is punched and printed as well as to increase the productivity of the operator by about 10%. Regarding the second characteristic, from one to four programs can be loaded into the Data Recorder by reading pre-punched program cards. Four program-level function keys are found on the keyboard. Programming provides control of field lengths, automatic skipping, automatic duplicating, upper/lower shifting functions, and file or word erase operations. In addition, verifying cards is a standard function of the IBM 5496 Data Recorder.

Key-to-Tape (Stand-Alone). The above punching devices are capable of handling large volumes of input. However, there is a considerable amount of time and expense involved. During the past several years, manufacturers have developed input equipment to remedy deficiencies. Among the various data-entry devices to record data directly onto magnetic tape is the Honeywell Keytape (Figure 7-3d). Some key-to-tape stand-alone devices use cassettes or cartridges as an intermediate medium, but generally data are sorted onto half-inch computer-compatible tape.

During data entry with a typical key-to-tape method, a complete record is key entered and stored before it is released to the magnetic tape. This feature simplifies and increases error correction. Errors sensed by the operator while keying data from the originating document can be corrected immediately by back-spacing in memory and keying in the correction. The same correction method is applicable to verification. Studies indicate that an operator's productivity is increased by approximately one-third over regular punching methods. These improvements in operator efficiency primarily result from quieter operation, quicker setup, and simpler verification.

Key-to-Disk. Despite the immediate benefits available for a typical keyboard to magnetic tape device discussed above, someone must gather the magnetic tapes from the many data input devices and process them on the computer for a merge and a sort operation of the input data. To overcome this processing problem, manufacturers have developed key-to-disk entry systems, one of which is the Key Processing System developed by the Computer Machinery Corporation (Figure 7-4).

A minicomputer controlled key-to-disk system is more efficient than key punches or key-to-tape machines (stand-alone). As data are entered through the keyboard, they are processed by the system's minicomputer and stored on a magnetic disk in locations appropriate to the keystation of original entry. Once recorded data are verified, completed batches can be transferred automatically from the disk onto a single reel of magnetic tape. Finally, this tape reel is the input for any computer batch-processing run. In order to visualize this system versus the keypunch and the key-to-tape (stand-alone) methods, a comparison of input data processing methods is depicted in Figure 7-5.

figure 7-4. Key-to-disk system. (Courtesy Computer Machinery Corporation.)

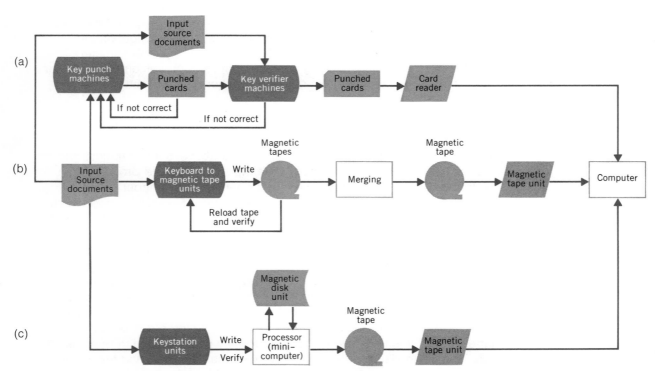

figure 7-5. Three different methods of preparing data for computer entry: (a) keypunch, (b) key-to-tape, and (c) key-to-disk.

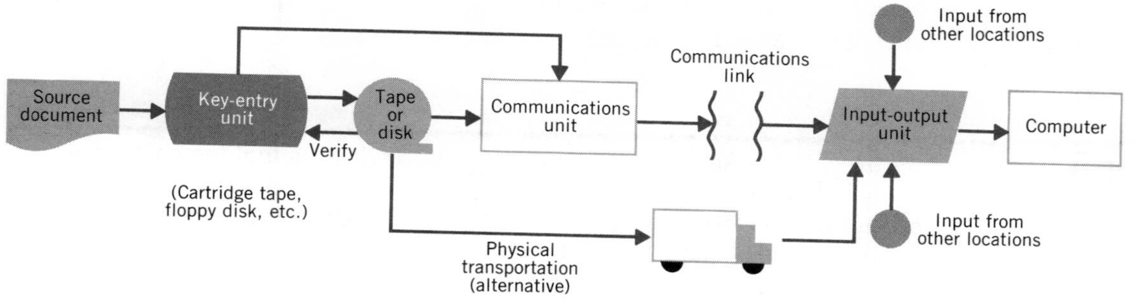

figure 7-6. Current method of preparing data for computer entry—distributed data entry.

Key-to-Floppy Disk. In addition to key-to-disk devices, there are also key-to-"floppy" disk units where data are recorded on only one side of the diskette. Illustrated in Figure 7-3e is the IBM 3741 single-station unit with a display (at left) for preparing data input as well as computer programs. The output from data-entry devices (diskette) is fed into the IBM System/370 (360) series computer through a 3540 diskette peripheral unit which simulates a card reader/punch. Additionally, there are "flippy floppys" which allow both sides of the disk to be used.

Distributed Data Entry. The current phase in data entry is toward distributed data-entry systems whereby a single or multiple data-entry units are distributed at various company locations. As illustrated in Figure 7-6, data-entry units are used to capture input data on either magnetic tape or disk which are then communicated on-line to input devices of a computer system. To speed up the process, data from the key-entry units are communicated directly to the computer for on-line processing. A slower alternative as illustrated is to transport the tapes and disks to the computer center for processing. Thus, a distributed data-entry approach brings flexibility to an organization's data-entry operations.

---

batch-oriented computer equipment

Basic data processing functions, enumerated in Chapter 3, are applicable to the individual components of a batch-oriented computer system as well as an interactive computer system. The input-storage-processing-control-output (ISPCO) cycle is associated with a computer's components as follows:

1. INPUT data are read by various *input devices*.
2. STORAGE is available as high-speed, *primary storage* for storing program instructions and data or slower *secondary storage* for storing file data.
3. PROCESSING is accomplished through the *arithmetic/logical unit*.
4. CONTROL over processing is provided by the *CPU* (central processing unit) *control unit*.
5. OUTPUT information is produced by various *output devices* (recording and printing).

These hardware components are explained in subsequent sections of the chapter for a batch-oriented computer system.

input/output devices

An essential characteristic of input/output devices is that they are connected on-line to the central processing unit. They are activated under the control of the stored program and can transmit data to or receive data from the memory unit of the central processor. Many of these devices can be utilized as both input and output devices. In addition to the standard input/output devices, there is great use of remotely located devices, such as teletype devices and visual display (CRT) units, to transmit data over conventional telephone lines to the computer. These devices are generally operated on-line. Other input devices, such as optical character recognition and transaction recorders, are capable of reading data directly into the computer. The discussion below will center around the standard input/output devices found in batch-oriented computer installations.

Buffer Storage. In order to speed up the slower input (output) computer equipment, manufacturers have developed additional features on their equipment. For example, temporary storage areas, referred to as *buffer storage,* have been added to the equipment. Their function is to store temporarily data that are read or ready to be written. Thus, when the computer is ready for data, it is provided by the high-speed buffer.

Card Readers and Punches

Punched cards are used as input and output for many computer systems. Card readers that serve as input devices vary widely in their reading rates. Reading speeds range from as low as 100 cards per minute up to 2000 cards per minute, the average speed being between 450 and 1200 cards per minute. Although this input rate seems high, the central processor is capable of processing at a much faster rate than the card reader can feed data into the system.

Operation of Card Reader. Computer card readers are either of the brush or photoelectric type. In the *brush-type reader,* cards are mechanically moved from a card hopper, through the card feed unit, and under reading brushes. The reading brushes sense the presence or absence of holes in each column of the card. This electric sensing converts the data to electrical impulses that can be utilized by the card reading unit for storing information. Some card readers have two sets of reading brushes (Figure 7-7a) whereby each card is read twice as it moves through the card feed unit. This procedure checks on the validity of the first read station. After the cards are read, they are moved from the card feed unit and selected under program control in the appropriate stacker.

The *photoelectric card reader* (Figure 7-7b), the second type, performs the same functions as the brush type, the difference being the method of sensing the holes. Photoelectric cells are activated by the presence of light. As the punched card is passed over a light source in the reader, light passing through the punched holes activates photoelectric cells (one cell for each column of the card) for recognizing and storing input data.

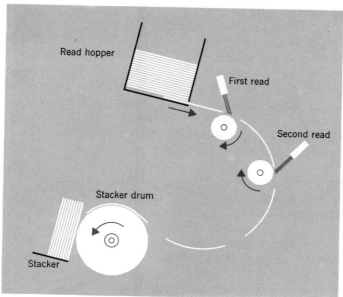

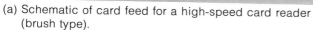

(a) Schematic of card feed for a high-speed card reader (brush type).

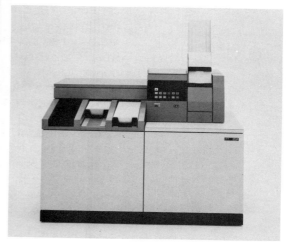

(b) IBM 3505 Card Reader.

(c) IBM 2540 Card-Read Punch.

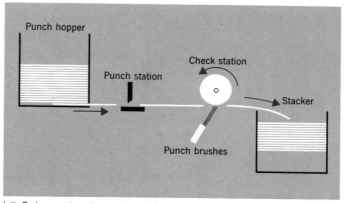

(d) Schematic of card feed for computer card punch.

figure 7-7. Read and punch units—input/output units for computer systems. (Courtesy International Business Machines Corporation.)

(e) IBM 3525 Card Punch.

Operation of Card Punch. The speed of output card devices, ranging from 60 to 500 cards per minute, is slower than that of readers, the average being between 100 to 300 cards per minute. As shown in Figure 7-7d, the card punch unit moves blank cards automatically, one at a time, from the card hopper under a punching mechanism. The data received from storage are punched into the card. The card is moved to the checking station where the data are read and checked with the information received at the punching station. The card is then selected for the appropriate output stacker. Shown in Figure 7-7e is a typical card punch, operating at a rate up to 300 cards per minute.

Combination Read-Punch Unit. A card punching machine may be combined with the card reader into one machine, shown in Figure 7-7c for the IBM System/370 series. The long extension protruding from the read unit is known as a file feed, capable of holding up to 3100 cards. This card read-punch unit, with five output stackers, is capable of reading cards at a rate of 1000 cards per minute and punching at a speed of 300 cards per minute.

Another combination read-punch unit can be found on an IBM small-scale computer system. Depending on the Model—A1 or A2—it can read 96 column cards at the rate of 250 or 500 cards per minute and punch 60 or 120 cards per minute, respectively. This Multi-Function Card Unit (MFCU) consists of two input stations, a read station, two wait stations, single punch, cornering and print stations, and four output stackers. While under the control of the central processing unit, it can perform any of the following, individually, or in various combinations: read cards from two separate card files, collate, gang punch, summary punch, reproduce, interpret, punch calculation results, replace older master cards with new or updated ones in the proper file sequence, punch a card while the previous card is being printed, and print data on a card that are not punched in the card. Thus, a series of separate operations can be consolidated and processed into one or a few computer runs.

Punched Paper Tape Readers and Punches

The paper tape reader reads data represented as punched holes in paper tape. The speed of reading ranges from 10 to as many as 2000 characters per second, depending on the type of paper tape reader. Mechanical readers can perform at speeds over 100 characters a second. For higher processing speeds, photoelectric-sensing techniques are generally employed. The tape reader moves or feeds the tape past a reading unit. The presence or absence of holes in the tape is sensed and converted to electronic impulses that are used as data by the computer system. Accuracy of reading is determined by making a parity check on each character.

Just as data can be read by a paper tape reader, data from the computer system can also be recorded as punched holes in paper tape by an automatic tape punch. Data received from main storage are converted to a tape code and punched in a blank tape as the tape is moved through a punching mechanism. Accuracy of data recorded is verified by a parity check for each character. Because of the electromechanical action usually required to produce the holes in the tape, the tape speed is approximately 300 characters a second.

figure 7-8. NCR Paper Tape Reader. (Courtesy The National Cash Register Company.)

There are many punched paper tape readers, punches, and combination units available. Figure 7-8 shows a computer operator placing a punched paper tape onto the tape reader. It should be pointed out that output is not restricted to punched paper tape only since there are paper-tape to magnetic-tape converters. Conversion to magnetic tape is obtained by photoelectric reading of the paper-tape input.

OCR Readers

Currently, there is a proliferation of optical character recognition equipment that can be connected on line to a computer system or can be used off line. Off line refers to devices not under the direct control of the computer's central processing unit. On-line and off-line equipment can be classified as follows: optical reader card punch, optical mark reader, optical journal tape reader, and optical character reader. Each piece of equipment is capable of reading one or more machine-printed or hand-printed documents of various sizes, including adding machine and cash register tapes. Likewise, the speeds of these OCR readers varies according to the technology employed.

An integral part of OCR equipment is the *scanner* whose principal function is to convert the printed input to electrical signals for analysis by the recognition unit. (The hardware that most directly affects the way data are recognized as well as the cost of the reader is the *recognition unit*.) While early OCR equipment implemented the recognition logic in hardware, newer equipment employs combinations of hardware and software. With the latter approach, the recognition logic becomes more flexible, but speed decreases and cost increases because of the addition of a minicomputer. However, speed reduction is not a critical problem because of the mechanical limitations of readers.

When an OCR device is operating in an on-line mode, it acts like a high-speed card reader. The IBM 3886 Optical Character Reader, illustrated in Figure 7-9, reads typewritten or machine-printed alphanumeric data and hand-printed numbers into the computer from a wide range of

figure 7-9. IBM 3886 Optical Character Reader. (Courtesy International Business Machines Corporation.)

pages, forms, and other documents. Since the reader operates in conjunction with an IBM System/370 computer under programmed control, the data are directed by the program to any computer-driven recording device, such as a magnetic tape unit, a high-speed printer, or a card punch. Through a distributed processing approach, an OCR reader can also be linked with other computers and peripheral devices at remote locations. Thus, OCR readers can be utilized as input devices (under computer control) for scanning turnaround documents that have been previously prepared as output by a computer system. Utility companies, mail-order houses, insurance firms, and the airlines are examples of those reaping the benefits of OCR equipment by using turnaround documents as input to their business information systems.

Magnetic Tape Units

Most computer manufacturers have a series of magnetic tape units that are compatible with their own computer lines. They differ basically in two ways: the speed in reading or writing data on tape and the data density (number of bits, digits, or characters per inch) of the tape. Regarding the tape's speed, magnetic tape has a very fast data transfer rate with speeds ranging up to about 1,250,000 characters or bytes per second for either input or output. Many tape units can read tape as they move in either direction.

Referring to the tape's data density, early recording devices placed 200 parallel characters per inch on tape. Current systems allow 6,250 bits per inch. Latest developments in serial recording provide capability for 80,000 bits per inch. This increase in capacity has been the result of improved magnetic tapes and magnetic heads, and to increased sophistication of the methods used to record and recover data.

Magnetic tape drives use magnetic tape, which is made from a very strong and durable plastic. The tape is coated with a substance that can be easily magnetized. Data are recorded on the tape surface by means of

figure 7-10. Magnetic tape—7-bit alphanumeric code.

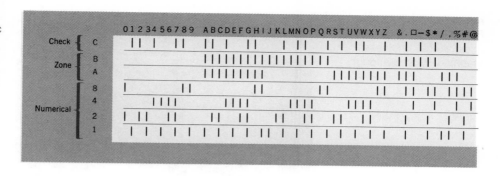

magnetized spots. As indicated in Figure 7-10, numbers, letters, and special characters can be recorded by using the 7-bit alphanumeric code. A single reel of tape is usually $\frac{1}{2}$ to 1 inch wide and 2400 feet long.

Current Magnetic Tape Units. The foregoing fundamentals of magnetic tape units apply to models on the market currently. For example, the IBM 3420 magnetic tape unit (Models 3 and 8) reads and writes data at densities up to 6,250 bits per inch on one-half inch magnetic tape. It is under the control of the 3803 control where several tape drives can be combined (Figure 7-11a). In the latest magnetic tape units, such as the IBM 8809 (Figure 7-11b), tape speed and tension are controlled electronically as opposed to control by a constant speed motor and vacuum columns.

figure 7-11. (a) IBM 3420 magnetic tape units and 3803 tape control and (b) IBM 8809 magnetic tape unit.

(a)

(b)

On-Line Printers

A most important characteristic of an on-line printer is that it produces a large amount of readable output. With very fast printing speeds currently, a computer system can literally bury a user in printed output. Generally, a print buffer holds data temporarily in storage, and thereby frees the computer for other processing while the line is being printed. Vertical spacing is basically under program control or punched tape loop.

On-line printers are capable of printing cards in addition to continuous paper forms. Shown in Figure 7-12 is the IBM 1404 Printer Model 2 which can print continuous paper forms at a speed of 600 lines per minute or print cards at a maximum rate of 800 cards per minute. In the area of very

figure 7-12. IBM 1404 Printer Model 2. (Courtesy International Business Machines Corporation.)

fast on-line printers, the IBM 3800 Printing Subsystem can print as high as 13,360 lines per minute.

Impact Printers. Many of the on-line printers are impact printers; that is, they print by pressing the paper and ribbon against the proper type as it passes in front of the paper. For each print cycle, all the characters in the print set move past each printing position and a magnetically actuated hammer presses the paper against an inked ribbon at the instant the selected character is in position.

Impact printers go beyond furnishing the user with readable output. They are utilized for printing data on cards and forms that are designed to be returned by the sender, known as turnaround documents (mentioned previously for OCR readers). Upon return, documents can be batched and fed into optical character recognition equipment. The data, in turn, can be read directly into a computer system or recorded on some magnetic storage medium.

Nonimpact Printers. Much faster printing, up to 18,000 lines per minute, can be attained by use of nonimpact printers. Some of these printers produce an image by electrical charges that are transferred to the paper for a visual record. Even though these devices are much faster than the impact printers, they are not capable of producing simultaneous multiple copies.

Console Devices

Practically every computer system has a visual display or typewriter device (cable connected to the system) that permits some form of manual entry into, and control over, the central processor. The keyboard (Figure 7-13) allows the operator to instruct the computer and, in turn, the computer reports back in visual form the specific data requested. The visual display unit can receive data sent under computer control in response to programmed instructions. Its input speed is dependent upon the ability

figure 7-13. Visual display console (3278-2A) with printer that allows the operator to interact directly with the IBM 4331 and 4341 processors via a keyboard. (Courtesy Internation Business Machines Corporation.)

of the computer operator while output is limited by the capabilities of the equipment.

Other Input/Output Devices

There are many other important input/output devices available to batch-oriented computer systems. They include: transaction recorders, voice response systems, graph plotters, and display systems.

Transaction Recorders. Point of origin transaction recorders can be operated off-line or on-line. In an on-line mode, the transaction recorder transmits data directly to a computer system. This permits updating available airline seats, account balances, payroll records, inventory records, and similar items that must be maintained on a current basis. While some transaction recorders come equipped with slots for inserting fixed input data and entering variable data by keys, dials, or levers, others have only a keyboard for entering input data (Figure 7-14).

Voice Response Systems. A somewhat similar terminal communication device is the voice response system. This system consists of a message handling unit, a number of touch-tone telephone units, and standard telephone lines for an on-line mode. The audio response unit has a vocabulary tailored to the user's needs. A major advantage of a voice response system is the quick-verbal response from a computer system by means of remotely located and multipurpose telephone terminals.

figure 7-14. IBM 1062 Teller Terminal used to transmit transaction data. (Courtesy International Business Machines Corporation.)

figure 7-15. Cal Comp Model 1012 Drum Plotter. (Courtesy California Computer Products, Inc.)

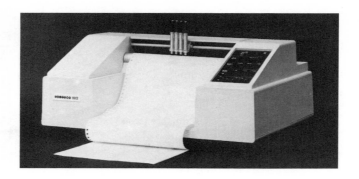

Graph Plotters. Automatic graph plotters (Figure 7-15) are utilized where graphic or pictorial presentation of computer data are meaningful and easier to use than extensive alphabetic or numeric listings. They are indispensable for output when the volume of graphic presentation makes it uneconomical or impossible to perform the task manually. Generally, there is some restriction on format; however a pictorial representation may include any desired combination of axes, lines, letters, and symbols with an unlimited choice of scale factors, letter and symbol sizes, and printing angles.

Display Systems. A display unit that is capable of on-line displaying, updating, and manipulating drawings and alphanumeric data is found in Figure 7-16. This IBM 3278 Display System also can be used as a system operator console, which substantially reduces the time needed for transferring messages between the operator and the system. Specific applications include the display of engineering drawings and the display of intermediate and/or final results of scientific calculations in the form of curves, plotted points, bar graphs, or symbols. The display unit can be individually addressed by X and Y coordinates.

The light pen, as illustrated in Figure 7-16 enables the operator to identify a particular point, line, or character in the displayed image to the

figure 7-16. IBM 3278 Display System with the optional Selector Light Pen. (Courtesy International Business Machines Corporation.)

program. The operator moves the penpoint to the part of the image the individual wants to identify. The photodetector associated with the pen, sensing light at that point, generates a signal for the program. The light pen can be used alone or in conjunction with a keyboard to rearrange or delete information, or to add lines from a base point already lighted by the CRT beam.

central processing unit

The central processing unit contains the memory or primary storage, the arithmetic/logical unit, and the CPU control unit. Primary storage and the CPU control unit may be in the same or separate housing unit, depending on the computer system. Some CPU's have a control console as a part of the unit itself while other central processors have a separate console with a visual display device (Figure 7-17).

Advancements in computer design and programming has reduced the need to utilize the console in computer processing. Some of the functions once required of the computer operator are now contained in the system's circuitry and components, or are a part of the program itself. These improvements result in less set up time and running time when processing a specific computer program.

figure 7-17. IBM Model 3032 central processing unit with attached visual CRT devices. (Courtesy International Business Machines Corporation.)

primary storage devices

Memory devices that are in integral part of the central processing unit must be capable of moving data at extremely fast rates. Early computers made great use of magnetic drums that operated in the millisecond (1/1,000 of a second) range. Magnetic core and large-scale integration (LSI) now operate at microsecond (1/1,000,000 of a second) and nanosecond (1/1,000,000,000 of a second) speeds. Faster memory devices currently under development will make it possible to operate in picoseconds (1/1,000,000,000,000 of a second), making internal processing speeds even faster. Each time there is an increase in operating speeds, the computer becomes even more input or output bound, depending upon the speed of the slowest unit. Thus the speeds of internal memory devices are not always the basis for selecting a particular computer for business and industrial applications. Consideration must be given to the throughput ability of the computer system.

the punched card:
• 80 column card—punching positions from top of the card to the bottom are 12 or Y, 11 or X, and 0 through 9 for digits, alphabetics, and special characters.
• 96 column card—punching positions from top of the card to the bottom are divided into three parts—upper half, columns 1–32; middle half, columns 33–64; and lower half, columns 65–96. The 6-bit binary coded: decimal (BCD) system is used.

data-entry equipment:
• card punch—most common method in the past for converting source data into punched card.
• key verifier—most widely used verifying method for the card punch.
• data recorder—resembles the card punch but has a memory that serves as a buffer before the card is punched.
• key-to-tape (stand-alone)—allows a complete record to be key entered and stored before it is released to magnetic tape.
• key-to-disk—permits data to be recorded on magnetic disk and verified before transferring completed batches to magnetic tape.
• key-to-floppy disk—allows data to be recorded on diskettes.

input/output devices:
• card readers and punches—speeds range from 100 cards per minute up to 2000 cards per minute. Current trend is to combine reading with punching into one device.
• punched paper tape readers and punches—speeds range from 10 to as many as 2000 characters per second. These can be combination units.
• OCR readers—speeds vary according to the type of equipment. They are utilized for scanning turnaround documents in an on-line or off-line mode.
• magnetic tape units—speeds of transfer rates range up to 1,250,000 characters or bytes per second for either input or output. Tape density can be as high as 6,250 bits per inch.
• on-line printers—speeds can be from several hundred lines per minute up to 18,000 lines a minute. The user's needs determine what printer is best.
• console devices—input speeds are dependent upon the ability of the computer operator. They permit some form of manual entry into and control over the central processor.
• transaction recorders—input speeds are dependent on the ability of the operator.
• voice response systems—speeds are the same as for normal speech.
• graph plotters—speeds vary according to the type of equipment employed.
• display systems—speeds vary according to the type system used.

**first self-study
exercise
of chapter 7**

True-False:

1. (   ) The most popular size for the punched card is 90 columns.
2. (   ) For an 80-column card, an E is represented by a 12 punch and a digit 5 punch.
3. (   ) The 96-column card uses the EBCDIC system.
4. (   ) The keypunch method was the most widely used one for capturing source data.
5. (   ) A key-to-disk system is slower than the traditional key punch method.
6. (   ) The ISPCO cycle concept is applicable to input/output devices only.
7. (   ) The function of buffer storage for key punch units is to store data temporarily.
8. (   ) A punched paper reader is a much faster form of input than magnetic tape.
9. (   ) Nonimpact printers are faster than impact printers.
10. (   ) Generally, a display system is capable of being used as a system operator console.

Fill-In:

11. Each vertical column in an 80-column card contains twelve punching positions. The top three punching positions or 12, 11, and 0 of the card are the _____ punches while 0 through 9 are the _____ punches.
12. _____ _____ punches 12 and 8 in any one vertical column of an 80-column card indicate the letter H.
13. Up to 128 characters can be printed on the face of a _____ _____ card. The 6-bit _____ _____ _____ system is the method of coding data.
14. Basically, card readers used in a computer system are of the _____ type or employ _____ cells for reading data.
15. Card readers and punches can be stand-alone units. However, the trend is toward combining the _____ and _____ functions into one unit.
16. The basic problem of _____ _____ input and output for computer systems is their slow rate of speed.
17. _____ _____ provides a much faster input and output transfer rate than card or punched paper tape.
18. A _____ coded pattern of 0 and 1 bits is utilized for reading and writing data onto magnetic tape.
19. High-speed computer printers can be classified as _____ and _____.
20. _____ _____ systems are capable of giving quick verbal responses to its users from remote locations.

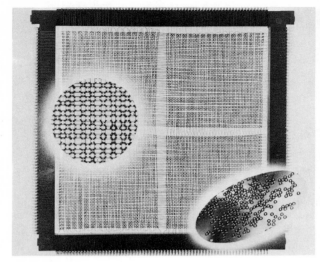

(a) Magnetic core plane.

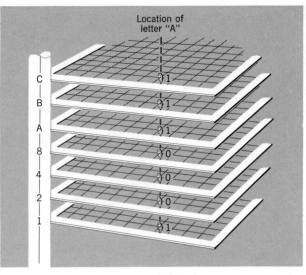

(b) A core stack showing the BCD character representation for the letter A.

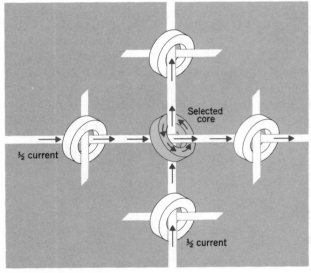

(c) Selecting a core.

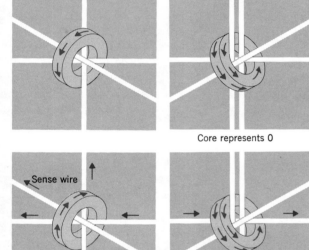

(d) Core sense wire.   (e) Core inhibit wire.

figure 7-18. Magnetic core—a type of primary storage.

Magnetic Core

A magnetic core is molded from a ferrite powder into a doughnut shape comparable to the size of a pin head. These tiny cores are, in turn, strung on wires in much the same manner as beads on a necklace in order to form a core plane (Figure 7-18a). Several core planes are stacked on top of one another to form a core stack (Figure 7-18b). Many thousands or millions of cores are used in main storage, depending upon the size of the computer's memory.

A core can be easily magnetized in a few millionths of a second and it retains its magnetism indefinitely. When a strong enough electrical current is sent through the wire, the core becomes magnetized. The direction of current determines the magnetic state of the core. Reversing the direction of current changes the magnetic state. The two states can represent on or off, plus or minus, yes or no, 0 or 1.

Selecting a Core. Two wires run through each core at right angles to each other. When half the current needed to magnetize a core is sent through each of the two wires, only the core at the intersection of the wire is magnetized, as illustrated in Figure 7-18c. No other core in the string is affected. Even though there are a large number of cores strung on a screen of wires, a single core can be selected for storage without affecting the others.

A third wire, called a sense wire, runs through each core and is needed to read back the stored information (Figure 7-18d). This wire is used to detect the small current created when an electric pulse reverses the polarity of a core. It can be determined from the current whether the core was originally positive or negative. When a core is read by reversal of its polarity, the act of reversing the original positive or negative state of the core destroys the information stored in it. This is referred to as a "destructive read out," that is, all 0's are changed to 1's. To overcome this destructive read out, there is an automatic resetting of cores after they have been read out. The computer attempts to put 1's into all previously read positions even though some of them may have been 0's. A fourth wire, called an inhibit wire, is run through each core to prevent the writings of 1's into those positions that previously contained 0's before they were read (Figure 7-18e). The net result of the four wires passing through each core is a nondestructive read out, but destructive read in.

Large-scale Integration (LSI)

Large-scale integration (LSI), sometimes called monolithic integrated circuits, has two basic approaches. One employs *biopolar integrated circuit techniques.* The other uses *metal oxide semiconductor* (MOS) *techniques.*

Characteristics of LSI. The bipolar techniques are favored since their speeds give them an edge over MOS circuitry in main memory units of large scale and scientific computers. However, their circuits use more current; hence, they heat up more. MOS can compete with bipolar in the newer desk-top electronic calculators and in mini- to medium-scale computers where nanosecond speeds seldom are necessary. These were the key factors in IBM's decision to use MOS/LSI or MST (monolithic system technology) circuitry for the entire main memory of its small- to medium-scale System/370 Models.

MOS circuits are complex, precision-etched silicon slivers encased in metal, plastic, or ceramic. Some are the size of aspirin tablets, others as big as matchbooks. More important, while bipolar devices operate at higher speeds, MOS utilizes less power which means its components can be crowded more compactly onto the silicon before a critical heat problem arises. Thus, their great attraction is their size.

As indicated, MOS circuitry is used in minicomputers. For the IBM 5110 Portable Computer (discussed and illustrated in Chapter 9),

figure 7-19. MOSFET (Metal-Oxide Semiconductor Field-Effect Transistor) technology with ROS (Read-Only Storage) chips is used in the IBM 5110 Portable Computer —minicomputer illustrated in Chapter 9. (Courtesy International Business Machines Corporation.)

MOSFET (Metal-Oxide Semiconductor Field-Effect Transistor) technology is employed. Its ROS (read-only storage) chips are .23-inch square, containing 48K bits; they are shown in Figure 7-19.

Latest Primary Storage Technology

The latest technology employed for primary storage is the 64K-bit chip (IK = 1024 bits) which is a convenient shorthand for referring to the chip's density. Actually, 65,536 bits or binary digits of information can be stored on a $\frac{1}{4}$-inch square. Packaging density comes to a quarter-million bits when four of the 64K chips are mounted on a module 2.5 centimeters (one inch) square. What this means is that a large processor memory can be housed in a very small space. Additionally, the larger the central processor, the fewer times data from a piece of peripheral equipment has to be transferred into primary storage.

The 64K-bit random access memory (RAM) chip is illustrated in Figure 7-20. Notice how small its size is when compared to a coin. The new chips allow fabrication of modules with different density and performance ranges containing up to 512K bits. For example, when compared to IBM's previous main memory modules, the new modules provide up to 32 times improvement in module density. Overall, the objective of this new processor technology is to provide high-density memory chips that have high performance characteristics, are small in size, are simple in process, and can be mass produced and sold at low cost.

figure 7-20. 64K-bit chip used for primary storage of current computer systems, such as the IBM Models 4331 and 4341. (Courtesy International Business Machines Corporation.)

Internal Operating Speeds

Core memories have cycle times over 500 nanoseconds; they have a minimum cycle time potential of approximately 350 nanoseconds. On the other hand, integrated circuits or large-scale integration seem to have an average time under 150 (about 120 nanoseconds), the minimum cycle time being below 50 nanoseconds. These present speeds are truly remarkable when compared to older computers.

A more realistic approach in measuring internal operating speeds is to think in terms of "throughput performance" rather than in nanoseconds. Of great importance to the user is the number of instructions that can be performed within a certain period of time. The new benchmark for computer measurement is mips (million instructions per second). Currently, super-computers operate at the rate of approximately 6 to 15 mips. Other more advanced systems are operating between 100 million and 900 million instructions per second.

secondary storage devices

The need for fast access storage, which serves as an extension of the computer's primary storage, has resulted in the development of several mass data files. Secondary (auxiliary) storage devices have the capability of storing data in either sequential or random sequence, depending on the type of storage unit. Their design is such that they may be directly accessed by the computer for use within the central processing unit. Data in secondary storage are not as accessible as information in primary storage since they must be routed through memory first before calculation and manipulation can occur.

Magnetic tape, one of the input/output devices described previously, can also serve as auxiliary storage devices. Applications, however, are limited for this storage device. The more universally used storage units currently are magnetic disks and magnetic drums. A more recent addition to this listing is the mass memory system. Only these most popular secondary devices are discussed.

Magnetic Disk

The magnetic disk, similar to a phonograph record, is coated on both sides with a ferrous oxide recording material. Information is recorded as magnetized spots on each side of the disk. On an IBM 2316, six magnetic

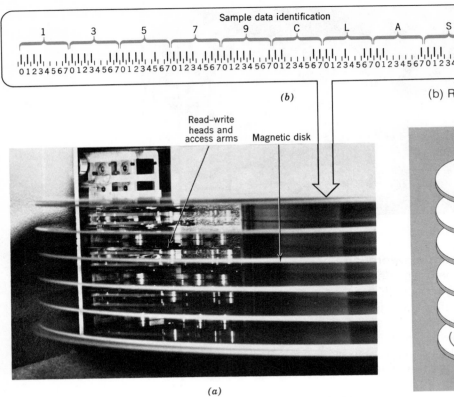

(b)

(b) Representation of data on disk.

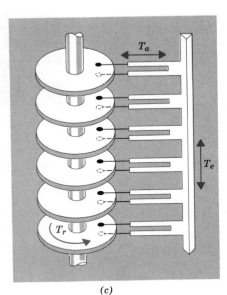

(a) Closeup picture of an IBM 2316 removable disk pack (utilizes six magnetic disks).

(c)

(c) Access motion time (T_a) and rotational delay time (T_r) to disk storage.

figure 7-21. Magnetic disk—a type of secondary storage. (Courtesy International Business Machines Corporation.)

(d) IBM 3344 Direct Access Storage Device

(e) IBM 3330 Disk Storage
   Factility and 3830
   Storage Control Unit.

(f) IBM 3370 Direct Ac-
   cess Storage Drive
   (DASD).

disks are mounted together as one unit, commonly referred to as a disk
pack (Figure 7-21a). The disk pack can be easily removed from the magnetic disk unit and be replaced with a new disk pack. This has made
disks very much like magnetic tapes.

Rather than storing data by columns of characters, they are recorded
serially bit-by-bit, eight bits per byte along a track. In Figure 7-21b, data
are stored serially, using the extended binary coded decimal interchange code (EBCDIC). The absence of parity bits in the illustration should
be noted. The technique of checking for parity in each byte is generally not
used with direct access devices.

Operation of Magnetic Disk. As shown in Figure 7-21a, enough space
is available between each disk to permit access arms to move in and
read or record data. Access arms generally have two read/write heads
for retrieving or recording on either side of a disk. To read or write data,
an access arm must be positioned on the disk over the desired location.
The arm moves in and out to locate the correct storage location. If there
is no arm for each magnetic disk, the arm must move out from the stack
of disks and up or down to the correct disk (shown as T_e in Figure 7-21c).
As might be expected, the greater the number of heads, the faster the
data may be. read or written.

Figure 7-21c depicts a simplified, single-module storage with one comb-like access mechanism. Access to one specific track on a given recording surface is accomplished by the lateral movement of the whole access mechanism from a current track location. The time required for this movement is called access motion time (T_a) and is related to the lateral distance the arm moves. In addition to access motion time, there is another timing factor, known as rotational delay time (T_r). Rotational delay time is the time required for the disk to position the desired record at the selected read/write head. Maximum rotational delay time is slightly more than the time required for one full revolution, average rotational delay time being one-half the maximum. Typical disk speed is 1800 revolutions per minute. The selection of the proper read/write head is performed simultaneously with access motion time. This is performed electronically and the time is negligible. Total data search time for disk storage includes the access time and rotational delay time.

Data are addressed on the disks by the disk number, the sector on the disk, and the track number on the IBM 2316. The disks, numbered consecutively from bottom to top, are assigned sectors on each side. Generally, they are assigned sector addresses 0 through 4 for the top side and 5 through 9 for the bottom of the disk. There are 200 tracks of recorded data on each side of the disk, having addresses 000 through 199. In some disk files, record lengths may be flexible enough to allow recording variable lengths of data records. As pointed out in Chapter 3, the advantage of variable record length capability is the more efficient use of storage space. Thus, the number of characters available per sector for each track varies with the density of the data stored.

Essential Features of Magnetic Disk. The storage capacity of magnetic disk packs varies; some have the ability to store many millions of characters of information. Even though access time is restricted to the revolving action of disks and the arm movements, the average search time for newer equipment (such as the IBM 3344 in Figure 7-21d) is about 25 milliseconds while the average rotational delay is about 10.1 milliseconds. The speed for the data transfer rate can be as high as 885,000 bytes per second, once the data are located by the read/write head.

Advantages of Magnetic Disk. An important characteristic of the disk is that an item of data is as quickly obtainable as any other. It is possible to skip over unwanted data. This is a decided advantage over magnetic tape as is the ability to process transactions without sorting the data previously. Also, several different but related data may be stored on disk files, thereby allowing a transaction to be processed against these files at the same time. For example, a customer order can be processed on line against the following magnetic disk files: credit check, inventory, accounts receivable, and sales analysis. In essence, disk is best for random access operations where input data are not arranged in any particular sequence before they are written on the disk. This direct accessibility feature plus its vast storage ability and relatively fast transfer rate have made them widely used in computer systems.

Current Magnetic Disk Units. Current multiple magnetic disk units include the IBM 3330 Disk Storage Facility (Figure 7-21e), which has a maximum storage capacity of 800 million bytes. It features modular con-

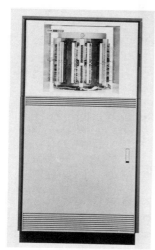

figure 7-22 IBM 2301 Drum Storage (utilizes the 2820 Storage Control Unit). (Courtesy International Business Machines Corporation.)

struction, allowing users to configure up to four dual disk modules as their requirements expand. In addition to the removable disks, there are fixed magnetic disks which cannot be removed. Designed for environments where data integrity is very critical, the sealed magnetic disk units have a large storage capacity. Since the heads do not move from track to track, as in moving-head units, these drives average access times of about 8.5 milliseconds. The fixed 3370 Direct Access Storage Device (DASD) pictured in Figure 7-21f has a maximum storage capacity of 571.3 megabytes per drive.

Magnetic Drum

In the earlier days of computers, magnetic drums were the basic means of primary storage. Today, they are used as on-line storage devices where fast access to secondary storage is required. Basically, a magnetic drum is a cylinder with a magnetized outer surface. The size of the drum limits the quantity of information that can be stored. Some magnetic drum units are capable of storing several million characters of data. The IBM 2301 Drum Storage (Figure 7-22), which utilizes the 2820 Storage Control Unit, can store to 4,100,000 bytes or 8,200,000 digits. The data transfer rate to and from the central processor may be up to 1,200,000 bytes per second or 2,400,000 digits per second while the rotational delay to a specific part of the track ranges from 0 to 17.5 milliseconds, averaging 8.6 milliseconds.

Operation of Magnetic Drum. Data are normally represented in standard binary coded decimal form, as depicted in Figure 7-23. Storage is in the form of invisible tracks around the cylinder as noted above. Each track is divided into sections which are, in turn, subdivided into character locations. The number of tracks, sections, and characters depends upon the size of the magnetic drum. As the drum rotates at a very fast speed, data are recorded or sensed by a set of read/write heads. These heads are close enough to the surface of the drum to magnetize it and to sense the magnetization on it.

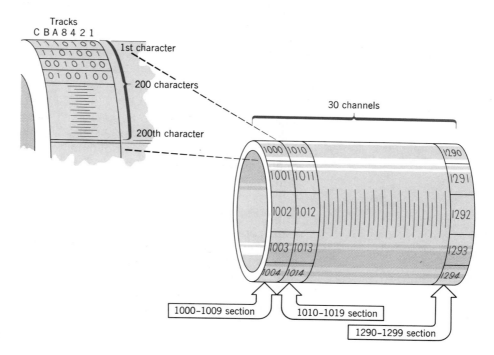

figure 7-23. Schematic for a typical drum storage.

**second summary
of chapter 7**

central processing unit:
The central processing unit contains the memory (primary storage), the arithmetic/logical unit, and the CPU control unit.

primary storage devices:
• magnetic core—molded from a ferrite powder into a doughnut shape, comparable to the size of a pin head. These tiny cores are, in turn, strung on wires to form a core plane. Several core planes are stacked on top of one another to form a core stack.

• large-scale integration (LSI)—microscopic elements that employ bipolar integrated circuit techniques or metal oxide semiconductor (MOS) techniques.

• latest primary storage technology—65,536 bits or binary digits of information can be stored on a 64K-bit chip (a $\frac{1}{4}$-inch square).

• operating speeds of primary storage devices:
  • millisecond (one thousandth of a second)—early computers operated in this range
  • microsecond (one millionth of a second)—magnetic core and large-scale integration memories operate in this range
  • nanosecond (one billionth of a second)—newer magnetic core and large-scale integration memories operate in this range
  • picosecond (one trillionth of a second)—memory devices under development operate in this range

• consideration for selecting a computer—internal memory speeds are not always the basis for selecting a particular computer for business. Rather, consideration must be given to the throughput ability of the computer system.

secondary storage devices:
• magnetic disk—speeds in terms of data transfer rates can be as high as 885,000 bytes per second while the average search time is about 25 milliseconds and the average rotational delay is about 10.1 milliseconds. Magnetic disk has the ability to process transactions without sorting the data previously—a decided advantage over magnetic tape. This direct accessibility feature plus its vast storage ability and relatively fast transfer rate have made them widely used in computer systems.

• magnetic drum—speeds in terms of data transfer rates can be as high as 1,200,000 bytes per second or 2,400,000 digits per second while the rotational delay to a specific part of the track averages 8.6 milliseconds. Magnetic drum, like magnetic disk, is used where fast access to secondary storage is required. However, magnetic drum cannot be removed physically from the storage unit. Hence, its storage capacity is more limited when compared to magnetic disk.

• mass storage system—a typical system holds 2000 tape cartridges which provide up to 16 billion characters of stored data—equivalent to about 6,400 tape reels or 200 disk packs.

second self-study exercise of chapter 7

True-False:

1. ( ) The central processing unit contains primary and secondary storage only.
2. ( ) Primary storage devices are the same thing as secondary storage devices.
3. ( ) Magnetic core memories are slower than LSI (large-scale integration) memories.
4. ( ) Currently, nanoseconds represent the fastest internal processing speeds of primary storage.
5. ( ) A recommended approach to measuring computer performance is the level of throughput performance.
6. ( ) Magnetic disk has the ability to process transactions without sorting the data initially.
7. ( ) Magnetic disk storage is used mostly for primary storage.
8. ( ) A common method of storing data on magnetic disk is to use the EBCDIC system.
9. ( ) Access motion time is the time required for the disk to position the desired record.
10. ( ) The operation of the read/write heads for magnetic drum is similar to magnetic tape.

Fill-In:

11. The computer's _____ _____ is a means of interacting with the computer during processing.
12. A very popular method of interacting with the computer via a paperless printout is with a _____ unit.
13. Primary storage devices that have been and are widely used for computers include magnetic _____ and _____.
14. A _____ _____, comparable to the size of a pin head, is molded from a ferrite powder into a doughnut shape.
15. Each core has four wires passing through it, making it capable of _____ read-out, but _____ read-in.
16. LSI (large-scale integration), sometimes called monolithic _____ _____, employ _____ and _____ techniques.
17. MOS (metal-oxide semiconductor) circuits have important advantages over prior circuits. They are faster, lower cost, more _____, and smaller.
18. The benchmark for measuring "throughput performance" today is _____.
19. _____ _____, which is similar in appearance to a phonograph record, makes it possible to skip over unwanted data.
20. _____ _____ is a cylinder with a magnetic outer surface that is used for secondary storage.

Essentially, the operation of the read/write heads is similar to magnetic tape. Spots are magnetized by sending pulses of current through the write coil. The polarity of a spot is determined by the direction of the current flow. In effect, magnetized spots can be read as either 0 or 1, depending upon their polarity.

Mass Storage System

Mass storage systems provide large secondary storage capabilities. Such systems provide significant improvements in operating efficiency and enhanced data security features over conventional computer tape libraries. For example, the CDC 38500 Mass Storage System (Figure 7-24) holds 2000 magnetic tape cartridges where each cartridge has a data storage capacity of 8 million bytes of on-line data. The system provides a maximum of 16 billion characters of stored data. System capacity is equivalent to approximately 6400 average tape reels or 200 disk packs.

The mass storage system may be under the control of up to four (IBM System/370) computers. Likewise, it operates through a data-staging technology, i.e., information is transmitted to intermediate disk storage devices for subsequent computer processing. Overall, such a system has the capability to meet the storage requirements of large computer installations.

figure 7-24. CDC Model 38500 Mass Storage System. (Courtesy Control Data Corporation.)

---

summary

After having explored the punched card and the various types of data-entry equipment, the basic components of batch-oriented computer systems were presented. These included input/output devices, central processing unit, primary storage, and secondary storage devices. Additional components will be described in the next chapter for time sharing computer systems. Although these components represent the *hardware* of a computer system, there are three other important elements in computerized business information systems. These are *software* (programming), procedures, and personnel which are the end result of a feasibility study. Each of these elements will be explored in subsequent chapters, i.e., Parts Five and Six.

---

questions

1. How do punch codes for the 80 and 96 column cards differ?
2. What are the essential differences between a key punch and a key verifier?

3. What are the important differences among the key-punch method, key-to-tape method, and key-to-disk method?

4. What is current trend in data entry? Support your viewpoint.

5. a. Describe at least four types of computer input.
   b. Describe at least four types of computer output.

6. How essential is an on-line printer and card punch in every computer installation? Explain.

7. Contrast the similarities and differences between a magnetic core and a large scale integration (LSI) memory.

8. What are the advantages and disadvantages of magnetic disk and magnetic drum as secondary storage devices?

---

answers to first self-study exercise

1. F 2. T 3. F 4. T 5. F 6. F 7. T 8. F 9. T 10. T 11. zone and digit 12. Hollerith code 13. 96-column and binary coded decimal 14. brush and photoelectric 15. read and punch 16. punched card 17. magnetic tape 18. binary 19. impact and nonimpact 20. voice response

---

answers to second self-study exercise

1. F 2. F 3. T 4. F 5. T 6. T 7. F 8. T 9. F 10. T 11. console device 12. CRT 13. core and LSI 14. magnetic core 15. nondestructive and destructive 16. integrated circuits, bipolar and MOS 17. reliable 18. mips 19. magnetic disk 20. magnetic drum

chapter eight interactive-oriented computer equipment

Although computerized batch processing procedures are utilized in processing the bills of Joe and Claudia Cosgrove (as described in the previous chapter), there is a different processing approach, that is, an interactive one, used when they shop for groceries. As they move through the aisles of their favorite supermarket, their selections are aided by computer-generated unit price information. At the checkout counter, a clerk moves the purchased items over a small electronic reader, making sure that the preprinted product code is in the proper position for reading. The product code identifies the brand as well as the size of the package. Once read, this product code information is sent to the store's computer where the current price of the item is found and stored temporarily.

After all purchases have been scanned, the clerk depresses a button and a detailed list of all purchases stored by the computer are printed. In turn, Joe presents his bank charge card which is inserted into a small card reader, similar to that used on a 24-hour bank teller. Almost instantaneously, funds are transferred from Joe's and Claudia's checking account to that of the supermarket. This interactive processing mode for buying and paying for groceries is quite different from that used in a batch processing mode for processing monthly bills.

After initially exploring the area of data communications and related channels, services, and equipment, the chapter focuses on interactive processing in a time-sharing mode, particularly, equipment currently available. Fundamentally, time sharing refers to a computer that is shared by many users through a number of input/output terminals. Although some of the time-sharing terminals may be close enough to use direct cable connections, others may not. This means that a typical time-sharing system may rely heavily upon a data communication system for linking its terminals to a minicomputer or computer.

data communications

In the past, the telephone has been utilized to transmit data for business purposes. Today, it has assumed a new role—one of linking people and machines in order that timely data can be received and sent as a by-product of a business information system. The growth of data communications is reflected by the number of data sets in the A.T.&T. system. The merging of high-speed electrical communications with DP has resulted in a data communication system which enables an organization to operate as if it is under one roof when, in reality, it is not.

Data communications, sometimes called *telecommunications* or *teleprocessing,* is an integral part of business information systems. Without data communication capabilities, time sharing would not have been possible. Its importance will be evident in the following sections.

Importance of Data Communications
The real importance of data communications lies in the time factor. Instead of waiting long periods for other means of communications, such as air mail and special delivery, data can be communicated by electrical transmission in a matter of seconds or minutes. This time reduction can mean more effective controlling of an organization's activities. The information received now as opposed to tomorrow or the next several days can be

figure 8-1. Data communications should be used up to a point where the value from the immediate movement of information is greater than its cost.

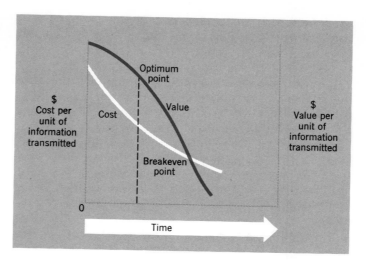

figure 8-2. The net benefit in dollars derived from information transmitted changes over time.

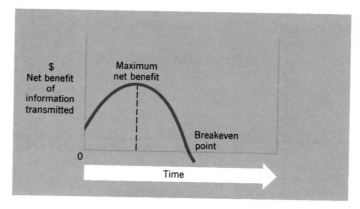

used to change existing conditions when subsequent action will have been too late. Data communications should be utilized up to a point where the value of the immediate movement of information is greater than its cost (Figure 8-1). Also, the net benefit in dollars derived from information transmitted changes rather significantly as the time factor increases (Figure 8-2). In the final analysis, the timeliness of information transmitted is of vital importance to an organization.

Links Data Processing Operations Together. Since data communications are capable of providing timely information, they have and will continue to have an important role in keeping an organization in touch with its own regions, divisions, and plants as well as with its customers and suppliers. Many times, data communications can help to reduce an organization's overall costs since billing, inventory, purchasing, payroll, and similar functions can be handled more efficiently on a centralized basis. By means of a data collection system, business data can be communicated to and processed by a central facility. Likewise, data communications can be used effectively in *distributed processing* which is an alternative to central processing of DP activities. Although most business applications can be handled by minicomputers and small general-purpose computers locally; nevertheless, data communications does provide a means for forwarding summary and critical information to the central processing center. Thus, data communications play a valuable role in linking DDP operations together.

Makes On-Line Inquiry Processing Possible. Data communication systems are an important part of inquiry processing. Essentially, inquiries are sent to the computer from an inquiry device connected via communication lines. After the data have been processed, the data are transmitted back to the inquiring terminal. Examples of organizations using on-line inquiry processing are airlines, banks, brokerage houses, hotels, and savings associations. Another example is a sales inquiry which automatically updates the inventory if merchandise can be shipped or initiates a production order if stock is not available.

Facilitates Computer Load Balancing. In a data communication network, a central computer facility is linked and accessed by a number of local and remote terminals that are capable of input and output. In a similar approach, two or more computers, not in the same location, are connected for the transmission of data in order to smooth out workloads. If one (or more) computer is overloaded, jobs on the one can be transmitted to another if time is available. Thus, computer load balancing can be a very important part of data communications.

data communication channels

When data are sent by a transmitting station to a receiving station, the latter must be in synchronization with the former. This is necessary in order that the signals be received correctly. If the receiving station does not begin at the proper point or does not maintain the identical time interval of the sending terminal, the coded pulses will not be interpreted correctly. In view of these difficulties, several techniques have been devised to keep the sending and receiving terminals in step, the more common ones are *synchronous transmission* and *start/stop synchronization*. The synchronous or bit stream method keeps the receiving station in step with the transmitting device by means of a special timing circuit. This method insures that the data are synchronized for both receiving and transmitting stations. With the start/stop method, a start signal is sent initially and a stop signal at the end of the data transmission. This method allows the irregular transmission of data, but requires extra bits to act as start and stop signals.

Data communication channels or *circuits* are divided into three basic types. These are:

1. simplex,
2. half-duplex,
3. full-duplex.

The *simplex* channel allows one-way transmission of data while the *half-duplex* channel can carry information in both directions, but permits the transmission of data in only one direction at a time. A remote receive-only device is an example of a simplex data communication channel. On the other hand, a remote send-receive unit is one for use in a half-duplex data communication channel. The last major mode of operation for communication facilities is the *full duplex* which has the ability to transmit information in both directions simultaneously.

A variety of channels for data transmission are available from the telephone companies. When consideration is given to designing an effective data communication system, the capacity of the channel should match the speed capabilities of the equipment associated with it. Data processing equipment speeds in bits per second range from slow (i.e., typewriter) to very high (i.e., central processing unit). Thus, there is a wide range of operating speeds.

| data communication services | *Data communication services* can be divided into three classes: |

Data communication services can be divided into three classes:

1. narrow-band,
2. voice-band,
3. broad-band.

These three bands are sometimes called *circuit grades*. The width of a band determines the maximum transmission speed since its width affects the frequency range. The higher the frequency rate, the faster is the transmission speed. Normally, bands are expressed as so many characters per second, bits per second, or words per minute. Various combinations of signals or absence of signals form codes which represent numerics, alphabetics, and special characters. These individual impulses are called bits. Five to eight bits represent one character, while a word is defined as five characters plus a space.

Narrow-Band Class. The narrow-band class of data communication service (first class) has a slower speed than that needed for voice transmission. For this reason, it is sometimes called a *subvoice grade channel*. The TWX (Teletypewriter Exchange Service) and the Western Union TELEX have employed the narrow-band for many years. The narrow-band is used for data collection systems since it is relatively inexpensive. Typical speeds are 45, 57, 75, and 150 bits per second while the transmission rate can go as high as 300 bits per second.

Voice-Band Class. Voice-band channels (second class) transmit the human voice over a range or band width of approximately 3,000 Hertz (cycles per second) for public lines and 4,000 Hertz for leased lines. Maximum data speeds range up to 2,400 bits per second. It is possible to obtain slower speeds by dividing into subvoice channels, consisting of bands of 150 to 200 cycles. The 100-Speed TWX Service makes use of the voice-band grade channel for reading, transmitting, and punching eight-channel paper tape at the rate of 100 words per minute. The Data-Phone as well as other data transmission equipment (presented later in the chapter) use the voice-band to transmit data from punched paper tape, punched cards, and magnetic tape. The cost for this type data communication service is comparable to a long distance telephone call. Still another service available over voice-band grade channels is WATS (Wide Area Telephone Service). It permits long distance telephone service among a large number of telephones and is more economical than regular long distance for large volumes. WATS is billed at a fixed monthly rate, allowing an organization to make a large number of outgoing calls throughout the month. Its lines may also be used in conjunction with the Data-Phone for data transmission.

Telephone noise is the major error source in most systems. It originates within the telephone switching equipment and can sometimes be heard on the line as clicks. Such noise prevents the receiving end from detecting a bit correctly sent from the transmitting end. *Parity schemes* are used to detect errors when they occur. Some codes are designed to detect the presence of errors, but more elaborate codes can actually identify what the error was, and even correct one or more errors. Although acceptance of bad data at the receiving end can be brought to a low probability, elaborate parity schemes reduce line efficiency since some time will be lost in sending redundant bits.

Broad-Band Class. The broad-band or wide-band class of data communication service (third class) has a higher band width than the voice-band width. It involves a microwave (radio relay) communication system that operates at frequencies above four million kiloHertz per second. Data must be continually amplified and repeated by stations (20 to 35 miles apart) which use dishlike antennas.

Satellites. An emerging candidate to ease the ever increasing data transmission traffic is the use of satellites. However, there are high costs involved. A satellite operator will need to spend approximately $15 million for NASA's launching of one satellite. Despite the costs involved, A. T. & T. and Western Union employ satellites for backing up their communications network. A current satellite model can accommodate 10,800 voice-grade channels. Little change in wide-band rates result from the use of satellites since rates must be based on the total investment in cables and microwave links as well as the satellites used in the Bell network.

data communication equipment

To achieve coding uniformity of data transmitted, the United States of America Standards Institute adopted a data processing code, known as the ASCII or the USASCII—U.S.A. Standard Code for Information Interchange (Figure 8-3). This seven-level code actually utilizes eight bits since the eighth bit is used for parity checking—verify that data transmission integrity has been maintained. In addition, there are a number of variations of the seven-level code as well as five-, six-, and eight-level codes. The EBCDIC code, for example, can be transmitted on channels designed for ASCII. However, standardization with USASCII facilitates the conversion and interchange of data among the data communication equipment available throughout the industry.

Data Communication System. No matter what code is employed, data are transmitted in five stages through the use of data communication equipment and lines. Basically, the data are sent:

1. from an input device,
2. to a transmitting terminal,

figure 8-3. ASCII coding chart where each character is represented by seven bits.

				b7→ 0 b6→ 0 b5→ 0	0 0 1	0 1 0	0 1 1	1 0 0	1 0 1	1 1 0	1 1 1
Bits	b4↓	b3↓	b2↓	b1↓	Col.→ Row↓	0	1	2	3	4	5	6	7
	0	0	0	0	0	NUL	DLE	SP	0	@	P	\	p
	0	0	0	1	1	SOH	DC1	!	1	A	Q	a	q
	0	0	1	0	2	STX	DC2	"	2	B	R	b	r
	0	0	1	1	3	ETX	DC3	#	3	C	S	c	s
	0	1	0	0	4	EOT	DC4	$	4	D	T	d	t
	0	1	0	1	5	ENQ	NAK	%	5	E	U	e	u
	0	1	1	0	6	ACK	SYN	&	6	F	V	f	v
	0	1	1	1	7	BEL	ETB	/	7	G	W	g	w
	1	0	0	0	8	BS	CAN	(	8	H	X	h	x
	1	0	0	1	9	HT	EM	)	9	I	Y	i	y
	1	0	1	0	10	LF	SUB	*	:	J	Z	j	z
	1	0	1	1	11	VT	ESC	+	;	K	[	k	{
	1	1	0	0	12	FF	FS	,	<	L	\	l		
	1	1	0	1	13	CR	GS	—	=	M	]	m	}
	1	1	1	0	14	SO	RS	.	>	N	∧	n	¬
	1	1	1	1	15	SI	US	/	?	O	—	o	DEL

3. through an electrical transmission line,
4. to a receiving terminal,
5. and to an output device.

This is represented in Figure 8-4.

Referring to the five stages, the input device at the transmitting terminal may be a paper tape reader, card reader, magnetic tape unit, computer, keyboard, or special collection device (1). The sending terminal that transmits the data from the input device consists of several units, even though they are contained in a single cabinet and sold as a single communication terminal device (2). The input control unit accepts and stores data temporarily by means of a buffering device so that its speed is compatible with the communication facility. The error control unit detects and, sometimes, corrects errors that occur during transmission. The most commonly used methods for error control are validity checking and parity checking.

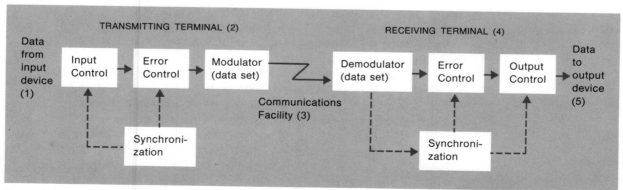

figure 8-4. Data communication system—flow of data.

While the former assumes the accuracy of character representation, the latter determines whether the number of bits received meets the established odd or even bit code. By means of the synchronization unit, transmitting and receiving units operate at the same frequency while data move. Before data can be sent over the communications facility, impulses generated by the terminal input device must be modified so as to be compatible with it. The transmitting terminal unit that performs the function is called a modulator (data set).

Once the data have been received over the communications network (3), the demodulator (data set) at the receiving terminal converts the signal back into a form acceptable to the output device. For two-way communications, the data set is a combination modulator-demodulator unit, often called a *modem* (MOdulating-DEModulating equipment). The error control unit checks the data pattern to make sure it meets the validity check or parity check. The last unit or the output control unit accepts and stores the data temporarily for transfer to the output device at an appropriate rate. For the receiving terminal, the synchronization unit assures that it is operating on the same frequency as the transmitting instrument (4). Finally, the output device at the receiving terminal may be a paper tape punch, card punch, printer, magnetic tape unit, computer, or display device (5).

data transmission terminal equipment

Data sets cannot only perform the functions set forth above, but also can be a means of dialing and providing a connection for the communications facility. Various types of data sets, used as data transmission terminal equipment, are furnished by communications carriers, depending upon their use. In the following material, several of the more common terminals and equipment will be explored.

Data-Phone. The best known transmitting system is the Data-Phone data set, manufactured by the Bell Telephone System. As shown in Figure 8-5a, it is basically a modified telephone which can be used either for voice or data transmission. A method for utilizing the Data-Phone is to dial the appropriate number to which information is being sent. When the Data-Phone set is answered at the other end, the transmitting party indicates the start of an information transmission. At this moment, both parties depress the "Data" button which automatically depresses the voice capability and allows data to be sent over the wires. In this manner, Data-Phone sets or modems can be either transmitters, receivers, or both.

Push-Button Telephone. The push-button telephone is another commonly used data set, shown in Figure 8-5b. A call is placed by depressing the buttons which correspond to the desired telephone number. Upon the completion of the call, the telephone can be used to transmit data or for normal voice communication. If data are transmitted to a receiving set connected to a recording device, such as a card punch or a punched paper tape, the receiving set accepts the call, transmits an answer tone, and connects the recording device to the transmission line. Input data are entered by depressing the buttons on the telephone. As the buttons are depressed, the data set converts the tones to electrical signals that are captured by the recording device.

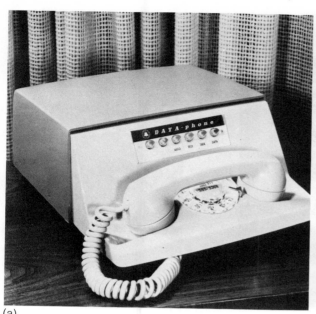
(a)

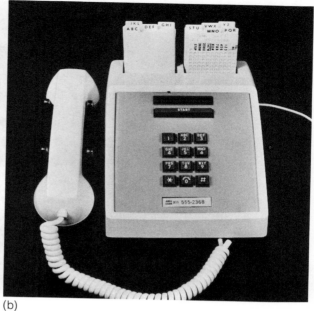
(b)

figure 8-5. (a) Data-Phone data set, and (b) telephone data set that allows dialing and data transmission by push button or punched plastic cards. (Courtesy American Telephone and Telegraph Company.)

In addition to the above procedure, the telephone data set has the ability to use punched plastic cards. This added flexibility allows customers or company personnel to enter orders quickly and efficiently. For example, a customer wishes to place an order. The individual simply dials the number of the vendor and identifies the firm by inserting a prepunched plastic identity card into the reading device of the telephone. The customer then feeds into the reader a punched plastic card describing the first item being ordered. Once the contents of the card have been transmitted via a tone signal to the sender, the quantity is entered by depressing the appropriate buttons. At the receiving end, a recording device produces a set of cards, punched paper tape, or other output. The same procedure is completed for the rest of the order. At the end of a certain time period, say a month, the vendor submits a listing of all orders entered and the amount billed for the customer. This procedure speeds up the ordering process and reduces the need for writing purchase orders.

Visual CRT Terminal. Visual CRT (cathode ray tube) display terminals have proven to be a necessity for many organizations desiring up-to-date information. For any CRT terminal, the keyboard is the means of inquiry for data which are stored on-line by the computer system. Coded signals are generated and transmitted by data sets and communication channels to the computer system. Once the computer interprets the signals and has retrieved the requested information, the data are transmitted again, using data sets, back over the communications channel to the visual display terminal in the form of coded signals (refer to Figure 8-4). The signals, in turn, are interpreted and displayed on the TV type screen. A typical display of data is illustrated in Figure 8-6a.

figure 8-6. Stationary visual CRT computer terminals.

(a) IBM 3270 Display Station with alpha-numeric keyboard. (Courtesy International Business Machines Corporation.)

(b) DATASPEED 40 CRT data terminal with hard copy output. (Courtesy Teletype Corporation.)

CRT Terminal Illustration. A representative application of CRT data terminals is a customer ordering procedure. Although some customer orders arrive through the mail and via Teletype, many are phoned in to the firm's sales office. Salespersons write the orders and hand them to an adjacent order entry typist. Flashed on the CRT terminal are a series of questions to be answered by the typist: customer account number, customer order number, date of order, phone or mail order, tax code (type of customer), inside salesperson, and job control number. Additional questions are flashed on the screen for an answer, depending upon the type of order. Sets of questions continue until the operator enters an L for "last." Each keyed-in answer appears on the screen opposite the question. There is one edit check for each item on the order and the operator verifies that an entry is correct by keying in OK (okay) or NG (no good). After an NG entry, the individual redisplays the particular item in question and enters changes. An editing program, stored in the computer, checks the answer against preestablished facts and limits, resulting in question marks being flashed on the screen when the program finds an answer unacceptable. When all questions have been correctly answered, the computer program checks the customer's credit. If credit is approved, a message is displayed on the screen. However, if the customer fails the credit check, a warning message is flashed on the terminal. Once the credit information is cleared, the computer program deducts stock requirements of the order from the company's inventories or if inventories are insufficient, a production order is immediately placed. When the foregoing procedures have been completed, the computer prints out an order set for notifying the customer and actual shipment of the goods. The above process takes about 5 to 10 minutes, depending upon the complexity of the order.

CRT Terminal with Printed Output. Data that are displayed can be printed if the visual display unit is equipped with an attached printer per Figure 8-6b or integrated within the CRT terminal. The number of applications is as wide as the CRT terminals being marketed. They include: credit check, accounts receivable, production scheduling, inventory, shipping information, sales data, administration data, stock prices, and similar business data. A feasibility study is needed to determine what CRT units best serve the organization since their capabilities and prices vary from manufacturer to manufacturer.

Portable Audio Terminal. Data communication equipment is not limited to stationary terminals. Portable computer terminals are becoming more popular since they perform the same functions as larger units and are reasonably priced. The IBM 2721 Portable Audio Terminal (Figure 8-7a), for example, allows the user to enter alphabetic and numerical data into a System/370 from any standard telephone. The unit communicates to the computer through an audio response unit and is designed for salespersons, insurance agents, personnel at manufacturing plants, and others with similar requirements.

An insurance agent, for example, fits a telephone handset at a prospect's home into the 2721's acoustic coupler, connecting it with a remote computer. With the keyboard, the agent would then enter the prospect's age, income, number of dependents, present insurance coverage, and other factors. The computer would then calculate the amount and type of protection needed to achieve the prospect's insurance needs. The computer's reply is heard over the terminal's built-in speaker (or through a set of earphones). The spoken words are selected by the computer from a vocabulary stored in its audio-response unit. Words are chosen from a library of most frequently used words for the specific application. A 32-word vocabulary is provided and can be expanded in 16-word increments, up to 128 words.

Portable CRT Terminal. A recent addition to the category of portable computer terminals is the combination CRT/keyboard terminal (Figure 8-7b). With this particular model, two operating modes are selectable by a front panel push button: Local mode—provides page transmission which allows editing and On-Line mode—transmits character by character identical to a teletypewriter. When the screen is full, the top line is deleted and the information remaining on display is shifted upward to allow new characters to be entered on the bottom of the display, just as a teletypewriter rolls up paper.

Portable Printer Terminal. Another portable computer terminal is illustrated in Figure 8-7c. This portable terminal produces full-page computer printout. Teletype compatible, it needs only a standard power outlet and a telephone to begin operating for entering or receiving desired information. Information is transmitted at 30 characters per second. At the heart of this unit is a microprocessor (a computing device to be explained in the next chapter).

Another portable terminal with hardcopy output, illustrated in Figure 8-7d, incorporates a memory as a mass-storage device. To illustrate its versatility over the previous ones illustrated in Figure 8-7, a salesperson can enter orders in the terminal throughout the day. At night, the individual can transmit the stored data to a computer. Additionally, this portable terminal makes use of a new storage technology called bubble memories which has the capacity to pack data bits in densities that range up to

(a) IBM 2721 Portable Audio Terminal. (Courtesy International Business Machines Corporation.)

(b) Portable CRT/keyboard terminal. (Courtesy Bendix Corporation.)

(c) Silent 700 Model 745 Portable Data Terminal with hardcopy output. (Courtesy Texas Instruments, Inc.)

(d) Silent 700 Model 765 Portable Memory Terminal with hardcopy output—uses bubble memory. (Courtesy Texas Instruments, Inc.)

figure 8-7. Portable computer terminals.

millions of bubbles per square inch. The basic memory stores 20,000 bytes which can be expanded in 20,000 byte increments to reach 80,000 bytes.

Teletype Terminals. Among the most widely used of all data transmission equipment today is the Teletype machine. What the telephone does for verbal data, the Teletype does for written data. It permits the transmission and receipt of data between two points by telephone lines. Tele-

(a) Inktronic RO (receive-only) set.

(b) Inktronic KSR (keyboard send-receive) set.

(c) Model 38 ASR (automatic send-receive) set.

figure 8-8. Teletype terminals.
(Courtesy Teletype Corporation.)

type produces various models in order to meet the specific needs of its customers. Basically, their equipment includes:

1. RO (receive-only) set,
2. KSR (keyboard send-receive) set,
3. ASR (automatic send-receive) set.

RO set. The Inktronic RO set (Figure 8-8a) is a remote typewriter output. It prints up to 1200 words per minute which is much faster than ordinary page printers in its class. The method of printing is through electrostatic deflection. Ink literally leaps to the page to form a character. Ink droplets carry a negative charge and are drawn to the page through a series of electrodes that cause it to trace out the shape of the character desired. Each character, then, is made up of a number of dots.

KSR set. A teletype machine similar to that of a typewriter (keyboard input and output) is shown in Figure 8-8b. The Inktronic KSR set provides keyboard data entry and printed page copy at both the sending and receiving ends. Also, data can be transmitted and received in eight-channel punched paper tape for direct input to a data processing system on those models that have the capability. This approach allows for preparing paper tapes in advance so that its accuracy can be checked as well as transmitting automatically at a more rapid rate than would be possible with manual typing.

ASR set. The Teletype Model 38 ASR set, illustrated in Figure 8-8c, offers the widest range of operational features. This model provides keyboard data entry, printed page copy, and paper tape capabilities. The keyboard-printer console can be used separately for sending input data or monitoring output per one of the above processing modes.

Teletype Applications. Numerous applications have been found for Teletype's data transmission equipment, namely, transmission of sales orders, invoices, production schedules, inventory, payroll checks, personnel data, quotations, internal reports, shipping data, and similar business data. Many organizations have replaced their traditional inventory replenishment method with a communications network that ties its distribution outlets and warehouses to its computer center via a Teletype ASR set. Teletype equipment is used to send and receive inventory data among warehouses, distribution centers, and a computer center. The computer analyzes the inventory at each location and considers past stock requirements as well as seasonal demand and, where applicable, possible obsolescence. It determines the stock needs and material requirements of each warehouse and distribution outlet. The Teletype ASR set transmits stock replenishment orders quickly and accurately which results in keeping inventories current and costs at a minimum.

Magnetic Tape Transmission Terminal. Another popular type of data transmission is one that uses magnetic tape transmission terminals. Each terminal is designed to read tape or write tape during transmission, depending on how the switch is set. Magnetic tape terminals read or write tape with a high density of characters per inch. They are capable of utilizing magnetic tapes from or preparing magnetic tapes for the most popular tape devices. There is generally no limitation regarding the length of each record transmitted.

Computer-To-Computer Transmission. Computer-to-computer transmission of data is possible by connecting transmission control terminals to the respective computers. The sending transmission control terminal converts data from computer storage to the transmission language, used for common carrier communication. The data may have originated from on-line storage, punched cards, magnetic tape, or paper tape, then manipulated before sending through the data set. On the receiving end of the transmission, the data set picks up the signals while the data transmission control terminal converts data from the transmission language to the respective language of the computer. The receiving computer is ready to manipulate the incoming data, such as update records in disk storage or prepare data for a printout. The real benefit of the computer-to-computer transmission is that it allows one computer center to back up another, especially during peak periods.

interactive processing modes

The basic types of interactive processing modes are:

- real-time
- time-sharing

Fundamentally, a real-time system is designed to fulfill the DP requirements for one organization as opposed to a time-sharing system that is oriented toward the problem solving needs of many users. Although user orientation differs between these two interactive processing modes, the computer equipment needed for operating both type systems are quite similar.

Inasmuch as the focus in Chapters 5 and 6 was on the BASIC language for a minicomputer system, accent will be placed on time sharing within this type of operating environment. In addition, the low cost of mini-computer systems have resulted in their widespread use not only by business, but also by academic institutions of all sizes. Thus, an introduction to time sharing within a minicomputer environment will permit the reader to understand the inner workings of larger time-sharing and real-time computer systems that are used for business purposes.

time sharing

The idea of time sharing began to develop during the late 1950's. The impulse came mostly from the frustration that developed among scientists and programmers bottlenecked by a batch-processing system. It was a British mathematician, Christopher Strachey, who gave the first public paper on time sharing at a UNESCO congress in 1959. In that same year, Professor John McCarthy wrote an internal memorandum distributed at M.I.T. These two men, working independently, were the first to go on record with specific solutions to the problems of time sharing. Important research began at M.I.T. where Professor F. J. Corbato developed what has since become, in Project MAC (machine-aided cognition or multiple-access computer), one of the most advanced time sharing systems at work in the country. The idea of time sharing spread to other colleges, notably Dartmouth and the University of California at Berkeley.

Reasons for Time Sharing
Before exploring the basic characteristics of time sharing, it would be helpful to explore the rationale for its rapid growth. There are many reasons, the most frequently mentioned ones being:

1. convenience and ease of getting started
2. application flexibility
3. faster programming with user-machine interaction
4. low cost

Implementation Factors. A remote terminal can be installed wherever there is electric power and telephone circuits. There are a number of portable terminals which can be operated from any standard telephone without special installation. In a similar manner, most users can acquire an on-line service in a matter of weeks or even hours while it may take months or years to install a computer in a conventional manner. Also, it is easy to divest oneself of this capability if it fails to meet the user's needs.

Application Flexibility. A time-sharing system has the added advantage of being a small computer to many users or a large dedicated system when required. One user may be using it as a desk calculator while another as a powerful system simulator. This application flexibility gained by the user is normally not available with a batch processing system. Thus, flexibility can be a significant reason for utilizing time sharing devices.

first summary
of chapter 8

data communications:
Links company personnel and computers together in order that *timely* data can be received and sent as a by-product of a business information system. Its important characteristics are:
- links data processing operations together
- makes on-line inquiry processing possible
- facilitates computer load balancing

data communication channels or circuits are divided into three types:
- simplex—allows one-way transmission of data
- half-duplex—permits two-way transmission of data, but in only one direction at a time
- full-duplex—allows two-way transmission of data in both directions simultaneously

data communication services or circuit grades are divided into three classes:
- narrow-band—has a slower speed than that needed for voice transmission
- voice-band—transmits the human voice over public and leased lines
- broad-band—has a higher speed than the voice-band width

data communication equipment:
Data communication systems consist of data being transmitted (1) from an input device (2) to a transmitting terminal (modulator) (3) through a data communications line (4) to a receiving terminal (demodulator) and (5) to an output device.

data transmission terminal equipment:
- Data-Phone—a modified telephone that can be used for voice or data transmission
- push-button telephone—a phone that allows dialing and data transmission by push button or punched plastic card
- stationary visual CRT terminals (with optional printed output)—on-line computer devices that have a keyboard for displaying data on a TV-type screen for sending input and receiving output from a computer system
- portable (audio, CRT, and printer) computer terminals—on-line computer devices that can be hand carried and operated from a standard power outlet and telephone for sending input data and receiving output from a computer
- Teletype (RO, KSR, and ASR) terminals—data transmission equipment for sending input data or receiving output depending upon the type of terminal used
- magnetic tape transmission terminals—data transmission equipment used to send or write magnetic tape during transmission from one location to another
- computer-to-computer transmission—a method of data communication for linking computers together for balancing out work loads

**first self-study
exercise
of chapter 8**

True-False:

1. (   ) The real importance of data communication lies in the time factor.
2. (   ) The net benefit in dollars derived from transmitted information does not change over time.
3. (   ) There is little need for the receiving station to be in synchronization with the transmitting terminal.
4. (   ) Full duplex allows one-way transmission of data only.
5. (   ) Data communication services can be classified as circuit grades.
6. (   ) Satellites are used by A.T.&T. as a part of their communications network.
7. (   ) The USASCII code was adopted to achieve uniformity of data transmitted.
8. (   ) For two-way data communications, the data set must be a modem.
9. (   ) CRT terminals are rarely used as data transmission terminal equipment.
10. (   ) The only type of Teletype terminal is the keyboard send-receive set.

Fill-In:

11. The transmission of data between two or more points is called _____ _____.

12. Data communications equipment should be used up to the point where the _____ from the immediate movement of information is greater than its _____.

13. Data communications channels that carry data in both directions, but permits the transmission of data in only one direction at a time, is termed _____-_____.

14. Data communications services range from the slow speed of _____-_____ to the high speed of _____-_____.

15. _____-_____ class service has the capability of transmitting the human voice over public lines.

16. In a data communications system, the receiving terminal unit that picks up data through a communications facility is called a _____.

17. In a data communications system, the transmitting terminal unit that sends data through an electrical transmission line is called a _____.

18. One of the best known transmitting systems is the _____-_____ which permits data to be sent over public lines by depressing the voice capability.

19. A transmitting system which allows the user to enter numerical and alphabetical data through its keyboard and receive a reply from the computer over the terminal's built-in speaker is called an _____ _____.

20. Teletype terminals that can produce printed output at both the sending and receiving ends are called _____ sets.

Faster Programming. With a conventional computer system, program development can be an extremely long, costly, and drawn out affair. The computer cannot be used for other processing when on-line computer debugging takes place. Time sharing can cut drastically into this delay of waiting for available computer debugging time. Many users report programs have been solved and running in less time than required for a batch machine since the problem solver can communicate directly with the machine in a user-machine interaction mode. This is in contrast with a batch-processing computer system where program cards must be converted to a computer input medium and proofed before entering the computer. An individual is not bogged down with intermediate steps, that is, one works directly with the programmed problem and the time-shared computer. The direct user-machine interaction frequently leads to ideas, insights, and an understanding of the relevant problem variables and interrelationships that are not possible with conventional methods. In essence, the programmer can ask questions during the on-line debugging process which were not foreseen in the beginning. Also, the individual can alter the framework of the problem, if necessary while it is being solved.

Low Cost. Low cost is an important reason for the growth of time sharing. A financial manager need not spend a considerable amount of time on a feasibility study. Quite often, the individual has the authority to expend several hundred to several thousand dollars per month for time-sharing computer services. Since CRT and typewriter terminals, computer time-sharing services, and telephone lines are rented, everything is expensed monthly without the need to go through the formal organizational channels for large capital expenditures. Thus, some of the growth of time sharing can be ascribed to the ease of financial procedures in acquiring the system.

Basic Characteristics of Time Sharing

The most basic of all time-sharing characteristics is the fact that local or remote terminals are connected directly on-line to the computer. In some cases, a communication system (telephone lines usually) is used for the connection. In other cases, the terminals are wired directly to the computer, thereby circumventing the need for telephone lines.

On-Line Processing. Time sharing allows many users to interact simultaneously with the computer. This capability allows the computer to become an "on-line" part of the task being performed. Any time-sharing service, then, is basically an on-line system that is shared by many users.

Multiprogramming Capability. Time sharing is an extension of the multiprogramming concept which permits the computer to work on many programs concurrently. This is the reason why a time-sharing system is referred to as a *multiple access system*. Having this capability, each user has one or more input/output terminals which are connected by communication lines (telephone lines) to a central computer. In turn, it responds as if the user is the only one utilizing the facility. Because of the speed of the central processing unit, the computer system can relay the output to the user almost immediately although the central processor is working on other programs at the same time. Thus, an essential characteristic of time sharing is the method of sharing the computer's main memory.

By and large, there are two methods for sharing the computer's central processing unit—*memory swapping* and *paging*. Under the memory swapping approach, the entire program is moved in and out of the computer's memory. This results in having only one program in memory at a time. A very short period of time is allowed in main memory before the next program is brought in for processing. With the second approach, each program is segregated into a group of instructions called pages. These may range from a small number of instructions to a subroutine of a program, depending upon the size of the computer. When a specific program is to be run, a page (or group of pages) is (are) brought into the computer's main memory and executed. As a page is executed, its memory space can be released to the next page of the program. Pages from time-sharing programs may be in memory simultaneously which allows the computer's arithmetic logical unit to switch back and forth among the programs.

Executive Program Control. No matter what memory allocation approach is used, there is need for a supervisory program, sometimes referred to as an *executive program*. It schedules the processing of programs submitted by the terminals in use and copes with the problems of memory allocation.

Overhead Time. A fundamental characteristic of time sharing is "overhead" time. This is defined as that part of the system's execution time which is not devoted directly to the execution of problems submitted by users. It is the time necessary for the system to engage in certain coordinating and recording activities each time the processing of a problem is interrupted for memory swapping or paging. Based upon past studies, swap time (time spend transferring data from main memory to auxiliary memory and back because of program interrupts) represents 20% to 30% of the total time in a time-sharing system. Also, overhead computation is approximately 5% of the total available time, leaving normal computation time anywhere from 60 to 70%. However, the execution of a problem is increased by approximately 20% for the inclusion of relocatability of the memory. This means that additional overhead time on direct execution of user problems has to be considered. Hence, about 20% of the 60 to 70% of normal computation time mentioned above or approximately 12% must be added to the total overhead time. Total overhead time, then, can be as high as 40% for a typical time-sharing system.

User Data Files and Programs. The user's data files are maintained at the time-sharing computer center where the user's instructions identify the files to be employed. This security feature prevents a user from making unauthorized entry into the files of another user. In like manner, each user has a set of programs which are stored by the time-sharing system or are read via the time-sharing terminal through its punched paper tape attachment (if available). Also, there is a library of time-sharing programs which are available to users.

Wide Range of Applications. Among the more prominent applications are: mathematical calculations (most common usage), statistics, programming, debugging, and simulation. Other areas include: accounting, budgeting, education, forecasting, investment analysis, market research, mechanical design, project planning, reliability, scientific research, and sales analysis.

**time-sharing
terminal devices**

There is a wide range of terminal devices for a time-sharing system. The user operates terminal devices which are connected by communication lines to a time sharing computer system. Data are inserted into the terminal from which output is obtained by means of programmed instructions. Basically, time-sharing input/output devices are divided into four types:

1. visual CRT terminals,
2. portable terminals,
3. typewriter terminals,
4. multifunction terminals.

Visual CRT Terminals. A time-sharing terminal device, explored in a prior section, is the visual CRT display unit, shown in Figure 8-9. It is popular due to its speed and flexibility, that is, the capability to display printed and graphic information at a much faster speed than typed information. An added advantage is its ability to delete and change characters or words selectively in desired records or files. Its disadvantages are slightly higher costs and lack of hard copy in most cases.

Portable Terminals. Portable terminals, previously shown in Figure 8-7, allow the user to travel to the problem itself and solve it right on the spot. For example, it allows one to take a physical inventory at some remote location and report the items after they have been counted for an immediate comparison to the perpetual inventory maintained on-line.

Typewriter Terminals. A typewriter terminal for time sharing, operating at 30 characters per second, is depicted in Figure 8-10. Other terminals

figure 8-9. VT52 DECscope—(CRT display unit) for a DEC PDP-11 minicomputer. (Courtesy Digital Equipment Company.)

figure 8-10. LA36 DECwriter II (typewriter terminal) for a DEC PDP-11 minicomputer. (Courtesy Digital Equipment Company.)

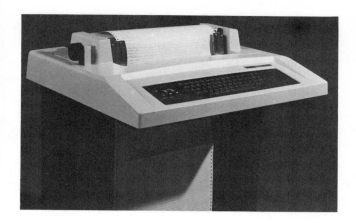

figure 8-10. LA36 DECwriter II (typewriter terminal) for a DEC PDP-11 minicomputer. (Courtesy Digital Equipment Company.)

widely used for time sharing are those produced by Teletype, illustrated previously in Figure 8-8.

Multifunctional Terminals. The foregoing time-sharing terminals may not be flexible enough for large time-sharing installations. For such systems, there are a few time-sharing devices that combine a reasonably fast printout and card reading with the use of a typewriter and paper tape input/output. Shown in Figure 8-11 is a UNIVAC DCT 2000 remote input/output batch terminal which consists of a card reader, card punch, and a printer. As indicated in its name, it is capable of remote batch processing. Even though these input/output devices are slow when compared with similar computer equipment, their speeds approach the limit of the standard voice-band grade channels which are sufficient for the average time-sharing user.

figure 8-11. UNIVAC DCT 2000 Multifunction Remote Input/Output Batch Terminal. (Courtesy UNIVAC Division of the Sperry Rand Corporation.)

**second summary
of chapter 8**

interactive processing mode:
• real time — oriented toward the DP requirements for one organization
• time sharing — oriented toward the problem-solving needs of many users, such as students at a college using the same computer.

time sharing:
Time sharing, which is based on an user/machine interactive processing mode, was developed in the 1950's. It was a response to resolving the frustrations caused by bottlenecks of batch-processing systems.

reasons for time sharing:
• convenience and ease of getting started
• application flexibility for desired level of computing facilities
• faster programming with user-machine interaction
• low initial capital outlays and low operating costs
Of the foregoing, the growth of time sharing can be ascribed, in many cases, to the ease of financial procedures in acquiring the system.

basic characteristics of time sharing:
• on-line processing — refers to the capability of users to interact simultaneously with the computer.
• multiprogramming capability — permits more than one program to reside in main memory at the same time and be executed concurrently by means of an interweaving process.
• executive control program — schedules the processing of programs submitted by users and copes with the problems of memory allocation.
• overhead time — refers to that part of the system's execution time that is not devoted directly to the execution of problems submitted by the users.
• user data files and programs — refers to each user having a set of data files and programs that is restricted from use by others.
• wide range of applications — these include numerous business as well as nonbusiness areas.

time-sharing terminal devices:
• visual CRT terminals — permits the display of printed and graphic information
• portable terminals — allows the user to solve problems in the field
• typewriter terminals — permits the user to receive hard-copy output
• multifunction terminals — combines processing of input data with various forms of output within one unit

**second self-study
exercise
of chapter 8**

True-False:
1. (   ) The computer equipment needed for real-time and time-sharing systems are similar.
2. (   ) The SAGE system is the American Airlines reservation system.

3. ( ) A user-machine interaction mode is not available with time sharing.

4. ( ) Initial capital outlays for time sharing are extremely high.

5. ( ) One form of multiprogramming utilizes memory swapping.

6. ( ) Overhead time in a time-sharing system can be around forty percent.

7. ( ) There is no need for security features in a time-sharing system.

8. ( ) Generally, programming is faster in a time-sharing environment versus a batch-processing one.

9. ( ) Most time-sharing devices are multifunction terminals.

10. ( ) Time-sharing systems are widely used in colleges for instruction purposes.

Fill-In:

11. A _____-_____ processing mode is found in a typical time-sharing system.

12. _____ _____ allows users in different locations to share the same computer via input and output devices linked by telephone lines.

13. Most computer programs can be solved and running in less time in a time-sharing environment versus a _____-_____ mode since the problem solver can communicate directly with the computer.

14. There are two methods of sharing the computer's central processing unit, namely, _____ _____ and _____.

15. Time sharing which is an extension of the _____ concept permits the time-shared computer to work on many programs concurrently.

16. The _____ _____ schedules the processing of programs submitted by users and copes with the problems of memory allocation.

17. One drawback of time-sharing computers is the _____ time, that is, the time not devoted directly to the execution of problems submitted by users.

18. Generally, each user has its own set of programs and _____ _____ which are stored by the time-sharing system.

19. There is a variety of time-sharing _____-_____ devices that are available to suit the user's needs.

20. _____ are widely used today for time-sharing systems.

summary

The introduction of data communication equipment and interactive computer systems has greatly increased the flow of business information. Data communications have made possible the development of real-time business information systems while time-sharing systems have brought the on-line capabilities of computers to the smallest user. This timely flow of business data, sometimes referred to as "now" information, will undoubtedly add to a more efficient operation of an organization's activities. Information that tells what is happening now is generally more beneficial to management that that which produces needed operating data at a later date.

As interactive processing continues to grow, it will reach a point where it will be used to solve most simple business problems. Whether it be in academic, business, engineering, research, or other areas, it will become an accepted way of life. It has the potential to enrich the quality of the environment by providing answers to problems on the spur of the moment which, because of their complexity, may not be solvable in days or weeks using manual methods. Hence, interactive computing has the potential of affecting the world in which we live.

questions	1. How important is data communications in the field of business data processing today?
	2. What is the function of a data set or modem?
	3. Distinguish between data communication channels and services.
	4. Describe the three basic types of communication channels.
	5. What is the significance to a potential user regarding the types of communication channels and grades of circuits which are available? Explain.
	6. Describe five types of data transmission terminal equipment.
	7. (a) What is meant by time sharing? Explain thoroughly. (b) What are the important reasons for the rapid growth of time sharing? Explain.
	8. State and explain the basic characteristics of time sharing.
	9. Of the many basic types of time-sharing devices available, what are the advantages and disadvantages of each?
	10. How does a time-sharing computer system differ from a batch-processing system?
	11. (a) Define the term multiprogramming as used in a time-sharing system. (b) Can multiprogramming be an important part of a batch-processing system? Explain.

answers to first self-study exercise

1. T 2. F 3. F 4. F 5. T 6. T 7. T 8. T 9. F 10. F 11. data communications 12. value and cost 13. half-duplex 14. narrow-band and broad-band 15. voice-band 16. demodulator 17. modulator 18. Data-Phone 19. audio terminal 20. KSR

answers to second self-study exercise

1. T 2. F 3. F 4. F 5. T 6. T 7. F 8. T 9. F 10. T 11. real-time 12. time sharing 13. batch-processing 14. memory swapping and paging 15. multiprogramming 16. executive program 17. overhead 18. data files 19. input-output 20. minicomputers

chapter nine

minicomputers and business-oriented computer systems

As indicated in the previous interactions between the computer and the Cosgroves, there are many ways that computerized systems can be configured to meet specific user needs. As additional examples, consider the following scenario. As Joe and Claudia drive through the city on their way to their vacation destination, the traffic signals are computer controlled to facilitate traffic movement. When they enter the turnpike, the card Joe receives on entering and returns on leaving the toll road will be eventually processed by the state's computer system to determine revenue and usage of the toll road as well as other statistical data.

Once they reach their destination, a motel room that was previously reserved by the motel's computer system will be waiting, thereby simplifying their sign-in procedures. Also, when they turn on the television to watch a baseball game in the motel room, the amusing antics of cartoon characters will be displayed on the million-dollar, computer-controlled scoreboard. Throughout the game, several reports are given on the progress of the nation's latest space flight. Such space exploration would be impossible without the assistance of sophisticated computer controlled systems. Thus, computer systems of various types come in direct contact with Joe and Claudia Cosgrove whether they are in town or away on a vacation.

In the prior two chapters, the accent has been on batch- and interactive-oriented computer equipment that is found in business information systems. In this chapter, the focus is initially on minicomputers and how they function, followed by a presentation of minicomputers and peripheral equipment as found in typical time-sharing systems. Hence, this chapter brings together a configuration of computer equipment for a time-sharing system that satisfies a particular set of specifications per a feasibility study.

In a similar manner, several configurations of batch-oriented computer equipment, currently being marketed, are illustrated. These systems range from small scale to large scale, their differences being that of speed and ability to handle varying volumes of input, throughput, and output. Within these typical business information systems, data bases are discussed since they house important business data that are usable by many functional areas of an organization. This background sets the stage for presenting two different approaches to a computerized accounts receivable application. Lastly, the availability of computing power by virtually all businesses regardless of size is explored in terms of service bureaus and computer utilities.

---

microprocessors

A *microprocessor* is the smallest version of a computer today; it is, in effect, a miniature computer. It manipulates data by interpreting and executing coded program instructions. This general-purpose DP device is contained on large-scale integrated (LSI) circuits, which are produced by means of metal-oxide semiconductor (MOS) technology (see Chapter 7). Fundamentally, a microprocessor consists of an accumulator, an arithmetic-logic unit, a very small memory, a register (a device that is capable of temporarily storing a specified amount of data while or until it is used in an operation) for instructions and a decoder for these instructions, an input/output bus (to be discussed under minicomputers), and controller for

Figure 9-1. Intel 8080A microprocessor. (Courtesy Intel Corporation.)

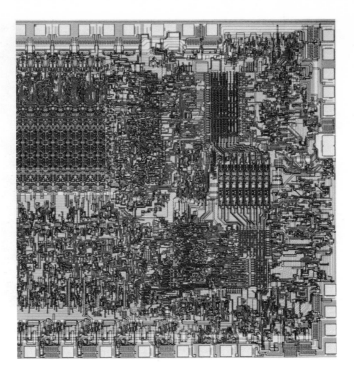

inputing and outputting of data. A typical microprocessor is shown in Figure 9-1.

Potential applications for microprocessors are immense. Present applications include intelligent peripherals, point-of-sale units, CRT terminals, printers, data-entry devices, and a variety of other input/output units that have a broad range of new capabilities as a result of microprocessor technology. Similarly, there will be numerous applications outside the computer field. Microprocessors will be found in automobiles and trucks to warn drivers of malfunctions. Likewise, they are currently found in household appliances, such as microwave ovens and sewing machines. Thus, the microprocessor is a means of assisting data entry into any computer system whether it be small-, medium-, or large-scale as well as being a means for controlling many other devices not connected directly to a computer. It is the hardware that makes various types of input/output terminal devices programmable (to a certain degree); hence, the term *intelligent terminal* has come into being.

As microprocessor prices fall, the number of potential applications will increase. This situation is reminiscent of the soaring markets that occurred for electronic calculators as their prices fell.

microcomputers

Going beyond the capabilities of the microprocessor and below the processing capabilities of minicomputers is the *microcomputer.* Although the microcomputer is a smaller version of a minicomputer, there is a tendency to blend the two kinds of computers into a virtually indistinguishable product line. However, there are certain distinguishing characteristics. Microcomputers tend to differ from minicomputers by having a

figure 9-2. PDP/03 Microcomputer shown below a CRT display unit. (Courtesy Digital Equipment Company.)

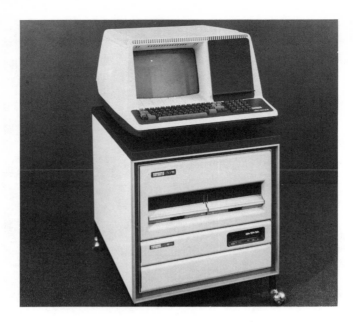

smaller word size for processing data, a slower memory cycle time, a more limited instruction set, a lower price, utilize less power, and customfitted controls for specific applications.

Based upon these foregoing features, a microcomputer can be defined as a microprocessor affixed with memory and input/output logic or circuits so that it can perform a useful function. A typical one is illustrated in Figure 9-2. Some companies produce complete microcomputers—CPU, data-storage memory, program memory, and input/output circuitry—on one or two MOS-LSI circuits. The tendency in such cases is to call the unprogrammed circuits a microprocessor system.

Due to the steady advances in circuitry sophistication and miniaturization, the logic and memory circuits of a microcomputer are the size of a fingernail. It is possible to have tens of thousands of components on a single chip requiring only milliwatt power. Based upon their size and capabilities, it is expected that microcomputers will have an impact on our lives similar to that of electric motors. Growth is assured since prices are destined to decrease.

A listing of present and future applications for microprocessors and microcomputers is shown in Figure 9-3. Like minicomputers, both will be an important part of distributed processing, thereby leading to greater decentralization of DP operations. Some industry experts see the large computer system emerging as simply a central memory system with many processors, like microcomputers and minicomputers, addressing it. Hence, their mass use will result in computational functions being distributed throughout an organization's business information system.

minicomputers

A minicomputer is exactly what its name implies—a small computer. Some models are not much larger than a typewriter (Figure 9-4). Additionally, a minicomputer is one that is low priced (prices ranging from several

Areas	Examples
Store sales information systems	Point-of-sales terminals, electronic registers, billing machines, inventory control equipment, cash dispensers, accounting equipment for medical facilities, and systems for gas stations.
Information processing systems	Intelligent terminals, community antenna television terminals, ID card readers, optical character recognition equipment, and graphic displays.
Measuring systems	Semiconductor testers, blood analyzers, automatic meteorological measuring devices, and environmental pollution measuring devices.
Control systems	Process control equipment, industrial robots, control of traffic lights, and control of elevators.
Education and home systems	Programmed instruction machines, games, central heating control, and control of electric household appliances.
Other systems	High-performance electronic calculators, control devices for automobiles, devices for aircraft, and air traffic control.

figure 9-3. Present and future applications for microprocessors and microcomputers.

hundred to several thousand dollars), mass produced, maintained by the user's staff, and normally programmed and operated by people who are not experts. Typically, a minicomputer has a small-bit word size and a small to medium size memory. It is capable of accepting a wide variety of peripherals, such as magnetic tape units, disk storage, and line printers. Likewise, it can communicate with other devices, such as time-sharing computers and plant machinery.

Importance of I/O Bus. The basic means for transferring data between the computer and the input/output devices is generally referred to as the I/O bus. Other names that may be used to designate this facility include

figure 9-4. Hewlett Packard 21MX minicomputer with 4K MOS memory. (Courtesy Hewlett Packard.)

figure 9-5. I/O bus—data transfer under program control.

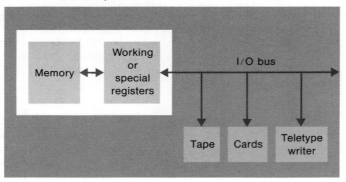

Mini-computer

Party Line (Varian Associates) and Multiplexer Bus (Interdata). The I/O bus is usually offered as standard equipment and included in the price of the basic processor. Functionally, the I/O bus permits the transfer of data between the input/output units and the working registers of the computer. Some computers have dedicated registers for I/O transfers. Figure 9-5 shows how the I/O bus interfaces with various components of a mini-computer system. The number of devices that may be connected is determined by the size of the address field of the computer's I/O instruction, and correspondingly, the number of address lines in the I/O bus.

Minicomputers Versus Time-Sharing Terminals. Many of the tasks currently handled by a minicomputer were previously handled by a time-sharing terminal linked to a computer. The reason is that the cost of mini-computer is less than the annual rental cost of a time-sharing terminal. Of equal importance to the user is the question of reliability. Control of output from time-sharing terminals are wholly dependent on the computer to which they are connected. Should a failure occur in that unit, all terminals and the machines to which they are connected are out of service until repairs are made. Should a minicomputer fail, only the task to which it has been assigned is affected. It can be replaced with a spare minicomputer in matter of minutes. Generally, a minicomputer is not subject to the time delays prevalent in some time-sharing systems.

An alternative to a time-sharing terminal is the IBM 5110 per Figure 9-6, which is designed for problem solvers in business, engineering, and scientific disciplines. BASIC and/or APL (All Purpose Language) are the interactive programming languages employed. Included as a part of the 5110 are a combination typewriter-like electronic keyboard and a 10-key char-

figure 9-6. IBM 5110 Portable Computer—minicomputer. (Courtesy International Business Machines Corporation.)

acter pad for data entry; a 1,024-character CRT display; a processing unit with from 16K to 64K positions of main storage, and a tape cartridge for storing programs and/or data. An optical communications capability for the 5110 allows the unit to operate as a communications terminal to remote IBM System/370 computers. In effect, this minicomputer is capable of performing many tasks that a terminal is capable of accomplishing when interacting with a time-sharing computer system. Such a portable computer, then, is an alternative to time-sharing operations. The user has a dedicated computer versus one shared by a number of users.

Minicomputers in a Total System. In Figure 9-7, several minicomputers and a small time-sharing system can be linked to a centrally located computer in order to form a hierarchical network. The minicomputer on the production line, for example, may send data, such as part counts, rejection rates, and machine performance to a central computer for filing. In a similar manner, business and engineering data can be controlled from time-sharing devices by a minicomputer before entering a time-sharing computer. All data within Figure 9-7 are finally directed to a larger computer. The larger computer, then, can issue commands to the different equipment connected on-line. Its responses will be based upon information received. If irregularities, for example, are reported from a machine station, the central computer will immediately direct the minicomputer to shut down the machine or assign necessary corrective measures. This hierarchical approach using minicomputers is a typical example of a distributed processing network.

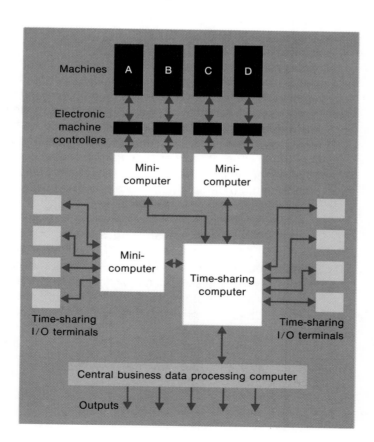

figure 9-7. Hierarchical network using minicomputers.

figure 9-8. Hewlett Packard Distributed System/3000 (mini-computer). (Courtesy Hewlett Packard.)

time-sharing computer systems

Within a time-sharing environment, terminals may be located nearby or hundred of miles from a computer capable of performing time-sharing functions. These terminals can communicate with a central computer facility in several ways. They can be linked to a minicomputer which, in turn, communicates with the time-sharing facility or they can communicate with a time-sharing system directly or over common carrier channels. Only the latter type machine configuration for time sharing is discussed below. Hence, the use of minicomputers to perform in an interactive processing mode is emphasized.

Hewlett Packard Distributed System/3000. The Hewlett Packard Distributed System/3000 is pictured in Figure 9-8. Not only is this system designed for time sharing, but also is an important link in a *distributed processing* network. Specifically, paper-tape readers, magnetic tapes, and magnetic disks can operate on line with the system processor (system console) for processing current data. In a similar manner, card readers, line printers, and terminals can be linked with the system processor through the communications processor for local processing. Also, data can be communicated to and from a computer system, say an IBM System/370. This interactive HP system, then, is capable of servicing local DP needs, fulfilling the time-sharing needs of local and remote users, and meeting the requirements of regional or central headquarters in a distributed processing network.

DEC PDC-11/45 Time Sharing System. The hardware components of the Digital Equipment Company's (DEC) PDP-11/45 Time Sharing System (minicomputer), pictured in Figure 9-9, differs somewhat from the prior Hewlett Packard System. A major difference is that all data and instructions come to the 11/45 processor over one of two independent busses. One, the UNIBUS (analogous to the I/O bus mentioned earlier), is used to transfer data between the processor, core memories, and peripheral devices. The second is used exclusively for transfers between the processor and the monolithic solid-state memory and is totally unaffected by the data transfers on the UNIBUS. They proceed in parallel. When the processor must go to core memory for data, the transfer is automatically interleaved with ongoing peripheral data transfers.

An overview of the UNIBUS in relation to the PDP-11 processor, memory,

figure 9-9. DEC PDP-11/45 Time-Sharing System (minicomputer). (Courtesy Digital Equipment Company.)

and terminals is illustrated in Figure 9-10. As shown, the main processor is connected by the UNIBUS to terminals or modems (full duplex) in 16-line groups through asynchronous multiplexers. Because the system is asynchronous, the UNIBUS is compatible with devices operating over a

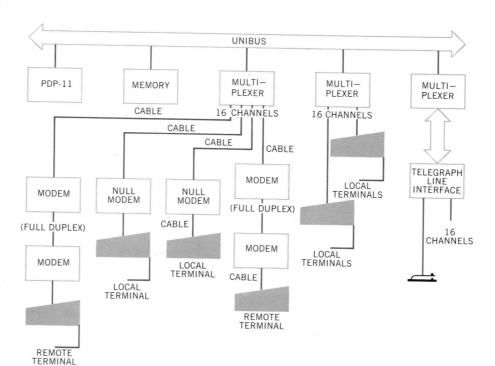

figure 9-10. Schematic of DEC PDP-11/45 Time-Sharing System (minicomputer). (Courtesy Digital Equipment Company.)

wide range of speeds. The maximum transfer rate on the UNIBUS is one 16-bit word every 400 nanoseconds or 2,500,000 words per second. Hence, a very fast transfer rate is available within this minicomputer time-sharing system.

The PDP-11/45 Time-Sharing System can handle up to 40 simultaneous jobs with 48 connected terminals—writers, CRT terminals, teletype, or remote modems. Also, the system utilizes disk storage as well as industry-compatible magnetic tape, that is, programs may be written to read or write in a format of another computer. Using BASIC-PLUS (the programming language covered in Chapters 5 and 6), it automatically checks all program commands for accuracy when they are entered. Thus, this system is an ideal candidate for solving a wide range of business problems in an inter-active processing mode.

**first summary
of chapter 9**

microprocessor:
A microprocessor is the smallest version of a computer today. It consists of an accumulator, an arithmetic-logic unit, a very small memory, a register for instructions and a decoder for these instructions, an I/O bus, and controller for inputing and outputting data. Examples of microprocessors are found in Figure 9-3, such as intelligent terminals and OCR equipment.

microcomputer:
A microcomputer goes beyond the processing capabilities of microprocessors and below those of minicomputers. Fundamentally, it is a small version of a minicomputer since it has a smaller word size, a slower memory cycle time, a more limited instruction set, a lower price, less power required, and custom-fitted controls for specific applications. Examples of microcomputers are found in Figure 9-3, such as industrial robots and air traffic control.

minicomputer:
A minicomputer is basically a small computer system. It has a small-bit word size, small- to medium-size memory, and is capable of accepting a wide range of peripheral devices, such as magnetic tape units, magnetic disk storage, and line printers. An I/O bus, usually offered as standard equipment, permits the transfer of data between the input/output units and the working registers of the computer. Examples of minicomputers include those used as stand-alone units, as part of a hierarchical distributed processing network, and as a time-sharing computer system.

time-sharing computer systems:
These systems allow many users located nearby or hundreds of miles from the computer to communicate in an user-machine mode for solving a wide range of problems. Time-sharing computer systems can utilize mini-computers as well as general-purpose computers that operate in an interactive processing mode. Batch-processing computer systems that permit interactive processing are noted in the next section of the chapter.

first self-study exercise of chapter 9

True-False:

1. (   ) The largest version of a computer today is the microprocessor.
2. (   ) The prices of microprocessors are expected to fall in the future.
3. (   ) Generally, microcomputers use custom-fitted controls for specific applications.
4. (   ) Input/output terminals can utilize microprocessors as part of their hardware.
5. (   ) Generally, minicomputers are higher in price than microcomputers.
6. (   ) Time-sharing terminals are always preferred over stand-alone minicomputers.
7. (   ) A popular programming language for minicomputers is BASIC.
8. (   ) A distributed processing network using minicomputers is an important DP direction now.
9. (   ) All time-sharing systems utilize minicomputers exclusively.
10. (   ) Time-sharing systems are mainly devoted to a batch-processing mode.

Fill-In:

11. _____ are currently used in input/output terminal devices that are programmable to a certain degree.
12. A _____ is defined as a microprocessor affixed with memory and input/output circuits such that it performs some useful function.
13. A typical _____ system is capable of utilizing a wide variety of peripherals, such as magnetic tapes, magnetic disks, and line printers.
14. Small stand-alone minicomputers are used currently as an alternative for _____-_____ terminals.
15. The _____ _____ of minicomputers permits the transfer of data between the input/output units and the working registers.
16. Minicomputers have became an important part of hierarchical _____ _____ networks as found in business information systems today.
17. Within a time-sharing environment, minicomputers are employed to perform in an _____ _____ mode.
18. Some time-sharing computer systems are capable of operating not only in an interactive processing mode, but also in a _____-_____ mode.
19. One of the major programming languages for the DEC PDP-11/45 minicomputer is _____-_____.
20. The _____ of the DEC PDP-11/45 minicomputer is comparable to the I/O bus of other minicomputers.

batch-oriented computer systems

As with time-sharing systems, several of the basic equipment devices illustrated previously are normally brought together and integrated into a batch-oriented computer system. Computer configurations available for business information systems include:

- minicomputers (see prior section)
- small-scale systems
- medium-scale systems
- large-scale systems

A small-scale system can rent for as low as $1000 per month while a large computer system can carry a monthly rental of well over $100,000. In between these two monthly rentals, there are literally thousands of different computer configurations that can be developed for the specific requirements of the user.

Small-Scale Computer Systems

There are a wide range of small-scale computer systems available from the computer manufacturers. Many of these are oriented toward distributed data processing. The IBM 8100, for example, is such a system. Its memory utilizes a new silicon chip technology with up to 64,000 bits or elements of information per chip (refer to Chapter 7 on the 64K-bit chip). This system includes a choice of two processors, a storage unit, a display station, a magnetic tape unit, and a line printer.

In a large organization, the new system can be linked to an IBM System/370 processor as well as to other 8100s as part of a cooperative network processing plan. With the Distributed Processing Control Executive, for example, DP personnel at headquarters can assemble and distribute programs to 8100 locations to provide greater productivity and consistency throughout the organization. On the other hand, with the Distributed Processing Programming Executive, programs can be prepared locally using high-level languages, or with a special 8100 capability called Development Management System. This application development aid enables users to define screen formats, enter data or access files on the spot, and develop entire programs without the assistance of programming professionals. Thus, the 8100 goes beyond the capabilities of many previous small-scale computer systems, making it the computer of the 1980s for local processing. Shown in Figure 9-11a is the IBM 8100 Information System.

Medium- to Large-Scale Systems

If an organization has need for a larger computer system, it can acquire a medium-scale computer system. Not only are the central processor and peripherals faster, but also the amount of storage and the number of attached units are larger. If a medium-scale system is inadequate for meeting an organization's DP needs, a large-scale system can be acquired. Most computer manufacturers offer medium- to large-scale computer systems. Generally, these sized systems are capable of operating not only in a batch-processing mode, but also in an interactive mode.

Of the many systems currently offered by computer manufacturers, the most widely used are the IBM computers. A typical medium-scale computer system is the IBM Model 4341. This system is especially attractive when an organization needs to increase existing performance or capacity, extend distributed processing capabilities, or improve problem-solving capabilities. With up to four million characters of main memory, this processor offers ample capabilities for advanced on-line applications and interactive problem solving. As with most computer systems, a wide range of peripheral

(a) Model 8100—a small-scale computer system.

(b) Model 4341—a medium-scale computer system.

(c) Model 3032—a large-scale computer system.

figure 9-11. Various sized business-oriented computer systems. (Courtesy International Business Machines Corporation.)

equipment is available. Shown in Figure 9-11b is a machine configuration that includes the central processing unit plus a wide range of peripherals, such as computer CRT console, disk and tape storage, printer, and card input/output.

One of the largest computers is the IBM Model 3032 (Figure 9-11c). This computer system gives large-scale computer users not only extensive interactive and batch-processing capabilities, but also is capable of multi-programming and multiprocessing. *Multiprogramming* is defined as a technique whereby more than one program may reside in main memory at the same time and be executed concurrently by means of an interweaving process. To state it another way, it refers to the ability to process several programs at one time in what appears to be simultaneous operations to the users. On the other hand, *multiprocessing* is a method whereby multiple central processing units (situated in the same location or in a remote loca-tion) have the capability of communicating with each other so as to utilize the additional processing capabilities of those CPU's that might otherwise stand idle. In addition, features found on other System/370 series are available.

Virtual Storage. An important feature of larger computer systems is *virtual storage* or *virtual memory*. To understand this concept, it is helpful to relate it to real or actual storage. With *real storage,* an entire program generally occupies storage space in main memory while the program is being executed. However, with *virtual storage,* only those parts of the program actually needed at any given time occupy the computer's main memory. The rest of the program is kept on disk files, ready for use when needed.

Each element of a program stored in main memory must have an address—a location where it can be found. In real storage, each address is usually reserved for one element throughout the program. On the other hand, with virtual storage, program elements are brought in from disk files, placed in the computer's memory, and transferred back to the disk files when no longer needed. Thus, during the execution of a program, the same element may occupy different addresses and the program may refer to it as if it were at its original address. This is made possible by a facility called *dynamic address translation,* working in conjunction with the operating system and with the program being executed. (Fundamentally, an operating system is defined as software that controls the execution of computer programs.) The entire process takes place automatically, without any need for intervention by the user.

Overall, more programs, i.e., longer ones, can be run under virtual storage, thereby potentially expanding the capabilities of computers. Individual programs, however, may require more time for execution under virtual storage. Virtual storage, then, is a technique found in computer systems that allows the user to treat secondary (disk) storage as an extension of main memory, thereby giving the "virtual" appearance of a larger main memory to the programmer.

common data bases

An integral part of a business-oriented (time sharing and batch) computer system, as presented in this chapter, is some type of on-line data files, commonly referred to as a *common data base.* The data base may be stored on magnetic disk, magnetic drum, mass storage as well as magnetic tape. No matter what type or combination of secondary storage is employed, the data processed by a computer have access to the data base for making appropriate changes. For example, during an inventory updating run, inventory quantities stored on the data base can be adjusted (added to and subtracted from) before an inventory report is printed by the system.

In the past, system design approaches utilized files structured for individual applications. Because of this individualistic approach, there was a great deal of redundancy, that is, the same data were carried in a number of files. Common keys which provided a means of referencing file data, such as employee number, were mandatory because they were the only method of cross-referencing two or more files. The redundancy information, however, extended far beyond the mandatory keys and included employee's name, department number, and the like, as depicted in Figure 9-12a.

The duplication of information in a variety of files is costly because excessive amounts of secondary storage capacity must be provided and a greater amount of magnetic disk, drum, or tape manipulation is required. A much more critical aspect, however, lies in the updating of multiple files. It is not difficult to conceive of one file being updated while the status of

Payroll File Employee No.	Name	Department	Payroll Data

Earnings File Employee No.	Name	Department	Earnings Data

(a)

Personnel File Employee No.	Name	Department	Personnel Data

(b)

Common Data Base Employee No.	Name	Dept.	Payroll Data	Earnings Data	Personnel Data

figure 9-12. (a) Redundant data files with past system approaches versus (b) a common data base approach.

the same record on a second file, a third file, or other files remains unchanged. To overcome this problem, a preferred approach is illustrated in Figure 9-12b — the *single-record concept*. Basically under this concept, all relevant information which formerly appeared in multiple files now appear in the common data base.

Structuring a Common Data Base. Before the size of the common data base can be determined, a number of items must be considered. Generally, one should know as much as possible about the data being considered in building the common data base — types of data files, the number of data items per data file, and the number of characters per data item. Also, consideration must be given to the number of different application programs that are to be developed. Hence, there must be a balance of available on-line storage space with cost and other critical factors when structuring a common data base.

To assist in structuring the common data base, several important questions are detailed in Figure 9-13. Of all the questions, the second one is probably the most difficult to answer, that is, the determination of what data to retain on line and for how long.

The design of the data base will dictate, or in some situations, be constrained by, the type of storage devices to be used, the data management system chosen to manipulate the data base, the degree of security that

---

1. What is the scope of the data base? What application areas will be included?
2. What data should be retained and for how long? What priorities are applicable to these data in terms of response time required from the system?
3. How should the various types of data be organized?
4. What security controls are required to protect sensitive data?
5. What storage medium should be selected? Is direct-access memory required or are other storage media suitable alternatives?
6. What is the optimum method for entering data into and selecting data from the storage medium? What controls are required for these data to insure accuracy?
7. What allowances can be made for growth of data records?

figure 9-13. Questions to assist in structuring a common data base.

must be built into the sytem to protect the data for management inquiries, and other important considerations. No matter what the constraints are, the data base elements should be integrated (as illustrated previously in Figure 9-12b). However, where data are too long for one record, related elements should be capable of being referenced for appropriate information with a minimum of time.

The preferred method of structuring the common data base, then, is the single-record concept, in which utilization of on-line secondary storage devices improves the accessibility of information for computer users. Because the data base contains much of the information needed throughout the entire processing cycle—from the receipt of a customer order to the issuance of an invoice—the number of points at which information is entered into the system is minimized. This approach tends to reduce bottlenecks in the processing of data.

computer system applications

Utilizing the foregoing presentation of computer systems and a common data base, it would be helpful to illustrate a typical computer application as a means of bringing together the prior material. For this reason, an accounts receivable application using magnetic tape (batch oriented) and magnetic disk (interactive oriented) is presented below. Not only are the essential steps for each method of storage (common data base) enumerated, but also the benefits of one method over the other are contrasted. In this manner, the reader can get a feel for a typical application found in computerized business information systems.

Accounts Receivable Application—Batch Oriented

In small- to large-size batch computer systems that are magnetic tape oriented, much of the processing time is devoted to maintaining files. Typically, sales analysis, inventory, payroll, accounts payable and accounts payable records must be continually updated. At periodic intervals, say daily, weekly, and monthly, reports and other desired output are printed from these files. As an example, a batch-oriented magnetic tape approach for updating accounts receivable daily is shown in Figure 9-14. This system flowchart indicates that four steps are involved in updating a master accounts receivable file with a tape system.

The first step, as illustrated, is keypunching and verifying accounts receivable input for the current day, namely, customer payments, charges, credits, and miscellaneous adjustments. In the second step, transaction cards are written onto magnetic tape. For this conversion process, a relatively simple program reads the cards, processes the data, and writes an accounts receivable transaction tape. In the processing phase, the program edits for valid input data. *Editing* includes tests to ensure that numeric fields contain numeric data, account numbers are correct using self-checking digits, numeric fields do not contain blank, transaction codes are valid, and contents of each field are within reasonable limits. As part of the output, an error listing is printed that contains all invalid transactions. In turn, these transactions are not written on the output tape so that processing can continue. Also, as output, control totals for customer payments, charges, credits, and miscellaneous adjustments are printed for checking with predetermined totals.

figure 9-14. System flow-chart for updating the master accounts receivable magnetic tape file.

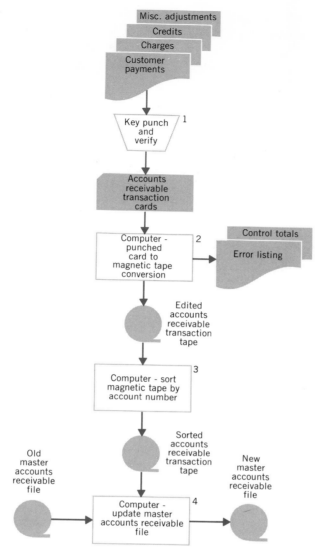

In the third step, the transactions are sorted into the same sequence of the master file, i.e., customer account number. For the sorting process, three or more tape drives are used (even though the system flowchart per Figure 9-14 shows only one input tape and one output tape). During the execution of the sort program, each of the tapes will be read and written several times before the file is finally sorted.

The fourth and final step is the updating run. In the updating process, the old master accounts receivable file and the sorted transaction tape are read into memory for processing by the computer program. If one or more transactions apply to a master file record, the appropriate changes are made to the master record before it is written on the new master accounts receivable file. For those master file records that have no transactions for the day, the master record is written unchanged onto the new tape file. Thus, the new tape file consists of all records—those that were changed and those that were not changed.

figure 9-15. System flow-chart for continuous up-dating of master accounts receivable file.

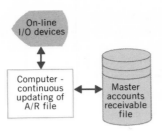

Accounts Receivable Application—Interactive Oriented

Because of the capabilities of magnetic disk, the foregoing steps common to a batch-oriented approach can be eliminated with an interactive mode that uses magnetic disks. As illustrated in Figure 9-15, the key punching and verifying phase, the card to tape conversion, the tape sort, and the final updating run are dropped and replaced by one step. This step entails the updating of the accounts receivable's data base as transactions occur throughout the day. In terms of customer payments, they can be posted individually as they are received or can be batched periodically and posted at one time. Similarly, charges, credits, and miscellaneous adjustments can be posted individually or accumulated for processing against all accounts on some periodic basis. In essence, the number of steps in an interactive mode is much less than for a batch-processing mode.

From the foregoing comparisons of the two approaches, it seems that the interactive mode is preferable over a batch-processing mode, especially when consideration is given to the number of processing steps. However, there are other important considerations. The cost of magnetic tape processing is considerably less than that for comparable magnetic disk. Also, it is easier to handle large volumes of data with magnetic tape. Overall, there are trade-offs between the two methods.

For the typical accounts receivable application mentioned above, an interactive processing mode is preferred where there is a lot of file activity. The ability to answer questions now about the status of an account goes a long way to improving customer relations. Also, where the accounts receivable balances are large, the interactive mode is preferred. On the other hand, for a large accounts receivable file that has very little activity and low account balances, the batch-oriented approach is generally preferred. Thus, the attendant circumstances must be surveyed to determine the service level that is desired at a certain cost for maintaining customer accounts.

service bureau

For the organization not having the need or expertise for on-site computer systems that may or may not employ a common data base, a service bureau is a viable alternative to meeting an organization's data processing needs. A *service bureau* is a profit-making organization that operates computer equipment for the benefit of organizations other than its own on a stated fee basis. For all practical purposes, a service bureau can be defined as an organization which provides data processing functions for other organizations, in particular, the actual processing of the data itself for some meaningful output.

The key factors in deciding whether a computer service bureau should be utilized or not are the needs of management and the cost aspects. Regarding the latter point, it is necessary to know how much is being spent presently on clerical operations which will be taken over by the service bureau. An important consideration is the additional volume that can be handled by the outside data center at a small increase in cost—less than the cost of adding personnel to handle the same work in the customer's office. Quite often, management will elect to use a service bureau even when little or no dollar savings are expected. Improved service and accuracy of reporting are the determining factors. Thus, management's needs can be a far more important consideration than slightly higher costs. The key question is, can the use of a service bureau improve the organization's ability to operate in a more efficient manner that will add to profits?

Services Provided

Although computer service bureaus vary widely in their ability and size, their service is particularly suited to the needs of small- and medium-sized organizations with or without computer equipment of their own. Of particular interest to this group is the fact that it is not necessary to prepare data input manually. Input media, such as punched paper tape, OCR type font, and magnetic strip ledger cards can be produced on comparatively inexpensive office machines as a by-product of accounting machines and various types of terminal devices. By sending their by-product media to a data processing center, timely and updated management reports can be prepared at nominal costs.

Complete Processing of Data. Services provided by a DP service center go far beyond the familiar ones of payroll, sales statistics, and routine reports. It is possible for the data service bureau to process all the paperwork required from the receipt of customer order through shipment, invoicing, and updating of accounts receivable; from bill of materials for purchasing through production control schedules, costing records, maintenance of accounts payable, and updating of perpetual inventory records; and from cash receipts and disbursements ledgers through the posting of the general ledger. Many of the procedures can be handled by utilizing time-sharing devices for updated information in order to control the organization's operations.

Programming and Implementation. When a time-sharing device is used for routine accounting applications, such as customer billing, accounts receivable, and updating inventory records, certain prescribed procedures must be followed. Specialized forms must be used, controls over procedures established, and comparable methods must be clearly set forth since change is not likely to occur. One method for getting a new user started on a time-sharing basis with a service bureau is to define the processing and file requirement and let the service center design an appropriate system by working with the client. Programs are written or library routines are used while the client's records (programs and files) are recorded on a computer access medium. After terminal devices have been installed and clerks have been trained, a cut-off point is established for converting to the new time-sharing system. There should always be a short period of parallel operations as a safety factor so the new system can be thoroughly checked for deficiencies. Many times, the terminal devices are a teletypewriter and an auxiliary printer since this method allows for entering new information via the keyboard while other data are being produced by the printer. The data entered through the console are transmitted, checked, and transmitted back for printing by the auxiliary printer. This procedure assures that invalid data are not being typed. If an operator notes an error before an entry is completed, it can be erased before transmission by depressing a control key. It should be noted that there is no need to dial the computer center to start processing, since the leased line provides for a continuous connection to an on-line terminal.

computer utility

The computer utility concept has made great gains in the DP service industry. In fact, there has been a steady evolution toward this concept since the early days of computers. A *computer utility* is basically a data processing service organization that provides a number of computer services, ranging from a fast response to a slow response time for solving a wide range of business problems. The computer services are far different from those of a traditional service bureau. However, some computer service organizations have expanded to the point where they are supplying computer utility services. By bringing together large-scale computing power, common data bases, and a vast communication equipment network, the computer utility surpasses in capability what can be achieved with most in-house computer systems. Current large computer utilities include Computer Sciences Corporation, Electronic Data Systems, University Computer Company, and Computing and Software.

Facilities Management

A more recent direction of the computer utility concept is contracting the entire responsibility for an organization's data processing department to an independent "facilities management" group. This outside computer utility is responsible for normal in-house data processing activities. A contract, normally arranged on a five-year basis, would be signed for supervising all DP operations, including equipment, people, and functions. Experience has indicated that facilities management is well suited for those organizations who have problems procuring and keeping capable data processing personnel because of the tight labor market for good DP people. A facilities management firm is in a better position to attract and hold qualified personnel since it is able to pay higher salaries as well as use the person's experience and talents on more than one processing facility. From this viewpoint, the facilities management organization is better able to guarantee the success of a new data processing operation than many small- and medium-sized organizations are capable of doing by themselves.

Computer Network

Since there is a need for large-scale computing ability, computer utilities rely on large and powerful computer equipment. Many of the major computer manufacturers are currently providing the required large-scale computing equipment as well as the advanced operating systems to permit multiple methods of access to remote users. Control Data Corporation, for example, has its supercomputers, which reflect their commitment to large computers serving the nucleus of a *distributed network*. Other computer manufacturers are capable of providing computer services in real-time, remote-batch, and multiprogram batch on large-scale computing equipment.

CYBERNET. The Control Data Corporation has established a computer utility network, called CYBERNET, which links computers in cities of the United States and countries abroad (Figure 9-16). This network enables the user to take full advantage of the firm's fast computer power, data base capabilities, and many other data processing services through its CYBER-PAK data service. With CYBERPAK, it enables users to purchase fractional portions of a CDC computer system with accompanying support services. Thus, customers can acquire up to a complete super-scale computer system with full support services and wide range of proprietary software application packages. Problems that normally take hours or days on medium-sized computers are solved in seconds or minutes with one of their supercomputers—a factor that could mean substantial savings in both time and costs to the user.

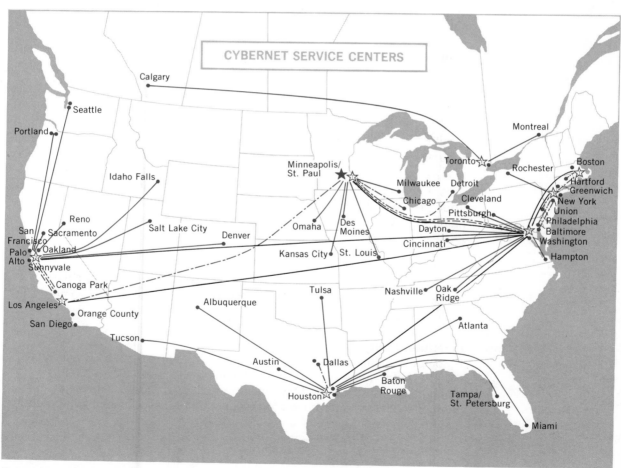

figure 9-16. CDC CYBERNET System—a computer network linking cities in North America. (Courtesy Control Data Corporation.)

**second summary
of chapter 9**

batch-oriented computer systems:
These systems require that data be batched before processing can occur. As with interactive processing systems, basic computer equipment devices are brought together and configured as a business information system. Such configurations are:

- minicomputer systems
- small-scale systems
- medium-scale systems
- large-scale systems

Several features of larger batch-oriented computer systems include:
- multiprogramming—capability of the CPU to process several programs at one time in what appears to be simultaneous operations.
- multiprocessing—capability of multiple CPU's to communicate with each other so as to utilize the processing capability of idle CPU's.
- virtual storage—capability to treat secondary storage as an extension of primary storage, thereby giving the "virtual" appearance of a larger memory.

In addition, larger systems are generally capable of both batch and inter-active processing.

common data bases:
A data base is some type of on-line data files that are stored on magnetic disk, magnetic drum, mass storage, or comparable secondary storage mediums. The size of the data base is determined by the following:
- types of data files
- number of data items per data file
- number of characters per data item

The preferred method of structuring the data base is to utilize the single-record concept, i.e., all relevant information to one data item which formerly appeared in multiple data files appears in one data file in order to eliminate redundant data and increase data accuracy. Also, data items are accessible to all users.

service bureau:
A service bureau is a profit-making organization which provides data processing functions for other organizations that have need of some meaningful output.

computer utility:
A computer utility is a profit-making DP service organization which provides a wider range of computer services than a service bureau. It is analogous to any public utility since it provides the user with large-scale computing power, data base capabilities, and a vast communication equipment network.

facilities management:
A facilities management firm provides the capability of taking over a company's internally run DP department where there are processing and personnel problems.

---

second self-study exercise of chapter 9

True-False:

1. (   ) Batch-oriented processing is available on small-scale computer systems only.
2. (   ) Minicomputers are always found in large-scale computer configurations.
3. (   ) The only benefit of large-scale computer systems is their fast computing speeds.
4. (   ) Operating systems are found only in minicomputer systems.
5. (   ) Magnetic disk and drum are used as secondary storage mediums.
6. (   ) It is best to have multiple data processing files of the same data items.
7. (   ) Good data base design should allow for variable-length records.
8. (   ) Good data base design should provide for some type of lockout feature.
9. (   ) The Control Data Corporation utilizes a computer utility network.
10. (   ) Facilities management is simply a fancy name for service bureau.

Fill-In:

11. The IBM _____ _____ is an example of a small-scale computer system.
12. An important language for small-scale, batch-oriented computer systems is _____.
13. _____ allows more than one program to reside in memory at one time in what appears to be simultaneous operations.
14. With _____ _____, an entire program generally occupies storage space in main memory only.
15. _____ _____ can occupy space in both primary and secondary storage.
16. Another name for on-line storage of data files is a _____ _____ _____.
17. The _____-_____ concept states that all information relevant to one data item appears in one file for multiple users.
18. A well-designed data base should allow for _____ of data files.
19. Firms that operate computer equipment for the purpose of processing data and providing meaningful output to its customers on a stated fee basis are called _____ _____.
20. A _____ _____, an enlargement of the service bureau concept, gives the user large-scale computing power, common data bases, and a vast communication equipment network.

summary

The fundamentals of microprocessors, microcomputers, and minicomputers were presented in the chapter. As part of a general overview of business-oriented computer systems, typical configurations of minicomputers and peripheral equipment within a time-sharing environment were illustrated. Similarly, typical configurations of batch-oriented computer systems ranging from small scale to large scale were presented. No matter the processing mode, an organization can upgrade its installation by adding (or eliminating) input and output devices as well as primary and secondary storage without the need for reprogramming.

Within a typical business information system, the common data base which has taken on new importance was discussed. Special emphasis was placed on design considerations for an on-line data base. For those organizations not having the need or expertise for on-site computer systems that may or may not utilize data bases, outside organizations, such as service bureaus and computer utilities, offer an excellent way to utilize modern DP methods and procedures—the last subject for discussion in the chapter.

questions

1. Distinguish among minicomputers, microprocessors, and microcomputers.
2. What is the function of the I/O bus in a minicomputer?
3. How important is the minicomputer currently in time-sharing computer systems?
4. Distinguish between time-sharing computer systems and batch-oriented computer systems.
5. What important factors must be taken into consideration when designing an efficient common data base?
6. How important is security within a computerized data base environment? Explain.
7. How does a computer utility differ from a traditional service bureau?

answers to first self-study exercise

1. F 2. T 3. T 4. T 5. T 6. F 7. T 8. T 9. F 10. F 11. microprocessors 12. microcomputer 13. minicomputer 14. time-sharing 15. I/O bus 16. distributed processing 17. interactive processing 18. batch-processing 19. BASIC-PLUS 20. UNIBUS

answers to second self-study exercise

1. F 2. F 3. F 4. F 5. T 6. F 7. T 8. T 9. T 10. F 11. 8100 system 12. RPG 13. multiprogramming 14. real storage 15. virtual storage 16. common data base 17. single-record 18. security 19. service bureaus 20. computer utility

part five

designing and implementing data processing for business

In order to implement a business information system, there is need to undertake a feasibility study. The first step of the study is basically an analysis of the present system (systems analysis). It culminates in an exploratory survey report that is reviewed by top management regarding the feasibility or infeasibility of undertaking a systems project. Systems design, the second and most creative step of the feasibility study, involves determining new system requirements. This includes working with people and resolving problem areas. Both of these steps are covered in Chapter 10. The third and last step of the feasibility study is equipment selection. Once the equipment has been integrated as a part of a new business information system, commonly referred to as systems implementation, it must be reviewed periodically for improvements—the subject matter for Chapter 11.

chapter ten

feasibility study— systems analysis and design

The foregoing vignettes of Joe and Claudia Cosgrove with the computer have centered around presently installed computer systems. However, there is a constant search via a feasibility study to implement new systems that will help the company and the environment in which it operates. For example, due to the current energy crunch, the company for which Joe works has programmed its computer to suggest possible car pools by matching home addresses and work schedules. Based on the computer program, Joe is a member of a four-person car pool. One month ago, he did not know any of his three fellow riders. Hence, Joe pulls into the service station less frequently for a fill-up.

When he does purchase a full tank of gas, he signs a sales slip that has been imprinted with his credit card number and amount of gas purchased. This slip, in turn, is eventually used by the oil company's computer for billing Joe. As with all systems, a feasibility study must be undertaken to insure that a workable and economical system is installed.

The purpose of this chapter and the next one is to explore the steps of a feasibility study and the implementation of a system project. The feasibility study encompasses these major steps:

1. systems analysis, including an exploratory survey report,
2. systems design,
3. equipment selection.

The first step focuses on systems analysis which is a thorough and comprehensive review of the present system. This analysis allows the feasibility study committee to make valid comparisons among the many feasible system alternatives with the present system, thereby providing a basis for preparing an exploratory survey report to top management.

Once a decision has been made to implement a newer business information system, the details of the system must be specified. The second step of the feasibility study is systems design. Imagination and creativity are a must for this phase: otherwise, some of the basic weaknesses and related problems of the existing system will be duplicated unconsciously by the data processing group. It should be noted that the third and final step of the feasibility study—equipment selection—is covered in the next chapter.

purpose of the feasibility study

The primary purpose of a feasibility study is to determine the feasibility or infeasibility of applying newer data processing procedures and/or equipment to selected functional areas of an organization. In general, a system project is started in response to some problem. In the area of marketing, the sales manager might state: "We're losing business because of our poor customer service, not to mention the number of times that we are out of stock." Or in production, a manufacturing manager might complain as follows: "It is difficult to plan production if sales forecasts are off by twenty percent each month." Or in accounting, the accounts receivable manager might state: "Our monthly statements to customers are not current and they are full of errors." Any of these problems may lead to a system study that will, in turn, lead to a modification of the present system or the development of a new one.

After a thorough analysis of all the facts regarding the problem(s), the feasibility study group can reach one of two conclusions. One is that the present business data processing system is superior to any of the new systems studied. The other conclusion is that one or more new systems, when consideration is given to their financial aspects, appear to be superior to the present system. In the second case, the feasibility study proceeds to the next step—systems design. In the first case, the data processing group may go back and examine additional systems or study new equipment developments that have come on the market since the analysis was initiated. If the answer is still negative, the feasibility study will cease, awaiting developments in the field.

The importance of doing a thorough job cannot be overemphasized. It is extremely essential for the future well-being of an organization that this time-consuming process be performed accurately and methodically. A fast and half-hearted attempt will often lead the organization to a premature conclusion about a new system. Only after installation do the real facts come to light, often resulting in major data processing problems and/or higher data processing costs. Thus, the need for a careful and systematic approach is a must for installing a successful business information system; there are no legitimate shortcuts.

establishment of a feasibility study committee

To initiate a system project, top management must establish a feasibility study group. Normally, an executive committee is established to give direction to this group. Many times, members of the executive committee include one or more of the following: chairman of the board, president, executive vice-president, and vice-presidents—marketing, manufacturing, purchasing, finance, engineering, personnel, and research and development. This high-level committee not only oversees what the feasibility study committee is doing, but also enhances the chances of success because of its rank and status.

Once the membership is established, the executive committee's initial task is to issue a written statement that a feasibility study committee has been formed. This statement should state adjustments in personnel and jobs may be required to make the change. Some employees may have to be retrained and reassigned for new data processing jobs, some of which may be higher, lower, or the same as the present ones. It should be emphasized to all personnel that no one will be fired or asked to resign. This first memo to all employees should indicate that periodic written statements will be issued regarding the progress of the feasibility study.

A concurrent task with the preparation of the written memorandum from the executive committee is the selection of a feasibility study committee. This latter committee will have the authority and responsibility for evaluating and possibly implementing a new business information system. It, in turn, will be held accountable for its actions. The number of participants will depend on several factors, the following being the most important: the organization's size, the number of divisions and departments, the degree of centralization or decentralization, the number of business functions considered for new DP applications, the skills of the organization's personnel, budget constraints, and time considerations. Typical study groups range from four persons up to a dozen or more, depending upon the above factors.

If a business information system cuts across the entire organization, a member from each of the functional areas should be selected. If at all possible, each person selected should have several years of experience, be an objective thinker, and capable of creative thinking. Also, the individual should be familiar with major problem areas. Generally, those who have the background and hold responsible positions have not had the opportunity to keep up with the latest developments in data processing equipment. For this reason, it is necessary to have persons with computer and programming experience within the feasibility study who, generally, do not know the organization's methods and procedures. This may mean going to outside consultants if the organization lacks the technical expertise in data processing. Whether the individuals selected are from inside or outside the organization, this committee will function best when people with the required knowledge are present. It is recommended that at least one person devote full time to the feasibility study. This individual will head the group and direct the study to maintain its momentum. Other members may work full time or part time, depending upon the magnitude of the feasibility study.

define the scope of the feasibility study

The determination of who will comprise the two committees (executive and feasibility study) leads to the question of what will be included in the feasibility study. It is up to the executive committee to define the scope of the data processing study. This top-level group might ask the feasibility study committee to restrict its activities to production, marketing, finance, or some other functional area. On the other hand, the study might be very broad in scope so as to include the entire organization. Again, the scope might be somewhere in the middle of the above two approaches.

Once the overall scope has been set forth by the executive committee, the feasibility study committee undertakes the next steps of the exploratory survey. This consists of:

- selection of desired objectives
- definition of the problem
- determination of a realistic schedule

Selection of Desired Objectives

The formulation of objectives is the joint effort of the executive committee and the feasibility study committee. Not only do objectives force top management to do some serious thinking about the organization's future, but they also bring to light problems that might have been overlooked. For the study team, it provides a framework from which to operate. The constraints and limitations under which the project must function are clearly set forth. Experience has indicated that a feasibility study has gone much more smoothly when a formal statement of objectives has been clearly defined.

The objectives desired by management can take many directions, as set forth in Figure 10-1. Objectives can center around a cost savings approach.

- Increased efficiency in the organization's operations
- Reduction in data processing costs
- More timely information for management decisions
- Improved customer service and relations
- Increased flow of data for meaningful information
- Uniform and accurate handling of data with a minimum of human intervention
- Elimination of conflicting and overlapping services
- Improved internal control
- Improved employee and public relations
- Increased managerial development and efficiency
- Efficient utilization of personnel and equipment
- Increased overall net income from operations

figure 10-1. Selection of desired objectives for a system project.

In such situations, consideration should be given to tangible and intangible benefits in order that the evaluation is complete and realistic. Other objectives can emphasize faster and more timely information for management decisions. In reality, this approach is aimed at cost reduction as well as faster service for customers. Ideally, a new system is one that is able to meet as many objectives as possible and, at the same time, reduce organization costs.

In addition to reduction in costs, more timely decisions, and improved service to customers, the following are also representative of objectives desired by management. The utilization of advanced data processing equipment speeds up the flow of data. This permits instantaneous information to be generated about the status of customer orders. It allows production to be scheduled more effectively and notifies the customer of any shipping changes or delays. Also, faster billing procedures are available. The uniform and accurate handling of data is available without the problems of human intervention. All these benefits improve customer relations and enhance the firm's competitive position.

Top management might consider other objectives, such as the elimination of conflicting and overlapping services within the organization. A very important objective is the employment of checks and balances as the data are processed, eliminating the need for manual checking. This would be part of internal control for the new system.

The above listing of objectives is by no means complete, but is a cross section of objectives that can be set forth by the executive group for the feasibility study committee. Usually, the selection of many desired objectives results in the need for more advanced data processing equipment which can be more costly than the present system. No matter what objectives are included as a frame of reference, an important one of any feasibility study is a resulting larger net income to the company after consideration of all the tangible and intangible factors involved. It should be remembered that the desired objectives can be changed if they are found to be unrealistic later in the study.

Definition of the Problem

Once the objectives have been determined, the feasibility study committee defines the problem more precisely. It is the job of the study team to specify the areas that will be explored in greater detail. When doing so, the group must make sure that the scope of the feasibility study is compatible with the objectives. If the objectives and the scope of the study are in conflict, this is the time for the two groups to resolve the difficulties. For example, the objective — provide immediate information to customers on orders placed — is difficult to achieve with a batch-processing system while it would be relatively easy for a real-time system. A conference between the two committees would resolve the problem.

Having defined the problem as accurately as possible within the scope of the study, the study team should have little doubt as to the areas to be covered by the investigation. It is advisable to state these findings in writing. A written memorandum by the feasibility study group ensures the accomplishment of what was originally intended and reduces the problem of "going off on a tangent." A carefully laid out plan for areas to be explored indicates where the study will cut across original lines and where authority is needed for changes in systems, methods, procedures, forms, reports, or organization.

Determination of a Realistic Schedule

The next step in the exploratory survey is the preparation of a time schedule for the entire systems study. Such a study may take place over a long period of time, ranging from many months to several years. Experience has shown that there is a tendency to underestimate the time element of the feasibility study as well as all other succeeding steps. The time factor is a function of the objectives desired and problem definition. For a successful study, it must be covered in sufficient depth and be as thorough as possible. This means the time factor is of secondary importance. If time becomes the important consideration, the results will usually mean that an optimum decision for the organization's DP needs will probably not be made.

When developing a time schedule, the feasibility study committee must determine the amount of work involved in each step of the systems change and what resources in terms of personnel and skills will be needed. Likewise, consideration must be given to the following areas: training, programming, program testing, delivery of the equipment, physical requirements and installation of the equipment, files development, delivery of new forms and supplies, and conversion activities. The foregoing includes the major items that must be included in a realistic schedule.

Major Parts of a Systems Project. An overview of time, stated in percentages, for the various steps in a feasibility study and systems implementation, is given in Figure 10-2. These percentages should not be construed as absolute values, but rather as a general guide for a typical system project that would take approximately two years. Depending on the complexity of the project, a Gantt chart or a PERT/Time network can be used to control the activities. Normally, a feasibility study comprises more than one-third of a system project.

The period required for systems implementation comprises about two-thirds of the total effort required for a system change. This is where the hard work and long hours really begin. It is unfortunate that many in top management feel the real work has been completed when the feasibility

Feasibility Study:

Systems analysis, including exploratory survey report	12%
Systems design	15%
Equipment selection	10%

Systems Implementation:

Training personnel—programmers and all others	8%
Flowcharting and using decision tables	10%
Programming and desk checking	10%
Program compiling and testing	20%
Parallel operations for checking new system	5%
Final conversion to new system	10%
	100%

figure 10-2. Major steps of a system project, stated as a percent of total time.

study is over when, in reality, the reverse is true. This attitude by top management often explains the hurry to get the equipment installed and running during the systems implementation phase. This is particularly true when the rental on the equipment starts and management sees no production for the large cash outlays. The end results are incomplete, inefficient, and ill-conceived programs that are a disappointment to all involved in the systems project. Expected benefits will never be realized under these circumstances.

Feedback on Systems Project. The study group that is responsible for scheduling should not only prepare a realistic timetable, but also be in a position at all times to report whether the study is ahead, behind, or on schedule. The feasibility study committee should issue reports periodically to the executive committee on the status quo of the project. Included in the reports should be information that is critical to the study, such as problem areas and delays. The utilization of the "exception principle" in progress reports is needed to control the project.

systems analysis— detailed investigation of present system

The detailed investigation of the present system, commonly referred to as systems analysis, is the next job for the various study groups or systems analysts of the feasibility study committee. It involves collecting, organizing, and evaluating facts about the present system and the environment in which it operates. Generally, the study teams devote full time to this undertaking because it is so time consuming. Survey of existing inputs, methods and procedures, data flow, outputs, files, and internal control, to name the more important ones, should be more than a casual one. It should be an intensive review in order to understand fully the present system and its related problems. No area should be excluded unless it has no relationship to the scope of the study in terms of desired objectives and the problem definition. Hence, the search should be comprehensive and include these areas:

- *Review of historical facts*—identifies the major turning points and milestones that have influenced the organization over time. Not only must historical data be analyzed, but also current and future plans must be examined in order to relate their impact on a new business information system.

- *Analysis of inputs*—identifies where source documents are used to capture originating data. An understanding of the nature of the document, what is contained in it, who prepared it, where it was initiated, when it was completed, and its distribution is important since outputs from one area serve as inputs for other areas. A sample list of input records for three major functional areas of a manufacturing firm is found in Figure 10-3a.

- *Review of methods and procedures*—assists in understanding the relationship between inputs, files maintained, and outputs. The series of procedural steps by which data processing operations are accomplished can be examined to determine what action is required, who is required to act, and when the action is to be undertaken.

- *Review of files maintained*—permits an understanding of the number and size of files maintained by departments, where they are located, who uses them, and the number of times they are referenced. The maintenance of files is a function of their values versus their costs of storage plus satisfying legal requirements.

- *Analysis of outputs*—determines how well present reports are meeting the organization's needs. The questions of what information is needed and why, who needs it, and when and where it is needed are ones that must be answered. Additional questions concerning the sequence of the data, how often the form is used, how long it is kept on file, and the like must be investigated. A typical list of outputs for the functional areas of a manufacturing firm is shown in Figure 10-3b.

- *Review of internal control*—indicates control points that are critical to maintaining efficient data processing operations. Locating these control points allows one to visualize the essential parts and the overall framework of a system.

- *Analysis of present personnel requirements*—assists in pinpointing the present personnel in terms of type, by skill, and by pay scale. Basically, these data can be obtained from personnel records, monthly reports, and interviews. Every effort should be made to understand thoroughly this most important element of DP operations, since the same people will normally be involved in the new system.

- *Review of present work volumes*—identifies average and peak workloads as well as the workload at month's end. If work volumes are low and the processing procedures are complex, the feasibility of applying new DP equipment is unlikely. On the other hand, if large work volumes require straight forward processing, the chances of using new equipment is very high. Additionally, work volume analysis is helpful to determine whether a particular work station is a control, storage, or terminal point in a system.

- *Review of other requirements and considerations*—helps in locating important items that may be critical to the present system. Items, such as the effects of exceptions and errors on the present system, seasonal or other cyclical characteristics, current production facilities, and present financial resources, should be investigated if these are critical factors for current operations.

Functional Area	(a) Sample Inputs	(b) Sample Outputs
Marketing	Sales quotations, salespersons reports, sales forecasts, sales invoices, listing of customers, advertising budget, and customer credit information.	Marketing sales analysis, sales by products and product lines, comparison of company sales to industry sales, monthly budget versus actual, and salespersons commissions and salaries report.
Manufacturing	Production orders, receiving reports, shipping reports, purchase orders, time cards, stock records, stock requisitions, personnel records, and time standards.	Production control report, production shipping schedule, inventory control report, quality control report, spoilage and scrap analysis, departmental budget versus actual, and factory personnel turnover analysis.
Finance	Vendor invoices, cash receipts, fixed asset records, tax returns, stockholder listings, and insurance records.	Cash flow analysis, monthly budget versus actual, monthly balance sheet and income statement, capital project study, and aging of accounts receivable.

figure 10-3. List of sample (a) inputs and (b) outputs for three major functional areas of a manufacturing firm.

Flowchart the Present System

The best method to organize the facts obtained from the above investigation is to utilize some form of flowcharting. The system flowchart is suitable for tracing the origin of input data, through each phase of processing and communication, into files, and finally out of files for desired outputs—many in the form of reports. The flowcharting of the present operations not only organizes the facts, but also helps disclose gaps and duplications in the data gathered. It allows a thorough comprehension of the numerous details and related problems in the present operation. In essence, the knowledge, gathered to date, is brought together in a meaningful relationship for members of the feasibility study committee. It should be noted that flowcharting need not be undertaken separately, but generally is combined with systems analysis.

Present System Costs and Benefits

One of the major reasons for reviewing the present operation is to determine its cost. Cost should be analyzed by department since this is the most common basis for reporting and provides an excellent means of comparing new system costs.

Existing costs are not the only ones determined. Present system benefits must be set forth for comparison at a later date with each proposed alternative. These include the present level of service to customers, the value of reports, return on investment, rate of profit, ability of the present system to grow with the organization, and inventory turnover. Many of these benefits can be measured precisely while others are intangible by their very nature which require subjective evaluation. For the final evaluation of the present system and the proposed alternatives, costs and tangible benefits are compared first. If the proposed alternative system meets the organization's established return on investment, there is no problem. However, if the proposed alternative falls below the acceptable level for the investment, the intangible factors are critical for a final answer.

Five-Year Cost Study. The usual cost projections for the proposed system in a feasibility study is a five-year period, starting with implementation of the new system. The rationale is this: if a computer is selected, it will not be processing on a daily basis for about a year from the day of equipment selection (the final step of the feasibility study). Also, the equipment must be capable of handling the organization's workload from at least three years up to about five years. Thus, a five-year cost projection that starts after completion of the feasibility study is a realistic approach for the present and proposed systems. Attempting to go beyond five years is undesirable in view of the guesswork and assumptions that must be made about newer equipment.

proposed system alternatives

Inasmuch as each functional area of the present system that is germane to the study has been carefully analyzed, a feasible set of processing alternatives are developed in order to select the best one from the set. Each alternative will not be developed in the same depth as was undertaken to understand the present system. Otherwise, such an effort would increase the time and manpower requirements of the study beyond its intended scope and budget.

Before feasible system alternatives are developed, proposed system specifications must be clearly defined. These specifications, which pertain to each functional area of the feasibility study, are determined from the desired objectives set forth initially in the study. Likewise, consideration is given to the strengths and the shortcomings of the existing system. Required system specifications, which must be clearly defined and in conformity with the study's objectives, are as follows.

1. Input data from original source documents for processing by the system.
2. Methods and procedures that show the relationship of input data to files and files to outputs of the data processing system.
3. Files to be maintained with automated data processing equipment (or otherwise).
4. Outputs to be produced, with great emphasis on managerial reports that utilize the "exception principle."
5. Work volumes and timing considerations for present and future periods, including peak periods.

A starting point for compiling the above specifications is to work with the outputs first. After they have been determined, it is possible to infer what inputs and files are required and what methods and procedures must be employed. Future workloads of the new system must be defined for inputs, files, and outputs in terms of average and peak loads, cycles, and trends.

Flexible System Requirements
for Developing System Alternatives

The requirements of the new system may appear on the surface to be fixed. A closer examination often reveals that the study group should think in terms of these specifications having flexibility. For example, the objectives set forth in the study state certain computer files or a common data base must be updated once a day. Perhaps the best data processing solution is to utilize an interactive computer system where the files or a common data base are updated as actual transactions occur. This approach is within the constraints as initially set forth and introduces a new way of maintaining files. The important point is that alternative methods are available which may have the outward appearance of being fixed. With this in mind, it is possible to design a number of different systems with varying features, costs, and benefits. In many cases, additional data processing systems can be investigated and analyzed when flexible system requirements are considered.

Consultant's Role in Developing and Selecting a System Alternative.

A clear understanding of the new system requirements is the starting point for developing feasible system alternatives. By far, this phase is the most important and difficult undertaking of the study to date. Experience of the outside consultant is a great value to the study group. The individual's knowledge can help immeasurably to reduce the number of promising solutions. Too often, a study group "goes off on a tangent" about a specific system that should have been discarded initially as not feasible. Also, the consultant can point out the shortcomings of a certain approach that may have been strongly pushed by certain individuals. Such an individual can act with the head of the feasibility study committee to resolve conflicts that tend to divide the team when particular members like their approaches over others presented. The consultant's objectivity can enhance the organization's chances of developing viable system alternatives and selecting the optimum one when judging the merits and weaknesses of a new system. Thus, the key to developing promising system alternatives and selecting the optimum one is to employ the talents and experience of the study group to its fullest capacity.

Costs and Tangible Benefits
of Each System Alternative

The next step after developing feasible system alternatives is to determine the anticipated savings and incremental costs for each one, like those set forth in Figure 10-4. The difference between the estimated savings and estimated incremental costs represents the estimated net savings (losses) to the organization before federal income taxes. *Estimated savings,* sometimes called *cost displacement,* are: reduction in the number of personnel; sale or elimination of some equipment; reduction in repairs, maintenance, insurance, and personal property taxes; lower cost rental and utilities, and elimination or reduction in outside processing costs.

Incremental costs are segregated into two categories, namely, "one-time" costs and "operating" costs. Major *one-time costs* are those relating to the feasibility study, training of programming and operating personnel,

Grosse Manufacturing Company
Feasibility Study System Alternative #9
Estimated Net Savings
Rental Basis—Five-Year Period
198–

	Years from Start of Systems Implementation					Five-Year Total
	1	2	3	4	5	
Estimated Savings:						
Reduction in personnel (including payroll taxes and fringe benefits)	$120,200	$400,500	$440,300	$490,500	$540,500	$1,992,000
Sale of equipment	120,000					120,000
Rental (space) savings	25,000	51,000	54,500	58,000	61,800	250,300
Elimination of rental equipment	2,050	4,380	4,690	5,000	5,300	21,420
Other savings	3,000	3,060	3,210	3,370	3,540	16,180
Total Estimated Savings	$270,250	$458,940	$502,700	$556,870	$611,140	$2,399,900
Estimated One-Time Costs:						
Feasibility study (for this year and prior year)	$95,000					$95,000
Training	50,000					50,000
Systems and programming	255,500					255,500
Master file conversion	262,500					262,500
Other conversion activities	75,500					75,500
Site preparation	55,400					55,400
Other one-time costs	22,300					22,300
Total Estimated One-Time Costs	$816,200					$816,200
Estimated Operating Costs:						
Data processing equipment rental (include maintenance)	$110,000	$120,800	$127,400	$134,100	$141,000	$633,300
Additional personnel for new system (includes payroll taxes and fringe benefits)	34,000	60,700	62,300	63,400	64,600	285,000
Program maintenance	20,000	30,700	32,200	33,800	36,000	152,700
Forms and supplies	10,000	21,500	23,000	24,500	26,000	105,000
Other additional operating costs	4,400	12,400	12,800	13,200	17,600	60,400
Total Estimated Additional Operating Costs	$178,400	$246,100	$257,700	$269,000	$285,200	$1,236,400
Net Savings (Losses) before Federal Income Taxes	($724,350)	$212,840	$245,000	$287,870	$325,940	$347,300

figure 10-4. Feasibility study system alternative #9 for net savings (losses)—five-year period (rental basis).

detail flowcharting of all feasibility study applications, programming and testing of programs for the new system, parallel operations where the old and the new system operate concurrently, file conversion, site preparation, conversion activities from existing system to new system, and other equipment and supplies. In a similar manner, *operating costs* include monthly rental or depreciation of computer and related equipment; maintenance of equipment; wages and salaries, payroll taxes, and fringe benefits of DP personnel; program maintenance; forms and supplies of computer and related equipment; and miscellaneous additional costs.

Accurate figures for a five-year period are of great importance to the feasibility study committee, indicating the need for the accounting department's assistance. Many times, the best way to increase the accuracy of the figures compiled by the study group is to have the outside consultant assist in their preparation and review.

When computing the estimated savings and incremental costs, the trend of growth or cutback in the organization's workload should be analyzed and projected for the next five years. These data can, then, be utilized to project savings and costs, similar to the analysis found in Figure 10-4. In this feasibility study for alternative #9, consideration has been given to higher future costs. Salaries and wages are generally increased by 6 to 8% per year.

Discounted Cash Flow. Since the projected savings and costs factors in a feasibility study are for five years (starting with systems implementation), the difference between the two sums after taking into account federal income taxes should be discounted back to the present time. The purpose of the discounted cash flow method is to bring the time value of money into the presentation. This is shown for system alternative #9 in Figure 10-5. Notice that the net savings after federal income taxes of $180,596 over the five-year period (anticipated life of the system), when discounted, shows a negative present value for this alternative, amounting to $22,897. On the basis of a discounted 20% return on investment for this alternative, it should not be undertaken (the cutoff point for capital investments is 20%). Even though the revised discounted rate of return is approximately 16%, consideration should be given to additional benefits.

Grosse Manufacturing Company
Feasibility Study System Alternative #9
Discounted Cash Flow — 20% Return After Federal Income Taxes
Rental Basis — Five-Year Period
198–

Year	Net Savings (Losses) Before Federal Income Taxes (per Figure 10-4)	Federal Income Tax @ 48% Rate	Net Savings (Losses) After Federal Income Taxes	At 20% Present Value of $1	Present Value of Net Savings (Losses)
1	($724,350)	($347,688)	($376,662)	.833	($313,759)
2	212,840	102,163	110,677	.694	76,810
3	245,000	117,600	127,400	.579	73,765
4	287,870	138,178	149,692	.482	72,152
5	325,940	156,451	169,489	.402	68,135
Totals	$347,300	$166,704	$180,596		($22,897)

figure 10-5. Feasibility study system alternative #9 — discounted cash flow based on 20% after federal incomes taxes (rental basis).

figure 10-6. Feasibility study—intangible benefits, considerations for newer DP systems.

Improved customer service by using better techniques to anticipate customer requirements, resulting in less lost sales, less overtime in the plant for rush orders, and similar considerations.

Better decision-making ability in the areas of marketing, manufacturing, finance, purchasing, personnel, engineering, and research and development through more timely and informative reports.

More effective utilization of management's time for planning, organizing, directing, and controlling because of the availability of timely data and information.

Ability to handle more customers faster with more automatic data processing equipment.

Closer control over capital investments and expenses through comparisons with budgets or forecasts.

Improved scheduling and production control, resulting in more efficient employment of personnel and machines.

Greater accuracy, speed, and reliability in information handling and data processing operations.

Better control of credit through more frequent aging of accounts receivable and analysis of credit data.

Reversal of trend to higher hiring and training costs arising from the difficulties in filling clerical jobs.

Help prevent a competitor(s) from gaining an eventual economic advantage over the firm.

Improved promotional efforts to attract new customers and retain present ones.

Greater ability to handle increased workloads at small additional costs.

Enhanced stature in the business community as a progressive and forward-looking firm.

Other Tangible Benefits. Other tangible benefits may be available in order to justify the system project. Among these are: reduced investment in the amount of inventory carried, less spoilage and obsolescence of inventory, lower purchasing costs through automatic reordering with data processing equipment, lower insurance costs and taxes on inventory, fewer number of warehouses needed, lower transportation costs, and less interest charges on money needed to finance inventories. More effective inventory control can have a pronounced effect on this large balance sheet item.

In a similar manner, a more accurate projection of cash needs will reduce charges for short-term money. Other large asset items should be evaluated in order to determine if tangible savings are available through more effective control. All these values discounted to the present should be added to Figure 10-5. If the present value of net savings for a system alternative is still negative after adding these tangible benefits, the intangible benefits must be explored. This situation will occur in most cases for a newer data processing system.

Intangible Benefits for Each System Alternative

A number of intangible benefits or qualitative factors will be uncovered by studying the potential contributions of the new system to the organization's activities and problems. A list of these factors is found in Figure 10-6. Even though qualitative factors are nonquantifiable initially, their ultimate impact is in quantitative terms, reflected in the financial statements.

An analysis of Figure 10-6 indicates that these benefits offer two major benefits ultimately to the organization. They are increased revenues and decreased operating costs. Better customer service and relations should enhance the organization's chances of increasing sales to its present customers and to many potential ones who are looking for these characteristics in its vendors. A new system change not only affects it externally, but also internally in terms of faster and more frequent reporting of results. In addition to accuracy, speed, and flexibility, automatic data processing equipment allows management more time to plan and organize activities and, in turn, direct and control according to the original plan. This is in contrast to many older systems that do not facilitate the functions of management. In summary, the qualitative factors, upon close examination, can have a pronounced effect upon the evaluation of each system alternative.

Comparison of Each System Alternative to Present System

The feasibility study committee is in a position to compare the system alternatives to the existing system once a thorough analysis of the important factors has been accomplished. There are two approaches to evaluation of alternatives: identifying and listing the relevant costs and benefits (tangible and intangible) or utilizing simulation techniques of operations research to determine the outcome of the system alternatives. Although either approach can be effectively employed for a definitive conclusion to the feasibility study, only the first one will be explored below.

Decision Table to Evaluate Systems Alternatives. The first approach can take the form of a decision table, shown in Figure 10-7. The conditions in the upper part of the table represent the important facts assembled in the study while the middle part contains the possible courses of action. Each rule or system alternative represents a set of actions corresponding to a certain set of conditions. Rule 3 (system alternative #3) indicates a whole series of no (N) answers to the stated conditions with a low 16% return on investment. A similar situation applies to system alternative #6. Further study for these alternatives should be discontinued. Rule 7 (system alternative #7) indicates a high return for an interactive processing system when compared to the last two alternatives (#8 and #9). The important action required is a reevaluation of the values used in calculating the return on investment after federal income taxes for this system alternative. The last rule or system alternative #9 meets all the conditions except the one pertaining to return on investment. The action required for rule 9 is the employment of an additional consultant for the study.

exploratory survey report to top management

At the conclusion of the foregoing studies, ample information has been accumulated to make a final recommendation to top management. The exploratory survey report, authored by the feasibility study committee, should be a signed report to the executive committee. It should be financially oriented since large sums of money are involved. Important information that has a direct or indirect reference to finances must be included.

**first summary
of chapter 10**

purpose of the feasibility study:
The main purpose of the feasibility study is to determine the feasibility or infeasibility of applying newer data processing procedures and/or equipment to one or more functional areas of an organization.

establishment of a feasibility study committee:
The feasibility study committee consists of organizational personnel from the functional areas being investigated, the DP section, and generally one or more outside consultants. It is established by a high-level executive committee which gives direction to this study group.

define the scope of the feasibility study:
The scope of the feasibility study which centers on what functional areas to be included may be very narrow, very broad, or in between as determined by the executive committee. Within this defined scope, desired objectives are selected, the problem is defined, and a realistic schedule is determined. Generally, one-third of the total project time is spent on the feasibility study (systems analysis, systems design, and equipment selection) and two-thirds on systems implementation.

systems analysis—detailed investigation of present system:
Systems analysis, being a detailed survey of the present system installed, involves a comprehensive investigation of these areas:
* review of historical facts
* analysis of inputs
* review of methods and procedures
* review of files maintained
* analysis of outputs
* review of internal control
* analysis of present personnel requirements
* review of present work volumes
* review of other requirements and considerations

The best method to organize the above facts in a logical manner is to utilize *flowcharts*. Not only does the preceding analysis give the feasibility study committee an understanding of the present system, but also assists in determining its costs and benefits.

proposed system alternatives:
A most important task of the feasibility study committee is to develop feasible system alternatives. An integral part of each alternative is developing a financially oriented, five-year study, i.e., savings, costs, and tangible benefits. Likewise, consideration is given to intangible benefits. A thorough analysis of all facts finally leads to the selection of the best system alternative.

**first self-study
exercise
of chapter 10**

True-False:

1. (   ) The main purpose of the feasibility study is to determine the best system.
2. (   ) To initiate a new system, there is need to establish a study committee.
3. (   ) An example of a desired system objective is increased DP costs.
4. (   ) Program checking and testing precede selection of the DP equipment.
5. (   ) Analysis of inputs determine how well present reports are meeting user needs.
6. (   ) During systems analysis, there is no need to review internal control.
7. (   ) One method of organizing current facts is to use flowcharts.
8. (   ) A five-year study of savings and costs should ignore discounted cash flow.
9. (   ) A decision table is a reliable method for evaluating system alternatives.
10. (   ) Intangible benefits are not considered in a feasibility study.

Fill-In:

11. The _____ _____ encompasses three major steps, the first being systems analysis that includes an exploratory survey report to top management.
12. In a data processing system project, the most profound changes occur in the area of _____.
13. Normally, the _____ _____ _____ includes those from the functional areas of an organization, the data processing section, and generally one or more outside consultants.
14. The formulation and selection of desired _____ is an important part of the first phase of the feasibility study.
15. Once the objectives have been reduced to writing, the feasibility study committee specifies a clear _____ of the _____ as far as it is possible, that is, within the scope of the study.
16. In most system projects, the _____ _____ takes approximately one-third of the total time while _____ _____ consumes about two-thirds.
17. The objectives of systems analysis is to understand the _____ _____, in particular, its exceptions and problems.
18. Analysis of _____ involves asking the questions—who, what, where, when, and why about current information being generated.
19. A recommended method that brings together all the data collected during the systems analysis phase is _____.
20. A final part of the first step of the feasibility study consists of determining the _____ _____ _____ plus their savings and costs.

Decision Table	Table Name: Feasibility Study — Exploratory Survey								Page 1 of 1			
	Chart No: FS-ES-1				Prepared By: Robert J. Thierauf				Date: July 25, 198–			

Condition	Rule Number												
	1	2	3	4	5	6	7	8	9	10	11	12	13
Tangible Benefits:													
Meets return on investment criteria −20% after taxes*	Y	Y	N	N	N	N	N	N	N				
Reduced order processing costs	Y	Y	Y	Y	Y	Y	Y	Y	Y				
Lower investment in inventory, all types	N	N	N	Y	Y	Y	Y	Y	Y				
Less cash requirements in the future	N	N	N	N	N	Y	Y	Y	Y				
Intangible Benefits:													
Improved customer service	N	N	N	N	N	Y	Y	Y	Y				
Improved promotional efforts	N	N	N	N	N	N	Y	Y	Y				
Ability to handle more customers faster	N	N	N	N	N	N	Y	Y	Y				
Better decision making ability	Y	Y	Y	Y	Y	Y	Y	Y	Y				
More effective utilization of management's time	N	N	N	N	N	N	Y	Y	Y				
Improved scheduling and production control	N	N	N	Y	Y	Y	Y	Y	Y				
Closer control over capital investments and expenses	N	N	N	N	N	Y	Y	Y	Y				
Better control of credit	N	N	N	N	Y	Y	Y	Y	Y				
Ability to handle more volume at low costs	N	N	N	N	N	Y	Y	Y	Y				
More accuracy and reliability of data	N	N	N	Y	Y	Y	Y	Y	Y				
Action													
Utilizes a newer batch processing system	X	X	X	−	−	−	−	−	−				
Utilizes a time-sharing processing system	−	−	−	X	X	X	−	−	−				
Utilizes an interactive processing system	−	−	−	−	−	−	X	X	X				
Minor changes of inputs and outputs	X	X	X	−	−	−	−	−	−				
Substantial changes of inputs and outputs	−	−	−	X	X	X	X	X	X				
Need for new files (common data base)	−	−	−	X	X	X	X	X	X				
Moderate revision of methods and procedures	X	X	X	−	−	−	−	−	−				
Complete revision of methods and procedures	−	−	−	X	X	X	X	X	X				
Employ an additional consultant for study	−	−	−	−	−	−	−	−	X				
Recruit new data processing personnel	−	−	−	X	X	X	X	X	X				
Re-evaluate benefits of system alternative	−	−	−	−	−	−	X	−	−				
Discontinue feasibility study of system alternative	−	−	X	−	−	X	−	−	−				

Other Information:
*1−22%; 2−20%; 3−16%; 4−18%; 5−18%; 6−16%; 7−19%; 8−17%; 9−16%

figure 10-7. Feasibility study – decision table for appraising feasible system alternatives.

Generally, the approval for one of the recommended alternatives must come from the board of directors or top management.

The contents of this report must be as objective as possible so that the best business information system is selected. The equipment should meet the needs of the system that has been developed rather than the system being altered to meet the capabilities of certain equipment. Consideration must be given to a fundamental fact that a computer-oriented system is in a far better position to absorb growth in volume with a slight increase in operating costs as opposed to other systems. Comparable data processing principles should be embodied in the system recommended for a constructive report to management.

Feasibility (or Infeasibility) of Applying Data Processing

The feasibility of implementing a newer system is a difficult undertaking when numerous alternatives are available. A comparison of many proposed systems is a formidable task. Using the data in Figure 10-7, the feasibility of a systems change is promising for all proposed systems, except alternatives #3 and #6 which are poor candidates when compared to the seven others. More benefits and higher returns are available with other proposals. When consideration is given to tangible and intangible benefits in the example, the remaining seven appear to be promising candidates. Thus the feasibility of applying newer data processing equipment and techniques has been established. The question, then, becomes one of determining which proposal is best when all critical factors are appraised.

Since the committee's primary job is to select the best feasible system alternative, the weighing of quantitative and qualitative factors with emphasis on the organization's future—growth patterns and related problems—can assist in resolving this dilemma. For the specific organization, the attendant circumstances must be analyzed for a definite conclusion.

In the example, an examination of the data in Figure 10-7 indicates that alternatives #7 through #9 are best. In terms of tangible and intangible benefits, there are more affirmative answers for an interactive processing system than for a newer batch-processing system and a time-sharing processing system. The returns on investment are comparable for the most part, except for alternatives #1 and #2. Now, the question is, which one of these alternatives (#7 through #9) should be implemented? On the surface, all three have about the same benefits, except that alternative #7 gives a higher return on investment. However, a review of these three systems reveal that only alternative #9 utilizes optical character recognition equipment (also applies to alternative #3). Conversion today to OCR equipment will mean no or minimal conversion costs in the future for this area. With this added advantage in mind, the feasibility study committee feels that the future cost savings justifies accepting a lower return. Its recommendation to top management has been finally resolved.

When agreement has been reached among the group about one particular system alternative, a comprehensive report must be prepared that states this recommendation. A suggested listing for the final exploratory survey report is depicted in Figure 10-8. The report gives management an opportunity to examine the data and appraise their validity and merit. It also provides management with a sound basis for constructive criticism of the system project.

1. Scope of the study in which the objectives are stated and the problem is clearly defined.

2. Overview of the existing system which points out its weaknesses and problems.

3. Adequate description of the recommended system alternative, indicating its tangible and intangible benefits, its superiority in eliminating or reducing the deficiencies of the present system, and its general impact on the organization.

4. Financial data on the recommended system alternative, similar to that found in Figures 10-4 and 10-5.

5. Reference to other feasible system alternatives which were investigated, giving reasons for their final rejection. Decision table, similar to Figure 10-7, should be included.

6. Financial data on system alternatives that were not selected, similar to that found in Figures 10-4 and 10-5.

7. Schedule of funds required for specific periods of time during systems implementation.

8. List of additional personnel needed to implement the new system and personnel requirements during conversion.

9. Accurate time schedule for the remainder of the system project.

10. Other special factors and considerations.

figure 10-8. Suggested listing for a final exploratory report to top management.

A considerable expenditure of time, effort, and cost on the exploratory survey may result in the infeasibility of applying newer data processing equipment and techniques. This conclusion can be caused by initially limiting the scope of the study. Instead of extending the problem definition to many areas of the organization, the study was restricted to areas where progress in terms of new technical improvements has been slow or non-existent, the area does not lend itself to newer data processing equipment, or some other reason. (When an opportunity exists for technical improvement, a broader approach is desirable for the most part.) This situation can be avoided with the help of outside consultants or personnel from within who are knowledgeable on data processing and are capable of suggesting fertile areas for a feasibility study. To blindly start on the exploratory survey without any idea of the results is wasteful and does not speak well of top management.

systems design— determine requirements for new system

Even though a system alternative has been established in the exploratory survey report, there are innumerable approaches available to the systems designer within this framework. These can be utilized to fit the particular circumstances and can be adapted from past experience as well as from a broad knowledge of approaches that have been successful in other installations. The almost infinite variety of alternative designs makes the task a challenging one. For example, the decision to install an interactive processing system that cuts across the entire organization offers many possible design alternatives. In such a system project, the systems analyst is offered countless opportunities for imaginative systems design.

The participants of the exploratory survey report to management are generally the ones to undertake the design of the recommended alternative. If systems designers are not part of the group, they should be brought in. Additional personnel to represent the various departments affected by the system change are needed. This is necessary because participation and cooperation of all functional areas, represented by departmental personnel, is the key to implementing successfully a new system. It is much easier to redesign a system at this stage to accommodate their constructive suggestions than at a later date. Too many installations have faced embarrassing situations, only because appropriate departmental personnel were not given an opportunity to evaluate the systems design as it progressed.

Review Data on Present and New Systems

Generally, many weeks will have elapsed since data have been compiled on the present and new systems. One purpose of the review is to recall pertinent facts about the present system, in particular, its problems, shortcomings, and exceptions. Certain questions can be used for determining the deficiencies and shortcomings of the present system. Basically, they are:

1. Can inputs, files, outputs, methods, and procedures be improved so as to accomplish the organization's objectives to the highest degree possible?

2. Are all operations necessary? Does this result in duplicate or overlapping operations, files, and the like?

3. Is there a faster, simpler, and/or more economical way of processing the data?

4. Are data recorded in a manner that is compatible with their final use?

5. Is it possible to reduce the work volume by modifying or changing policies, organization structure, files, departmental functions, or other established practices?

6. Can the system be improved through work simplification?

These may not be new or revealing to the reader, but are necessary for an in-depth review. These same basic questions will be asked time and time again by the systems designer as the new system is developed in detail. The designer will discard certain designs as a result of the above questions in order to devise a more efficient one. The creative talents of the systems designer can now be appreciated.

New System Requirements

After the systems designer has reviewed data on the present system and information contained in the exploratory survey report, in particular, the new system recommendation, the requirements for the new system must be determined. The major ones include:

- *New policies consistent with organization objectives* — relates to reducing the complexity and the number of exceptions in the system. Examples are simplifying pricing and discount policies to conform to

figure 10-9. Systems design—considerations for new procedures.

Can the procedure be improved to realize more fully organizational objectives?
Are all steps in the procedure necessary?
Is it possible to simplify the procedure through modification of existing company policies, departmental structures, practices of other departments, or similar considerations?
Is there too much handling of the document in the procedure?
Does the procedure route the document through too many operations and/or departments?
Can the procedure be performed in a faster and a more economical manner?
Does the procedure make a contribution to the quality or flow of the work?
Is the cost of the procedure greater than its value to the organization?
Are all of the forms used in the procedure necessary? Can the forms be combined?
Does duplication of work exist in the procedure?
Are the steps in a logical sequence for the greatest efficiency in the procedure?
Are there parts of the procedure that functionally belong to another activity?
Is the new procedure really essential to the organization's operations?
What would happen if one or more steps in the procedure were eliminated?

organization objectives, thereby keeping exceptions to a minimum in the new system.

- *Planned inputs*—focuses on capturing source data initially in a machine processable form. The elements of time constraints on the inputs and variations in input volume are important considerations when designing a new system.

- *New methods and procedures*—relates to the design of new methods and procedures to produce desired output given certain inputs and data files. DP operational procedures should be tested for practicability, efficiency, and low cost. In addition, since each functional area or activity is related to others, there must be a compatibility of methods and procedures in the new system. Questions for testing the validity of any procedure are set forth in Figure 10-9.

- *Data files to be maintained*—revolves around the amount of data to be contained in the files whether they are on-line or off-line. Efficient systems design dictates keeping storage data at a minimum.

- *Output needs*—centers on developing output that meets the user's requirements. It is advisable that information users work with systems designers so that the format, detail desired, the degree of accuracy wanted, and the frequency of the report can be specified. Questions that relate to testing the validity of a report are set forth in Figure 10-10.

- *Internal control considerations*—relates to establishing checks at control points to insure what has been processed is accurate. Likewise, internal control focuses on making certain that no one person has full responsibility over an entire operation. This should be apparent in such areas as cash and payroll since one person with complete responsibility can defraud an organization without too much difficulty.

A thorough understanding of the foregoing areas gives the study team a basis for designing the new system.

It should be noted that the new system should be designed in general terms. To design a system with only one equipment manufacturer in mind is restrictive, reduces the potential of the system, and often reduces the

figure 10-10. Systems design—questions to test the validity of a report.

Is the report necessary to make decisions to plan, organize, direct, or control organizational activities?

Is the "management by exception" concept incorporated in the report?

What would be the effect if operating personnel got more or less information than presently?

How would work be affected if the report was received less frequently or not at all?

Is all information contained in the report utilized?

How often is all or part of the information contained in the report utilized after its original use?

Can data on this report be obtained from another source?

How long is the report kept before discarding?

Is the report concise and easy to understand?

How many people refer to it?

Can the department function without the report?

Are there other reports prepared from pertinent data on the report?

Does utilization of the data justify the preparation cost of the report?

Is the report flexible enough to meet changes in the firm's operating conditions?

Is the report passed to someone higher or lower in the organization structure?

When and where is the report filed?

---

ultimate success of the system project. Equipment is important at this stage, but only in terms of classes and types of equipment.

Human Factors

The foregoing requirements for a new system are not complete until the human factors in coding and data representation are considered. For example, research indicates that while a machine can read documents numbered "A4B" as easily as those coded "AB4," a human being cannot. Systems designers must consider the human element as well as procedures, data, and machines before finalizing any design. When trade-offs are deemed necessary, the human element should be given preference over the machines.

Error rates with various coding schemes increase as the number of characters in the data code increases. It is suggested that longer codes be divided into smaller units of three or four characters, such as 123–456 instead of 123456, to increase the reliability of coding. Characters used in data codes should be those in common use. Special symbols, such as Greek letters and diacritical marks, should be avoided. Also wherever a number of data-entry errors appears, the errors should be studied to see if there is a systematic pattern. Systematic errors, to the extent that they can be detected, should be identified. Factors that contribute to their occurrence should be considered in designing data codes.

Going a step further, a system should also be designed to interface with anyone who may come into contact with its results. This requirement applies equally to the needs of employees as well as customers. If employees can understand what the system requires from them and, at the same time, the system is helpful to them, the end result can only be improved operating efficiency. If a customer can easily understand and process the invoices rendered, then improved customer relations will result. In the final analysis, less time and money will be spent dealing with customer inquiries and similar matters.

design the new system

Determining the above requirements is performed concurrently with designing the new system. After all, a system is nothing more than a total of all its parts. The design of a system involves making decisions about each of its parts—planned inputs, files to be maintained, outputs desired, and data processing methods and procedures that link input with output. An integral part of systems design work is answering many questions, like those set forth in Figures 10-9 and 10-10 for new procedures and reports.

Modular (Building Block) Concept. The design of a new system should be approached from the outset with modularity or the building block concept in mind. This involves identifying all of the foregoing system requirements. At this point, all of the requirements are placed in a functional block diagram, but these are only the highest level functions and seldom represent an optimum functional breakdown of a supporting computer-based system. Each of these functions is broken down into individual functions, applying the process iteratively from the top down. The resulting analysis is represented by an inverted tree diagram, wherein major functions at the top are successively broken into separate data processing functions in the lower branches of the tree.

As the breakdown continues, two important phenomena are observed: (1) the branches are beginning to terminate (they do not lend themselves to further breakdown) and (2) some of the functions are turning up in more than one place (duplicated modules). When the process is complete, a thorough functional analysis is obtained even though the system has not been fully designed. It should be noted that an analyst often finds alternative ways to break a function down into its component parts. A great deal of time will be spent on changing and filling in details which were considered unimportant on an earlier pass. But time spent here is worthwhile since this step forms the heart of the new system.

When the functional analysis is complete, the system designer creates a system structure for the functional modules that will operate within whatever hardware constraints are imposed. This modular approach allows the bringing together of individual modules that are capable of standing alone. The net result is that the complexity of an overall system is reduced since many of the duplicated modules are eliminated. Also, this modular approach facilitates modification or updating of the system that may be necessary during succeeding stages of systems design as well as in the future.

Steps in Systems Design. The various steps involved in systems design are set forth in Figure 10-11. The first two steps have been treated in determining and designing the new system. The remaining steps treat the method for resolving the final systems design. Basically, flowcharts are drawn to appraise the merits of many modular system alternatives with appropriate company personnel. After considering as many system designs as possible, it will become apparent that some are more appealing than others. The more promising ones should be investigated further. It should be noted that alternative system designs not covered in the original survey report can be evaluated before selecting a final one. This permits a comprehensive review of all other promising system alternatives that come

figure 10-11. Systems design—steps for one of the firm's functional areas.

Determine tentative inputs, files, and outputs and their related basic content.
Devise many systems design possibilities through a modular or building block approach, including detailed methods and procedures as well as giving consideration to internal control and other parts of the system.
Prepare flowcharts showing the modular relationships of inputs, files, methods, procedures, and outputs for the various alternatives.
Review systems design alternatives with appropriate personnel.
Select the more promising alternatives with the aid of properly designated personnel.
Compare the tangible and intangible benefits of the promising alternatives with the final exploratory survey report. Cost factors, volumes, and requirements for equipment and personnel should be carefully analyzed to check the report's validity.
Select the systems design that best meets the study's requirements from among the promising alternatives.
Prepare final system flowcharts and/or decision tables for the recommended system design and relate it to all other parts of the business information system.
Document the final design for bid invitations to equipment manufacturers.

to light when the creative talents of the systems designers are being employed to their fullest.

Exception Reporting on Systems Design. Once the final design has been resolved by the study groups based upon the existing tangible and intangible benefits, any significant deviations from the findings of the exploratory survey report must be reported to the executive committee. It is the function of these top managers to make a final decision on the feasibility or infeasibility of applying the recommended data processing system under changed conditions. This is why the feasibility study is a continuing one even though the feasibility study committee has endorsed a proposed system in the exploratory report. The feasibility study is formally concluded with equipment selection, the initial subject matter of Chapter 11.

flowchart and document the new system

An important step (as stated in Figure 10-11) is preparation of final system flowcharts for the recommended new system. These flowcharts are drawn without specifying the equipment to be ordered. Accuracy, simplicity, and ease of understanding are the essential components since nontechnical personnel will be reviewing and evaluating them.

Since all data compiled on the new system will be needed for submitting bid invitations to equipment manufacturers and preparing program flowcharts, detailed documentation is necessary. In regard to the first item, documentation is needed for the following: data origination and communications, planned inputs, files to be maintained (common data base), methods and procedures, output needs, and special requirements of the system. Also included in the bid invitation are system flowcharts depicting the interrelationships of the various parts to the entire system and those showing each area under study. Without this documentation, the feasibility study committee is vulnerable since data can be easily forgotten and personnel can leave for a number of reasons.

In order to prepare program flowcharts for coding at a later date, it is necessary to develop the appropriate logic. Block diagrams or program flowcharts can be prepared for a detailed documentation of the new system. In other cases, decision tables can also be employed to show the complexity of the programming effort during systems implementation.

second summary of chapter 10

exploratory survey report to top management:
Once agreement has been reached among the feasibility study group about the selected system alternative, an exploratory survey report to top management is prepared that states this recommendation. The content of this report focuses on an adequate description of the selected system, particularly, in financial terms and comparison to other feasible system alternatives. Personnel requirements, capital outlays, a time schedule, and other important factors are contained in the report.

systems design—determine requirements for new system:
Systems design, being the act of devising new system approaches, centers on determining the requirements for a new system. After system designers have reviewed data on the present system and information contained in the exploratory survey report, they must specify the following:
- new policies consistent with organization objectives
- planned inputs
- new methods and procedures
- data files to be maintained
- output needs
- internal control considerations

The foregoing requirements for a newly designed system are not complete until the human factors are considered.

design the new system:
It is recommended that a methodical approach to systems design be undertaken initially during this critical phase. A recommended approach is the *modular* or *building block approach* wherein major functions at the top are successively separated into distinct data functions at the lower levels. When the functional analysis is complete, the designer creates a system structure for the functional modules that are capable of operating within whatever hardware constraints are imposed. The net result of the modular approach is that duplicated modules, i.e., data processing tasks, are eliminated and the complexity of the overall system is reduced.

flowchart and document the new system:
An important last step when designing a new system is the preparation of system flowcharts. Likewise, documentation is needed for those items determined during the systems design phase—refer to the above listing.

**second self-study
exercise
of chapter 10**

True-False:

1. (   ) Basically, the exploratory survey report to management is a waste of time.
2. (   ) By and large, the exploratory survey report is not financially oriented.
3. (   ) Systems designers should not review data compiled on the present system.
4. (   ) Systems designers should employ simplified methods and procedures.
5. (   ) Planned inputs focus on capturing source data in a machine-processable form.
6. (   ) Internal control of a new system centers only on the problems of fraud.
7. (   ) Data files in a new system can be in an on-line, an off-line mode, or both.
8. (   ) Generally, designers are not concerned about human factors in new systems.
9. (   ) A good way to design a new system is to utilize the modular concept.
10. (   ) Final system documentation can be used for submitting invitations to equipment manufacturers.

Fill-In:

11. A desired system design approach is having knowledge of the _____ _____ without letting these facts override the designer's creative ability of the new business information system.
12. A starting point for systems design involves reviewing data on the present system as contained in the _____ _____ phase and examining material developed on the new system per the _____ _____ _____.
13. Good systems design demands that _____ of information, functions, and comparable items be eliminated or kept to a minimum.
14. A principle of good systems design dictates that methods and procedures should _____ data processing tasks, thereby keeping repetitive motion and tasks to a minimum.
15. Reviewing the present system brings to light _____ that should be avoided in the new system.
16. A principle of good systems design dictates that organization's objectives be made compatible with its _____.
17. A principle of good systems design dictates that the organization's _____ be considered first before developing methods, procedures, files, and inputs.
18. A principle of good systems design dictates that _____ _____ be an integral part of the new system in order to handle inaccuracies, fraud, and other data processing irregularities.
19. Good systems design requirements are not complete until the _____ _____ in coding and data representation are considered.
20. The modular systems design concept requires breaking the system down into its lowest-level component parts and examining for _____.

designing and implementing data processing for business

summary

The importance of the exploratory survey cannot be overemphasized since a thorough analysis of all promising and feasible data processing systems is undertaken. This permits the feasibility study committee to recommend the best system, under the attendant circumstances, to the executive committee. A quick and unsophisticated undertaking will result generally in the selection and implementation of a mediocre system. The need for a thorough exploratory study is important to the organization's future success.

After the basis of the feasibility study has been determined—what will be covered, who will be involved, when it will be done, and how it will be accomplished, the study team, then, concentrates on the detailed investigation of the present system or systems analysis. This phase is very time-consuming. Analysis of costs and benefits, both tangible and intangible, forms the basis of the exploratory survey report to top management or the executive committee. In this comprehensive report, the feasibility or nonfeasibility of applying newer data processing equipment and techniques is explored.

The design of an effective business information system is related directly to the creative ability of the systems designer(s). This individual relies upon intuition, experience, and inventive talents to develop promising system alternatives. Each alternative is analyzed by a representative group to determine its benefits and resulting impact on the organization. The most promising system alternative, then, is chosen and documented with system flowcharts. The basis for selection is the successful accomplishment of organization objectives and attainment of quantitative and qualitative factors set forth in the exploratory survey report.

questions

1. What is meant by a feasibility study?
2. (a) Why is it that the growth of the data processing system will lag behind the corresponding growth of the organization?
   (b) What effect does this have on the feasibility study?
3. What are the steps involved in a systems project?
4. Explain the relationship among the following in a feasibility study: selection of desired objectives, definition of the problem, and the determination of a realistic schedule.
5. If you were assembling an ideal data processing committee for a typical manufacturing firm, who would be the members?
6. What part of the detailed investigation of the present system is most important from a managerial point of view?
7. What are the problems associated with calculating net savings after federal income taxes for feasible system alternatives?
8. What questions must the systems analyst answer if the present system is to be improved?
9. Why have an exploratory survey report? Why not save this expense and procure a newer generation computer to effect a system change?
10. Many organizations have found that initial estimates of new system benefits are too high and costs too low. What are the major factors contributing to this condition and how may they be overcome?

11. What are the questions that a systems analyst must ask when designing a new system?

12. (a) Why should the systems designer consider reporting requirements first when designing a data processing system?
    (b) What is the relationship between reporting requirements and file design?

13. What important factors must be taken into consideration when designing efficient and economical files?

14. What are the typical steps a systems designer should follow when designing a new system?

---

answers to first self-study exercise

1. T 2. T 3. F 4. F 5. F 6. F 7. T 8. F 9. T 10. F 11. feasibility study 12. personnel 13. feasibility study committee 14. objectives 15. definition and problem 16. feasibility study and systems implementation 17. present system 18. outputs 19. flowcharting 20. feasible system alternatives

---

answers to second self-study exercise

1. F 2. F 3. F 4. T 5. T 6. F 7. T 8. F 9. T 10. T 11. present system 12. systems analysis and exploratory survey report 13. duplication 14. simplify 15. weaknesses 16. policies 17. outputs 18. internal control 19. human factors 20. duplication

chapter eleven

feasibility study— equipment selection and systems implementation

chapter objectives

- To explore the final step in the feasibility study, namely, equipment selection.
- To determine the best approach for acquiring a computer and related equipment.
- To set forth the critical items in evaluating proposals from equipment manufacturers.
- To examine the steps involved in implementing a business information system.
- To determine the need for periodic reviews of a business information system.

chapter outline

Joe and Claudia Cosgrove are sports enthusiasts, and they spend considerable time watching college football games on television, particularly on the weekends. On a recent sports program, there was a discussion of how the computer is used to rate football players who are eligible for the professional draft. Although the technical aspects of the presentation were slighted, Joe and Claudia were fully convinced that such a system is easily implemented. The real plus factor for the computerized system is that it allows for comparing their subjective ratings to the computer's objective ones for their favorite football stars.

The implications of computers for sports need not stop here. Some teams use the computer to analyze an opponent's past games and predict the most likely plays in certain situations. Sport equipment, such as golf clubs and tennis rackets — as used by Joe and Claudia, are designed with the assistance of computers. In actuality, computers can be active participants in sport activities.

With the completion of the first two steps of the feasibility study, namely, systems analysis and systems design, the feasibility study committee is ready to undertake the last major step of the feasibility study, which is the selection of data processing equipment. The final selection of the most suitable equipment will probably require some systems modification. In effect, the exploratory survey report to top management may have to be modified sometime during this step. It is possible these modifications may be major, but generally they are not. This is the rationale for including equipment selection within the framework of the feasibility study. The feasibility or infeasibility of applying newer data processing equipment is not completely established until the order(s) is (are) placed with the respective manufacturer(s).

In addition, significant factors involved in selecting DP equipment are discussed as well as important data on systems implementation. Periodic review of the new system for possible improvements is the final subject of discussion.

---

approaches to equipment selection

The equipment selection approach taken by the feasibility study committee is important for a successful conclusion to the study. There are two basic methods of selecting equipment. Only one is recommended.

Recommended Approach. The recommended approach is to submit flowcharts and decision tables to each manufacturer where the specifics of the new system are outlined. General information on the company, its future processing plans, and list of new system specifications should be forwarded to the competing manufacturers. The particulars of these specifications will be covered in subsequent sections.

Alternative Approach. The second approach is basically illogical since it disregards the data compiled by the feasibility study to date and requests that the equipment manufacturers start from scratch. Briefly, the manufacturers bring in their own system personnel who will study the present system and devise a new system tailored to their own equipment. The operations will be timed and cost savings will be calculated on this basis.

Generally, different approaches by each equipment manufacturer result in making a final evaluation virtually impossible when placed on a common basis. Most manufacturers will direct their proposals to highlight the specific features of their own equipment over their competition.

The problem of time is another important consideration since each manufacturer must conduct a lengthy system review. For example, assume five manufacturers are involved and each spends a month to review the present system. This means about one-half year of lost time plus continuous disruptions to current operations. After department heads, supervisors, and operating personnel have been through the same set of questions five times, their attitude toward a system change, needless to say, is negative. Likewise, their morale has reached an all-time low. Even after all the manufacturer's efforts, one month is still not ample time to learn an organization's system in sufficient detail, especially when it comes to exceptions and problem areas. Because of the manufacturer's inability to gather all the pertinent facts in the time allotted, their recommendations can be poor and, many times, impractical systems are advocated. Thus, the second approach should be discarded.

equipment selection

Equipment selection should be undertaken by the study group upon the completion of systems design. Its basic steps include:

1. determine equipment manufacturers,
2. submit bid invitations to manufacturers,
3. evaluate manufacturer's proposals,
4. select equipment manufacturer(s).

determine equipment manufacturers

Before submitting necessary data to equipment manufacturers, their representatives should be contacted and invited to an orientation meeting on the proposed new system. During the course of the meeting, they should be instructed about the areas to be converted, general problems that will be encountered, approximate volumes—present and future, and other pertinent data. Each manufacturer should indicate in writing whether it wishes to receive a bid invitation. The reason for this approach should be obvious. There is no need to prepare a packet of specifications, flowcharts, decison tables, and comparable material if the manufacturer has no interest in bidding on the newly designed system.

Most organizations, undertaking a data processing system project, have some type of computer equipment under consideration based on the exploratory survey report. Since they have computer and related peripheral equipment salespersons calling at various times, they have had previous contact with most of the manufacturers. The major manufacturers of complete business computer systems are: Burroughs Corporation, Control Data Corporation, Honeywell Information Systems, International Business Machines Corporation, National Cash Register Company, and Sperry Rand Corporation (UNIVAC Division). All these organizations have sales offices in the larger cities. Chances are that outlying cities and towns are close enough to be handled by an office in a large city.

figure 11-1. Contents of a bid invitation to an equipment manufacturer.

I. *Company General Information*
- Description of the company and its activities.
- Overview of present data processing equipment and applications.
- Unusual data processing exceptions and problems.
- Other important general information.

II. *Future Data Processing Plans*
- Listing of areas encompassed by the new system.
- Target date for installation of new system.
- Deadline date for submitting proposals.
- Equipment decision date by the company.
- Criteria to be employed in analyzing and comparing manufacturers' proposals.

III. *New System Specifications*
(A) Planned Inputs:
- Where data originate within the system.
- Name and content of input data, such as documents and forms.
- Hourly rates of input data.
- Volume of inputs, including high and low points.

(B) Methods and Procedures for Handling Data:
- Transmission of local and distant data.
- Types of transactions handled.
- Computations and logical decisions required.
- New data generation within the system.
- Control points to test accuracy of data and eliminate processing of fraudulent data.

(C) Files to be Maintained:
- Where data are to be stored—on-line and off-line.
- Name and contents of files to be maintained.
- Methods and procedures for updating files.
- Size of files to be maintained.

(D) Output Needs:
- Name and content of output, such as reports and summaries.
- Timely distribution of output data.
- Hourly rates of output data.
- Volume of outputs, including high and low points.

(E) Other Requirements and Considerations:
- Changes in policies to conform with new system.
- Compatibility of common data processing language.
- Special internal control considerations.
- Ability to handle the company's future growth.
- Lease or cost of equipment not to exceed a stated figure.
- Additional special requirements and considerations.

submit bid invitations to manufacturers

Now that letters of intent are on file from equipment manufacturers, the company submits bid invitations to the interested equipment suppliers. The preferred approach, when sending bid invitations, is to mail the same set of data to all competing manufacturers. This permits bids to be placed on an unbiased basis, informs the manufacturers what requirements they must meet, keeps the number of questions to a minimum, and is a valid base for comparison of equipment. The manufacturers will probably need additional information and assistance from the prospective customer as they progress with the preparation of their proposals. Generally, one person from the data processing group will perform this consultative function for a specific manufacturer.

figure 11-1. (*continued*)

IV. *New System Flowcharts*
- Brief description of the system approach for each functional area under study.
- System flowcharts and accompanying decision tables (if applicable) for each area.
- System flowcharts that show the interrelationships of the various areas for the new system.
- A flowchart that gives an overview of the new system.

V. *Data to be Forwarded by Each Manufacturer*
- (A) Processing time for each area on the equipment.
- (B) Proposed Computer Hardware:
  - Basic equipment and components—its capabilities and technical features.
  - Peripheral equipment—its capabilities and technical features.
  - Expansion ability of the data processing equipment (modular concept).
  - Purchase price and monthly rental figures on an one, two and three shift basis for basic and peripheral equipment.
  - Alternative purchase and lease option plan (third party leasing).
  - Estimated delivery and installation data.
  - Number of magnetic tapes and/or disk packs required and their cost.
  - Equipment cancellation terms.
- (C) Site Preparation and Installation Requirements:
  - Amount of space needed.
  - Electrical power, air conditioning, and humidity control requirements.
  - Flooring requirements and enclosure of equipment.
- (D) Extent of Manufacturer's Assistance:
  - Cost of manufacturer's personnel to assist in the installation and for how long.
  - The availability and location of programming classes.
  - The possibility of on-site training classes.
  - Availability of procedure-oriented languages, compilers, programming aids, and program libraries.
  - Nearest testing facilities and on what shifts.
  - Amount of equipment time for compiling and testing programs without charge.
- (E) Maintenance service to be provided.
- (F) Equipment support for emergency processing.
- (G) Other pertinent information.

Utilizing this approach, the respective manufacturers should have ample information to familiarize themselves with the company and its peculiar data processing problems. The recommendations made in their proposals should show clearly how the equipment will meet the customer's needs. If the specifications lack clear definition from the beginning, the bid invitations will come back as proposals with standard approaches that are applicable to any and all potential customers. In essence, all the organization's preliminary work has been a waste of time. The equipment manufacturers cannot prepare proposals tailored specifically for a particular customer if the data contained in the bid invitation are deficient. It is of utmost importance that data submitted to manufacturers be as complete and self-explanatory as possible.

New System Specifications. Much of the material needed for the bid invitation can be taken directly from the data contained in the exploratory survey report and developed during systems design. The contents of the bid invitation include these areas:

1. company general information,
2. future data processing plans,
3. new system specifications,
4. new system flowcharts,
5. data to be forwarded by each manufacturer.

The detail for each major topic is shown in Figure 11-1.

In Sections I and II, the narrative should be brief so that attention can be focused on the remaining parts of the bid invitation. Data that are necessary for a thorough study are contained in Sections III and IV and form the basis for the manufacturer's proposal. Section III is composed of five essential parts: planned inputs, methods and procedures for handling data, files to be maintained, output needs, and other requirements and considerations for the new system. Material developed for Section IV was discussed in Chapter 10. If proper documentation was undertaken for systems design, the time to complete the area will be at a minimum since much of the material can be used in its present form.

Design of New System. New system flowcharts are contained in Section IV of Figure 11-1. Not only are system flowcharts needed for each functional area under study, but also for showing the interrelationships among the areas. Decision tables (if applicable) should accompany the bid invitation. This will enable the manufacturer to have a complete understanding of the programming effort envisioned and help determine the hardware that is needed under the existing conditions. The New System Flowcharts section of the bid invitation should contain a flowchart that depicts the overall aspects of the new system. This allows the equipment manufacturer to obtain an overview of the system and its subsystems.

In the final section (V) of the bid invitation, data to be contained in each manufacturer's proposal are listed. Specifying in advance what the proposals should contain insures that comparable information for a final evaluation will be forthcoming.

Conferences with Manufacturers. Even though bid invitations specify the numerous details of the new system, legitimate questions will be raised by the various equipment firms. Many of the questions center around those areas which may have need of modification. This is necessary sometimes to take advantage of the equipment's special features. The result may be favorable benefits to the organization in terms of cost savings. Conferences between the manufacturer and the potential customer, then, can prove beneficial to both parties.

---

evaluate manufacturers' proposals

The manufacturers should be given a reasonable amount of time to prepare their proposals. In most cases, approximately 60 days is adequate although large and advanced systems may take several months. When the proposals are completed, several copies are mailed to the customer for review which is, then, followed by an oral presentation by the manufacturer's representatives. At this meeting, the salesperson will stress the important points of the proposal and answer questions. After this procedure has been followed by all competing manufactuers, the feasibility study committee is prepared to evaluate the information contained in the various proposals.

There are many criteria that can be developed for evaluating a manufacturer's proposals. Among these are:

- *Extent of automation proposed*—refers to the amount of newer DP equipment proposed for the new system. This criterion gives the study group an overview of what is being advocated by each equipment manufacturer.

- *Throughput performance*—relates to the amount of data that can be processed by the computer system within a specific time period. In view of the difficulties with running computer programs, such as malfunctions of the computer's components, paper jams, error stops, input/output units out of cards, etc., most experienced DP managers add 50% to the manufacturer's time estimates for processing computer programs. To test the validity of times after a 50% time adjustment, a *benchmark* problem approach can be employed which consists of selecting a representative job to be performed by the new system. The results of the benchmark test are evaluated on how well the equipment meets the specified application in terms of total processing time, i.e., throughput performance.

- *Type of equipment*—focuses on the make, model number, and quantity of basic and related peripheral equipment along with their capabilities, operating characteristics, and technical features. Data on internal memory, operating speeds, storage capacity, and hardware controls are a part of the manufacturer's proposals on computers and related equipment.

- *Rental, purchase, or other basis*—refers to the method of acquiring DP equipment which currently include rental, outright purchase, option to buy, and third-party leasing (lease back arrangements). The decision to purchase or lease can be based on a number of factors, such as availability of capital funds, obsolescence of equipment, and the usage factor.

- *Delivery of equipment*—relates to a definite delivery data along with ample time to check out the equipment on the user's premises. Delivery dates run from several weeks to two (or more) years. This is contingent normally upon the manufacturer, the type of hardware, and the order date.

- *Installation requirements*—references the dimensions and weight for each piece of equipment along with necessary power and wiring requirements. The latter refers to false-floor, underfloor, or overhead wiring necessary to connect the computer units together. Most computers require air conditioning and humidity control.

- *Manufacturer's assistance*—refers to the amount and types of assistance that can be expected from the equipment manufacturers. Assistance includes: programmers, analysts, and engineers to implement the new system; training schools for the client's managers, programmers, and operators; software packages to simplify programming; and equipment for program testing prior to the installation. It should be noted that services for DP education and systems engineering are billed separately to the user.

- *Availability and quality of software* — centers on the software to support the hardware. Software includes: programming languages for business and scientific applications; program packages for reading and punching cards, reading and writing magnetic tapes, sort and merge routines, and others; compilers to assist in writing the final programs; routines to aid the computer operator during program debugging and to handle successive programs during production runs; and routine programs for handling specialized problems. The availability of reliable software cuts the user's time and expense since the DP staff can work at a reasonably high level of programming efficiency.

- *Maintenance contracts* — relates to maintaining the equipment in good operating condition. It is provided free normally under a rental contract, but not when the equipment is purchased. For small equipment installations, the maintenance function will be performed from the manufacturer's sales office. For large machine systems, the manufacturer may assign maintenance personnel to one or more systems.

- *Other considerations* — includes the ability to handle exceptions and unusual items, nearness to compatible machines for processing data on an emergency basis, overtime costs, and similar items.

Compliance with Terms of Bid Invitation. One last consideration revolves around how well each manufacturer has complied with the terms of the bid invitation. This involves completeness, clarity, accuracy, and responsiveness. Does each proposal cover all points set forth in the bid invitation? Is the proposal clear in every respect? Are all estimates of time and cost for peak, medium, and low workloads accurate? Does the proposal reflect a proper understanding of the bid? Failure on the manufacturer's part for any one of these points indicates a weakness that may be indicative of potential problems in the future. Final equipment evaluation, then, should include compliance with the original bid terms.

select equipment manufacturer(s)

Selection of the equipment manufacturer(s) is a difficult task for the feasibility study committee. The selection process is much easier if the equipment proposed is identical for all practical purposes. In such cases, the choice is normally based on the lowest cost equipment. However, this approach is generally not used since most manufacturers have certain equipment features that differ from their competitors. This results in a slightly different approach to the customer's proposed system that can utilize somewhat dissimilar equipment. In order to resolve this dilemma among the various competitors, various methods have been developed for evaluating and selecting equipment. They include the decision table and the weighting method, each of which are discussed below.

Decision Table for Evaluation Process. One method of evaluation is utilization of a decision table, shown in Figure 11-2. A decision table for a final evaluation not only defines the important criteria in compact notation, but also permits an objective evaluation since the values have been determined before receipt of the manufacturers' proposals. In the illustration, the highest possible score is one hundred points for each of the five com-

figure 11-2. Criteria to select equipment manufacturer in the feasibility study.

DECISION TABLE	TABLE NAME: CRITERIA TO SELECT EQUIPMENT MANUFACTURER		PAGE 1 OF 1
	CHART NO: FS-SEM-1	PREPARED BY: ROBERT J. THIERAUF	DATE: FEB. 25, 198–

CONDITION		RULE NUMBER													
		1	2	3	4	5	6	7	8	9	10	11	12	13
Major Criteria: High degree of automation proposed		Y	Y	Y	N	Y								
Low-cost throughput performance	√	Y	Y	Y	Y	N								
Expandability of equipment	√	Y	Y	Y	N	Y								
Monthly rental within amount set forth in the exploratory report	√	N	Y	Y	Y	N								
Availability of equipment when needed		Y	Y	N	Y	Y								
Capable of meeting installation requirements		Y	Y	Y	Y	Y								
Adequate programming assistance available		N	N	N	Y	N								
Good quality training offered		Y	Y	Y	Y	N								
Dependable and efficient software for proposed equipment	√	Y	Y	Y	N	Y								
Available equipment for compiling and testing programs (initially)		N	Y	Y	Y	N								
Adequate equipment maintenance		Y	N	Y	Y	Y								
Equipment backup in local area	√	N	Y	N	Y	Y								
Availability of operating personnel	√	Y	Y	Y	Y	Y								
Compliance with terms of bid invitation		Y	Y	Y	N	Y								
ACTION															
Subtract 5 points for each no (N) answer		X	X	X	X	X								
Subtract an additional 5 points for each no (N) answer checked		X	—	X	X	X								

Other Information:
Total points = 100 (14 criteria × 5 pts. + 6 criteria × 5 pts. = 100)
Competitor's total points:
1—70; 2—90; 3—80; 4—70; 5—65

peting manufacturers. A value of five points is deducted for each "no" answer while an additional five points is subtracted for an item that is checked. The checked questions represent criteria that have long run effects on the organization in terms of profits and return on investment. Thus, the deduction of ten points indicates greater importance attached to this particular criterion. Values for another organization might be different from those found in Figure 11-2. For the study currently undergoing evaluation, this is a realistic and precise approach in making this final decision for an interactive processing system. Thus, equipment manufacturer #2 with the highest score of 90 should be selected to receive the equipment contract.

Weighting Method for Evaluation Process. An alternative approach for evaluating and selecting equipment is the weighting method which consists of assigning different weighting factors to each criterion. Each manufacturer is given a score for each weighting factor. In most cases, the score is lower than the absolute value of the weighting factor. The values of all criteria are totaled which represent the total points for each manufacturer. As with decision tables, the competitor with the highest score is selected.

Signing of Equipment Contract. The signing of the equipment contract by a top-level executive, who has been the guiding force for both committees, brings the feasibility study to a formal close. However, before the official signing, the executive would be well advised to submit the contract to a lawyer for interpretation and the addition of user-protecting addendums.

Systems analysis, systems design, and equipment selection, being the major steps of the feasibility study, represent approximately one-third of the total time expended on a systems project. In the period just ahead, not only will more time be involved than in the feasibility study, but there will also be more involvement of organizational resources in terms of its operations and personnel. The problem of how to coordinate and control the activities during this interim period is a challenging task even for the most seasoned data processing manager.

systems implementation

The task of systems implementation is generally a major undertaking if it cuts across the entire organization structure. This results in a great need for implementation planning. A logical starting point for this type of planning involves knowledge of the following areas: personnel needs, programming, equipment selected, physical requirements, and conversion activities. An understanding of these areas establishes the specific tasks that must be undertaken and the relationship among them. Also, knowledge of the problems and exceptions is needed. This background permits detailed planning of the various tasks that must be incorporated into a schedule with specific deadlines. The scheduling method should follow the natural flow of work to be undertaken. The usual questions of who, what, where, when, how, and why must be answered in developing the schedule. Implementation planning should include a method for reviewing completed and uncompleted tasks so that it can be a control tool for the entire system project.

The major steps for systems implementation can be summarized as:

1. preparatory work of new system,
2. operation of new system,
3. periodic review of new system approaches.

These basic elements and their related subcomponents are the subject matter for the remainder of the chapter.

---

preparatory work of new system

The three basic steps of the feasibility study provide a starting point for the preparatory phases. System flowcharts, decision tables, and the manufacturer's proposal constitute the major material necessary to get work started. Even though the data have been compiled and documented properly, the time and personnel requirements for the system project are just beginning. Thus, it is necessary that the data processing manager be alert to keep costs at a minimum and within the confines of the exploratory survey report.

The preparatory work that must be accomplished before the new system can operate on a day-to-day basis include:

- *Scheduling the installation* — relates to scheduling the installation work in sufficient detail so that each important activity can be controlled. The scheduler must determine appropriate starting and completion dates for each activity so that ample time is allowed before the equipment is delivered.

- *Selecting qualified personnel* — refers to selecting qualified personnel for systems implementation and normal operations. Normally, the head of the DP group becomes or is the data processing manager who is given the authority and responsibility for staffing the organization. If qualified personnel cannot be found within the organization, it may be necessary to go outside the organization.

- *Training personnel* — focuses on giving organizational personnel the necessary formal training to operate the new system. Similarly, it is quite helpful to complement formal training with on-the-job training. By no means is training limited to those who will operate the system. Management, too, must have a good grasp of what data processing is and how it can be applied effectively. Otherwise, a gap will exist between management and DP technicians.

- *Realignment of personnel* — relates to reassigning personnel once parallel operations begin. During the systems implementation step, both the new and old systems are running in parallel in order to check the new system. Hence, personnel realignment begins on a massive scale while converting the functional areas set forth in the feasibility study.

- *Physical requirements and alterations* — refers to getting the physical premises ready for conversion to the new system. Alterations may be needed to handle new inputs, data files, and outputs. New methods and procedures may require physical modifications to many departments. Overall, new departments may replace older ones while other departments may be in need of extensive modifications or be eliminated.

**first summary
of chapter 11**

approaches to equipment selection:
There are two basic methods for selecting equipment. The recommended approach is to forward the same materials compiled during the feasibility study to each manufacturer where the specific details of the new system are outlined. The alternative approach which is not recommended is to have each manufacturer start from scratch.

equipment selection:
Systems analysis, systems design, and equipment selection constitute the three main parts of the feasibility study. The major sections for equipment selection are:

• determine equipment manufacturers—the selection process of determining which manufacturers should receive bid invitations.

• submit bid invitations to manufacturers—the submission of bid invitations to selected equipment manufacturers should include these areas:
  • company general information—overview of company and DP operations
  • future data processing plans—areas to be implemented, completion dates, etc.
  • new system specifications—planned inputs, methods and procedures for handling data, files to be maintained, output needs, and other important items
  • new system flowcharts—for each functional area to be implemented and an overview of the proposed system
  • data to be forwarded by each manufacturer—proposed computer hardware and processing times, site preparation requirements, manufacturer's assistance, and other important information

• evaluate manufacturers' proposals—the criteria that can be developed for evaluation purposes include:
  • extent of automation proposed
  • throughput performance
  • type of equipment
  • rental, purchase, or other basis
  • delivery of equipment
  • installation requirements
  • manufacturer's assistance
  • availability and quality of software
  • maintenance contracts
  • other considerations

• select equipment manufacturer(s)—the task of the selection process is relatively easy if the equipment proposed is identical. If the equipment proposals are somewhat dissimilar, the selection process can be difficult. Whether the proposals are somewhat alike or totally different, the dilemma can be resolved by utilizing a decision table or the weighting method. The manufacturer(s) scoring the highest number of points is (are) selected.

first self-study exercise of chapter 11

True-False:

1. ( ) There is no preferred approach to equipment selection.
2. ( ) The focus of the bid invitation is on future data processing plans.
3. ( ) Solving benchmark problems is an important part of the bid invitation.
4. ( ) Throughput performance is an important criterion for evaluating proposals.
5. ( ) Third-party leasing refers to a lease back arrangement.
6. ( ) Quality software permits a high degree of programming efficiency.
7. ( ) Compliance with terms of bid invitations by manufacturers is unimportant.
8. ( ) Decision tables are poor vehicles for selecting a particular manufacturer.
9. ( ) The equipment selection process represents one-third of the total project time.
10. ( ) Signing of the equipment contract brings the feasibility study to a close.

Fill-In:

11. The next major step after systems design in a feasibility study is _____ _____.
12. The recommended approach to equipment selection is submitting _____ and related information on the new system to each equipment manufacturer.
13. Each equipment manufacturer should indicate in writing whether it wishes to receive a _____ _____ on the system's hardware.
14. A list of new _____ _____ contained in a bid invitation is taken directly from the systems analysis and design phases.
15. The last major area to be covered in a bid invitation relates to data that are to be forwarded by each equipment manufacturer, in particular, equipment _____ times.
16. A logical starting point for evaluation of manufacturers' proposals is the extent of _____ proposed.
17. One method of determining _____ _____ of proposed equipment is by employing benchmark problems.
18. Often, equipment manufacturers are dropped from the evaluation process due to long _____ times.
19. An important consideration in evaluating manufacturers' proposals is the availability of reliable _____ since it allows the programming staff to work at a reasonably high level of efficiency.
20. One method of evaluating manufacturers' proposals is the utilization of a _____ _____ that defines the important criteria in compact notation as well as permits an objective evaluation.

figure 11-3. Detailed steps involved in developing an operational, batch-oriented computer program.

1. The problem is clearly defined in terms of system flowcharts and related items (inputs, files, logic, internal control, outputs, and other important considerations for coding).
2. The program flowcharts are the basis for detailed programming.
3. Procedure-oriented or problem-oriented languages are employed for the entire programming effort.
4. The flowcharts and coded program are desk checked for logical and clerical programming errors.
5. Program cards are prepared and verified to keep manual errors at a minimum.
6. A compiler is used to compile the input program.
7. Errors, as indicated on the initial compiler printout, are corrected and the program is recompiled.
8. Testing of the program necessitates a sample transaction deck which is representative of input data for the program being tested.
9. Logical and clerical programming errors are corrected as testing takes place and the program is recompiled.
10. An optimum program, recompiled after all programming errors have been remedied during detailed testing, is utilized for systems testing.
11. Parallel operations are run for the new and old systems in order to detect programming errors that have not appeared in step 10.
12. Conversion to daily operations from the old system to the new system is undertaken.
13. Documentation of the computer program is essential for review and control purposes. This last step should be an integral part of the prior steps.

- *Testing and acceptance of new equipment* — pertains to the testing of equipment by the manufacturer's field service engineers. Only the manufacturer has the necessary diagnostic routines to test the major equipment components. A common method is to utilize field service programs that are capable of testing the various hardware components. This method can be supplemented with a company computer program that has been thoroughly proven and operational.

- *Programming and testing* — refers to the major task of any new system, i.e., programming and testing computer programs. The detailed steps involved in developing a computer program were discussed at some length in Chapter 4. Briefly, the steps for developing an operational program are summarized in Figure 11-3. These steps are indicative of the formidable task in systems implementation for a batch processing mode.

- *File conversion* — centers on conversion of data files from one medium to another long before programming and testing is completed. Thus, there is a great need for adequate controls, such as record count controls and control totals, during file conversion.

operation of new system

The completion of optimum computer programs is shown per step 10 in Figure 11-3. Even though these programs have been systems tested, there is no way of duplicating the actual flow of work with all its exceptions and timing considerations. The best way to prove the new system is to implement these areas (to be explained below):

- run parallel operations
- conversion to new system
- provision to make necessary changes
- scheduling equipment and personnel
- alternative plans in case of equipment failure

Run Parallel Operations. Parallel operations consist of feeding both systems the same input data and comparing files and output results. This is depicted as step (11) in Figure 11-3. Despite the fact that the best possible systems testing was undertaken during the preparatory work phase, related conditions and combinations of conditions are likely to occur that were not envisioned. Last minute computer program changes are necessary to accommodate these new conditions.

The data processing department must keep the entire organization posted on parallel operations and conversion activities. This can be accomplished via a series of bulletins which started at the inception of the feasibility study. Departmental personnel should be informed when they are to start on systems implementation and what specific activities will be required of them. Department heads should be informed before the actual date of conversion activities so that anticipated problems can be worked out before they occur. The time spent instructing personnel on parallel operations or conversion activities is well worth it. Otherwise, wasted motion and time will be the order of the day, resulting in a cost that will exceed the original study figures. Activities must be organized, directed, and controlled around the original plan of the feasibility study.

During parallel operations, mistakes often found are not those of the new system, but are the result of the old system. These differences should be reconciled as far as it is economically feasible. Those responsible for comparing the two systems should establish clearly that the remaining deficiencies are caused by the old system. A poor, detailed checking job at this point can cause undue harm later when complaints are received from customers, top management, salespersons, departments, and other parties. Again, it is the responsibility of the data processing manager and assistants to satisfy themselves that adequate time for dual operations has been undertaken for each functional area changed.

When implementing a real-time project, the process of running dual operations for both new and old systems is more difficult than for a batch-processing system. The problem is that the new system has no true counterpart in the old system. One procedure for testing the new real-time system is to have several remote input/output terminals connected on-line and to have them operated by supervised personnel who are backed up by other personnel operating on the old system. The outputs are checked for compatibility and appropriate corrections are made to the on-line computer programs. Once this segment of the new system has proven satisfactory, the entire terminal network can be placed into operation for this one area. Additional sections of the system can be added by testing in this manner until all programs are operational.

Conversion to New System. After files have been converted and the new system's reliability has been proven for a functional area, daily processing can be shifted from the existing system to the new one. This is step (12) in Figure 11-3. A cutoff point is established so that all files and other data requirements can be updated to the cutover point. All transactions initiated after this time are processed on the new system. The data processing manager and delegated assistants should be present to assist and answer any questions that might develop. Considerations should be given to operating the old system for a short time. This permits checking and balancing the total results of both systems. All differences must be reconciled. If necessary, appropriate changes are made to the new system and its computer programs. The old system can be dropped as soon as the data processing group is satisfied with the new system's performance. It should be remembered that it is impossible to return to the old system if significant errors appear later in the new system. The operation of the existing system provides an alternate route in case of system failure during conversion.

Provision to Make Necessary Changes. Operating procedures per the final step (13) in Figure 11-3 should be completely documented for the new system. This applies to both programming and operational procedures. Before any parallel or conversion activities can start, operating procedures must be clearly spelled out for personnel in the functional areas undergoing changes. Information on input, files, methods, procedures, output, and internal control must be set forth in *clear, concise, and understandable terms* for the average reader. Written operating procedures must be supplemented by oral communication during the many training periods on the system change. Despite the many hours of training, many questions will have to be answered during conversion activities. Brief meetings where changes are taking place must be held in order to inform all operating employees of a change that has been initiated. Having qualified data processing personnel in the conversion area to communicate and coordinate new developments as they occur is a must. Likewise, revisions to operating procedures should be issued as quickly as possible. Consideration of these factors enhances the chances of a successful conversion.

Once the new system has been completely converted, the data processing section should spend several days checking with all supervisory personnel about their respective areas. As with every new installation, minor adjustments can be expected. The system as initially designed should be flexible enough to accommodate the changes. Channels of communication should be open between the data processing section and all supervisory personnel so that necessary changes can be initiated as conditions change. There is no need to get locked into a rigid system when it would be more beneficial to make necessary changes. Thus, the proper machinery for making necessary changes must be implemented.

Scheduling Equipment and Personnel. Scheduling data processing operations of a new system for the first time is a difficult task for the data processing manager. As the individual becomes more familiar with the new system, the job becomes more routine. The objectives of scheduling which relate to both personnel and equipment are depicted in Figure 11-4.

Schedules should be set up by the data processing manager in con-

figure 11-4. Objectives of scheduling personnel and equipment.

- Maximize utilization of personnel and machines to further organizational objectives.
- Meet deadlines for reports and output desired.
- Increase productivity of personnel by including time for formal training and on-the-job training.
- Facilitate the planning of proposed new applications or modifications of existing applications for new and/or existing equipment.
- Reduce conflicts of several jobs waiting for a specific piece of equipment which may result in delays of important outputs or unnecessary overtime.

junction with the departmental managers of the operating units that are serviced by the equipment. The master schedule for next month should provide sufficient computer time to handle production runs that occur daily, weekly, semimonthly, monthly, or some other periodic basis. Daily schedules should be prepared in accordance with the master schedule and should include time for reruns if necessary, program compiling and testing, special nonrecurring reports, and other programs. In all cases, the schedules should be as realistic as possible.

Scheduling a real-time system is more difficult than a batch-processing system. Even though the "executive program" handles the allotted time for each random inquiry of the system, the total time for these inquiries may vary from a few seconds to several hours. The time to assign remote batch programs under these conditions is a problem since the number of interruptions that will occur is generally unknown. There is an alternative approach to this problem. It is to assign a block of time each day for operation of remote input/output consoles. If this arrangement is not feasible, the data processing manager must rely on past experience. When total random and sequential demands are not high, the machine will have sufficient capacity to complete all scheduled work even though batch-processing runs will be stretched out by random system inquiries.

Just as the equipment must be scheduled for its maximum utilization, so must the personnel who operate the equipment. It is imperative that personnel who enter input data and handle output data be included in the data processing schedule. Otherwise, data will not be available when the equipment needs it for processing. It is essential that each person follow the methods and procedures set forth by the data processing group. Noncompliance will have an adverse effect on the entire system. Effective supervision of personnel enhances compliance with established procedures and scheduled deadlines.

Alternative Plans in Case of Equipment Failure. Alternative processing plans must be employed in case of equipment failure. It does not matter who or what caused it to happen. The fact is that the data processing system operation is down. Priorities must be given to those jobs that are critical, such as billing, payroll, and inventory. Critical jobs can be performed manually until the equipment is functioning again. For obvious reasons, the preferred method is using identical hardware at another location. The failure of a real-time processing system for any length of time may mean starting over for certain areas, such as inventory and sales analysis. There is not sufficient time to enter all the information that is necessary to update the files, say for one week. This amounts to establishing a cutoff date and starting from there.

Documentation of alternative plans is the responsibility of the data processing manager and should be a part of the company's systems and procedures manual. It should state explicitly what the critical jobs are, how they are to be handled in case of equipment failure (use identical equipment at another location, manual methods, or some other data processing method), where compatible equipment is located (includes service bureaus), who will be responsible for each area during downtime, and what deadlines must be met during the emergency. A written manual of procedures concerning what steps must be undertaken will help expedite the unfavorable situation. Otherwise, panic conditions will result in the least efficient method being employed when time is of essence.

periodic review of new system approaches

Just after the system is installed, the data processing manager should review the tangible and intangible systems benefits set forth in the exploratory survey report. The purpose of such a review is to verify that these benefits are, in fact, being achieved. Discussions with managers of operating areas being serviced will determine how well the new system is performing. Tangible benefits, such as clerical reduction and lower inventory, and intangible benefits of improved customer service and more managerial information are open to constructive criticism. Typical comments will be along the following lines: certain areas have been improved significantly, some are about the same, and others are not as good as before. The task of the data processing section, then, is to make the necessary adjustments to accomplish the quantitative and qualitative goals of the feasibility study. It may take from several months up to one year or more to effect the changes which may include reprogramming the most frequently used programs for greater efficiency.

As time passes, the workload for the present data processing system increases. Factors that were not previously problems can become significant. Can the equipment run longer hours or should additional equipment be obtained? Can modification of methods and procedures be made to reduce processing time and cost? Can noncritical processing be shifted to another time? How does the time differential affect the manning of a system that is operating within the continental limits of the United States? Answers to these questions must be evaluated by the data processing section through a periodic review of the existing system. The ultimate aim of such an investigation is system improvements. In essence, it may be necessary to undertake a feasibility study periodically in order to devise an optimum system for changed operating conditions.

summary

The final step of the feasibility study revolves around equipment selection. Bid requests or invitations which describe the important aspects of the new system provide the basis for receiving proposals from manufacturers. Proposals are, then, compared for selected criteria which have specific numerical values assigned to them. All things being equal, the manufacturer who has the highest score is awarded the contract. The ultimate responsibility for determining equipment, however, is not the manufacturer, but the user. The same is true for the advanced planning that is necessary to install the equipment.

Systems implementation begins after the formal signing of the equipment contract. While the feasibility study consists of three steps—systems analysis, systems design, and equipment selection—systems implementation involves two steps—preparatory work and operation of new system with a provision for periodic review of systems improvements. Time for a typical system project is one-third for the feasibility study and two-thirds for implementing the system. The number of operating personnel outside the data processing group is substantially increased for the latter phase. Also, an organization will experience high costs during systems conversion.

Programming and testing, the mainstay of the preparatory work phase, is time consuming and costly. Advanced programming techniques and programming languages should be utilized to assist in developing computer programs and reduce programming costs. Once a program has reached the operational stage, dual operations should be initiated to check for abnormal conditions that might have not been present during program and systems testing. This phase culminates in conversion of all activities for daily operation. Consideration must be given to alternative plans in case of unforeseen difficulties during conversion as well as at a later date.

Periodic review of the system should follow the installation which involves examination of new system approaches, new equipment, and cost factors. Many times, an evaluation of the existing system may signal the need for a new feasibility study. In essence, the system project cycle must start again. This permits making system changes that reflect the existing business environment.

---

questions

1. What are the steps involved in determining what DP equipment the organization should procure?

2. Are there any problems associated with having various computer manufacturers draw up the new system specifications for an organization and having them submit bids on this basis?

3. What are the most important factors when selecting computer equipment?

4. (a) What kinds of personnel problems accompany the change from one system to another?
   (b) How can they be overcome?

5. Once the equipment order has been signed, what type of training problems are likely to occur? Explain.

6. (a) What programming difficulties can be experienced by the data processing section during the preparatory work phase?
   (b) Explain how each can be resolved.

7. When installing a new computer system, what physical facilities are necessary?

8. How important is parallel operations for a simple computer program and a complex computer program? Explain.

9. Why should an organization review periodically its system for improvements? Explain.

**second summary
of chapter 11**

systems implementation:
Implementation of the new system begins after the formal signing of the equipment contract. Time for a typical system project is one-third for the feasibility study and two-thirds for systems implementation. The major parts of implementing a system are:

• preparatory work of new system — represents the work that must be undertaken before day-to-day operations of the new system can begin. They include:
  • scheduling the installation
  • selecting qualified personnel
  • training personnel
  • realignment of personnel
  • physical requirements and alterations
  • testing and acceptance of new equipment
  • programming and testing
  • file conversion

• operation of new system — focuses on day-by-day operations of the system. Even though computer programs and operational procedures have been systems tested, there is no way of duplicating actual operations with all their exceptions and irregularities except by following these steps:

  • run parallel operations — consists of feeding both systems (old and new) the same input data for comparison of updated files and output results.

  • conversion to new system — is the process of shifting one area from the existing system to the new one after files have been converted and the new system's reliability has been proven.

  • provision to make necessary changes — provides for making minor program and system adjustments that are deemed necessary for improving operations.

  • scheduling equipment and personnel — refers to setting up daily equipment schedules that involve organization personnel to operate the equipment efficiently.

  • alternative plans in case of equipment failure — involves giving preference to those jobs that are critical in case of equipment downtime for extended periods of time.

• periodic review of new system approaches — recognizes that the ultimate business information system will never be installed; hence the need for undertaking a feasibility study periodically to devise an efficient and economical system for changed operating conditions.

**second self-study
exercise
of chapter 11**

True-False:

1. (   ) There is little need of preparatory work for a new DP system.
2. (   ) Scheduling the installation is the least important of preparatory activities.
3. (   ) For the most part, file conversion is a costly and time consuming task.
4. (   ) Computer programming and testing requires little time in a system project.
5. (   ) Documentation is the least important step in programming and testing.
6. (   ) Parallel operations is the next step after systems testing.
7. (   ) Mistakes found during parallel operations may be those of the old system.
8. (   ) Most firms find parallel operations a waste of time and money.
9. (   ) Scheduling equipment and personnel is an important task of the DP manager.
10. (   ) Generally, there is no need for plans in case of equipment failure.

Fill-In:

11. The task of _____ _____ is generally a major undertaking if it cuts across the entire organization structure for a system project.
12. The major undertaking of a computer project is _____ and _____.
13. The costs and problems of _____ _____ are significant whether they be manual, magnetic tape, magnetic drum, or magnetic disk files.
14. The steps involved in developing an operational, _____-_____ computer program are long and drawn out.
15. Even though computer programs have been _____ _____, there is no way of duplicating the actual flow of work except with day-by-day operations.
16. _____ _____ consist of feeding the present system and the new system with the same input data, thereby allowing a comparison of files and output results.
17. Daily _____ of personnel and equipment must be undertaken if an efficient data processing operation is to be maintained.
18. Generally, the scheduling of a _____-_____ system is more difficult than that for a batch-oriented computer system.
19. Alternative plans must be employed in case of _____ _____ in order to give priorities to jobs that are the most critical.
20. Generally, it is necessary to undertake a _____ _____ in order to maintain an optimum system for an organization's changed operating conditions.

answers to first self-study exercise

1. F 2. F 3. F 4. T 5. T 6. T 7. F 8. F 9. F 10. T 11. equipment selection 12. flowcharts 13. bid invitation 14. system specifications 15. processing 16. automation 17. throughput performance 18. delivery 19. software 20. decision table

answers to second self-study exercise

1. F 2. F 3. T 4. F 5. F 6. T 7. T 8. F 9. T 10. F 11. systems implementation 12. programming and testing 13. file conversion 14. batch-oriented 15. systems tested 16. parallel operations 17. scheduling 18. real-time 19. equipment failure 20. periodic review

part six

the impact of data processing on the individual and the organization

The growth of the computer industry has opened up
challenging career opportunities for high school and
college graduates—to be explored in Chapter 12.
The individual must be willing to learn new methods
and procedures as more computers are introduced
in business organizations.

chapter twelve: the human element and its organization

To obtain an understanding of the computerized world around them, Joe and Claudia Cosgrove will be taking a short-term course on computers. This course will be offered next semester at the local community college. On Saturday morning, which is registration time, they drive to the college. The registration process consists of filling out a number of computer-readable forms. These forms become the input for class registration.

Although there was a lot of personal contact between the college and the Cosgroves, the same will not be true behind the scenes since all registration from this point on will be handled by the computer. This information will then become the basis for billing and keeping track of payments on account. Overall, the computerized aspects after registration can be just as effective as a manual system, since the interface between Joe and Claudia and the community college will be principally by mail, that is, it will consist of making payments on account. However, if there is need for a human interface, that is, for answering calls about the status of their account, consideration must be given to this important factor for an effective system.

This chapter focuses on the human element, a common factor in all DP systems. It covers those aspects dealing with human and morale factors plus those treating organization and conversion activities. Not only is each subject surveyed, but attention is also given to related problems and constructive comments to alleviate these shortcomings. In the final analyis, the only successful approach to data processing is a positive one that involves imaginative people with leadership qualities and technical ability.

human factors

As organizations install newer business information systems, they are confronted with the human factor and its related problems. The lower-level and middle-level managers fear some part of their control will be lost because tasks will be assigned to the computer or advanced data processing equipment. Likewise, the fear of job displacement, the loss of job security, or the individual's inability to cope with a new job are faced by office employees. These attitudes create an environment that is not conducive to an efficient operation. It is up to management to anticipate these human problems and provide ready answers as they arise.

Even though management understands and anticipates the human aspects of a new system, a certain amount of dislocation and hardship will be encountered. By planning effectively for these conditions, the amount of hostility and dissension can be kept to a minimum. In general, management plans should include not replacing certain clerical personnel as they leave (starting with the time that the equipment is on order). Not only is normal turnover effective for reducing personnel, but also routine jobs tend to have higher turnover of personnel than jobs requiring higher skills. Also, plans should be given to increased data processing work caused by growth factors. Often, this results in a need for additional employees in supporting information system activities. More new job openings may be created than were eliminated. Although many jobs will be different, management plans must consider what training is needed, who is to be trained, or what new personnel must be hired.

The Individual

Office employees are generally group-oriented compared to their immediate supervisor and those above them. The individual is more susceptible to the influence of fellow workers, especially their opinions on the new system. Other human factors that are important to the individual are: a need for recognition, affection, and attention; status in the eyes of co-workers; the social need for working in groups; the necessity to lean on others for support and encouragement; and reassurance as to job security. Research has indicated that the individual has a natural tendency to resist changes, tends to believe rumors versus the real facts, needs continuous motivation, is concerned with short-range goals, and is influenced by key workers. In essence, the individual is more concerned about social and ego needs as opposed to economic needs when it comes to a system change (Figure 12-1). It should be noted that economic, social, and ego needs are based upon Maslow's hierarchy of needs.

Social acceptance in a new environment is of great importance. Will new working conditions mean isolation from the individual's present friends? In a similar manner, the office worker is wondering how the new job will meet his or her ability and talents. Will the newly created positions present too much of a challenge or will it mean that the individual must look elsewhere for work since he or she lacks the appropriate skills?

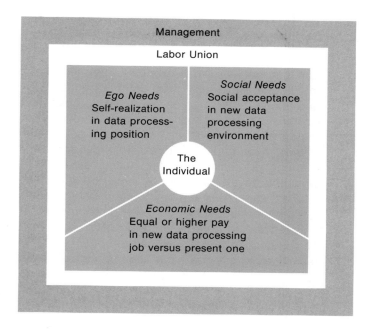

figure 12-1. The focal point of any business information system is the individual needs which are constrained by the labor union and management.

Need to Keep Individual Informed. Based upon these human considerations, it is not surprising that employee resistance increases as time passes. The common fear of machines displacing office workers is ever present. The feasibility study group cannot prevent these basic human reactions from occurring since it will take a long time to substitute new values for old ones and satisfy the individual as much as humanly possible. However, if the data processing section is aware of these powerful forces at work (as it should be), it can offset them in certain cases and minimize them in others. This can be accomplished by several methods, one being an effective communication process. The importance of keeping the individual informed is paramount. They need reassurance as to their job security, opportunities under the new system, and procedural steps to be followed during the coming period.

An essential part of management's plans when deciding on more advanced data processing equipment, then, is advising all individuals whose jobs are affected as early as possible about the change. This gives individuals a chance to think over their future and how they fit into the new information system. An early statement, preferably in writing, followed by subsequent ones should further clarify the organization's direction with newer data processing techniques and how this will affect the individual. Frank statements about groups that will be dislocated, jobs eliminated, and like matters permit the individual to develop future plans with the assistance of an immediate supervisor. This planned approach is in contrast to saying nothing or very little to the employee until the time comes for actual conversion activities. Under these conditions, the informal structure (grapevine) can give a distorted view of the true facts, especially in terms of personnel losing their jobs.

Need to Gain Individual's Confidence. Perhaps the best way to gain the individual's confidence is to relate the organization's general system problems to the work area. Employees who are opinion leaders in the informal organization should be convinced of the present system's shortcomings and should be sold on the merits of the new system. They, in turn, can become salespersons to their fellow employees. In all cases, individuals should be given ample opportunity to air their views in formal and informal meetings as the system project develops. This approach demonstrates to all individuals that the organization is concerned about their jobs and their future. By showing genuine interest in individuals, many of their initial and subsequent fears can be overcome. With an "open door" approach, personnel problems associated with dual operations, conversion, and day-to-day operations will be kept to a minimum so that the ultimate success of the new system will not be impaired.

With the introduction of newer data processing equipment, office employees should be advised and prepared for greater rigidity in their jobs. This is caused by the very nature of EDP equipment. Interdepartmental teamwork, which may have been unnecessary in the past, must be encouraged and enforced by the data processing section in order to insure a smooth work flow. Otherwise, bottlenecks will occur. Any tendency on the part of the individual to blame the system for errors can create serious operating problems, resulting in loss of confidence under the new system. This negative reaction on the part of organization personnel can be avoided by continuous checking during systems implementation. Any possible source of a system breakdown should be eliminated immediately before potential trouble spots become major problems. An alternative systems design technique that is effective in preventing previous system breakdowns in building some flexibility into the system. This approach permits adjusting to unforeseen contingencies without the need for formal system changes.

Labor Union

Any time a major new system is installed, top management must consider its effect on the labor union. Even though most office workers are not unionized, this is an opportune time for labor unions to publicize the fears and uncertainties that accompany further automation of the office. Thus, as time passes, more office unions can be expected since many data processing conversions have been far from ideal in the eyes of office workers.

Need to Work with Union Leaders. Once management must deal with a union of office employees, it must clarify the system project being undertaken and areas that are to be computerized. The system impact on all union members must be candidly discussed. Management should not attempt to conceal pertinent facts since they will be eventually known to all employees. Having set forth all important data to the union's satisfaction, it is much easier to handle any permanent layoffs or job reassignments that are necessary during the conversion period. If management is tactful and honest in its dealings with the union, it can obtain the cooperation it needs to handle the forthcoming changes. To do otherwise normally will result in numerous problems that can be damaging to the organization.

Union leaders are crucial to the success of systems implementation since they often act as interpreters of the new system. They can be one of the most effective forces for securing cooperation and acceptance from the organization's office members. In order to obtain their individual support, management must see that they are receptive to its training problems. A well-directed training course provides an excellent opportunity for convincing union officials that newer DP equipment is not to be feared. It can also provide a means of disseminating information about improved job opportunities and pay for its members.

Ideally, the union representatives will attend the same meetings and courses as those for the firm's supervisory staff. By placing them on the same level as supervisory personnel, the union leaders will be natural candidates for participating in system developments from the very outset. Although they will be looking out for the interests of their union members, they can be a tremendous help to management in seeing that system changes are adequately and carefully planned. Under these favorable conditions, union leaders can provide the necessary assistance during the many difficult phases of systems implementation.

Management

Just as an understanding of the human factors at work is necessary for the individual and the labor union, the same can be said of lower and middle management. Personnel at this level hold the key to the ultimate success or failure of the new system. Top management relies heavily on these two levels because they represent top management in the eyes of employees. Most nonsupervisory employees reflect the attitudes that flow downward from these supervisory personnel. Since their subordinates are quick to follow them, the DP section must obtain their acceptance and complete cooperation.

Lower and middle management levels present a number of special problems to those engaged in the system project. Often, these managing groups have a rather narrow perspective of overall operations. Since they are so immersed in their own respective areas, they lack the time and foresight to see what else is going on around them. Typically, there is an increased resistance to change as they grow older since they are reluctant to alter established work patterns. These management personnel fear their inability to compete with younger people. In a similar manner, lower and middle management levels fear a new system since any reduction in the number of employees is more than likely to reduce their span of supervision. Other human factors involved are: inability to learn and supervise new procedures, tendency to blame the new system for errors, and an abnormal amount of pressure during systems implementation.

Need to Reassure Lower and Middle Management. The previous list of human problems for lower and middle management should be solved by the data processing group as early as possible. Even before the actual feasibility study has begun, a written memorandum from top management is needed to allay their fears. The first announcement and subsequent reports must contain assurances of job security and other considerations that are deemed important by this group, such as reasons for the change and emphasis on the benefits available to all personnel. Reports to lower and middle management can be the same reports to their subordinates or can be separate ones, depending upon the attendant circumstances.

The same methods used for working with nonsupervisory personnel can be employed for these levels of management. The interview, in particular, gives DP personnel one of its best opportunities to obtain their cooperation and reduce their fears. Systems personnel can lessen the manager's fears of loss of status by stressing a direct relationship to the new system. These include: receiving better information for more exacting decisions, increased role as a trainer of new methods and procedures, utilization of the individual's experience, and treating the individual as an intelligent equal — capable of understanding the system and its problems. The process of winning over lower and middle management is a must since this group offers more resistance to system changes than all the employees reporting to them.

Need to Evaluate Top Management's Attitude Toward the New System. Lower and middle management are quick to form their opinions about a new system project. Most of the time, their attitudes reflect those of top management. If the management at the very top has interest in the project and is actively supporting it, chances are that the same attitude will prevail at the various management levels below. This is the reason why it is extremely important for the data processing group to evaluate the top management climate immediately. If there exists an environment that is conducive to teamwork among the various functions and departments, delegation of responsibility with the corresponding amount of authority, and the challenge of problem solving, the group can concentrate on the technical aspects of the project. On the other hand, if there are rigid departmental barriers, reluctance to keep employees informed on company plans, and the communication process has been restricted, attention first must be focused on the human element. The data processing group must educate top management about the importance of "working through people" in order to accomplish a successful system installation. To ignore the human factor under these adverse conditions and concentrate solely on the technical factors is a waste of time. The whole project is doomed to failure from its inception.

Top management must make assurances about job security, equal or better pay, opportunities about training, and guidelines to be followed for reassignment of lower and middle management jobs. An early statement of its policy on these critical matters to management and nonmanagement employees is an important plus factor in achieving a successful system. Top management's plan should include not only statements on the job area, but also specific details on all other data processing changes that affect the entire organization.

the human element	Too often, many DP installations have failed or have come to the brink of failing in the past. Management efforts to obtain acceptance of newer data processing equipment and procedures by its personnel were either lacking or ineffective. Cases where employees were slow in meeting deadlines, magnified the difficulties of conversion activities, and compiled data unwillingly were common. Group resistance or reluctance to cooperate fully led to disappointing results in terms of a new business information system. These problems were generally not connected to equipment difficulties, but rather were associated directly with the human element.

Because no system is "an island unto itself," it needs people to run it efficiently. What kind of personnel are needed? There is a great need for *imaginative people who have the required technical ability and have positive attitudes toward data processing.* They, in turn, must have the necessary *cooperation from all organizational members* who are directly or indirectly associated with DP activities, *in particular, top management.*

The investment of time and effort in acquiring and maintaining good employee relations is actually not very great. The various methods set forth earlier in the book, that is, written memorandums, posting of new jobs, formal training, and on-the-job training, are necessary to avoid employee hostility and a complete breakdown in good employee relations. No system is capable of producing good results on its own. It must have the complete cooperation of those who are in a position to make it operational. Thus, it should be emphasized that the human element—a group of imaginative DP personnel—interacts with environmental factors in order to produce a successful business information system (Figure 12-2).

Imaginative People With Technical Ability
Imaginative people with the required technical ability are a prerequisite for an efficient business information system. Not only are imaginative personnel needed for daily operations but they are also needed for developmental activities, in particular, systems design. Systems designers should be the most creative and imaginative of all DP personnel when it comes to developing newer systems. If the organization has not selected capable systems designers, it will eventually show when the system change is effected.

figure 12-2. The relationship of important business information system factors to the human element — the key to successful data processing.

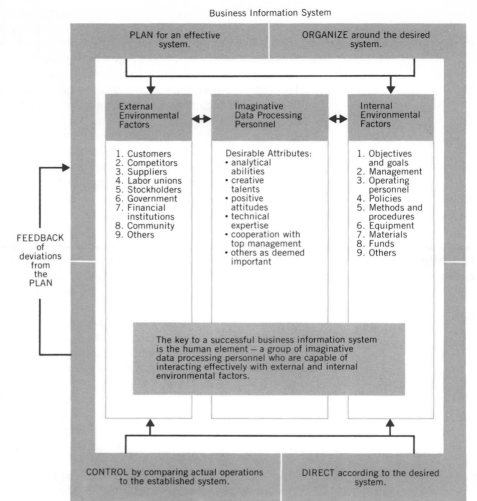

Business Information System

PLAN for an effective system.

ORGANIZE around the desired system.

External Environmental Factors

1. Customers
2. Competitors
3. Suppliers
4. Labor unions
5. Stockholders
6. Government
7. Financial institutions
8. Community
9. Others

Imaginative Data Processing Personnel

Desirable Attributes:
• analytical abilities
• creative talents
• positive attitudes
• technical expertise
• cooperation with top management
• others as deemed important

Internal Environmental Factors

1. Objectives and goals
2. Management
3. Operating personnel
4. Policies
5. Methods and procedures
6. Equipment
7. Materials
8. Funds
9. Others

FEEDBACK of deviations from the PLAN

The key to a successful business information system is the human element — a group of imaginative data processing personnel who are capable of interacting effectively with external and internal environmental factors.

CONTROL by comparing actual operations to the established system.

DIRECT according to the desired system.

To implement a successful system, management should place its imaginative personnel who meet the technical qualifications of specific jobs in key positions for several reasons. First, these people can sense in advance adverse conditions that can affect the human factor and other elements important to a smooth flowing operation. Being highly imaginative, they can correct the situation themselves or offer constructive comments for rectifying the problem immediately. Second, these high-caliber people can offer solutions that are highly practicable, but more importantly, ones that are simple to implement and use on a day-to-day basis. Instead of complex methods, procedures, and programs, imaginative people concentrate their efforts on simplified approaches, knowing that average people will be implementing these approaches. A simplified procedure goes a long way to establish good employee relations. A third consideration for strategically placing imaginative people is their positive attitude toward environment factors. If they take a positive approach toward their work and people around them, their subordinates will likewise reflect this same attitude since their supervisors are looked upon as the ultimate authority in their respective jobs. Lastly, imaginative people are not locked in their day-today habits, but have an open mind that is necessary for evaluating newer system approaches. They are constantly on the lookout for improvements.

Positive Attitude Toward Data Processing

Of all the personnel in the organization, management must have a positive attitude toward whatever system has been or is to be installed. It must be knowledgeable of what the system is capable of doing for them. Management must overcome the fear that the computer poses a threat to their office and realize that it, when properly installed, can increase control by making new information available when needed. They must recognize that their subordinates must work in a more disciplined manner in order to derive the maximum benefits of advanced equipment. Management's overview of the system should include a knowledge of the system's time and cost requirements which should be reviewed periodically. Otherwise, false expectations have a way of reappearing even when data on the new system have been clearly disseminated.

A positive attitude toward data processing is a requirement for anyone who desires to move up the management ladder, starting with the lowest level. It is acquired by taking formal courses, attending seminars, and working on the job. The aspiring individual is exposed to DP experts whose enthusiasm will be instrumental is dispelling any negative opinions and attitudes on the subject. This is in contrast to company personnel who may have a negative outlook about newer data processing activities. The basic reason for this condition is that they have had little or no exposure in the data processing area, either through the organization's fault or their own. The individual's negative attitude is conditioned by lack of DP knowledge. By educating the employee and supplementing this education with other positive motivators, such fears gradually disappear. The changing of the human element from a negative outlook to a positive one provides an essential key to successful data processing.

Cooperation with Top Management

Imaginative data processing personnel with technical ability and a positive attitude must be augmented by another important consideration, that is, cooperation with top management. Many computer studies have shown that rising computer expenses are not matched by comparable economic returns. The reason is that too many firms are leaving the job of computer implementation to the technician and not to top management. One study conducted by Booz, Allen & Hamilton, Inc. of 108 corporations has indicated one main reason for computer success—top management has taken charge of DP operations.*

Another study by McKinsey & Company, Inc. examined the common denominator for a profitable computer operation and found there were three essential principles involved.† They include (1) the rule of high expectations (top management demands profitable results from its com-

* N. J. Dean, "The Computer Comes of Age," *Harvard Business Review,* January–February 1968, pp. 83–85.
†D. B. Hertz, "Unlocking the Computer's Profit Potential," *Computers and Automation,* April 1969, p. 33.

puter applications), (2) the rule of diversified staffing (assignment to the corporate computer staff, along with the usual operations research specialists and other professionals, of at least one capable person from each of the firm's major functions), and (3) the rule of top management involvement (the profit potential of computers is assured if top management is in charge versus computer technicians).

first summary of chapter 12

human factors:
• the individual—susceptible to the influence of fellow workers, especially their opinions on the new system. The individual is more concerned about social and ego (higher-level) needs than economic (lower-level) needs.

• labor union—further automation of the office provides an opportunity for labor unions to publicize the fears and uncertainties of a system change. Hence, union representatives should be given the same information and training as those for the company's supervisory staff.

• management—lower and middle management present a number of special problems to those undertaking a system project. These include reluctance to alter established work patterns, inability to compete with younger people, and reduction in their span of supervision. Likewise, top management can be a barrier to undertaking a system project if there are rigid departmental barriers, a reluctance to keep company employees informed, and a restriction of the communication process.

the human element:
• imaginative people with technical ability—management should place these type people in key DP positions for several reasons. They are capable of:

  • rectifying a problem immediately.
  • offering highly practical solutions using simplified procedures.
  • radiating a positive attitude to people around them.
  • keeping an open mind necessary for evaluating new approaches.

• positive attitude toward data processing—recognizes that a new DP system, when properly installed, can increase managerial effectiveness by providing decision-making information when needed.

• cooperation with top management—studies have shown that the main reason for a successful computer installation is the involvement of top management. One study named these principles for a profitable computer operation:

  • the rule of high expectations, i.e., top management demands profitable results from its computer.
  • the rule of diversified staffing, i.e., assignment of capable people from each of the organization's major functions to the computer staff along with specialized technicians.
  • the rule of top management involvement, i.e., the profit potential of computers is assured if top management is in charge versus computer technicians.

**first self-study
exercise
of chapter 12**

True-False:

1. (　) The human factor is the least important one when undertaking a system change.

2. (　) Ego needs relate to satisfying the individual's salary requirements.

3. (　) There is little need to keep employees informed about system changes.

4. (　) Labor unions tend to publicize the fears and uncertainties that accompany a system change.

5. (　) Lower and middle management present special problems to those engaged in a system project.

6. (　) There is no need to evaluate management's attitude toward a system change.

7. (　) For a successful system, there is need for imaginative people with technical ability.

8. (　) Generally, a new DP system is "an island unto itself."

9. (　) For a successful information system, top management must be in charge.

10. (　) A computer installation will experience difficulties if the technicians have the final word.

Fill-In:

11. For a successful data processing system, specific attention should be focused on the _____ _____.

12. The focal point of any business information system is the _____ who is constrained by fellow workers and management.

13. The economic, social, and ego needs of the individual are based upon the hierarchy of needs as set forth by _____.

14. Perhaps the best way to gain the individual's _____ for the need of a system change is relate the organization's general system problems to the individual's work area.

15. With the introduction of newer data processing equipment, office employees should be advised and prepared for greater _____ in their jobs.

16. Any time a major system change occurs, the _____ _____ finds this to be an opportune time for publicizing the fears and uncertainties that accompany further automation of the office.

17. Lower and middle _____ hold the key to the ultimate success or failure of a new system project since they represent top management in the eyes of organization employees.

18. Sometimes, it is necessary that the data processing group undertake corrective action in _____ before starting a system project.

19. The key to a successful business information system is the human element, that is, a group of _____ _____ with technical ability who are capable of interacting effectively with the _____ factors.

20. In order to reap the benefits of DP, _____ _____ must form a team with its data processing technicians.

Many computer installations have been and are still in trouble because top management has abdicated their managerial responsibility. As noted in a trade publication, "Top managers have failed to achieve greater computer effectiveness because they abdicated control to staff specialists — excellent as technicians but lacking the operational experience to know the jobs that need doing and the authority to get them done right."* In essence, data processing personnel have neither the operational experience to know the projects that must be undertaken to further company objectives nor the authority to get them performed in an efficient manner.

A most important key to successful data processing, then, is teamwork between management and data processing personnel. Top management must exert leadership and operating managers must actively cooperate with computer specialists in order to form an effective team to implement business information system. Only when managers get involved, cooperate with data processing personnel, and relate their problems to the computer equipment can the computer's potential be realized.

organization for successful data processing

The human factor as a part of a business information system cannot operate in a vacuum, but must operate within an organization structure. As an organization grows, the degree of adherence to the DP organization structure changes. The structure that was loosely knit in the past becomes more structured and formal, reflecting the larger number of people to be supervised. Also, more rigid lines of communication must be employed to accomplish the many tasks.

The changes necessary to accommodate a new system vary from one organization to another. How computer activities are organized depends on the size of the organization and the complexity of the system. A system for a small company (say sales of $20 million) will be different from a medium-sized one (say sales of $100 million) or a large-sized one (say sales of $1 billion). Within every one of the foregoing categories, the application of the latest data processing equipment can vary because of the approach used. One may be a batch-processing system, an interactive system, or some other type system. The degree of hardware and software sophistication in an organization should be one that will best serve its needs.

The differences between the organization structure of a batch-processing system and an interactive processing system are not too significant. The interactive processing system still needs the same organizational units as a batch-processing system. Despite the fact that there will be fewer personnel preparing input data in a comparably-sized interactive system, there is still a need for input data on a remote batch-processing basis. Personnel will be needed to send and receive data to and from the many on-line I/O terminals. There will be less need for computer console operators in an on-line processing mode since a continuous series of processing runs will not be scheduled. Rather, interactive computer operations must perform a monitoring function in order to maintain an operational system. Even with these changes, the organization structure for an advanced interactive processing system is not too much different from preceding systems. The major difference is the number of personnel and the kind of equipment being employed.

* "Who Should Boss the Computer? You Should!," *Industry Week*, September 13, 1971, p. 45.

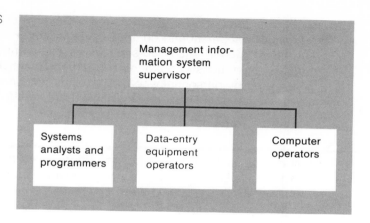

figure 12-3. A typical MIS organization chart for a very small firm.

MIS Organization Chart for Very Small Firms. It is impossible to design a data processing organization that fits all organizations and their respective needs. Nevertheless, it is worth while to discuss a "DP organization chart" for a typical firm of varying sizes. Illustrated in Figure 12-3 is a MIS (management information system) organization chart for a very small firm whose total annual sales are several million dollars. Equipment rental is generally under $5000 per month. All operating personnel report directly to the management information system supervisor.

MIS Organization Chart for Small- to Medium-Size Firms. A management information system organization chart for a small- to medium-size firm is depicted in Figure 12-4 where equipment rental costs can range up to $20,000 a month. Four supervisors report to the management information

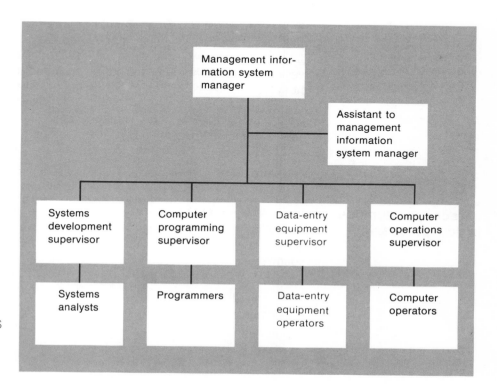

figure 12-4. A typical MIS organization chart for a small-size to a medium-size firm.

system manager or an assistant to the MIS manager. Two supervisors—systems development and computer programming—direct the system and programming effort. Also, two supervisors—data-entry equipment and computer operations—control daily operational activities. All supervisors are assisted by personnel who perform their assigned tasks. As noted in the illustration, the levels of management are kept to a minimum.

training of data processing personnel

Most organizations require a college degree as a prerequisite for those undertaking systems analysis, systems design, and most programming work. They prefer personnel who have taken several courses in computer data processing. Organizations require that prospective applicants take appropriate tests which measure mathematical and programming aptitudes. Computer manufacturers provide programmer's aptitude tests that can assist in making a final decision on applicants.

Once the organization has selected its applicants, it will send them to the manufacturer's programming school. Based upon the individual's performance in school, some will become systems analysts, programmers, or placed where needed. No matter where they are placed in the organization, the new trainees are assigned to and guided by more experienced personnel. Within one year on the job after programming school, the individual should be capable of undertaking assigned work.

Operations personnel are generally recruited from within the organization and are given some formal training. However, most of their training will be on the job. Training for data-entry equipment operators may be given by the respective manufacturer. In those cases where the manufacturer does not provide formal training, the organization's own supervisory personnel must develop and teach courses for the specific areas, utilizing the manufacturer's course materials.

Although personnel training in data processing activities is initially formal, acquiring new knowledge about their respective jobs should never end. Once the learning process stops, the organization will suffer since newer ideas and techniques are not being introduced to maintain an efficient system. A system which might be the answer for today's needs, many times, will not be the ideal one for tomorrow. Only by a continual updating process within the DP section will the organization maintain an efficient system. To think that the ultimate system has been installed is unrealistic and can be a significant barrier to progress.

career opportunities in data processing

As more and more DP systems are introduced, especially in the smaller organizations, additional trained DP personnel will be required at all levels. Major personnel categories, depicted in Figure 12-4, can be broken down as follows:

- management
- systems analysts
- programmers
- operations personnel

The appropriate background for these career opportunities is enumerated in the following sections.

Management

The management of a business information system is responsible for the data processing activities occurring throughout the entire organization. A certain level of technical and administrative skills is necessary to supervise the work of others. Most of this management group have moved into their high-level positions after performing exceptionally well as systems personnel or programmers. Almost without exception, they have the ability to get work done through others with the minimum of problems occurring. DP management people should have a college degree; a master's degree is highly desirable. Without a college degree, other managerial candidates from within and outside the organization appear to be, at least on paper, better suited for an opening in data processing management. The required course of studies will be dictated by the type of installation, that is, a business-oriented computer system versus a scientific-oriented one. The former would require a major in some business area, preferably data processing, accounting, or management. The scientific installation would require a degree in mathematics, engineering, statistics, or some other field, depending upon the type of system. No matter what installation is being considered, all management personnel should have had management, higher mathematics, statistics, and data processing courses, supplemented by practical job experience. All candidates for DP management jobs should possess leadership qualities.

Systems Analysts

The number of systems analysts is almost equal to the number of programmers. Although system developmental tasks can be divided into those of systems analysis and systems design, the established trend is to use one title, namely, *systems analyst*. Generally, systems analysis work is undertaken by junior systems analysts while the senior members of the systems development section are responsible for systems design. The highly abstract work of devising new systems requires creative talents and the ability to think logically through the many alternatives and component parts. A college graduate is best suited for this creative job. As above, the course of college study is dependent upon the specific installation. A desirable background for a business installation includes courses in data processing, higher mathematics, management, and courses that explore an organization's functional areas. Formal exposure and experience in marketing, production, and finance are necessary to design systems that cut across the entire organization.

Programmers

With the increasing number of computer installations, the demand for programmers is continually rising. Programmers can be split into two groups, namely, those dealing with business or scientific applications. Within each of these two groups is found another classification, namely, senior and junior programmers. The highly experienced personnel or senior programmers direct the efforts of junior programmers and other personnel involved in a programming project.

Because of the tremendous demand for programmers in the past, many business programmers did not possess a college degree. However, many organizations use the college diploma as a screening device for applicants. In addition, since most colleges are offering computer science and information system degrees, the high school graduate or one from a private programming school is finding it more difficult to procure programming jobs in the better firms. No matter whether the individual is a high school or a college graduate, the essential requirement for programming is a logical mind that can determine the necessary detailed activities for a specific program. Based upon this consideration, the need for a college business degree is not mandatory. Many of the best programmers have liberal arts and science degrees.

The background necessary for a scientifically oriented computer system is quite different from that required for business. In this area, a degree in mathematics, engineering, or a comparable discipline is a must. For highly sophisticated scientific applications, a master's degree is absolutely essential, especially when working with advanced engineering and mathematical models. Thus, for a better position in programming scientific projects, the programmer must have the appropriate degree and experience.

Operations Personnel

Data processing operations offer many career opportunities for graduates. Many openings are available for computer operators whose principal duty is to keep the machine operating in an efficient manner. Many computer operators formerly operated punched card equipment. Avenues of training for this job include: high schools, technical schools, private data processing schools, and colleges. However, many operators have obtained their skills through on-the-job training and schools conducted by equipment manufacturers.

An interesting career is being a key-to-disk operator or an input/output terminal operator. These jobs consist basically of working with original source data. Another promising opportunity in data processing is working with optical character recognition equipment for processing input data. A high level of manual dexterity, accompanied by practical thinking, is a prerequisite for doing an effective job.

certificate in data processing

Just as the fields of accounting and law, among others, have programs for certifying the professional capabilities of its members, the same has been accomplished for data processing personnel. The Certificate in Data Processing (CDP) has been developed by the Data Processing Management Association. Ever since the first examination was held in June 1962 (New York City), the test has been offered each year (normally in February) nationally and in some foreign countries at a number of university and college test locations. It covers the following categories: data processing equipment, computer programming and software, principles of management, quantitative methods, and systems analysis and design. All candidates are advised of pass or fail. Those who fail are told in which sections they scored below passing and are permitted to retake those sections.

Current Requirements. Current requirements to sit for the five-hour, 300-question exam include five years' proven experience in the field (or its equivalent in part-time work) and character references. Data processing management, systems development work, programming, and data processing teaching count toward meeting the experience requirement while clerical, keypunch, and direct sales experience are not acceptable.

Since 1974, the exam has been administered by the Institute for the Certification of Computer Professionals (ICCP). Information can be obtained from ICCP, 304 East 45th Street, New York, N. Y. 10017.

| certificate in computer programming | In addition to the annual examination for the Certificate in Data Processing, there is another called the Certificate in Computer Programming (CCP). The Registered Business Programmer was discontinued and replaced in 1977 by this certificate. The CCP examination is administered in three categories: business, scientific, and systems programmer. It is also administered by the ICCP, 304 East 45th Street, New York, N. Y. 10017. |

summary

Human factors, among other things, are important considerations for a successful system project. The cost and time involved in developing and maintaining good employee relations are nominal as opposed to those that are necessary to rectify a bad management-employee relationship. Methods used to prepare employees for system changes are written memoranda, newsletters, posting of new data processing jobs, formal training, and on-the-job training. These methods are applicable to office employees as well as to lower and middle management.

The organization structure changes as newer business information systems are installed. Likewise, organizational changes necessary to accommodate a new system vary from one organization to another. Comparable firms within the same industry and sales volume often have varying types of systems. Nevertheless, they have common personnel problems which can make or break any operating system.

The key to successful data processing is the human element. It takes more than imaginative people who work as a team with top management and have the required technical "know-how." It also requires a positive outlook toward data processing, especially when referring to all levels of management. This is particularly true for middle management levels since lower levels of management and nonsupervisory employees are quick to reflect attitudes that flow downward, especially if it is a negative one concerning a new data processing system. Thus, organizational personnel must overcome the attitude that the computer is a threat to them. They must replace this outlook with a positive one, that is, the computer is a powerful tool for providing timely and useful information for greater decision-making ability.

**second summary
of chapter 12**

organization for successful data processing:
• MIS organization chart (two-level) for a very small firm consists of a management information system supervisor who is assisted by systems analysts, programmers, data-entry equipment operators, and computer operators. Example: refer to Figure 12-3

• MIS organization chart (three-level) for small- to medium-size firms consists of a management information system manager who is assisted by a systems development supervisor, computer programming supervisor, data-entry equipment supervisor, and computer operations manager. In turn, each supervisor has one or more personnel under them in the same area. Example: refer to Figure 12-4

training of data processing personnel:
Training of DP personnel will depend upon the job to be accomplished. In some instances, personnel will have the proper background; in other instances, equipment manufacturers will be utilized for appropriate training purposes. In others, on-the-job training will be employed. Hence, the attendant circumstances will dictate what type of training will be used.

career opportunities in data processing:
• management—the individual should be able to get work done through others with a minimum of problems and have a college degree; a master's degree is highly desirable.

• systems analysts—each person should be creative and be able to think logically through several alternatives to a new system; a college degree is recommended.

• programmers—each person should have a logical mind that can determine the necessary detailed activities found in a computer program; a college degree can be used as a screening device.

• operations personnel—each person should be capable of practical thinking and, in many cases, a high level of manual dexterity is required.

certificate in data processing:
Current requirements are five years' proven experience in the field and character references.

certificate in computer programming:
The Registered Business Programmer was discontinued and replaced by the Certificate in Computer Programming. It is administered in three categories: business, scientific, and systems programmer.

second self-study exercise of chapter 12

True-False:

1. (   ) An interactive and a batch-processing system need the same DP organizational units.
2. (   ) The number of organizational levels is always the same for small- and medium-size firms.
3. (   ) The computer operations supervisor is assisted by systems analysts.
4. (   ) A form of data processing instruction is full-time training on the job.
5. (   ) There are more job opportunities as programmers versus programming managers.
6. (   ) Generally, senior members of the systems development section perform systems design.
7. (   ) A degree in mathematics is required for all programmers.
8. (   ) Many interesting DP career opportunities are available to high school graduates.
9. (   ) There are no requirements for the CDP exam.
10. (   ) The Registered Programmer Examination is a subsection of the CDP exam.

Fill-In:

11. The number of levels within the data processing _____ _____ is greater for a large organization than for a small one.
12. For a very small organization, the data processing supervisor is assisted by programming personnel, data-entry operators, and _____ _____.
13. In a medium-size organization, the systems development supervisor is assisted by several _____ _____.
14. Career opportunities in business data processing include DP management, systems analysts and designers, _____, and _____ _____.
15. The highly abstract work of devising _____ _____ systems requires creative talents and the ability to think through many alternatives.
16. Highly experienced personnel or _____ _____ direct the efforts of junior programmers and other personnel in a programming project.
17. For a highly sophisticated, scientific programming project, a _____ degree is essential in the scientific area being coded.
18. Interesting career opportunities are available for _____ _____ graduates, like an I/O terminal operator and a key-to-disk operator.
19. The _____ exam has been developed by the Data Processing Management Association to certify the overall professional capabilities of data processing personnel.
20. Current requirements for taking the CDP exam include five years proven experience in computer-based _____ _____ and high _____ qualifications.

questions

1. Of the three human factors mentioned in the chapter, which one causes top management the most problems when converting to a newer DP system? Explain.
2. What can an organization do to overcome personnel problems when a newer business information system is formally announced?
3. Do organization structures differ greatly for batch-processing and interactive processing systems? Explain.
4. Discuss the similarities and differences between the developmental and operational sections of a DP system.
5. How important is the staffing and training of DP personnel to the success of a business information system? Explain.
6. What is meant by the statement, "The key to successful data processing is the human element?"

answers to first self-study exercise

1. F 2. F 3. F 4. T 5. T 6. F 7. T 8. F 9. T 10. T 11. human element 12. individual 13. Maslow 14. confidence 15. rigidity 16. labor union 17. management 18. attitudes 19. imaginative people and environmental 20. top management

answers to second self-study exercise

1. T 2. F 3. F 4. T 5. T 6. T 7. F 8. T 9. F 10. F 11. organization structure 12. computer operators 13. systems analysts 14. programmers and operations personnel 15. business information 16. senior programmers 17. master's 18. high school 19. CDP 20. information systems and character

epilogue future impact of data processing on society and business

As demonstrated throughout this book, Joe and Claudia Cosgrove have benefited from the vast capabilities of the computer. However, recently when they were watching the evening news, a major topic of conversation was a charge that computers may have influenced the results of a recent city election. It was charged that many hours before the polls were officially closed, the computer, which was tabulating the election results, predicted the outcome based on an analysis of sample "key precincts." On hearing this prediction, Joe and Claudia decided not to vote, since they felt that their votes would have no effect either way on the final outcome. Did Joe and Claudia do the proper thing by not voting? Although this question cannot be answered with a definitive answer, it does raise an important issue about computers that will be explored to a large degree in this final part of the book.

In this Epilogue, the future impact of computers on society is initially discussed. This discussion serves as a background for developing a balanced approach to computers in society. Additionally, a balanced approach to the use of data banks is set forth to protect the privacy of the individual. In a similar manner, the future impact of computers on the human element in business is explored, with particular emphasis on the individual and the group as well as the various levels of management. After setting forth future computer developments, the Epilogue concludes with a discussion of how computers will affect the organization and society in the future. In effect, the conclusion highlights the major topics covered, i.e., the future impact of data processing on society and business.

impact of computers on society

To assess the impact of computers on society, it is necessary to examine their benefits and shortcomings. Needless to say, the benefits that society have received to date and will continue to receive from the employment of computers are many. Sample ways in which computers have and will continue to benefit society include:

- *New job opportunities* — refers to the proliferation of new computer firms and expansion of present computer companies in presenting new job opportunities for people of all ages. Many of these jobs were unheard of only a decade ago.
- *Increased leisure time and recreation* — relates to the fact that the computer has increased factory and office productivity, thereby allowing organizations to produce more goods and provide more services with less input of human labor. This benefit gives us more time to relax, travel, read, and to do our "own thing."
- *Improved educational instruction* — allows the student to interact directly with the computer via a terminal as part of an overall learning process. The student is given instructions, is asked questions, and receives responses within a *computer-assisted instruction* (CAI) environment.
- *Enhanced banking operations with the Electronic Funds Transfer System (EFTS)* — enables goods to be sold, merchandise purchased, employees paid, and funds deposited and withdrawn from banks without cash changing hands. The EFTS, sometimes shorted to *electronic money*, will change the time frame in which transactions and payments

are made, i.e., transactions will be posted immediately rather than waiting for bills and payments to be delivered through the mail. This system is made possible by linking the entire banking system together with a vast communication network.

- *Improved medical and health care*—focuses on using the computer to analyze medical data in order to recommend what action should be taken to overcome the diagnosed illness. But, more important, the computer has the capability of detecting illnesses before they occur so that preventive medicine can be applied.

Although this listing is far from complete, it does convey an idea of what the computer has and will continue to do for society. Additionally, this list demonstrates how the computer has touched our daily lives in some shape and form, i.e., in a positive way.

These benefits are but one side of the "computer coin." On the other side, there are certain shortcomings about computers that we should be aware of. They include:

- *Large-scale unemployment*—relates to the degree of unemployment caused by computer automation in the factory and in the office. Many times, this results in the necessity for relocating. Likewise, it can result in the need for extensive retraining of personnel.

- *Uncertainty about one's future*—centers on forced changes caused by more computerized automation. Alienation, distrust, and fear often result from such forced changes.

- *Proliferation of data banks*—focuses on the gathering of data about the individual. The dissemination of information into the wrong hands creates many problems and involves one's right to privacy.

- *Pressure toward uniformity and standardization*—refers to conforming to a certain mode of operation. For example, answers to questions must conform to one of those in the list so that proper identification can be made or your name must fit within the number of spaces alloted. This approach forces the individual into rigid molds.

- *Increased crime by the computer*—consists of such items as, entering fraudulent data into a computer, altering records to conceal cash thefts, or changing programs to print unauthorized checks. These crimes are generally undertaken by computer technicians.

Just as with the prior listing, these cautions about computers, although incomplete, are representative of those currently being discussed.

Balanced Approach to Computers in Society. The preceding benefits and shortcomings can be viewed from several perspectives. From an extreme view, one can conclude by applauding the present and prospective achievements of computers while demonstrating that their dangers or shortcomings are capable of being alleviated by sophisticated "technological fixes of some sort." In effect, there can be a plea for generous support of more and more computers in society. This is usually coupled with more or less subtle assertions that only computer scientists can "save the world."

A viewpoint at the other extreme is that the present benefits are much too grandiose and their shortcomings have been understated. From this view, one can conclude that less computerization of society will aid everyone and, therefore, reduce the technological change that is moving at a rapid rate. In addition, the individual will be less constrained by less uniformity and standardization of everyday life. The individual's rights to life, liberty, and the pursuit of happiness will be emphasized and will be capable of being realized.

Although arguments can be espoused for both viewpoints, neither one in itself represents a balanced approach to computers in society. A preferred viewpoint is one that incorporates the best features of both. Hence, the benefits of computers set forth above should result in enriching a person's everyday life and not result in encroaching on an individual's freedom. For example, the utilization of the Electronic Funds Transfer System will allow one to relegate the monthly drudgery of paying bills to this system. The time saved can be spent on more productive and rewarding items.

In a somewhat similar manner, the shortcomings can be viewed from a positive standpoint, that is, a computer is a "tool" to aid society in ridding itself of or in reducing its problems. As an example, a data bank on criminals can aid the police department in arresting suspects for various types of crimes. Another example would be the taking of a series of tests to determine an individual's aptitudes. A computerized profile from low interest levels to high interest ones can assist an individual in evaluating promising career opportunities. Overall, an enlightened approach to computers is utilizing their full potential for the benefit of society.

Balanced Approach to Use of Data Banks. Just as a balanced approach is needed for employing computers in society, so too there is need for a balanced perspective to the use of computer data banks. More recently, several laws have been passed at the national level to control the use of data bank information. The purpose of this legislation is to insure that an individual's privacy is not being violated when it comes to information contained in data banks. For example, it has been reported that there are five files on every living American which range from employment to social habits. Thus, the magnitude of the data files and their relationship to the invasion of privacy is a matter of great concern to the average individual.

Current legislation that has been passed to promote an intelligent approach to data banks is:

- Fair Credit Reporting Act—requires consumer credit agencies to follow reasonable procedures to safeguard credit information. It requires that the individual be informed when a credit investigation is being conducted.

- Freedom of Information Act—provides for an open flow of data in government and protects the public's right to know about government activities. A safeguard was built in to protect the rights of individuals, i.e., data of a personal nature could be withheld from the public.

- Federal Reports Act—forbids a federal agency from conducting or sponsoring the collection of identical items of data on ten or more persons, other than federal employees, without approval from the Office of Management and Budget.

- Privacy Act of 1974—requires each federal agency to publish a list of the systems of records it maintains. This list must include the name and location of the data system and the category of individuals on which records are maintained.

As more abuses and misuses of data banks are reported by the general populace, other legislation will be drafted by governmental officials so as to maintain a balance between the need for data banks and the invasion of privacy. As an example of the balance, the Internal Revenue Service maintains a data base on each taxpayer. However, the dissemination of income tax information to the wrong persons or organizations may create problems for the individual, thereby invading one's right to privacy. Data on individuals may be detrimental to one's employment opportunities, hinder one's ability to obtain credit, and so forth. On the positive side, data banks provide a valuable information resource for making sound managerial decisions. They provide factual, quantitative data for improving service, increasing efficiency, and reducing waste. Thus, a balanced approach to computerized data banks in society is a necessity; it may require some type of governmental regulation at times to maintain this balanced perspective.

impact of computers on the human element in business

Although the foregoing has focused on the impact of computers on society, this part of the Epilogue examines the impact of computers on the human element in business organizations. An overview of fundamental changes that are occurring assists the individual in understanding why they are

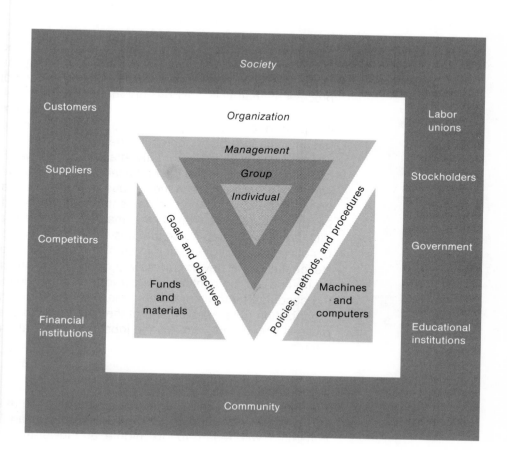

figure E-1. An overview depicting the individual, the group, and management as the focus of the organization.

happening. A basic understanding of innovations will, hopefully, help the individual adjust to the new data processing environment. As illustrated in Figure E-1, the individual as well as the group and management are the focus of an organization, thereby being most affected by newer DP operations.

The Individual and the Group

Because of the large number of computer systems installed, there appears to be a danger that the creative talents of many company personnel are and will be stifled. If there are computer programmed decision rules that optimize performance for basic decisions of an organization, it would appear that there is a tendency to rely completely on these decisions. This approach results in a "depersonalizing" effect on the organization's decision-making process. The individual carries out the decision determined by the computer program. Instead of discussing the factors that affect the decision with an immediate superior, the individual carries out the computer decision as is. The final result is that the hard and fast decisions of computers relieve the individual of all responsibility for an accurate decision, thereby making one feel frustrated. In effect, the individual's creative talents are being restrained. Clearly, such a condition is undesirable.

Although sophisticated systems will abound in the future, there will never be one that is 100% accurate for all decisions. Why is this so? There are always future conditions that arise which were not initially contemplated by the computer decision model. Among these are changes in the economy, unexpected contracts or sales, strikes, floods, and similar conditions. In essence, there will always be a need for the individual to recognize the changed condition and to override or modify the computer answer. This process of changing must be kept to a minimum. Thus, the individual does have the ability to utilize his or her creative talents by questioning computer decisions in light of changing business conditions that have not been considered by the computer decision model.

The group will also be greatly affected by the many sophisticated computer systems in the future. Instead of having large groups of personnel processing data in the various departments, many times they will be replaced by advanced equipment that utilizes a small nucleus of personnel to operate them. In this manner, the cost of processing will drop. With continued rising personnel costs and lower equipment costs, it is beneficial for an organization to employ more equipment and less people. Hence, future DP developments will dramatically affect the size of the group and the job content for each individual within the group. This changing condition for the individual, a member of the group, will allow an organization to take advantage of the rising educational level of its employees who do not want routine jobs, but ones that are a challenge to their talents.

Management

Although there is general agreement regarding the relationship of computers to the individual and the group, there is disagreement concerning computers with regard to top, middle, and lower management. Since the computer is a central figure in this controversy, George Kozmetsky, writing from the perspective of a twenty-first century manager, states: "By the year 2000, the top managers and the machines were directly responsible for virtually all decision making. The authority of middle managers was very limited."* One may ask how accurate this prediction will be. To answer this question and others like it, one may extrapolate from current trends, focusing initially on lower management.

Lower Management. To visualize the impact of computers on lower management, it is necessary to understand the nature of work carried out by this level of managers. For the most part, they manage workers who perform the most basic activities of an organization. Whether in the office or plant, the manager's task entails making decisions of a highly programmable nature, that is, those that are frequently occurring, rather homogeneous in nature, and routine in importance. Often they are so repetitive that the organization develops systematic ways of handling them. The computer has the capacity for handling these routine tasks: the monitoring of inventory levels, the preparation of a large payroll, or the systematizing of processing purchase orders. Thus, computer systems can easily facilitate the handling of highly programmable decisions.

Since so much of the lower manager's job entails making highly programmed decisions, the computer's application at this level is currently widespread. In such an environment, the manager's job becomes essentially one of supplying pertinent inputs to the various computerized systems with which the individual interfaces and of being able to use the computer's output to aid the daily task of short-range scheduling, establishing work priorities, coordinating effort, and the like. Because of the computer's impact on this first level of management, the number of first-line supervisors is expected to decline in the future. Nevertheless, the computer's existence creates staff or supportive functions so that the ultimate impact on the total number of first-level jobs will be negligible. What is affected, therefore, is the relative mix of line versus staff managers at the lower management level.

Middle Management. Lower management is characterized by highly programmed activities, but middle management activities are less programmed. Since middle managers represent a higher position in the administrative echelon, it is only logical that their work be more comprehensive, less routine, less structured, and more varied. It can be said, then, that less of middle management's work is conducive to computerization than that of lower management. Nevertheless, inroads continue to be made into programming certain aspects of the middle manager's job. The employment of computerized mathematical models are expected to increase in usage.

The debate over the impact of computer systems on middle management was begun by Harold Leavitt and Thomas Whisler, who set forth several predictions. Their predications include the following statements pertaining to the impact of the computer on middle management jobs:†

---

* George Kozmetsky, "The Reflections of a 21st Century Manager," *The Futurist,* June 1969, p. 74.
† Harold J. Leavitt and Thomas L. Whisler, "Managers in the 1980's," *Harvard Business Review,* November–December, 1968, p. 85.

1. Jobs at today's middle-management level will become highly structured. Much more of the work will be programmed, i.e., covered by sets of operating rules governing the day-to-day decisions.

2. A radical reorganization of middle-management levels should occur, with certain classes of middle-management jobs moving downward in status and compensation (because they will require less autonomy and skill), with other classes moving upward into the top management groups.

3. The line separating the top from the middle of the organization will be drawn more clearly and impenetrably than ever before, much like the line drawn in the last few decades between hourly workers and first-line supervisors.

Although these predictions have not come to pass, it would be helpful to explore the first one.

Jobs of middle management may become highly structured owing to the constraints of the computer system, because system methods dictate that certain of these functions must be performed in a certain way for computerized decision making. However, a middle manager must still solve nonprogrammable decisions, be a leader and a communication link with the work group, motivate subordinates, and supervise the ongoing organization activities. In summary, the computer can assist the manager by allowing the individual to relegate certain routine decisions to it, giving more time in other areas to increase effectiveness as a manager. This added "time" dimension may also allow more workers to be supervised in certain areas, resulting in fewer middle managers. Thus, the first statement is only partially true today, and may be only partially true tomorrow.

Our viewpoint is that middle managers may be fewer in number in the future, but they will need a greater knowledge of the surrounding environmental factors, a broader vision of their responsibilities, and a greater initiative to cope with changes. The computer will increase in importance by assisting middle management in certain areas of nonroutine decision making plus the traditional area of decision making.

Top Management. At the highest level of management, top managers are the interface between the external and internal environmental factors. They have the responsibility for monitoring and assessing external market opportunities and relating these opportunities to the organization's resources and capabilities. Consequently, the decisions they make are long range in perspective and comprehensive in scope. Top management engages in long-range planning much more than middle and lower management. In this area, the computer is going to assume an important role.

Computer usage over the past few years illustrates that top management decisions which were once based solely on intuition, judgment, and experience can be made amenable to computer application. These applications include use of heuristics, i.e., "rules of thumb," to solve poorly structured problems or of newer mathematical models. Although it is not anticipated that all problems can ultimately be solved heuristically, top management can quantify decision criteria that were once thought to be unquantifiable. Therefore, top managers will be able to assess market conditions, company resources, and economic parameters so that some of the "unknowns" of the past will become "knowns" of the future. As mathematical models are developed that more realistically depict real-world conditions, top managers will have available new capabilities that heretofore were unknown.

future computer developments

Just as opinions vary on the impact of computers on society and business, they also vary on forthcoming computer developments. A logical approach to predicting their future is to extrapolate from computing history and the state of the art of computer technology. Based on this approach, several factors indicating future changes in general-purpose business data processing are:

- Progress in lower-cost computer equipment and data communication technologies.
- Advancement in computer programming and testing of programs.
- Development of better user-machine interfaces (languages) that reduce the programming and testing of new computer systems.
- Added protection of data privacy, security, and integrity.
- Growth of data communication and data-sharing needs for organizations as well as for individuals.
- Development of economic, social, and legislative action that could ultimately result in either monopolization or decentralization of the data processing industry.

In keeping with past computer developments, the user will get more computing power and more storage capabilities for less money. Not only will small-, medium-, and large-scale computers abound in organizations, but also minicomputers and microcomputers will outnumber by far the traditional line of computers. In particular, microprocessors will be found everywhere: in automobiles, household appliances, TV sets, pocket calculators, and so forth. The numerous autonomous, application-oriented mini and small computing systems will have little or no need to communicate with other systems or external files (data bases). Processing and storage capacities of these systems will be comparable with present computer systems. They will be equipped with easy-to-use application programs, will require no operators besides the actual user, and will require minimum maintenance.

Overall, computer systems will be simpler to understand, use, and operate; current programs and data bases will not become obsolete. A possibility is that future computer systems, while offering a "compatible mode" with current programs and data bases, will strongly encourage use of high-level structured programming languages for development of new DP applications. Thus, new and exciting computer opportunities are available to users whose management wants to meet the challenge of the 1980s.

The question of the degree of centralization and decentralization in the future relates closely to computers. If centralization of computing and storage resources causes only a negligible increment in data communication cost, the economies of scale would favor centralization, leaving only

figure E-2. Classification
of computer costs—based
on several studies.

	Average (Approximate)
Equipment rental and/or depreciation costs	36%
Systems development—systems analysis, systems design, and programming of new applications	24%
Maintenance of current programs	16%
Operating expenses for daily activities	24%
	100%

the necessary input and output data terminals geographically distributed. There are, however, several important factors working against centralization. Most important are:

- The significant rise in communication costs that centralization requires.
- An increase in local response time that may be intolerable in some applications, such as process control found in manufacturing.
- Insufficient reliability of the communication line to the central facility.
- The rise in importance of distributed processing systems, particularly at the local and regional levels.

In essence, the economics may well dictate the best approach—centralization, decentralization, or some combination of the two in a distributed processing network. Future computer systems should be flexible enough to allow not only any desirable mode of operation, but also a nondisruptive transition from one mode to another.

Classification of Computer Costs. Analysis of current hardware, software, and operating costs that are indicative of their future trend, have been undertaken by many reputable consulting organizations. A composite of these studies (average values) is found in Figure E-2. The most costly aspect of a computer installation is the software expense that totals approximately 40% (24% for new applications plus 16% for current applications) versus about 36% for equipment rentals and/or depreciation charges. The importance, then, of software cost is evident.

With the trend toward the installation of more sophisticated business information systems, software for these types of systems is getting more complex and expensive. Because of this development, there is a marked tendency to acquire more advanced hardware. This is in opposition to spending great sums of money creating software that will maximize the efficiency of the hardware. In essence, the cost factors of the equipment itself affects directly the software that will be utilized in future business information systems.

conclusion

For an organization to be effective, it must change in response to the environment in which it operates. The changing environment revolves around the complexities of products, expanding markets, newer technology, aggressive labor unions, and increasing governmental authority. Likewise, it also includes newer computer equipment that is capable of handling the increasing load of business data. Data and useful information extracted from the organization's data base have become a vital resource for coping with internal and external changes. The availability and the capability of computers to extract meaningful reports and analyses means that managers are able to function more effectively in the ever-changing business world. In essence, the computer is a powerful tool now, but more so in the future for recognizing important changes in environmental factors that confront an organization.

Greater utilization of advanced computer systems in the future will not be confined only to business and government areas, but will be extended to most phases of society. This was evident in the prior discussion, especially on electronic money. It is also evident when applying for a job. The computer industry has displaced many boring, repetitive, and uninteresting jobs with newer and more challenging ones. Total employment will not be affected as was the case with automation in the plant. Jobs, displaced by a computer installation, are generally offset by jobs created by this growing industry. The final effect of future data processing advancements is that newly created jobs are more specialized than their predecessors. Those who lack these new skills are going to be unemployable since our computer-oriented economy has few openings for unskilled and uneducated people. Thus, our present problems of hiring the hard-core unemployed for administrative and office jobs will be further compounded by the increasing need for specialists.

Not only does society face additional problems of adapting to electronic money and continued technological unemployment resulting from computers, but it also faces the problem of invasion of privacy, as discussed in the first part of the Epilogue. Invasion of privacy and infringement on the freedom of the individual may well cause large numbers of people to turn away from our capitalistic system. This unfortunate "computer plague on society" can be clearly avoided by an intelligent use of central data banks, that is, the banks can be employed only for statistical analysis without identifying specific individuals. In essence, confidential information should not be used for spying on the general populace.

Computer advancements do not occur in a vacuum, but are implemented within a business information system that affects the individual, the group, management, the organization structure, the organization, and finally society. Society, in the final analysis, can accept or reject this new technology. It is interesting to note that this second technological revolution (automation was the first) is also meeting with opposition. Even though both are beasts of burden, computers are not being opposed because of unemployment problems as automation was and still is, but rather because of the impersonal nature of their operation. Ironically, this popular notion is not true since computer data banks have the ability to centralize all pertinent data on the individual through government banks and credit bureau data files. In reality, the computer has the capability of being more personal than any type system in the past. Proper use of computers and their data banks, then, is essential for preserving the basic tenets of our democratic society.

**summary
of epilogue**

impact of computers on society:

Benefits to be derived from computers, among others, include:
- new job opportunities
- increased leisure time and recreation
- improved educational instruction
- enhanced banking operations with the Electronic Funds Transfer System (EFTS)
- improved medical and health care

Shortcomings from using computers, among others, encompass:
- large-scale unemployment
- uncertainty about one's future
- proliferation of data banks
- pressure toward uniformity and standardization
- increased crime by the computer

Balanced approach to computers in society—recognizes that the benefits (set forth above) should result in enriching an individual's everyday life and not in restricting an individual's freedom. Similarly, the shortcomings (set forth above) should be viewed from a positive standpoint, i.e., a computer is a tool to aid society in ridding itself of or reducing its problems.

Balanced approach to data banks in society—recognizes that data banks provide factual, quantitative data for improving service, increasing efficiency, and reducing waste. However, dissemination of information to the wrong persons or organizations may create problems for the individual, i.e., invading one's right to privacy. Thus, specific legislation may be required, such as the following passed to date:
- Fair Credit Reporting Act
- Freedom of Information Act
- Federal Reports Act
- Privacy Act of 1974

impact of computers on the human element in business:
- the individual and the group—recognizes that individuals will be replaced by newer DP equipment which utilizes a smaller number of personnel to operate them.

- management levels—relates to the impact of computers on lower, middle, and top management. At the *lower* management level, the ultimate impact on the total number of first-level jobs will be negligible; however, the relative mix of line and staff positions will be affected. The number at the *middle* management level will be fewer while the number of *top* managers will remain about the same. However, more sophisticated computer programs will be utilized to help solve the myriad of problems at these two levels.

future computer developments:

Numerous developments will be forthcoming in hardware and software. Not only will hardware costs continue to drop, but also there will be greater use of DP equipment, particularly, at the data-entry level. Great emphasis will be placed on *Distributed Data Processing* at the local and regional levels as opposed to centralized processing.

**self-study
exercise
of epilogue**

True-False:

1. (　) New job opportunities are not available with further computerization.
2. (　) The Electronic Funds Transfer System will never be implemented.
3. (　) Use of computers requires a large degree of uniformity and standardization.
4. (　) There is no need for a balanced approach to computers in society.
5. (　) A positive view of computers is to aid society in reducing its problems.
6. (　) Currently, no legislation has been passed to restrict the use of data banks.
7. (　) Generally, groups in business organizations will not be affected by computers.
8. (　) In the future, the number of middle management positions will be less.
9. (　) Future computer developments will occur only in hardware.
10. (　) Equipment costs are always the highest of all DP costs.

Fill-In:

11. The ＿＿＿ ＿＿＿ ＿＿＿ system links the entire banking system together with a vast communications network.
12. Improved education instruction is available now as well as in the future by utilizing ＿＿＿-＿＿＿ ＿＿＿.
13. An intelligent approach to computers is to utilize them as a ＿＿＿ to aid society in ridding itself of or reducing its problems.
14. The ＿＿＿ ＿＿＿ of 1974 requires that each federal agency publish a list of the systems of records it maintains.
15. A ＿＿＿ ＿＿＿ is a necessity for the proper use of computerized data banks.
16. The increasing ability of the computer to make decisions gives rise to the feeling that the creative talents of the ＿＿＿ are and will be stifled.
17. The individual will still need to override computer answers due to ＿＿＿ ＿＿＿ not contained in computer programs.
18. Relegating many of management's routine tasks to a computer will allow more time to spend on the important managerial function of ＿＿＿.
19. High-level executives of the future will want to evaluate alternative long-range plans, pricing decisions, product lines, and comparable areas by having their assistants employ ＿＿＿ ＿＿＿.
20. The most costly aspect of a DP installation is the ＿＿＿ expense which comprises about 40% of all computer costs.

questions

1. From the individual's standpoint, set forth a desirable approach to computers that is compatible with the basic tenets of our democratic society.

2. Will our economy ever operate completely with electronic money in the future?

3. What is the proper approach to data banks that will best serve the interests of society and business? Explain thoroughly.

4. What is the relationship of the individual, group, and management to computers now and in the future? Explain thoroughly.

5. Are more changes likely to occur in management jobs or non-management jobs? Explain.

6. What major developments are expected in the future for the following:
   (a) computer hardware?
   (b) computer software?

7. When consideration is given to future data processing developments, what impact will they have on organizations? Explain thoroughly.

answers to self-study exercise

1. F 2. F 3. T 4. F 5. T 6. F 7. F 8. T 9. F 10. F 11. Electronic Funds Transfer 12. computer-assisted instruction 13. tool 14. Privacy Act 15. balanced approach 16. individual 17. extraneous conditions 18. planning 19. mathematical models 20. software

appendixes

appendix a operation of IBM 29 card punch

The IBM 29 Card Punch is a widely used means of data entry. Because of its widespread use not only in business but also in academia, its operational aspects are discussed below. They include:

- introduction to card punch
- punching without use of automatic features
- punching with automatic feed only
- punching with a program card

Also, a program card illustration is included.

Introduction to Card Punch

The IBM 29 Card Punch, illustrated below (Figure A-1a) and previously in Chapter 7, has a full keyboard (Figure A-1b). Because the alphabetical characters on the keyboard are identical to those on a typewriter, an individual who can type can keypunch without the need to relearn. However, the numbers 1 to 9 are arranged differently. They can be punched with three fingers of the right hand.

Since the card punch has features that perform certain functions automatically, the beginner may want to start by bypassing these automatic features. As more proficiency is developed, the individual may want to add these features to increase punching speeds. Hence, the operation of the IBM 29 Card Punch will be described (in the following sections) on this basis.

Punching Without Use of Automatic Features

The on-off switch for the card punch is located on the inside of the right leg. Once power is turned on, it is necessary to set six control switches (Figure A-1b) on the panel directly above the keyboard. For punching without use of automatic features, the AUTO (automatic) SKIP DUP (duplicate) switch (first to the left) is turned off (down) as are the next two switches—TWO PROG (program) SEL (selector) and AUTO (automatic) FEED. The PRINT switch is turned on (up) as is the LZ (left-zone) PRINT switch (suppresses the printing of leading zeros in a field). Lastly, the CLEAR switch is turned off. (This is a spring switch which causes all cards then in process to be moved through the stacker without feeding any new cards.) In addition, the program control lever, located in the upper part of the card punch, directly below the window showing a cylinder or program drum (Figure A-1c) is deactivated.

Once the foregoing switches have been properly set, the operator is ready to start punching. However, the operator must first understand how to utilize three keys, located at the right-hand side of the keyboard (Figure A-1b). These are the REL (release), FEED, and REG (register) keys that are explained below.

The first card to be punched is fed by key depression (depress FEED key) from the card hopper to the entrance of the punching station, per Figure A-1c. Depressing the REG key, the card is moved into position for punching. By striking the appropriate keys, the card is punched serially, that is, column by column. Because the keyboard operates normally in the alphabetic mode, all numerics and most special characters require the use of the numeric shift key at the lower left of the keyboard (Figure A-1b) while striking the keys. As with the typewriter, columns may be skipped by depressing the space bar. Once all punching has been performed, the card is moved to the reading station per Figure A-1c by depressing the REL key. If this is the only card that is being punched, pressing the REL and REG keys will move the card from the reading station to the card stacker where it can be removed (Figure A-1c).

If there is need to correct or duplicate a card, the card to be reproduced is inserted in the reading station (Figure A-1c). A blank card is brought from the card hopper by depressing the FEED key. Pressing the REG key will then register both cards. By depressing the DUP (duplicate) key on

(a) Card punch.

(b) Keyboard and control switches.

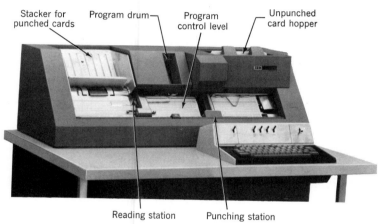

Stacker for punched cards — Program drum — Program control level — Unpunched card hopper

Reading station — Punching station

(c) Card path.

figure A-1. IBM 29 Card Punch. (Courtesy International Business Machines Corp.)

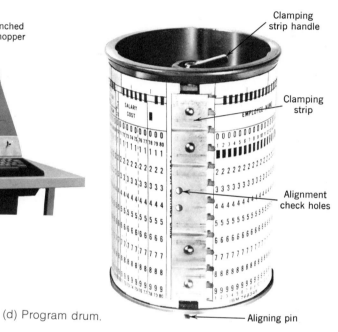

Clamping strip handle

Clamping strip

Alignment check holes

Aligning pin

(d) Program drum.

the keyboard, data read at the reading station from the first card will be punched automatically into the second and at the punching station. If one or more columns are to be omitted or altered from the first card, the operator depresses the space bar or keyboard characters respectively instead of the duplicate key.

Punching with Automatic Feed Only

To speed up the punching of many cards, the AUTO (automatic) FEED (Figure A-1b) can be used. When this switch is on, a continuous supply of cards is fed and registered each time the card being punched is released. However, if a card is to be corrected or duplicated per the above, the AUTO FEED switch must be turned off.

PROGRAM ONE ROW	FUNCTION	PROGRAM TWO ROW	WHERE PUNCHED	USED ON
12	Field Definition	4	Each column except first	Models A, B, C
11	Start Auto-Skip	5	First column only	Models A, B, C
0	Start Auto-Duplicate	6	First column only	Models A, B Model C only when in punch mode
0	11/12 Elimination	6	Necessary column only	Model C only when in interpret mode
1	Alphabetic Shift	7	Each necessary column	Models A, B Model C only when in punch mode
2	8-Column Left-Zero Field	8	First column only	Model B only
3	7-Column Left-Zero Field	9	First column only	Model B only
2,3	6-Column Left-Zero Field	8,9	First column only	Model B only
1,2	5-Column Left-Zero Field	7,8	First column only	Model B only
1,3	4-Column Left-Zero Field	7,9	First column only	Model B only
1,2,3	3-Column Left-Zero Field	7,8,9	First column only	Model B only

figure A-2. Program codes for IBM 29 Card Punch—Models A, B, and C. (Courtesy International Business Machines Corporation.)

Punching With a Program Card

An integral part of the IBM 29 Card Punch is the program unit, a device that permits some programming to assist the key punch operator. It controls (a) *automatic skipping* over columns not to be punched, (2) *automatic*

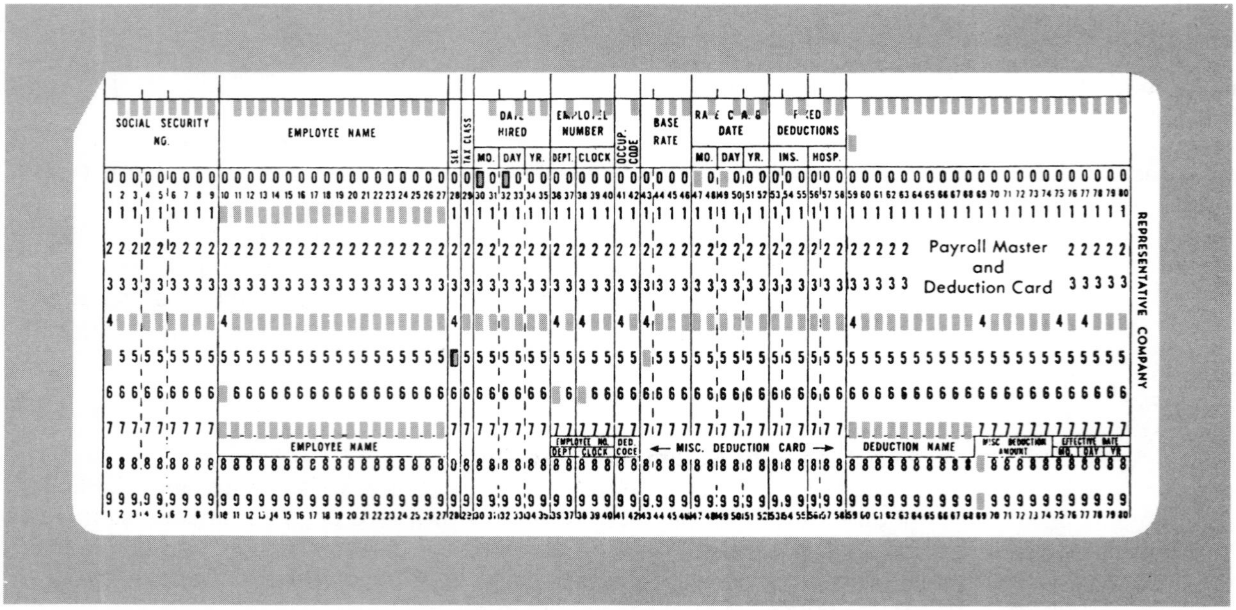

figure A-3. Program card—multiple functions for IBM 29 Card Punch. (Courtesy International Business Machines Corporation.)

duplicating of repetitive data, (3) *shifting from numeric to alphabetic* and vice versa, (4) *automatic insertion of zeros* to the left of the first significant digit in numeric fields (Model B only), (5) controls the *skipping of fields* that are not to be interpreted (Model C only), and (6) the *elimination of overpunches* from amount field columns (Model C only). These operations are controlled by the program card wrapped around the program drum, as in Figure A-1d. Generally, a separate program card must be prepared for each different series of cards being punched. On the 29 Card Punch with two program levels (one program drum), the program card can contain two totally different 80 column programs. Either program can be selected by setting a program selection switch. (Refer to Figure A-1b.) If it is desired to utilize both program levels for control punching on a single card, alternating from program to program can be made by program selection keys on the keyboard.

The program card is punched with code numbers that indicate to the key punch what it must perform for each of the card columns when passing

COLUMNS	FIELD HEADING	NORMAL PROGRAM	ALTERNATE PROGRAM
1–9	Social Security No.	Manual punch	Automatic skip
10–27	Employee Name	Manual punch, alphabetic	Automatic duplicate, alphabetic
28	Sex	Manual punch	Automatic skip
29	Tax Class	Manual punch	
30–35	Date Hired	Automatic duplicate	
36–40	Employee Number	Manual punch (Department and Clock coded as separate fields for error correction and zero suppression)*	Automatic duplicate (Department and Clock coded as separate fields for zero suppression)*
41–42	Occupation Code or Deduction Code	Manual punch	Manual punch
43–46	Base Rate	Manual punch	Automatic skip
47–52	Rate Change Date	Automatic Duplicate	
53–58	Fixed Deductions	Manual punch (Insurance and Hospitalization coded as separate fields for error correction and zero suppression)*	
59–68	Deduction Name	Automatic skip	Manual punch, alphabetic
69–74	Misc. Ded. Amount		Manual punch (left-zero insertion field)
75–80	Effective Date		Manual punch

Month and day in each date field are coded as separate fields for zero suppression*
*Left-zero print switch off

figure A-4. Program table for payroll master and deduction card per figure A-3. (Courtesy International Business Machines Corporation.)

the punch dies. A listing of program codes for all three models (A, B, and C) of the IBM 29 Card Punch is found in Figure A-2. The holes of the program card are detected by tiny starwheels that ride only on the top of the card as it rotates in unison with the card being punched. As a starwheel drops into a hole in the program card, it causes the key punch machine to perform one of the steps outlined in Figure A-2.

Program Card Illustration

To understand program codes for a multifunction (two) program card (Figure A-3), program one for the payroll master card has row 12, columns 2 through 9 punched for field definition of social security number (numeric to be punched manually) and row 12, columns 10 through 27 punched for field definition of employee name plus row 1, columns 10 through 27 for alphabetic shift (alphabetic to be punched manually). Referring to program two, for the deduction card, row 5, column 1 is the first column of the program card and row 4, columns 2 through 9 call for automatic skipping, that is, no data are to be punched in columns 1 through 9. For the second field, row 6, column 10 denotes the first column of this data and row 4, columns 11 through 27 are the required spaces for employee name. The equivalent alphabetic shift (alphabetic to be punched automatically) for program two is row 7, columns 10 through 27. The remaining columns in the example have been programmed in a similar manner (refer to Figure A-4 for programming of the remaining columns).

appendix b   glossary

Abacus. A manual calculating device that uses beads to represent decimal values.

Absolute coding. Coding that uses machine language instructions and can be directly executed by a computer without prior translation to a different form.

Access time. The time interval between the instant at which data are called for from a storage device and the instant delivery is completed—the read time. Also, the time interval between the instant at which data are requested to be stored and the instant at which storage is completed.

Accumulator. A storage device in the arithmetic unit in which the results of arithmetic and logical operations are formed.

Address. A label, name, or number identifying a register, a storage location, or a device from which information is received or to which it is transmitted.

Address modification. The process of changing the address part of a machine instruction by means of coded instructions.

Address register. A register in which an address is stored.

ADP. Automatic data processing is a term used to describe a minimum of manual operations in processing data.

Algorithm. A prescribed set of well-defined rules or processes for the solution of a problem in a finite number of steps.

Alphanumeric code. A system in which characters may be either letters of the alphabet, numerals, or special symbols.

Analog computer. A calculating device that operates on numbers represented by measurable physical quantities, such as the amount of voltage, temperature, and the like.

Analytical engine. The first general-purpose computer, developed by Charles P. Babbage.

Application package. A computer routine or set of routines designed for a specific application, such as inventory control, on-line savings accounting, and linear programming.

Applications programmer. A programmer who writes programs for the needs of specific applications.

Arithmetic unit. The part of a computer processing section that does the adding, subtracting, multiplying, dividing, and comparing.

ASCII. American Standard Code for Information Interchange.

ASR (Automatic Send Receive). A teleprinter unit that allows messages to be prepared and edited off-line on paper tape for automatic transmission.

Assembler language. A language intermediate between machine language and English, but closer to the former.

Assembly program. A computer program that takes sequential instructions written by the programmer in a nonmachine language and changes them to a machine language used by the computer.

Associative memory. A storage device whose storage locations are identified by their contents rather than by positions, as in computer storage devices.

Asynchronous computer. A computer in which each operation starts as a result of a signal generated by the completion of the previous operation or by the availability of the equipment required for the next operation.

Automatic programming. The process of using a computer to perform some stages of the work involved in preparing a final program.

Auxiliary (peripheral) equipment. Equipment not actively involved during the processing of data, such as input/output equipment and auxiliary storage utilizing punched cards, magnetic tape, disks, or drums.

Auxiliary operation. An operation performed by equipment not under continuous control of the central processing unit.

Auxiliary storage. A storage that supplements another storage.

Backup. Reserve equipment that takes over control when the computer is down.

Band. A unit of signaling speed equal to the number of signal events per second.

Bandwidth. The difference, expressed in the number of cycles per second, between the two limiting frequencies of a band.

Base address. A specified address (often held in a "base address register") that is combined with a relative address (usually contained in an instruction) to form the absolute address of a particular storage location.

BASIC. An acronym of Beginners All-purpose Symbolic Instruction Code. A widely used time-sharing language (developed by Professors Kemeny and Kurtz) that is similar in structure to FORTRAN.

Batch processing. A method by which a number of similar transactions or problems are grouped for processing during a single continuous machine run.

Baud. A unit of signaling speed that amounts to 1 bit per second.

Baudot code. A system of coding for transmission of data in which five bits represent one character.

Binary coded decimal (BCD). A decimal notation in which the individual decimal digits are represented by a pattern of ones and zeros, that is, in the 8-4-2-1 binary coded decimal notation.

Binary number system. A number system using the base two, as opposed to the decimal number system which uses the base ten.

Bit. The smallest unit of information in the binary number system. It is the abbreviation for the "binary digit" where a bit refers to one (on) and a no-bit means zero (off).

Block. A group of machine words considered or transported as a unit. In flowcharts, each block represents a logical unit of programming.

Block diagram. A diagram of a system, instrument, computer, or program in which selected portions are represented by annotated boxes and interconnecting lines.

Blocking. Combining two or more records into one block usually to increase the efficiency of computer input and output operations.

Branching. A computer programming term indicating that a sequence of steps has been completed or is to be broken and that the sequence is to be repeated or changed to a new one.

Breakpoint. A specified point in a program at which the program may be interrupted by manual intervention, or by a monitor routine.

Broadband. Data transmission facilities capable of handling frequencies greater than those required for high-grade voice communications.

Bubble memory. A method of storage that utilizes tiny magnetic bubbles for storing about a million bits of information per square inch.

Buffer. A temporary or intermediate storage unit used to hold data being transmitted between internal and external storage units or between input/output devices and internal storage.

Bug. A mistake in the design of a program or a computer system, or an equipment fault.

Bulk memory. Portion of the computer's memory located outside the central processing unit.

Bus. A circuit used to transmit signals or power.

Byte. A sequence of adjacent binary digits operated upon as a unit. It is the basic unit used in determining the memory size of a computer.

Calculator. A device that performs primarily arithmetic operations based upon data and instructions inserted manually or contained on punched cards.

Card code. The combination of punches employed to represent alphabetic and numerical data on a punched card.

Card design. The technique of determining the pattern to be followed in punching data into cards which will be processed by a data processing system.

Card feed. A mechanism that moves cards serially into a machine.

Card hopper. A device that holds cards and makes them available to a card feed mechanism.

Card jam. A pile-up of cards in a machine whether it be on-line or off-line equipment.

Card punch. A device or machine that punches holes in specific locations of a card to store data.

Card reader. A device for inputting information from punched cards into the computer system.

Card read-punch unit. A device that carries out the functions of a card reader and a card punch.

Card stacker. An output device that accumulates punched cards in a deck.

Card system. A system that utilizes only punched cards as the processing medium.

Cathode-ray tube (CRT). An electronic vacuum tube containing a screen on which output data may be displayed in graphic form or by character representation. Essential for many interactive processing systems.

Central processing unit (CPU). The unit of a computer system that contains the arithmetic, logical, and control circuits necessary for executing computer programs.

Chad. A portion of tape or card that is removed when a code is punched.

Channel. A path over which information is transmitted, generally from some input/output device to storage.

Character. A decimal digit, alphabetic letter, or a special symbol.

Check digit. One or more redundant digits in a character or word which depend on the remaining digits such that if a change of digits occurs in data transfer operations, the malfunction of equipment can be detected.

Checkpoint. A reference point to which error-free operation of the program has been verified and to which the program may return for restart in the event of subsequent failure.

Circuit. A system of conductors and related electrical elements through which electrical current flows.

Classify. The identification of each item and the

systematic placement of like items together according to their common features.

Clear. Program instruction to remove all information from a storage device of a machine and restore it to a prescribed state, usually zero or blank.

Closed loop control. The form of on-line control where the computer controls the instruments or controls certain valves without the intervention of the operator.

COBOL. Common business-oriented language is a coding language by which data processing procedures may be described precisely in a standard form. It is basically used for business programming.

Code. A set of rules that is used to convert data from one representation to another.

Collate. Two or more sets of related information, already arranged according to the same sequence, are merged into a single sequenced set.

Collator. A device to collate or merge sets of cards or other documents into a sequence.

Command. A group of signals or pulses initiating one step in the execution of a computer program—often called an instruction.

Common data base. Some type of on-line data files that are stored on secondary storage mediums, such as magnetic disk and drum.

Common processing language. A coded structure that is compatible with two or more data processing machines or families of machines, thereby allowing them to communicate directly to one another.

Communications executive. A systems software component that resides in the data communications processor and services the remote terminals.

Compiler. A programming system that produces a program from a series of source statements. It is capable of replacing single entries with a series of instructions or a subroutine that produces an expanded translated version of the original program.

Computer. An electronic computing machine that accepts input data, processes the data internally within the machine, and provides output of some type.

Computer system. It is commonly referred to as simply a computer because it consists of one or more input devices, a central processing unit, and one or more output devices.

Computer utility. A time-shared computer system that is similar in concept to an electric utility.

Computer word. A sequence of bits or characters treated as a unit and capable of being stored in one computer location.

Conditional branching. An instruction that causes a jump depending upon the result of some operation, the contents of some register, or the setting of some indicator.

Configuration. A group of machines that are interconnected and are programmed to operate as a system.

Console. The component of a data processing system that provides facilities for manual control and observation of the system's operation.

Console operator. An individual who operates a computer system.

Constant. Data with a fixed value that is available for use throughout a program.

Continuous form. Paper or card forms attached for continuous feeding in an accounting machine or computer printing device.

Control card. A punched card that contains input data required for a specific application of a general routine, such as a generator or operating systems; e.g., one of a series of cards that direct an operating system to load and initiate execution of a particular program.

Control panel. The panel that contains the external wiring to govern machine operations.

Control program. A routine, usually contained within an operating system, that aids in controlling the operations and managing the resources of a computer system.

Control unit. The portion of the central processing unit that implements the programs and thus controls all the other units.

Converter. A unit that changes the representation of data from one form to another so as to make it available or acceptable to another machine, such as from punched cards to magnetic tape.

Corner cut. A diagonal cut at the corner of a card to facilitate identification by sight.

Core memory. A computer memory that utilizes tiny cores strung on wires to form a core plane which, in turn, are stacked on top of one another to form a core stack.

Counter. A device, register, or storage location for storing integers, permitting these integers to be increased or decreased.

Cycle. An interval during which one set of events or phenomena is completed.

Data. A general term used to denote any facts, numbers, letters, and symbols, or facts that refer to or describe an object, idea, condition, situation, or other factors.

Data acquisition. The automatic collection of operating data.

Data base. Data items that must be stored in order to meet the interactive information processing and retrieval needs of an organization.

Data collection. A system that records, in machine readable form, the data pertinent to a transaction at the time and place the transaction occurs.

Data communications. The transmission of data between two or more points.

Data file. A user file, either temporary or permanent, in which data information is stored.

Data processing. Any operation or combination of operations on data to achieve a desired result.

Data processing system. The integration of major functional subsystems into one organized system in order that meaningful output can be produced for making decisions.

Data reduction. The transformation of raw data into more useful form.

Data set. A hardware device that provides the necessary interface between input/output devices and telephone or communication lines.

Data transmission equipment. Equipment designed to transmit either card code or channel code over long distances by means of telephone lines or by radio.

Debug. To detect, locate, and correct mistakes in a computer program.

Decision. The process of making comparisons by use of arithmetic to determine the relationship of two terms.

Decision table. A table that combines "conditions" (if) to be considered in the description of a problem, along with the "actions" (then) to be taken. Decision tables are sometimes used instead of flowcharts to describe and document problems.

Deck. A complete set of cards that have been punched for a specific purpose.

Decoder. A matrix of switching elements that selects one or more output channels according to the combination of input signals present.

Demodulator. A device that receives signals transmitted over a communications link and converts them into electrical pulses or bits that can serve as input to a data processing machine.

Density. The number of characters that can be stored per unit of length.

Diagnostic routine. A specific routine designed to locate a malfunction in the computer or a mistake in coding.

Difference engine. A special-purpose computer developed by Charles P. Babbage to compute mathematical tables.

Digital computer. A calculting device that uses numbers to express all the variables and quantities of a problem. Its accuracy is generally 100%.

Direct access. A random access storage medium that permits direct addressing of data locations.

Direct address. An address that specifies the location of an operand.

Disk file. Form of bulk storage utilizing rotating magnetic disks.

Disk pack. A portable set of magnetic disks that may be removed from the disk drive unit, allowing another set of disks to be placed on the unit.

Disk storage. The storage of data on the surface of magnetic disks.

Display station. A device that provides a visual representation via a cathode-ray tube.

Distributed data processing. An approach to placing computing power at the proper places (local, regional, or central) in an organization and linking them together (where necessary) with a centralized computer via a communicative network.

Documentation. Documents that describe the program and its contents during its preparation, its approval, and any subsequent changes.

Downtime. The elapsed time when a computer is not operating correctly because of machine or program malfunction.

Drum memory. Form of bulk storage utilizing a rotating magnetic drum.

Dump. A copying or printing out of all or part of the contents of a particular storage device. Synonymous with memory dump.

Duplex channel. A channel that allows simultaneous transmission in both directions.

Difference engine. A special-purpose computer developed by Charles P. Babbage to compute mathematical tables.

Duplicating. The automatic punching of information from a card or tape into succeeding cards or tape.

Dynamic relocation. The movement of part or all of an active program from one region of storage to another, with all necessary address references being adjusted to enable proper execution of the program to continue in its new location.

EAM. Electrical accounting machine. Generally refers to punched card equipment.

EBCDIC. An abbreviation for Extended Binary Coded Decimal Interchange Code.

Echo check. A check upon the accuracy of a data transfer operation in which the data received are transmitted back to the source and compared with the original data.

Edit. Involves the deletion of unwanted data, the selection of pertinent data, and the insertion of symbols.

EDP. Electronic data processing. Generally refers to computer equipment.

EDVAC. Electronic Discrete Variable Automatic Computer, developed by the Moore School of Electrical Engineering as the first commercial electronic computer.

Electronic data processing system. The term is used to define a system for data processing by means of computers as opposed to punched card equipment.

Elementary statements. Basic statements that are

often used in the development of a computer program.

Emulator. A device, generally used in conjunction with special routines, that enables a computer to execute machine language programs written for another computer of dissimilar design, without prior translation.

Encode. To apply a code, frequently one consisting of binary numbers, to represent individual characters in a message.

ENIAC. The first all-electric general-purpose computer built in the early 1940's by Prosper Eckert and John W. Mauchly while at the University of Pennsylvania.

Erase. To replace all the binary digits in a storage device by binary zeros. To remove data from a magnetic surface or other memory unit.

Error routine. A prepared diagnostic program that searches for predetermined types of errors and advises, by computer output, the types of errors found.

Executive program. The principal program that supervises the implementation of all other programs.

Expression. A method of assignment of values from one side of an equal to sign to the other side.

External label. An identifying label attached to the outside of a file media holder identifying the file. For example, a paper sticker is attached to the reel containing a magnetic tape file.

External storage. The storage of data on a device, such as magnetic tape which is not an integral part of a computer, but is in a form for use by a computer.

Facilities management. All EDP operations (equipment, personnel, and functions) are performed by a computer service facility instead of having the firm operate its own in-house computer processing system.

Feedback. The process of returning portions of the output of a machine, process, or system for use as input in a further operation.

Ferromagnetics. In computer technology, the science that deals with the storage of information and the logical control of pulse sequences through the utilization of the magnetic polarization properties of materials.

Field. A set of one or more columns of a punched card consistently used to record similar information.

File. A collection of related records treated as a unit.

File maintenance. The processing of information in a file to keep it up-to-date.

Firmware. Software that is stored in a fixed or firm way, usually in a read-only memory.

Fixed length record. A record that always contains the same number of characters.

Fixed point. An arithmetic system in which all numerical quantities are expressed in a specified number of places with the radix point implicitly located at some predetermined position.

Fixed word length. A storage device in which the capacity for digits or characters in each unit of data is a fixed length as opposed to a variable length.

Flip-flop. A circuit or device containing active elements capable of assuming either one of two stable states at a given time.

Floating point. A system of representing numerical quantities with a variable number of places in which the location of the point does not remain fixed.

Flowchart. A graphical representation of the definition, analysis, or solution of a problem using symbols to represent operations, data flow, equipment, and the like.

Foreground program. A program that requires real-time responses or has a high priority and therefore takes precedence over other concurrently operating programs in a computer system using multiprogramming techniques.

Format. The arrangement of data on a form or in storage.

FORTRAN. Formula translator. A programming language designed for problems that can be expressed in algebraic notation as well as other mathematical notation. The FORTRAN compiler is a routine for a given machine which accepts a program written in FORTRAN source language and produces a machine language object program.

Gangpunching. The automatic punching of data read from a master card into the following detail cards.

General purpose computer. A computer that is used to solve a wide variety of problems.

Generate. A generator is utilized to prepare a machine language program from a set of specifications.

Generator. A program for a computer that generates the coding of a problem.

GIGO. A contraction of "Garbage In, Garbage Out," which refers to the uselessness of invalid input data.

Half-duplex channel. A channel capable of transmitting and receiving signals, but in only one direction at a time.

Hard copy. A record presented in a permanent and readable form.

Hardware. A term applied to the mechanical, electrical, and electronic features of a computer system.

Hash total. A sum of numbers in a specified field of a record or batch of records used for checking or control purposes.

Head. A device that reads, writes, or erases data on a storage medium. For example, an electromagnet is used to read, write, or erase data on a magnetic drum or tape.

Header card. A prepunched record of the basic information pertaining to a specific individual or form which is used to create automatically the upper portion of a document.

Header label. A machine-readable record at the bebinning of a file containing data identifying the file and data used in file control.

Hexadecimal numbering system. A numbering system using the equivalent of the decimal number sixteen as a base.

Hierarchical control. Form of control in which computers are distributed at different levels of a system and each is controlled by the computer at the level above it.

Higher-level languages. Languages, like COBOL and RPG, that allow programming in procedure- or problem-oriented languages versus machine language.

High-order position. The leftmost position of a number or word.

Hollerith code. A standard 12-channel punched card code in which each decimal digit, letter, or special character is represented by one or more rectangular holes punched in a vertical column.

Housekeeping routine. Routine usually performed only at the beginning of machine operations which establishes the initial conditions for instruction addresses, accumulator settings, switch settings, and the like.

Idle time. The time that a computer is available for use but is not in operation.

IDP. Integrated Data Processing. Generally means the integration of several functional areas of data processing with the purpose of reducing or eliminating duplicate recording of data.

Indexing. A method of address modification that is performed automatically by the computer system.

Index register. A register whose contents can be added to or subtracted from an address prior to or during the execution of an instruction.

Index word. A storage position or register, the contents of which may be used to modify automatically the effective address of any given instruction.

Indirect address. An address that specifies a storage location containing either a direct address or another indirect address.

Information retrieval. The methods and procedures for recovering specific information from stored data.

Initialize. To set up program variables, such as addresses, counters, and program switches to zero or other starting values at the beginning of, or at prescribed points in, a computer routine.

Input device. The mechanical unit designed to bring data to be processed into a computer, e.g., a card reader, a tape reader, or a keyboard.

Inquiry. A request for information from storage.

Instruction. A set of characters which, when interpreted by the control unit, causes a data processing system to perform one of its operations.

Instruction register. The register that stores the current instruction governing a computer operation.

Intelligent terminal. A terminal that contains an integral processor and memory is capable of a limited amount of programming to edit, recall constant data, detect errors, etc., independent of the CPU.

Interactive processing. Transactions and inquiries into the system are processed as they occur, generally in no particular order.

Interface. A boundary between two systems or devices.

Interleave. To insert segments of one program into another program so that during processing delays in one program, processing can continue on segments of another program; a technique used in multiprogramming.

Interlock. A protective facility that prevents one device or operation from interfering with another.

Internal control. The plan of organization and all of the coordinate methods and measures adopted within a business to safeguard its assets, check the accuracy and reliability of its accounting data, promote operational efficiency, and encourage adherence to prescribed managerial policies.

Internal functions. Library functions that are supplied by the computer system.

Internal storage. Storage facilities that are an integral part of the computer and directly controlled by the computer.

Interpret. To print at the top of a punched card the information punched in it, using a machine called an interpreter.

Interrupt. A break in the normal flow of a system or routine whereby an operation can generally be resumed from that point at a later time.

Iterative. Pertaining to the repeated execution of a series of steps.

Joggle. To align a deck of cards by jostling them against a plane surface.

K. 1 K equals 1024 units of storage capacity. The units are bytes for most business computers.

Key. One or more characters associated with a particular item or record and used to identify that item or record, especially in sorting or collating operations.

Key punch. A keyboard-operated device that punches holes in a card to represent data.

Label. One or more characters used to identify or describe an item of data, record, message, or file.

Language translator. A general term for any assembler, compiler, or other routine that accepts statements in one language and produces equivalent machine language instructions.

Large-scale integration (LSI). The accumulation of a large number of circuits on a single chip of a semiconductor—basically for read-only memories.

Leased channel. A point-to-point channel on line that is contracted for the sole use of a leasing customer.

Library. A collection of standard proven computer routines, by which problems or portions of problems may be solved.

Limit check. A check written into a computer program to call attention to any data exceeding or less than certain predefined limits.

Line feed. A teletypewriter control character that causes the rotation of the teletypewriter platen to the next line down.

Line printing. The printing of an entire line of characters as a unit.

Linear programming. A mathematical technique of operations research for solving certain kinds of problems involving many variables where a best value or set of best values is determined.

Line speed. The maximum transmission rate of signals over a circuit expressed in bits per second.

Linkage. Coding that connects two separately coded routines.

Listing. A record of a program in machine language and either assembler or compiler language.

Literal. A symbol that names and defines itself.

Load. To place data into a register or into internal storage. Also, means to place a magnetic tape onto a tape drive or to place cards into a card reader.

Load-and-go. An operating technique in which there are no stops between the loading and execution phases of a program and which may include assembling or compiling.

Log. A record of the operations of data processing equipment.

Logarithm. The exponent of a number, indicating how many times the number must be multiplied by itself to produce another given number.

Logical operations. Nonmathematical operations, such as selecting, sorting, matching, and comparing.

Longitudinal parity check. A parity check performed on the bits in each track of magnetic tape or punched tape.

Loop. The repetition of a group of instructions in a routine until certain conditions are reached.

Low-order position. The rightmost position of a number or word.

Machine language. The instructions written in a form that is intelligible to the internal circuitry of the computer.

Machine-oriented language. A language in which there is a general one-to-one correspondence between the statements of the source program and the instructions of the object program.

Machine-sensible. Term denoting information in a form that can be read by one or more machine(s).

Macro instruction. A symbolic instruction in a source language that produces a number of machine language instructions.

Magnetic card. A card with a magnetic surface on which data can be stored by selective magnetizations of portions of the flat surface.

Magnetic core. A small doughnut-shaped piece of ferromagnetic material, about the size of a pin-head, capable of storing one binary digit represented by the polarity of its magnetic field.

Magnetic disk. A storage device by which information is recorded on the magnetizable surface of a rotating disk. A magnetic disk storage system is an array of such devices, with associated reading and writing heads mounted on movable arms.

Magnetic drum. A rotating cylinder whose surface is coated with a material on which information may be recorded as small magnetic spots representing binary information.

Magnetic film. A layer of magnetic material, usually less than one micron thick, used for logic or storage elements.

Magnetic ink. An ink that contains particles of a magnetic substance whose presence can be detected by magnetic sensors.

Magnetic ink character reader. A device capable of interpreting data typed, written, or printed in magnetic ink.

Magnetic ledger card. A ledger sheet or card that has stripes of magnetic receptive material in which magnetic type coded data can be stored and read by machine.

Magnetic tape. A tape or ribbon of material impregnated or coated with magnetic material on which information may be placed in the form of magnetically polarized spots.

Magnetic tape unit. A device for writing information onto and reading information from magnetic tape.

Magnetic thin film. A layer of magnetic material used for logic or storage elements.

Management information system. A computer and communication system designed to furnish management personnel with data for decision making.

Manual entry unit. An elementary keyboard device for putting information into the system.

Mark I. A first-generation computer, developed by Howard G. Aiken of Harvard University in 1944.

Mark sensing. A technique for reading special electrographic pencil marks on a card and automatically punching the data represented by the marks into the card.

Mass storage. An auxiliary storage medium whereby data are magnetically recorded in tracks or channels on the surface of cards or strips stored in demountable cells or cartridges.

Master card. The first card of a group containing indicative information for that group.

Master file. A file of records containing a cumulative history or the results of accumulation.

Matching. Checking two files to see that there is a corresponding card or group of cards in each file.

Mathematical business model. A mathematical representation of the behavior of the business world.

Matrix. An *n*-dimensional array of quantities. Matrices are manipulated in accordance with the rules of matrix algebra.

Memory. The part of a computer that stores the program and holds intermediate results plus various constant data. Also known as primary storage or main storage.

Memory dump. A copy of the contents of all or part of storage, usually from an internal storage into an external storage.

Merge. To combine items from two or more similarly sequenced files into one sequenced file. The order of the items is unchanged.

Message switching. The technique of receiving complete messages and forwarding the messages at a switching center.

MICR. Magnetic ink character recognition. Machine recognition of characters printed with magnetic ink.

Microcomputer. A microprocessor affixed with memory and input-output logic or circuits so that it can perform a useful function.

Microprocessor. A computer processing unit contained in a single plug-in semiconductor chip.

Microprogramming. A method of operation of the control unit of a computer in which each instruction, instead of being used to initiate control signals directly, starts the execution of a sequence of "micro instructions" at a more elementary level.

Microsecond. One-millionth of a second.

Microwave. Very short electromagnetic waves used in high capacity communication networks for transmitting voice or data messages at ultra-high speeds.

Millisecond. One-thousandth of a second.

Minicomputer. A low-cost, general-purpose digital computer.

Mnemonic. Pertains to a technique used to assist human memory. Most symbolic assembly languages use mnemonic operation codes. For example, ADD is used for addition, SUB is used for subtraction, and so forth.

Modem. A contraction of MOdulator DEModulator. Its function is to interface with data processing devices and convert data to a form compatible for sending and receiving on transmission facilities.

Modifier. A quantity used to alter the address of an operand.

Modify. To alter an instruction per the address of the operand; to alter a subroutine according to a defined parameter.

Modularity. The ability of the user to expand or contract a computer system without the need to reprogram.

Modular programming. A technique of writing computer programs in which the logical parts of a problem are divided into a series of individual modules so that each module can be programmed and tested independently.

Modulator. A device that receives electrical pulses or bits from a data processing machine and converts them into signals suitable for transmission over a communications link.

Monolithic circuits. Complete circuits produced in one manufacturing operation.

Multiplexer. A device that will interleave or simultaneously transmit two or more messages on the same communications channel.

Multiprocessing. A computer system consisting of multiple arithmetic and logical units for simultaneous use.

Multiprogramming. A technique whereby more than one program may reside in primary storage at the same time and be executed concurrently by means of an interweaving process.

Nanosecond. One-billionth of a second.

Narrow band channel. A channel that permits transmission of frequencies within the normal telegraph band of frequencies—lower than the voice-band channel.

Nondestructive read. A read process that does not erase the data in storage.

Normalize. In programming, to adjust the exponent and fraction of a floating point quantity so that the fraction lies in the prescribed normal standard range.

Numerical control. Pertaining to the automatic control of processes by the proper interpretation of numerical data.

Object language. A language that is an output from a translation process.

Object program. A program in machine language that has been converted from a program written in a programming language.

OCR. Optical character recognition. The machine recognition of printed and handwritten characters.

Octal. Pertaining to the number base of eight.

Off-line. Equipment or devices not under the direct

control of the computer's central processing unit.

Off-line storage. A storage device not under control of the central processing unit.

Off-punching. Punching not properly positioned in a card.

On-line. Peripheral equipment or devices in direct communication with the central processing unit, and from which information reflecting current activity is introduced into the data processing system as soon as it occurs.

On-line, real-time. Relates to a computer system which receives input data, processes them, and returns results in sufficient time to control the operating environment.

On-line storage. A storage under direct control of the central processing unit.

Open loop control. The form of on-line control where the operator is required to adjust the instruments on the basis of the computer's read-out.

Operand. An operand is usually identified by an address part of an instruction.

Operating system. Software that controls the execution of computer programs.

Operation. A defined action or one step in a procedure. The action specified by a single computer instruction. That which occurs when something is created, changed, or added to, such as writing, calculating, posting, or computing.

Operation code. The part of the command code of an instruction that designates the operation to be performed.

Operations research. The use of mathematical methods, models, and techniques for solving operational problems. The objective is to provide management with a more logical basis for making decisions.

Optical character recognition. The technique of using electronic devices and light in order to detect, recognize, and translate into machine language characters that have been printed or written on paper documents in a human-readable form.

Optical scanner. A device that optically scans printed or written data and generates its digital representation.

Output device. The part of a machine that translates the electrical impulses representing data processed by the machine into permanent results, such as, printed forms, punched cards, and magnetic writing on tape.

Overflow. On an arithmetic operation, the generation of a quantity beyond the capacity of the register or location that is to receive the result.

Overhead time. Refers to that part of the system's execution time that is not devoted directly to the execution of problems submitted by the users.

Overlay. To transfer segments of a program from auxiliary storage into internal storage for execution so that two or more segments occupy the same storage locations at different times.

Over punches. To add punches, usually control punches, to a card column that already contains one or more holes.

Pack. To store several short units of data in a single storage cell in such a way that the individual units can later be recovered.

Padding. Dummy characters, items, or records used to fill out a fixed length block of information.

Page. A segment of a program or data, usually of fixed length, that has a fixed virtual address but can, in fact, reside in any region of the computer's internal storage.

Paging. The separation of a program and data into fixed blocks so that transfers, such as between disk and core, can take place in page units rather than as entire programs.

Paper tape. A long strip of paper that carries information by means of holes punched into specific positions.

Parallel. To handle simultaneously in separate facilities. To operate on two or more parts of a word or item simultaneously.

Parameter. A quantity to which arbitrary values may be assigned but which remain fixed for each program. In a program generator, parameters specify certain machine hardware and data limits to be observed in the program being generated.

Parity bit. A binary digit appended to a group of bits to make the sum of all the bits always odd or always even.

Parity check. A check that tests whether the number of ones or zeros in a group of binary digits meets the established odd or even standard.

Password. A security feature used in time sharing that entails the use of a code known only to certain users.

Patch. A section of coding inserted in a program in order to rectify an error in the original coding or to change the sequence of operation.

Peripheral equipment. Units that work in conjunction with the computer but are not part of the computer itself. These include: tape reader, card reader, magnetic tape feed, high-speed printer, typewriter, and the like.

Photo-optic memory. A memory that uses an optical medium for storage. For example, a laser might be used to record on photographic film.

Picosecond. One-trillionth of a second.

Picture clause. Used in COBOL programs to indicate the size of an item, its class, the presence or absence of an operational sign, and/or an assumed decimal point.

PL/1. A procedure-oriented language designated to facilitate the preparation of computer programs to perform both business and scientific functions.

Plugboard. A removable panel containing an array of terminals that can be interconnected by short electrical leads in prescribed patterns to control various machine operations. It is also known as a control panel.

Powers code. A system of representing data by round holes punched in a 90-column card, invented by James Powers.

Problem analysis. A process whereby the problem is defined and all of the information needed for the problem's solution is identified.

Problem-oriented language. A language whose design is oriented toward the specification of a particular class of problems, such as numerical control of machine tools.

Procedure. A precise, step-by-step method for effecting a solution to a problem.

Procedure-oriented language. A language designed to permit convenient specification, in terms of procedural or algorithmic steps, of data processing or computational processes, i.e., COBOL.

Process control. A system in which computers, usually analog computers, are used for automatic regulation of operations or processes.

Processor. A machine language program that accepts a source program written in a programming language and translates it into an object program acceptable to the machine for which the source program was written.

Program. The sequence of machine instructions and routines necessary to solve a problem on the computer.

Program card. A punched card, punched with specific coding, placed around a program drum to control automatic operations in a card punch and a card verifier.

Program Evaluation and Review Technique (PERT). A technique for planning and controlling system projects.

Program file. A series of programming language statements beginning with line numbers.

Program flowchart. Designed to portray the various arithmetic and logical operations that must be accomplished to solve a computer problem.

Programmer. A person who prepares the planned sequence of events contained within the computer program for solving a problem.

Pseudo instruction. An instruction that has the same general form as a machine instruction, but is not directly executable by a computer.

Punched card. A heavy paper of uniform size and shape suitable for being punched with a pattern of holes to represent data and for being handled mechanically.

Punched tape. A tape, usually paper, on which a pattern of holes or cuts is used to represent data.

Queuing theory. A form of probability theory for studying delays or lines in interactive processing.

Quinary. Pertaining to the number base of five.

Radix. The base or the fundamental number in a number system, e.g., 10 in the decimal system, 8 in the octal system, 5 in the quinary system, and 2 in the binary system.

Random access storage. A storage device, such as magnetic core, magnetic disk, and magnetic drum, in which each record has a specific predetermined address that may be accessed directly. Access time in this type of storage is independent of the data location.

Raw data. Data that have not been processed. They may or may not be in a form acceptable by machines.

Read in. To sense information contained in some source and to transfer this information by means of an input device to internal storage.

Read-only memory. A memory that cannot be altered in normal use of computer processing. Usually, a small memory that contains often-used instructions, such as microprograms or system software as firmware.

Read out. To transfer data from internal storage to an external storage device or to display processed data by means of a printer, automatic typewriter, and similar equipment.

Real-time. The processing of data derived from a particular operation in a sufficiently fast manner so that time is available to influence the continuing operation.

Record. A collection of related items of data treated as a unit.

Record length. The number of characters necessary to contain all the information in a record.

Reentrant. Pertaining to a routine that can be used by two or more independent programs at the same time.

Register. A device capable of temporarily storing a specified amount of data, usually one word, while or until it is used in an operation.

Registration. The accuracy of the positioning of punched holes in a card.

Remote batch processing. Entering batches of data from remote terminals into a computer system.

Remote processing. A method of using a computer system from remote locations. The direct access connection can be accomplished by using conventional voice grade telephone lines to exchange information between the computer and terminals.

Report generator. A programming system for producing a complete report given only a description of the desired content and format of the output reports, and certain information about the input file and hardware available.

Reproducing. Duplicating punched information from one deck of cards into another.

Resource sharing. The sharing of one central processor both by several users and several peripheral devices. Principally used in connection with the sharing of time and memory.

Roll-back. A system that will restart the running program after a system failure. Snapshots of data and programs are stored at periodic intervals and the system rolls back to a restart at the last recorded snapshot.

Routing. A set of coded instructions arranged in a logical sequence and used to direct a computer to perform a desired operation or series of operations.

Row binary. A method representing binary numbers on a card where successive bits are represented by the presence or absence of punches in a successive position in a row as opposed to a series of columns.

Run. A single, continuous operation of a computer routine.

Run manual. A manual of documentation containing the processing system, program logic, controls, program changes, and operating instructions associated with a computer program.

Secondary storage. Storage that supplements a computer's primary internal storage.

Security controls. Safeguard techniques utilized in protecting computer programs, data files, and equipment.

Selecting. Removing cards from a file, or processing cards according to predetermined conditions.

Selector channel. A term used in certain computer systems for an input/output channel that can transfer data to or from one peripheral device at a time.

Semiconductor memory. A memory whose storage medium is a semiconductor circuit. Often used for high-speed buffer memories and for read-only memories.

Sequence checking. Checking items in a file to assure that they are all in ascending or descending order.

Sequential processing. The procedure of processing data records in the order that they occur.

Serial. The handling of data in a sequential fashion, such as to transfer or store data in a digit-by-digit time sequence, or to process a sequence of instructions one at a time.

Serial access. Pertaining to a storage device in which there is a sequential relationship between the access times to successive locations, as in the case of magnetic tape.

Serial operation. The flow of information through a computer in time sequence, using one digit word, line, or channel at a time.

Servomechanism. A device to monitor an operation as it proceeds and make necessary adjustments to keep the operation under control.

Set-up time. The time between computer or other machine operations that is devoted to such tasks as changing reels of tape and moving cards, forms, and other supplies to and from the equipment.

Shift. The process of moving characters of a unit of data to the right or left within a computer program.

Short card. A punched card of less than the regular number of columns.

Sight checking. Examining a group of cards for identical punching by viewing a light source through the punched holes.

Simplex. Pertaining to a communications link that is capable of transmitting data in only one direction.

Simulation. The representation of physical systems and phenomena by computers, models, or other means.

Snapshot. A dynamic dump of the contents of specified storage locations and/or registers that is performed at specific points or times during the running of a program.

Software. The programs and routines used to extend the capabilities of computers, such as compilers, assemblers, routines, and subroutines.

Solid logic technology (SLT). A microminiaturization of solid logic components and associated circuitry into very small units or blocks.

Solid state. Refers to electronic components that convey or control electron flow within solid materials, such as transistors, crystal diodes, and ferrite cores.

Sort. To arrange items of information according to rules dependent on a key or field contained in the items.

Source document. The original paper on which are recorded the details of a transaction.

Source language. A language that is an input to a translation process.

Source program. A program usually written in some programming language and intended for translation into a machine language program.

Special character. A character that is neither a numeral nor a letter; for example, #, $, /, and &.

Special purpose computer. A computer designed principally to solve a restricted class of problems.

Stacker. A receptacle or hopper that accumulates cards after they have passed through a machine.

Statement. In computer programming, a meaningful expression or generalized instruction in a programming language.

Storage. A device into which data can be entered, in which they can be stored, and from which they can be retrieved at a later time.

Storage allocation. The assignment of specific programs, program segments, and/or blocks of data to specific portions of a computer's storage.

Stored program computer. A computer that has the ability to store, to refer to, and to modify instructions in order to direct its step-by-step operations.

Straight line coding. Coding in which the use of loops and/or closed subroutines is avoided by repetition of parts of the coding when required.

String. A set of records in ascending or descending sequence according to a key contained in the records.

Structured programming. A technique for organizing and coding a computer program such that control paths are simplified in order to minimize programming complexity and resulting program errors.

Subprogram. A part of a larger program. Usually the subprogram can be converted into machine language independently of the remainder of the program.

Subroutine. A routine that is part of a program. A closed subroutine is stored in one place and connected to the program by means of linkages at one or more points in the program. An open subroutine is inserted directly into a program at each point where it is to be used.

Subset. A modulation-demodulation device designed to make the output signals of data processing equipment compatible with communication transmission facilities.

Summarizing. The accumulation of totals or amounts from data that have been classified and sorted into like groups.

Summary punch. A card-handling machine that may be connected to another machine, such as an accounting machine, and that will punch out on a card the information produced, calculated, or summarized by the other machine.

Supervisor. The general reference to the programs of a system that are responsible for scheduling, allocating, and controlling the computer system.

Switch. A point in a programming routine at which two courses of action are possible, the correct one being determined by conditions specified by the programmer.

Symbolic address. An address expressed in symbols that are convenient to the programmer.

Symbolic coding. Coding that uses the machine instructions with symbolic addresses.

Symbolic program. A program written in a language that makes use of mnemonic codes and in which names, characters, or other symbols convenient to the programmer are used instead of the machine language codes of the computer.

Synchronous computer. A computer in which each operation starts as a result of a signal generated by a clock.

System. A set or arrangement of entities that forms, or is considered as, an organized whole.

System flowchart. A flowchart that shows the sequence of major operations which normally summarizes a complete operation.

Systems analyst. A systems person who studies the procedures, methods, techniques, and the business in order to determine what must be accomplished and how the necessary operations may best be accomplished.

Systems programmer. A programmer who writes the programs that control the basic functioning of the computer.

Table look-up. The operation of obtaining a value from a table.

Tabulating system. Another term sometimes used to describe a punched card data processing system.

Tag. One or more characters attached to a particular item or record and used to identify that item or record.

Telecommunication. Any transmission or reception of signals, writing, sounds, or intelligence of any nature by wire, radio, visual, or any other electromagnetic means.

Terminal. Any input/output equipment that communicates with a central computer over a communications channel.

Test deck. A set of cards representative of all operations performed in a particular application. Used to test control panel wiring and computer programming.

Test routine. A procedure that shows whether a computer is functioning properly.

Thin film. A layer of magnetic material, usually less than one-millionth of an inch in thickness, which is deposited by a vacuum process onto plate or wire.

Throughput. The total amount of work performed by a data processing system during a given period of time.

Tine sharing. A computing system that permits many users to operate or use the system simultaneously or apparently simultaneously in such a way that each is unaware of the fact that the system is being used by others.

Top down programming. A technique for developing operational computer programs, starting at the highest level down to the lowest level, that allows planning and working with changes as they occur.

Trace routine. A diagnostic routine designed to check or demonstrate the operation of a program.

Track. The part of a data storage medium that is influenced by one head.

Trailer record. A record that follows another record or group of records and contains pertinent data.

Transaction code. One or more characters that form part of a record and signify the type of transaction represented by the record.

Transistor. A tiny, solid electronic device that performs the same function as a vacuum tube. In a vacuum tube, current flows through the gas and space within the tube. In a transistor, the current travels through solid materials only, which explains the familiar term "solid state."

Translator. A device or computer program that performs translations from one language or code to another.

Trap. An unprogrammed jump to a preset location, activated automatically upon the occurrence of a particular condition.

Truth table. A table that describes a logic function by listing all possible combinations of input values and indicating all the logically true output values.

Typer. A device similar to an office typewriter that enters typewritten information into the computer.

Unconditional transfer. An instruction that always causes a jump.

Unit record. A record in which all data concerning each item in a transaction are punched into one card.

Unit record equipment. Another name for punched card equipment.

Unpack. To separate short units of data that have previously been packed.

Update. To change a master file caused by current information or transactions.

User file. A file entered into a time-sharing system by a user.

User generated function. Gives the programmer the capability of developing specialized computer functions.

User number. A number assigned to users by the main-site installation to prevent unauthorized use of a time-sharing system.

User program. An object program file that has been loaded into memory for execution.

Utility program. Standard programs prepared and generally used to assist in the operation of a data processing system.

Validity check. A check based upon known limits or upon given information or computer results.

Variable. A quantity that may take on different values during processing of the program.

Variable length record. A record that may contain a variable number of characters.

Variable word length. Pertaining to a machine word or operand that may consist of a variable number of bits or characters. It is contrasted with fixed word length.

Verify. To determine whether a transcription of data or other operations has been accomplished accurately.

Virtual address. An address in a machine instruction that refers to a particular page that may be located in any region of the computer's internal storage.

Virtual storage. A technique that permits the user to treat secondary (disk) storage as an extension of core memory, thus giving the "virtual" appearance of a large core memory to the programmer.

Voice band channel. A channel that permits the transmission of frequencies within the voice band. A channel suitable for the transmission of speech, digital, or analog data.

Word. A set of characters that occupies one storage location and is treated by the computer circuits as a unit and transported as such.

Word length. The number of characters in a machine language word. In a given computer, the number may be constant, variable, or both.

Word mark. A symbol used in some variable word length computers to indicate the beginning or end of a word or item.

Working storage. A storage section set aside by the programmer for use in the development of processing results, etc.

X-punch. A punch in the second row, one row above the zero row, on a Hollerith punched card.

Y-punch. A punch in the top row, two rows above the zero row, on a Hollerith punched card.

Zero suppression. The elimination of nonsignificant zeros to the left of the integral part of a quantity before printing operations are initiated.

Zone punches. Punches in the Y, X, and O positions on a Hollerith punched card—used in combination with digit punches 1 to 9 to code alphabetic and special characters.

index